A HISTORY OF
DICKSON COUNTY
TENNESSEE

by

ROBERT EWING CORLEW

Southern Historical Press, Inc.
Greenville, South Carolina

This volume was reproduced from
An 1956 edition located in the
Publisher's private library,
Greenville, South Carolina

All rights reserved. No part of this publication may be
reproduced, stored in a retrieval system, transmitted in any
form, posted on to the web in any form or by any means
without the prior written permission of the publisher.

Please direct all correspondence and orders to:

www.southernhistoricalpress.com
or
SOUTHERN HISTORICAL PRESS, Inc.
PO BOX 1267
375 West Broad Street
Greenville, SC   29601
southernhistoricalpress@gmail.com

Originally published: Nashville, TN 1956
ISBN #0-89308-701-7
All rights Reserved.
Printed in the United States of America

In memory of my father

ROBERT EWING CORLEW

(1873-1930)

and

to my Mother

MARY ANN LEECH CORLEW

Several people have made financial contributions to aid in the research and publication of this volume, but had it not been for the generous assistance of Mrs. Beulah McLean Leech and Mrs. Beulah Leech Mayhew, who made their contribution in memory of their husband and father, WILSON BLAKE LEECH—lawyer, farmer, legislator, attorney general, financier, and business executive—it is highly probable that this book would never have been written and published.

INTRODUCTION

by

The Honorable J. B. White

President of the Dickson County Historical Society

There is nothing that unifies and strengthens a people like reading its own history. That history might be recorded in its books, embodied in its customs, engrafted in its institutions, or carved in its monuments.

Some writers find it more inviting to be influenced by legend and rumor than by truth which can be discerned only by diligent search. By yielding to such influence and repeating erroneous information, even from famed authors, one makes such mis-statement traditional to posterity. A true historian, however, owes to himself and to his readers objectivity, exactness, sincerity, and impartiality. He should be free from passion, unbiased by interest, and faithful to the truth which is the mother of history, the preserver of great actions, the enemy of oblivion, the witness of the past, and the director of the future.

Dr. Corlew's intimate knowledge of Dickson County and its people, and his ability clearly and concisely to state the facts as he finds them admirably fits him for writing a history of the county. The work itself shows that he has made an exhaustive and painstaking search for reliable authority for the statements made. The supporting footnotes throughout are evidence of the fact that he means to be exact. The context of the history shows that the only passion of the author is to relate the facts so that they might be preserved for future generations.

Within the pages of this volume is to be found an interest-gripping statement of the county's past from the time the first settlers located in its northeastern section to the present time. The life and habits of its people, the industries and trades in which they wrought, the opening and expansion of its roads and railroads, the founding and growth of its schools and churches, the birth and growth of its towns and villages, and the establishment and conduct of its government as well as the history of its financial and commercial institutions, all find liberal space and thought in this treatise.

As President of the Dickson County Historical Society, I believe that a reading of this work will reaffirm one's faith in the loyalty and devotion of our ancestors to the cause of establishing and developing the county, and of bestowing a noble heritage upon posterity.

FOREWORD

Dickson County is among the oldest of the Middle Tennessee counties. In the pages which follow I have sought to trace the history of this county from the days of the first white explorers to the present. The inhabitants have not been unique. For the most part they have moved within their own sphere of activity very much like the plain people which have inhabited the South and West in every stage of America's development. Politically and economically they have played a very important part in the development of the state and nation. In general they have been neither rich nor poor, and those of ante-bellum days fit well into Frank Lawrence Owsley's concept of the "plain folk" of the Old South. Like the lives of most plain folk, their lives have been simple and devoid of flamboyance. Men like Christopher Strong and George Napier wrote of their loves of God and man with no apparent desire for credit to themselves; and Joseph Dickson, William Norris, Jacob Lampley and others sought the best in life for their families without any apparent thought of their activities being an important part of the county's development. When the clarion call of battle was sounded, W. J. Mallory, Thomas K. Grigsby, Lucian Berry, William Luther Browning, Benjamin C. Sensing, Granville Stokes, and hundreds of others marched off to war with no other apparent thought than that they were doing no more than any other able-bodied American should do.

Source material for certain periods has proved difficult to locate. Nevertheless, I have found records of the activities of the people in many places, including the files of the various courthouse officials; the newspapers of Nashville, Knoxville, Clarksville, Columbia, and other cities, in addition to Charlotte, Dickson, and Burns; the United States Census Reports; the legislative proceedings; diaries, letters, and church records; and in a host of other places, including the minds of many elderly citizens.

In many ways much of the credit for this volume must go to others than myself. To my mother, Mary Ann Leech Corlew, who has lived her entire life in Dickson County, as did her parents, grandparents, and great-grandparents, I owe much, for it was she who instilled in me a respect for the history of my county, state, and nation. My wife, Mary Scott Corlew, has read and corrected portions of the manuscript. My uncle, Henry Collier Leech has encouraged me in many ways and has made available to me his valuable and extensive collection of source material which has added much to the richness of the history. The distinguished historian, Frank Lawrence Owsley, of the University of

Alabama, gave me much of my training in historical writing, and always has manifested much interest in the writing of this particular county history. I am also indebted for patient guidance and instruction to the Honorable Daniel M. Robison, formerly professor of history at Vanderbilt and now State Librarian; and to Professor Charles Summersell and Professor James Benson Sellers of the University of Alabama. Professor Frank B. Williams, Jr., of the history department of East Tennessee State College, has carefully read and corrected the entire manuscript. Professors Eugene Wiggins, William T. Windham, and Clayton James, of Middle Tennessee State College have read all or portions of the manuscript and have made suggestions. Many people in Dickson County, too numerous to mention, have supplied valuable aid. Particularly, among them are: Herbert Tallent, Leland Ishmael, R. A. Freeman, Clark Leech, Judge James A. Weems, J. B. White, Joe A. McMillan, J. M. Stuart, Ray Stuart, V. N. Loggins, Claude Powers, Mrs. Annie Lee Williams, Mrs. Joe B. Weems, Miss Mayme Myatt, Hartwell Gentry, and probably several hundred others too numerous to name. Mrs. Alice Hickman Davies, of Martin, gave much information on the Dickson Normal College. Mrs. Irene Charlesworth Johnson, of Greenbrier, supplied much valuable information on the Ruskin settlement. Mrs. Gertrude Parsley, of the State Library staff, made available much material which otherwise would not have become accessible.

State Historian Bob White willingly supplied much helpful advice and was of much assistance in a variety of ways.

Mention also should be made of the work of three pioneers in the writing of a history of Dickson County—W. Blake Leech, Joe B. Weems, and Frank Frazier. Each of these men dreamed of writing a history of the county, but each died before making substantial headway on his project.

The publication of this volume would not have been possible without the generous financial assistance of the Tennessee Historical Commission. Several private donors aided substantially. Mrs. Beulah McLean Leech and Mrs. Beulah Leech Mayhew, widow and daughter of W. Blake Leech, made a substantial contribution. The G. H. Weems Educational Fund, through Hon. James A. Weems, county judge, contributed liberally. Hon. Henry Collier Leech also made a liberal contribution. Several others made small contributions.

Errors may inadvertenly appear, for which the author assumes full responsibility.

ROBERT E. CORLEW
Charlotte, Tennessee
October 1, 1956

CONTENTS

Introduction (by J. B. White) v
Foreword vii
    I   The Coming of the Early Settlers 11
   II   The Establishment of Dickson County and the
          Coming of Montgomery Bell 19
  III   Early Economic Development 29
  IV   Early Religious Development 44
   V   Two Decades of Growth and Development, 1820–1840 57
  VI   The Expansion of Slavery 70
 VII   The Coming of the Civil War, 1840–1860 82
VIII   Civil War and Readjustment, 1861–1870 96
  IX   Growth and Development, 1870–1900 115
   X   A Socialist Colony Comes and Goes 137
  XI   Educational Development 153
 XII   Growth of Urban Areas and the Struggle for
          Political Supremacy 173
XIII   Dickson Countians in Two World Wars 193
XIV   Recent Developments 205
Footnotes 213
Appendix 226
Illustrations 33, 34, 51, 52, 108, 133, 134, 135, 136,
                                    169, 170, 171, 172, 191
Maps 10, 18
Index 235

Map of DICKSON COUNTY TENNESSEE

The Coming of the Early Settlers

Dickson County, Tennessee, lies in the center of the Western Highland Rim and directly west of Nashville. Originally it was a part of Davidson County when Davidson embraced over three fourths of Middle Tennessee, and it lay immediately adjacent to that county from its creation by legislative act in 1803 until the creation of Cheatham in 1856. Dickson and other counties carved from Davidson had a common frontier experience, and their early history is closely intertwined with that of Davidson.

When the first white men came early in the eighteenth century, they found in central Tennessee a hunters' and trappers' paradise. Oaks of tall and massive proportions graced the hillsides and wild animals of many varieties roamed the woodlands. Countless buffalo, wolves, panthers, bears, and bobcats filled the forests, and their weird calls could be heard on many a still night to wreak fear in the minds of explorers who might have come without nerves of steel and hearts full of courage.[1] Men like Jean de Charleville and his French associates saw in the furs of these animals a source of wealth and prosperity, and were in the Cumberland territory on trapping expeditions as early as 1714. They were said to have become quite wealthy from their sales of furs, and within a few years after their initial visits they had built a small settlement in the present area of Nashville, with headquarters near the "French Lick." Here was an area of salt deposits where animals often congregated in abundance, and where now is located "Sulphur Dell," a Nashville ballpark.[2] The story of the success of these early French explorers soon became noised abroad, and before long other explorers and trappers were coming into the territory in increasingly large numbers. Many who came carried back to their friends and associates in North Carolina and Virginia glowing accounts of the richness and vastness of the Cumberland country, creating within many a desire to push into the region to seek for themselves a fortune in furs or an economic state of independence from the cultivation of free land.

The whites, of course, were not the first inhabitants of Middle Tennessee. For centuries Indian tribes had coursed the hills and valleys by foot and had plied the streams in canoes. Living a primitive existence based largely upon the buffalo which he vigorously pursued but dearly loved, the red man had established many trails, homes, and towns throughout Tennessee by the time the white man came. One of the earliest of the tribes was known simply as "Moundbuilders," about whom little is known. The tribe did, however, leave evidence of its presence in Dickson and other counties of Middle and West Tennessee. They built large earth mounds in Dickson, Davidson, and other neighboring counties. The state capitol in Nashville, for example, is located on a mound said to have been built by these people during the Middle Ages.[3] The mounds served mainly as burial places, but sometimes were places where sacrificial offerings were made. The tribal chieftains generally were buried in them, and often several chiefs would be buried in the same mound over a long period of time, as more and more soil was piled upon each deceased leader. The Moundbuilders also built several villages along the Harpeth River, which were connected by trails. The exact locations of the villages is not known, but at least one trail was well-known and widely used at the time the white man came, and later became known as the "Chickasaw Trace."[4] In 1920, in order to determine as nearly as possible where the Moundbuilders had lived, an extensive survey was made by William E. Myers, a Washington archeologist; William L. Cook, Charlotte lawyer and circuit judge; and J. Benjamin Fuqua of Waverly. They determined that several villages had been erected along the Harpeth, and that a trail had been established, which moved in an east to west direction across Dickson County, and connected the various Indian villages. The trail crossed the Cumberland at the mouth of the Harpeth, and passed through or near the present communities of Bellsburg, Dull, and Promised Land. From there it followed a ridge north of Charlotte, through the vicinity of Sylvia, across Yellow Creek, thence through the present town of Ruskin and then into the adjacent county of Humphreys.[5] Cook, Myers, and Fuqua made no attempt to ascertain just when the Moundbuilders lived in central Tennessee, but it is safe to assume that by the time Columbus came to American shores these mysterious people had long disappeared and had been replaced by other Indian tribes.

The Indians inhabiting Dickson County at the time of the coming of the white man were of the Cherokee and Chickasaw tribes. The highest point between the Tennessee and the Cumberland rivers is a ridge which passes through the present city of Dickson, and this ridge, according to legend, was the dividing line between the claims of these warlike tribes. The Cherokees, claiming the territory west of the ridge, outnumbered the Chickasaws by about three-to-one, but because of the courageous and warlike nature of the latter the Cherokees were often overawed by them. The two tribes apparently got along reasonably well, however, and Dickson County served as a hunting ground for both.

The life of the red man in central Tennessee was soon to be disturbed, however, by the sound of the white man's gun and the bark of his dog. As mentioned earlier, explorers and traders visited and hunted over the vast Cumberland country long before permanent settlements were made. These early adventurers generally sailed up the Cumberland River and occasionally on the Harpeth, buying valuable furs from the

Indian chiefs in exchange for a few shiny trinkets, a gun, a knife, or a jug of firewater. The Spanish were the first to invade the Cumberland territory, but the French and the English were not far behind. Seeking gold, these Europeans found it in the form of rich and luxurious furs which brought high prices in the cities of their native continent.

The success of Charleville and his party of Frenchmen brought others, but information about these "long hunters" is sparse indeed. Kasper Mansker and his associates were in Middle Tennessee by 1770, and Timothy DeMonbreun and party came a few years later. Thomas Sharp Spencer (a man known to all Tennessee school children as a man with immense feet and as one who spent a winter in a hollow tree), and John Holliday, were two other explorers who were in the Cumberland country by the time that the Declaration of Independence was proclaimed in Philadelphia.

Settlers had come into the Watauga country of eastern Tennessee in the early 1760's, and by 1770 had established several thriving settlements. Many of those who settled in that region became dissatisfied after a few years, and wanted to move westward toward the Cumberland River. They felt that the Watauga settlement had grown too large for the amount of suitable farm land and wild game, and the stories of the plentifulness of wild game and fur-bearing animals were enough to cause many to express openly their dissatisfaction with the state of affairs in East Tennessee. Therefore, in 1779, James Robertson and eight companions set out for central Tennessee in the employ of Richard Henderson, who had purchased from the Indians a vast estate in central Kentucky and Tennessee. After traveling for two hundred miles through Cumberland Gap and along a trail blazed by Daniel Boone, Robertson found a beautiful country well drained by the Cumberland and lesser streams, and virgin forests filled with wild game. When he and his party reached the French Lick, the present site of Nashville, they decided to establish a settlement. Hastily they erected log cabins, cleared new ground, and planted corn. Robertson, later called "Father of Middle Tennessee," was joined by settlers from Kentucky in the same year, and visualized a large city on the banks of the Cumberland. The inexhaustible water supply, no doubt, caught his eye more than anything else, for just as easily he could have led his followers into the rich blue grass area of Kentucky which lay to the north. A good water supply, however, was of paramount importance and, too, the Cumberland offered an easy means of transportation in a day in which overland travel of lengthy distances was next to impossible except by those of sturdy constitutions and courageous heart.

After a few months on the Cumberland Robertson decided to return for his family and others who might desire to come. When he arrived he found that many were anxious to leave, but hesitant to make a move of such proportions. Robertson hastily explained that much of the land between Watauga and his settlement on the Cumberland was rough and undesirable, while the land around the Cumberland was fertile and well drained. The lengthy distance overland, however, still remained a major obstacle, and Robertson decided that he and the able-bodied men should take the overland route while the women and children should take a circuitous water route under the command of John Donelson. Robertson and the men were to drive as many horses, cattle, sheep, and goats as they could, while household supplies would be transported by boat. By mid-December, 1779, Robertson and party were in Middle Tennessee, and on January 1, 1780, crossed the Cumberland on the ice and began to erect forts and stockades in anticipation of the arrival of the women and children. Late in December, 1779, Donelson's small flagship called *Adventure*, accompanied by thirty flat boats, departed Fort Patrick Henry in the Watauga country and started on their journey. Donelson's intention was to float down the Tennessee to the Ohio River and, by the use of poles, push the boats up the Ohio a short distance to the mouth of the Cumberland. From there they were to move up the Cumberland to Robertson's fort. On the flagship with Donelson were Robertson's wife, Charlotte Reeves Robertson, for whom the county seat of Dickson County later was named; a sister of Robertson; Donelson's fifteen year old daughter, Rachel, who later became the wife of Andrew Jackson; and many others who later played prominent parts in the early history of Tennessee.

The many sufferings and hardships encountered by this hardy group of pioneers are known through the journal of John Donelson, which was a daily diary of the happenings on the voyage. The discomforts caused by the winter weather and the constant attacks from the land by the Indians, together with the smallpox epidemic which broke out on one boat, caused the journey to be slow and difficult. By March 12 the party had reached the shoals in northern Alabama, and a week later it had arrived upon the Ohio River. On April 24 those who had withstood the ravages of the journey reached Robertson's establishment amid great rejoicing by both groups.[6] By this time Robertson's party had finished a log fort on the Cumberland, had planted a crop of corn, and had taken other measures to insure the comfort and safety of the new settlers. Needless to say, all suffered greatly during the first year from marauding Indians, hunger, and other privations. Some died within a few months after they arrived, but others from Watauga and elsewhere came in large numbers to compensate for those lost by death and to swell the ever increasing population.

As in the case of the Watauga settlement, many who came into central Tennessee were not content to remain at Fort Nashborough but, despite the ever-present Indian menace, pushed out into the surrounding country and established farms and homes of their own. Robertson himself, always of a restless nature, by the early 1790's had explored the area later to become Dickson County, and by 1793 had established an iron furnace in the northern part of the county. All who left the immediate vicinity of the fort were in constant danger from marauding bands of Indians, however. After initial attempts to destroy the main forts had failed, the Indians reverted to aggression in small bands, often laying in wait along a trail for an unsuspecting man, woman, or child.

Most of those who farmed the hills and valleys of central Tennessee during this period did so with their trusty rifles by their sides.

The Cumberland settlements grew rapidly. As new settlers came and established homes, friends and relatives in the Watauga settlements and in Virginia and North Carolina would learn of their success, and wherever they gathered—whether at the neighborhood store, church, quilting party, corn shucking, or log rolling—a major topic of conversation must have been about the folk who had gone west. Among some of the people there was political and economic unrest, and this class hastened into the new settlements. Others who had served in the Revolutionary War were lured into the area by a gift of land. John Hogg, for example, a North Carolinian who had served as a private in the Revolutionary army, was among the first to receive a grant of 640 acres in what is now Dickson County. Hogg never took up his claim but, like many other Revolutionary War veterans, sold it to another. In 1813 Hogg and his brother Samuel were to be found in Bedford County. There they sold to John K. Wynne, of Wilson County, Hogg's 640 acres described as being located on Yellow Creek. They received only one dollar per acre for it.[7]

By the time Hogg's grant was made, doctors, lawyers, and ministers had moved into the Cumberland country. Davidson Academy, a school operated by Presbyterians, was incorporated in 1785, and by the following year the Reverend Thomas B. Craighead had established the first Presbyterian church in Nashville.[8] Also, by this date saloons were in abundance, and a distillery called "The Red Heifer" had been established in Nashville.[9]

As has been mentioned, James Robertson by 1793 had surveyed the area later to become Dickson County, and had concluded that the northern part contained rich ore banks suitable for the location of an iron furnace.[10] In some places iron ore could be detected on the surface, Robertson observed, and in other places vast banks could be uncovered with a minimum amount of excavation. Therefore, in 1793 he established the first iron furnace in Middle Tennessee and the second in the state. It was located near the present town of Cumberland Furnace, and was called, for awhile, the Cumberland Iron Works.[11] This furnace played an important part in the lives of the people of Dickson County for the next hundred years. From the beginning Robertson gave employment to many, which was one of the major reasons for the influx of settlers during the early 1790's. Shortly after the iron works was established, territorial Governor William Blount secured the opening of a good wagon road between East Tennessee and the Cumberland country, and this greatly facilitated the growth in population. On many days the road was crowded with immigrants moving westward in a steady stream.[12] This rapid growth continued to the time of the War of 1812, and for Robertson and the furnace it meant an ample labor supply and an expanding market. The wagon road, of course, made possible an economical means of procuring necessary supplies and of transporting the pig iron to markets in the East.[13] Both the furnace and the wagon road facilitated the development of slavery in the county, a topic which is to be discussed in a later chapter.

Before 1783 Dickson County was, politically speaking, a part of the vast "Cumberland country," an area sometimes termed for convenience merely "the area west of the mountains." In 1783, however, the county of Davidson was created by an act of the North Carolina legislature, and Dickson County was a part of that vast political subdivision. Three years later the northeastern part of Davidson had grown sufficiently to become a county within itself, and the general assembly of North Carolina created Sumner County from it. The population continued to grow rapidly, and two years later, in 1788, the legislature carved a second political division from Davidson, giving it the name of Tennessee County. Clarksville was designated the county seat, and this county included all the territory now within the boundaries of Dickson, Montgomery, Robertson, and Houston, as well as parts of Hickman, Humphreys, and Stewart.[14] In the following year North Carolina ceded her western lands to the federal government, and the Territory South of the Ohio was established to include all of the Tennessee counties. A territorial government was organized, and by 1795 many believed that the Tennessee territory had within its borders the required 60,000 people necessary for admission to the union as a separate state. Accordingly, the territorial legislature authorized the taking af a census, the results of which disclosed a population of nearly 67,000 whites and over 10,000 Negroes. The counties in central Tennessee had a total population of only 12,000, for the center of population was in East Tennessee. Immediately in the Cumberland country a movement arose to delay the admission of the state, for the Middle Tennessee counties, ever fearful that East Tennessee would gain complete control and domination, sought eventually to create a state of their own west of the Cumberland Plateau as soon as the population had reached the number required by law.[15]

A few months later when an election was held to determine whether the people of the entire territory favored immediate admission, over 2,500 people voted against it. Tennessee County, of which Dickson was a part, having a total population of 1,941, voted 231 to 58 against immediate admission.[16] The population was centered predominantly in East Tennessee, however, an area where almost to a man the immediate admission of the territory to statehood was desired. The people in that section voted solidly for admission, and the election results indicated a three-to-one majority in favor of statehood. Consequently, despite Federalist opposition in the nation's capital, Tennessee in 1796 became the sixteenth state. In that same year a constitutional convention was called to be held in Knoxville, and five representatives attended from Tennessee County. When it was decided that the state should receive the name of this county, Tennessee County was abolished and carved into Robertson and Montgomery.[17] Dickson remained a part of these local units of government until it was created by the state legislature in 1803. Thus, during the twenty year period of 1783–1803 the land which became Dickson County had been included within the borders of Davidson, Tennessee, Robertson, and Montgomery counties.

By the time Dickson was formed many settlers already had established homes and staked out claims to Dickson County soil. They applied the ax and the torch to the virgin timber, and cleared the land for crops. Such logs as were needed for cabins were notched and carefully laid one on top of another to form one-room cabins, but most of them were piled in large heaps and burned at the community "log rollings." Corn proved to be adapted to the soil, and this crop more than any other was raised in practically every cleared tract. Some cotton was grown but it was never profitable. Tobacco also was raised, and it met with more success than did cotton.

It is impossible to enumerate all those who had settled in Dickson County by 1803. However, it is known that by 1803 Montgomery Bell, John Nesbitt, Abraham Caldwell, and James Richard Napier had settled on Barton's Creek; that a Revolutionary soldier named Christopher Strong, together with Molton Dickson, James Martin, and Robert Harper, had settled on Jones' Creek; that George Tubbs and William Ward had settled on Johnson's Creek; that Minor Bibb, Edward Tidwell, John Brown, Milton Johnson, and William and Thomas Gentry had staked out claims on Turnbull Creek; and that William Hogins and Thomas Petty had established homes on Piney River. They were all farmers, and most of them had come from either North Carolina or Virginia. All were to occupy prominent places in the agricultural, political, and industrial development of the county. They were not to have the county to themselves, however, for scarcely a week passed but that a new family moved in and established a home. The population of the state of Tennessee more than doubled during the decade from 1800 to 1810, and Dickson County was an important part of this growth.

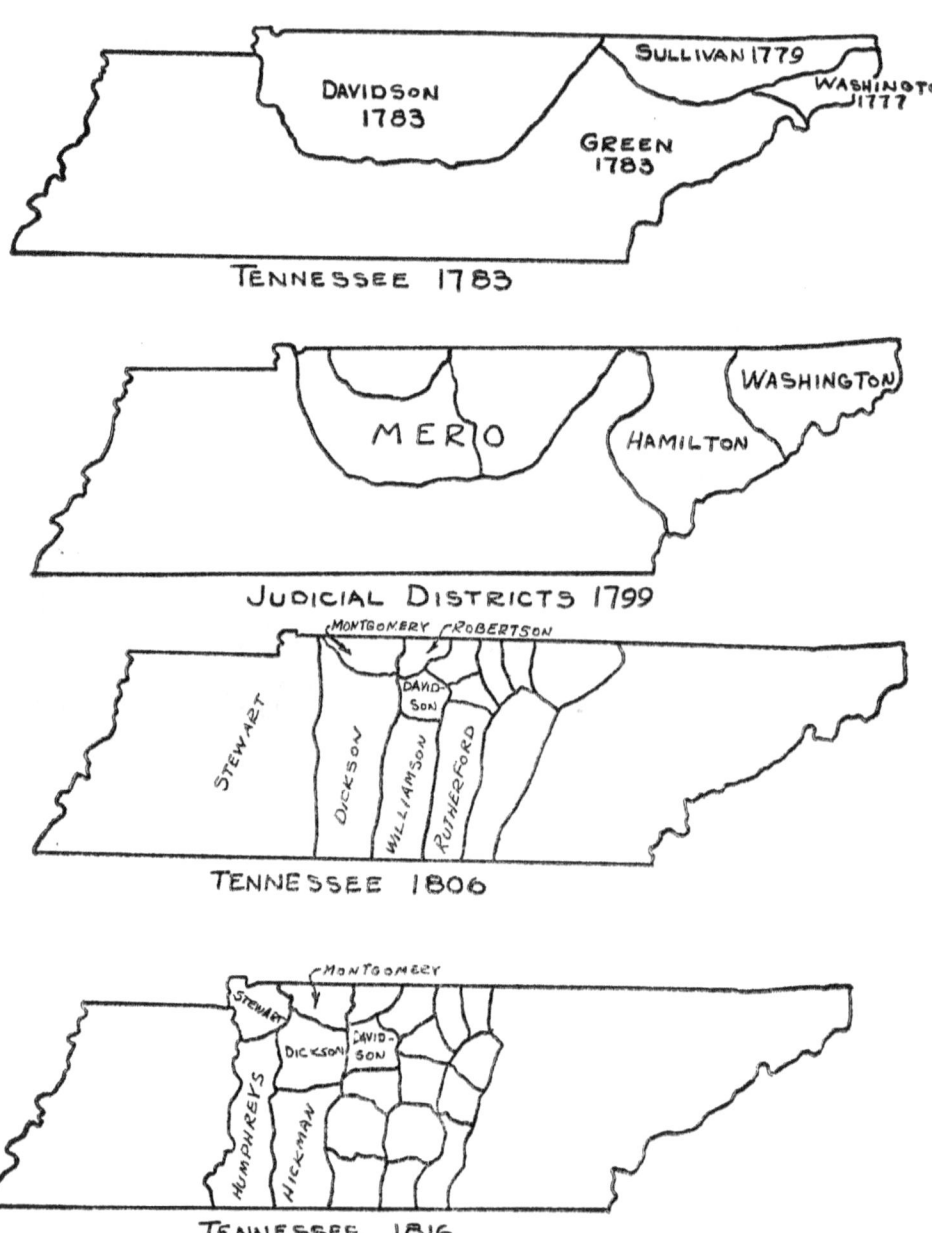

[FROM: TENNESSEE HISTORICAL MAGAZINE, VIII (1924-25), PP. 77-78]

(Maps show position of counties only. Boundaries are inexact.)

CHAPTER II

The Establishment of Dickson County and the Coming of Montgomery Bell

WHEN the legislature of 1803 convened, certain "citizens from Robertson and Montgomery Counties" filed a petition to create a new county.[1] The boundaries they proposed indicated plans for a vast sub-division. The northern boundary was to be Montgomery, the eastern limit was to be Davidson and Williamson, the southern boundary was to be the territory of Alabama, and the western border was to extend from the southeastern tip of Stewart County due south to the Alabama line. The petition was favorably acted upon and a bill was passed October 25, 1803, creating a new county by the name of Dickson.[2]

The county took its name from William Dickson, a young Nashville physician and statesman who was serving in Congress at the time. Dickson was born in Duplin County, North Carolina, in 1770. By 1795 he had studied medicine and had established a practice in Nashville. Good physicians were scarce on the frontier, and Dickson was able to build a large practice at once. As did most of the professional men who came into the western country, he began to participate in politics soon after his arrival. By 1799 he was not only a member of the state house of representatives, but was also speaker of that body. Two years later he advanced to Congress, where he served until 1807. He then returned to Nashville and resumed the practice of medicine, and there he lived until his death in 1816. He appears to have been well respected and to have exerted considerable influence in the affairs of Middle Tennessee. His interest in education was manifested in his willingness to serve as a trustee of the University of Nashville.[3] Although Dickson never lived in the county named for him, his cousin, Molton Dickson, and other relatives played important parts in its early development.

The pattern of settlement followed by the Dickson family was typical of that followed by many others who came from Europe and eventually into Tennessee. William Dickson's grandfather, John Dickson, was born in Ireland and came to Chester County, Pennsylvania, when quite young. After becoming accustomed to life in the new world he determined to move southward, settling next in Maryland, and later in Duplin (then New Hanover) County, North Carolina. He became a colonel in the North Carolina militia, and served in the colonial assembly of that colony. William Dickson's father, Colonel William Dickson, Sr., was one of nine children. He was born in 1739 when his parents were still in Pennsylvania, but moved to Maryland and thence in 1744 to North Carolina. While still in his teens he became a county surveyor, and afterwards was elected to the colonial assembly of North Carolina. He became an officer in the Revolutionary army, and afterwards a clerk of the county court for forty-four years. He was the father of nine children, several of whom in addition to William moved to Tennessee. Molton Dickson, a first cousin of William, served as county surveyor and state senator from Dickson County, and David Dickson, another cousin, was for many years county court clerk. The same pattern of settlement was pursued by Montgomery Bell, Edward Leech, Christopher Strong, and countless others who came into the county. Some would go from Pennsylvania into Kentucky and thence into Tennessee, but the usual path was down the Allegheny Mountains, into Virginia and North Carolina, and thence into Middle Tennessee.

The man for whom Dickson County was named was a friend of Andrew Jackson, correspondence between them reveals. Jackson, who was a young lawyer, politician, and Indian fighter when Dickson was in Congress, kept in close touch with his congressman during the latter's stay in the nation's capital.[4] In the feud which raged for several years between John Sevier and Jackson, Dickson took Jackson's part. Siding with the expansionists and those who advocated internal improvements at federal expense, Dickson fought for better transportation facilities for Tennessee and supported Jefferson's purchase of the vast Louisiana territory from Napoleon in 1803.[5] While Dickson was in Congress the Tennessee delegation did not cooperate because of local and sectional jealousies then existent among the people of East and central Tennessee. Dickson sought to pour oil on troubled waters, however; and when in 1806 the matter of establishing Cumberland Road came up, Dickson more than any other Tennessee congressman championed the cause of the measure.[6]

The legislative act which established Dickson County also named the members of the first county court and provided that they should convene for their first session at the home of Robert Nesbitt on Barton's Creek. The date of the first meeting was set for the first Monday of February, 1804, but inclement weather prevented the presence of a quorum. Those few who were present then decided to meet officially on March 19, by which time it was believed the roads would be in a passable condition. Consequently, on that date Montgomery Bell, William Doak, William Russell, Sterling Brewer, Gabriel Allen, Lemuel Harvey, Jesse Craft, Richard C. Napier, and William Teas met together at Nesbitt's home on Barton's Creek, about three miles north of Charlotte, and in a two-day session officially constituted the first county court.[7] In this the first session of the court there were at least two members who later gained wide recognition. Montgomery Bell, whose activities will be discussed presently, was to become one of the outstanding iron masters of the entire nation, and Sterling Brewer was to become speaker of the senate during the first administration of one of Tennessee's ablest governors, William Carroll. On the first day of the two-day session Robert Drake was appointed county court clerk pro tempore, and Drury Christian was named temporary sheriff. According to the record, this was all of importance which transpired on the first day. On the second day David Dickson, a cousin of William, announced his candidacy for the office of county court clerk, and was elected. Robert Weakley was named sheriff, James Walker was elected register of deeds, and Robert Drake was chosen commissioner of revenue. John Larkins was elected trustee, William Caldwell, ranger; James Fentress, county surveyor; and John Hall, coroner. N. A. McNairy was the first lawyer to be admitted to the bar, and was elected as the first county solicitor. A jury was appointed for the first session of the court, and a provision for a road to extend from the farm of William Teas on Yellow Creek to the Montgomery County line was voted upon, after which the court adjourned to meet again in June.[8]

In the original act no provision was made for a county seat or a courthouse. Therefore, on August 3, 1804, the state legislature empowered a commission composed of Montgomery Bell, Robert Dunning, Sterling Brewer, John Davidson, and George Clark, to study the terrain and seek a central and suitable location for a courthouse, prison, and stocks. Upon finding such a location the group was authorized to purchase not more than forty acres, which should be laid off into town lots. The lots then were to be sold and the income therefrom was to be used for the construction of the courthouse, jail and stocks. If the lots brought good prices, as many thought they would, the income would be sufficient to erect the county buildings, but if additional funds were needed the county court was authorized to levy a tax sufficient to make up the deficit.[9] Upon hearing of the needs of the county, however, a settler by name of Charles Stewart, who owned considerable property which included the area where now Charlotte is located, offered to donate to the county fifty acres for the new county seat. The offer was accepted by the commissioners, who then began a survey of Stewart's land in order to select the most desirable fifty acres for the county seat. The present location of Charlotte appealed especially to the commissioners. While examining the gently sloping hillside they stopped to rest at a spring under the hill on which the county jail now stands. Remembering, no doubt, that the legislative act had enjoined them in their search to have "due regard for good water," the commissioners saw in this spring and others nearby a sufficient water supply for hundreds of people, and they were convinced that the little valley nestled between two hills was the best site for the county seat. A man by the name of Ash was called in to lay out and plat the town, and settlers moved in rapidly. For the next half century it became one of the busiest county seats in Middle Tennessee.

The town was christened "Charlotte" after Charlotte Reeves Robertson, wife of the "Father of Middle Tennessee." While never residents of Dickson County, both husband and wife were well known throughout the Cumberland country. One of their daughters, Charlotte, married Richard Napier, an early settler in Dickson County. Charlotte Reeves was born in 1751, in Virginia, and was the daughter of a Presbyterian minister. At the age of seventeen she married Robertson, and they crossed the Appalachians to seek their fortune in the new Watauga settlement. Shortly after their marriage Robertson went west to explore the Cumberland country and, as noted earlier, his young wife joined him later when she went with the Donelson party to Fort Nashborough.[10] According to all accounts, Charlotte Robertson was a sturdy pioneer of great fortitude and courage. Of the many hardships she endured, one of the most interesting and trying was her participation in the Battle of the Bluffs at Fort Nashborough, April 2, 1781, in which by her quick action she helped repulse a fierce Indian attack. During the preceding night the Cherokees established themselves in ambush near the fort, at a point located at the present area of Church Street and First and Second Avenues, in Nashville. As morning dawned a small party of the tribe came to the fort and fired, and then hastily beat a short retreat but remained in full view. Most of the white men immediately grabbed their flintlocks and started in pursuit of the Indians, leaving the fort practically unguarded and in the hands of the women and a few men, who for various reasons were unable to engage in the pursuit. The Indians retreated and made a stand in the vicinity of what is now Demonbreun and Broad Streets. The whites were now a reasonable distance from the fort, and some fifty or more Indians, who remained just outside the gates unseen by the whites as they hastily pursued the enemy, now sought to batter down the gates and massacre those inside the fort. When it seemed that the few defenders could withstand the onslaught no longer, Charlotte Robertson decided to open the gates slightly and discharge about fifty fierce dogs, which already were whining and clawing at the gates in their desire to aid their masters. The dogs had been trained to hate even the smell of Indians, and their attack was like a modern blitzkrieg. The redskins were caught completely off guard, and were forced to give temporary attention to beating off the dogs, whose sharp fangs tore into their naked flesh. The attention of the Cherokees was diverted so that they lost the advantage of their excellent position, and the whites beat a hasty and successful retreat to the fort.[11] But for the quick thinking of Charlotte Reeves Robertson the history of Dickson County and Middle Tennessee might have been considerably different. Despite the many hardships which she endured, Charlotte Robertson lived to the ripe old age of ninety-two, and died at the home of her son-in-law, John B. Craighead, three miles west of Nashville, in 1843.[12] Her biographer, who knew her personally and who wrote of her a decade after her death, described her as being "kind and affectionate in her family, and a most devoted and loving mother.... In person she was rather above medium size with a symmetrical form, and regular, interesting, and expressive features."[13]

Of the many new settlers who came into the county around the turn of the century, the one who brought about the greatest industrial development was a young Scotch-Irish trader from Pennsylvania named Montgomery Bell, who was destined to become one of the greatest iron developers of the nation. As mentioned earlier, the Cumberland furnace had been first opened in 1793 by James Robertson and was the first iron furnace in the Cumberland country. Robertson had many interests besides iron manufacture, however, and did not develop the furnace to its full capacities. Bell, seeing the potentialities, purchased the furnace from Robertson in 1804 for $16,000 and began to expand it into one of the biggest industries of the South.

The story of Bell's success in Dickson County reads like an Horatio Alger novel. Born in 1769 in Chester County, Pennsylvania, Bell was reared in the vortex of the struggle and excitement of the American revolution. Receiving virtually no formal education, he set out on his own at an early age. After three years of work as an apprentice to a tanner, he joined an older brother who taught him the hatter's trade which he followed for several years with profit. In 1789 the young man, not yet twenty years of age, set out for Lexington, Kentucky, to join a sister whose husband's death had left her stranded in a strange place without funds. Almost overnight he built up a good hat business there, and within a short while employed as many as twenty hands in his business and paid for the education of his sister's children. Ever restless, however, Bell decided to push southward to seek his fortune. For years he had been interested in the development of water power, and the falls of the Cumberland country fascinated him. He saw that the streams of Middle Tennessee could be used to develop a thriving iron industry. It was at this point that he bought Robertson's furnace, and within a year's time increased the production several hundred per cent. Within a few years he had built additional furnaces on Jones' Creek, Turnbull Creek, Barton's Creek, and on the Cumberland and Piney rivers. He further indicated an interest in the establishment of a grist mill on Barton's Creek, and presented a bill to the county court requesting permission to erect a large dam on the creek for the purpose of creating sufficient power for his furnace and grist mill.[14]

Within less than a decade Bell was producing iron in large quantities. The extent of his operations may be gauged by the advertisement placed in a Nashville newspaper in 1808 for 5,000 cords of wood, for which he pledged to pay a price not to exceed fifty cents per cord.[15] This wood no doubt was to be buried and subjected to heat for about two weeks, after which it would become charcoal—a very necessary item in the iron business. In the same newspaper Bell also advertised for "eight or ten negro fellows," for which he agreed to pay a "generous price."[16] By the time these announcements were printed competitors had appeared in Middle Tennessee, but Bell was king of them all. In Dickson County, in addition to the Cumberland furnace, at least the following furnaces and forges were soon in operation, and most of them were owned by Bell: Carroll Furnace and Steam Forge near Bettstown on the Cumberland, Upper Forge on Jones' Creek, Piney Furnace on Piney

River, and Worley Furnace south of the present city of Dickson. In the adjoining county of Stewart, where Bell had limited interests, there were Randolph Furnace and Randolph Forge, Clark Furnace, Eclipse Furnace, Peytonia Furnace, Dover Furnace, Cumberland Rolling Mills, Rough and Ready Furnace, Bellwood Furnace, and Bear Spring Furnace. In nearby Montgomery, where Bell may have had interests, were Washington Furnace just over the Dickson-Montgomery line on the Charlotte to Clarksville road, Steele's Furnace on the south side of the Cumberland, Sailors' Rest Furnace located just south of Clarksville, Robinson Furnace near Palmyra, and Jones' Furnace and Mt. Vernon Furnace located on Budd's Creek.[17] Other furnaces and forges were probably in these counties in the early 1800's and also others in adjoining counties, particularly Hickman, where Bell had interests.

A thing which aided Bell greatly was a contract he made with the federal government to furnish it with cannon balls and other matériel of war. The agreement was made just before the War of 1812, and Bell is said to have made a small fortune from the contract. It is common legend in Middle Tennessee that practically all the balls used by Andrew Jackson in the Battle of New Orleans had been molded at Bell's Cumberland furnace. The ammunition probably was hauled by wagon to the Cumberland River, a distance of approximately fifteen miles, and there put on flatboats and shipped down the river to the Ohio, and thence to the Mississippi River. Once on the Mississippi, it was not long until it reached its destination.[18]

The most remarkable of all of Bell's undertakings was the harnessing of the Harpeth River at a point known as the Narrows of Harpeth, then a part of Dickson but now a part of Cheatham County. The Harpeth glides calmly and peacefully through the undulating plains of the Central Basin, but when it strikes the Highland Rim near Kingston Springs it makes several abrupt bends and winds round about for several miles. At the neck of one of the bends Bell resolved to cut a tunnel. At the point of his interest the river made a sweeping circuit of seven miles, but the distance across the hilly neck was only about 100 yards. Bell believed that if he could cut a tunnel through the neck he could develop a head of water sufficient to maintain a large furnace. When the undertaking was begun it was found to be a most difficult operation because of the presence of the subcarboniferous rock, through which drilling with the instruments of that day and time was a most laborious task. Bell had slaves to spare, however, and by working them for long hours seven days a week he was able to complete the project within a year. It is not known just when the operation was completed, but it probably was not long after the conclusion of the War of 1812. With the tunnel now cut, the river furnished about twice the water power which it had furnished before, and Bell built one of his largest furnaces there. He named it Pattison,[19] which was the maiden name of his mother. Not long after its completion Bell spoke of the work as "the justly celebrated . . . Narrows of Harpeth," which he believed "combined more water power and safety than any other on the western waters. . . ."

He described it as consisting of "a tunnel ... a distance of 96 yards, which is 15 feet wide and 6 feet high, by means of which a natural fall of water is gained of near 19 feet." The river, he explained was "bottomed on a smooth sound rock," with a solid bed of rock 250 feet high on one side, and "a band of still blue clay 22 feet high" on the other. This, he believed, would "admit the raising of a dam 12 feet high with perfect safety, thereby affording a head and fall of 30 feet of water. ..."[20] In the vicinity of this furnace Bell made his home for several years, and within a few miles of it he was buried in 1855.

The mining of ore was a comparatively simple operation for Bell, despite the fact that there were no steam shovels and heavy machinery. The pick and shovel in the hands of slaves scratched the ore from the shallow deposits, and wagons pulled by mules and oxen driven by slaves carried it to the washer. Here the early nineteenth century "rock crushers"—large sledge hammers in the hands of brawny Negroes—broke the rock into manageable size, after which it was washed under a steady stream of water. After a lengthy and thorough washing process, and after as much dirt and debris as possible had been cleaned from it, the ore was ready for the furnace. Many of the furnaces were heated by charcoal, and the following proportions were used to make pig iron once the furnace was in blast: eight hundred pounds of ore to eighty pounds of limestone, to twenty bushels of charcoal. These ingredients were called a "charge," and were put into the furnace in these proportions about every twenty minutes. The amount of pig iron obtained from a charge depended upon the purity of the ore. The temperature sometimes ran as high as 3,500 degrees Fahrenheit and the intense heat would melt the ore and transform the limestone into lime. The lime then would unite with the impurities of the ore and form a fusible impure glass which, being lighter than the melted iron, would float to the top and be taken off as slag. The iron, now settling to the bottom in a liquid mass, was drawn off at the bottom, while the slag was drained into a container lined with bricks called a "hot pot." The pot was emptied, or flushed, every thirty minutes. Entrance was gained to the lower opening periodically to permit the melted iron to run into small gutters made of sand, and called "pig beds." When a pig bed was filled the stream would be diverted to another bed, while the molten mass in the first pig bed was cooled with water. Once sufficiently cooled, the iron would be broken into pieces about eighteen inches long by men with sledge hammers. It was then ready to be cast into cannon, cannon balls, kettles, skillets, and a host of other objects.[21]

Although Bell was a man of great enterprise, his private and personal life was never exemplary and his greatness lies only in the fact that he succeeded materially in the American pragmatic conception of success. Early in life he learned to drive hard and shrewd bargains, to get the greatest amount of labor from the slave even if the whip and harsh treatment were necessary, to violate the law if such became expedient to the accomplishment of his ends, and to deceive friends if it appeared profitable. Leonard Lane Leech, who knew Bell personally, described him as a "shrewd, exacting trader," and one who would "never pay a debt unless sued."[22] The court records of Dickson County contain many suits against him. For example, Martha Dickson, a widow, was one who learned of Bell's character the hard way, and Francis Prince was another. Martha Dickson had answered one of Bell's advertisements for cord wood, and with her own hands had cut several loads and sold them to Bell. The iron master refused to pay her, however, and she was forced to bring suit in the circuit court of Dickson County for redress. Alleging that Bell "craftily intended to deceive and defraud" her, Martha sued Bell for her money. A jury granted her damages amounting to $114.40.[23] Prince made a contract with Bell and signed a negotiable instrument for $1,000 but in an issue of the Nashville *Impartial Review and Cumberland Repository* he found it necessary to insert the following announcement:

> All persons are forwarned from accepting a note drawn by me in favor of Montgomery Bell, for upwards of one thousand dollars, given last year, as I am determined not to pay up said note, on account of the said Bell not having fulfilled his contract therefor.[24]

Bell was said by some to have been kind to his slaves, and that many of them preferred to work for him rather than to have their freedom. He was said to have given them large allowances of food and clothing and to have permitted them many liberties. It was only in Bell's latter years, however, that he began to show a degree of tolerance for the slave. While he developed the Dickson County forges and furnaces it appears that he sought to wring from the slaves all that he possibly could, with little thought for their comfort. On several occasions slaves ran away from his furnaces. One such runaway was a black called "Billey," who made his escape in August of 1807. Bell offered a two hundred dollar reward to anyone who would apprehend the discontented runaway and bring him back in irons. He bought advertising space in a Nashville newspaper to herald the following announcement:[25]

> Ran-away on the 15th of the present instant from the subscriber at the Cumberland Furnace, Dickson County, state of Tennessee, a dark mulatto fellow, Called BILLEY, but will no doubt change his name; perhaps 34 or 5 years old, 5 feet 10 or 11 inches high, strong and actively formed, his countenance indicative of discontent, unless when he affects a smile; his features tolerably prominent without much flesh on his face, his clothing unknown, but will no doubt change them as he has an opportunity of pilfering others. He will I expect pass himself for a free man, has worked sometime at the coaling business, his direction is uncertain, but it is supposed he will bend his course toward Louisiana, Indiana Territory, state of Ohio, or Lexington, Kentucky. It is not to be supposed he will acknowledge who he belongs to, he was guilty of crimes previous to his elopement, for which he expected punishment. Any person apprehending him will iron him in the most secure manner, paying no regard to any promises he may make, lodge him in jail and inform me of it so that I can get him, or if they bring him to me secured in irons shall have the above reward and reasonable expenses paid by Montgomery Bell.

As late as 1845 Bell, then a man of advanced age and enfeebled condition, was having difficulty with runaway slaves. In that year he advertised in a Nashville paper for two blacks who had escaped from his Pattison Iron Works. One was called "Tom," an engineer, "about 24 years of age, well-formed, middle size." The other was "Jim," described as a blacksmith, "18 years old, and one leg shorter than the other, perceivable when he walks." Bell advised that there had been "two low white women" in the neighborhood with whom the boys had been friendly, and it was believed that they had encouraged the slaves to leave.[26]

"Low women" were not unknown to Bell himself. According to tradition the iron master numbered among his illegitimate children both whites and blacks. W. Blake Leech, recently deceased, could remember in the late 1870's when there were "many whites and mulattoes who claimed that they were Bell's children." While Bell contributed financially to the support of many, Leech believed that "he was held accountable for a great many sins that he did not commit."[27]

Among Bell's friends and relatives was one Edward Leech, who came to Pennsylvania at about the same time Bell did. Like the iron master, and also like the Dickson family for whom the county was named, Leech settled first in Chester County. Becoming interested in rich farm land in the South but not having visited the Kentucky-Tennessee area, Leech trusted Bell's judgment, for Bell made occasional business trips to Pennsylvania and New York. According to legend, Bell offered Leech a one thousand acre tract of his own land on Johnson's Creek for a valuable consideration, and at the same time gave Leech an exaggerated report of the value of the property. When Leech demurred, Bell offered the property to him in exchange for valuable property which Leech owned in Pennsylvania, and expressed the conviction that the Dickson County property was much the greater in value. Leech, took Bell at his word, and consummated the deal, only to find when he reached Dickson County that the Johnson's Creek property was by no means what Bell had represented it to be. Bell realized a handsome profit on this venture.

Bell spent over $150,000 on real estate alone in Middle Tennessee.[28] His holdings extended over Dickson, Davidson, Hickman, Stewart, and other Middle Tennessee counties. Among his Dickson County purchases, in addition to 10,000 or more acres in the vicinity of Barton's Creek, there were at least the following: in 1826, 640 acres "at Beaver dam fork at Turnbull Creek," and fifty acres "on the lead drain of Yellow Creek . . . opposite the head of Jones' Creek"; in 1828, 600 acres "on both sides of Turnbull Creek"; in 1832, 640 acres on "the waters of Jones' Creek"; and in 1837, 600 acres on Turnbull Creek and 55½ acres on Jones' Creek.[29]

Bell was thought by some to have brought money with him from Pennsylvania or to have received it by inheritance after coming to Tennessee. One careful student of Bell's life, however, believes that he started with nothing and received no help.[30] Only one time, apparently, in his business career did Bell experience financial difficulty, and that was during the early 1820's when the entire nation was engulfed in depression. In 1822 Bell asked for a large loan from the Bank of Tennessee, and the request was forwarded to a legislative committee for a decision. After "deliberate consideration and reflection . . . but with the deepest regret and concern," the committee decided negatively, stating that it would be "unwise and unsafe" for the state to make such a loan.[31] The amount Bell sought was not stipulated in the legislative *Journal*. The captain of industry, apparently frustrated by the lack of money and hard times in general, decided then to sell much of his property. In 1824 he purchased front page advertising space in the Nashville *Whig* and sought to dispose of some of his holdings. "The subscriber desirous of repose from the active pursuits in which he has long been engaged," Bell began, "proposes to sell on liberal credit" the following:

> 2 blast furnaces on the iron ore fork of Barton's Creek in Dickson County . . . with about 12,000 acres of well-timbered land. . . . Also a 5-fire forge on Jones' Creek . . . having the advantage of the most modern improvements . . . Also the justly celebrated Narrows of Harpeth. . . .

Much other property, in Davidson and Hickman, was also advertised for sale. Bell announced that if the property was not disposed of in eight months he would "then receive proposals for partnership for improving and carrying on the improved sites."[32]

The prosperity which followed the panic of 1819 and the early 1820's probably carried Bell along with it, and never again did he appear to have financial difficulty. He freed many slaves in his old age, and provided for their support in Liberia. He bequeathed $20,000 for an academy "for the education of children not less than ten or more than fourteen years old who are not able to support and educate themselves and whose parents are not able to do so."[33] An inventory of Bell's holdings, completed September 10, 1857, two years after his death, showed the iron master to have been worth $72,426.20 at the time of his death. Of this amount, $17,065.64 was on deposit in the Bank of Tennessee and the rest was in bonds and notes.[34]

Bell died almost a recluse, never having "lived in any sort of comfort."[35] According to one story, snow blew in on his deathbed through a broken window as he lay dying. He had few friends and was always a man of mystery. Park Marshall, of Franklin, who knew him, said of Bell that "he did not engage in public affairs or war . . . and was not one to bestow or win warm friendship."[36] Judge Robert Ewing of Nashville, another who knew him, saw in Bell a man "somewhat eccentric but of forceful character."[37] Leonard Lane Leech, who was at Bell's bedside when Bell died, saw in him a friendless man who always had difficulty in getting along amicably with his fellowmen.

While Montgomery Bell was exploiting Dickson County hills for its iron ore and its population for its labor, and at the same time causing the area to be widely recognized as an iron center, the county as a whole changed and developed phenomenally. Other furnace operations were to come and go, and many men of enterprise were to leave their marks upon the early history of Dickson County, but few rivaled the iron master of the Harpeth, Montgomery Bell.

CHAPTER III

Early Economic Development

THE early settlers found Dickson County land satisfactory for agricultural pursuits although not excessively fertile. The well-drained soil and moderate temperatures proved conducive to the raising of corn and tobacco, and many settlers also planted an annual crop of cotton despite the short growing season. They found most of the land covered with timber and underbrush, to which they hastily and vigorously applied the ax in order to make way for crops.

Practically all the pioneers settled in the rich bottom lands of the Cumberland and Harpeth rivers or in the creek bottoms of Johnson's, Jones', and Barton's, and it was they who obtained the best farm land of the county. Others found almost equally good soil, however, in the high table land which rises abruptly out of the bottoms. As mentioned, the county lies in the best part of the high dissected plateau known as the Highland Rim, which encircles the Central Basin where Davidson County is located. The ridge tops, especially in the northeastern area bordering the present area of Cheatham County, were smooth or gently rolling. In the southern part the settlers found a fairly fertile soil, consisting of a brownish-gray silt loam, underlain by a yellowish-red clay loam. This type was also on some of the ridges between the present towns of Charlotte and Dickson, as well as in the south central part in the present area of Burns and between Burns and Dickson. About fifty per cent of the soil of the entire county, the pioneers learned, consisted of a gravelly silt loam of a grayish color. In this kind of soil was found varying quantities of gravel, and in some of the hill land it proved too stony for profitable cultivation. This type was found throughout the county, occupying all except the lower slopes and the river valleys already designated. Corn, wheat, and tobacco were grown with some degree of success on this soil.[1]

The climate the settlers found to be characterized by moderate temperatures in both summer and winter, with a mean summer temperature of around 76 degrees, which was suited for most crops. In recent years it has been observed that the average frost-free season consists of about 188 days, and that killing frosts have occurred as early as October 2 and as late as May 2.[2] During the winter the temperature not infrequently dips below zero, but never for a sustained period. When James Robertson came into Middle Tennessee in 1779, he found the Cumberland River frozen so hard that men and cattle could pass over it with no danger. From time to time since then the Cumberland has frozen over, but this by no means has been a yearly occurrence.

For the proper growth of cotton it is well known that a long growing season is required and that soils of a sandy-spongy nature are those in which the crop flourishes. Although Dickson County could not adequately meet either test, still the farmers of the pre-Civil War period could not resist the temptation to grow all the cotton they could in order to reap some of the profits which were being realized from the staple. The invention of the cotton gin served as an impetus to the cotton culture, and by 1800 it was the chief money crop of the Cumberland Basin, with tobacco second.[3] Eli Whitney had invented the gin and secured a patent on it in 1793, and by 1799 his gins were used in some parts of the Cumberland country.[4] In 1803 the legislature passed a bill whereby the state could purchase from Whitney the right to manufacture and use the Whitney gin in Tennessee. In 1804, however, there appeared to be some doubt as to whether Whitney was the true inventor, and whether he had secured a legal patent for the gin. In that year the legislature rescinded the act until the title matter was cleared up. By 1806 it had been ascertained that Whitney was the true and rightful patent owner, and the legislature in that year enacted another law whereby a tax was levied for Whitney's benefit on all gins then in operation in the state. The legislators further requested the inventor to place a machine in Nashville by January 1, 1807 for the use and observation of the people of central Tennessee.[5]

By summer of 1807 there were at least fourteen cotton gins operating in Tennessee, and probably many more not on record.[6] In the same year Robert Jarman set up an establishment in Dickson County in which he manufactured gins. In June of that year he announced through a Nashville newspaper that he had erected a shop on Yellow Creek, ten miles west of Charlotte. He further stated that he would make gins "on a new plan, called the hollow neck teeth saw gins," and that his business would be carried on "very extensively." He explained that he was a stranger in Middle Tennessee, but in order to show that his gins were "superior to any now at work in this country," he submitted testimonials from James Robertson and Benjamin Joslin. Robertson declared that the gins were far superior to any he had ever seen, and from his personal observation he knew that Jarman's gins would pick "near twice as much in a day as the common gins in the country." Joslin likewise was lavish in his praise. He believed that Jarman was "the best gin maker in the country," and said that a fifty-saw gin which the craftsman had made for him had performed the unheard-of feat of seeding "fifty pounds of seed-cotton in five minutes."[7]

Although some of the cotton produced in the county was purchased locally, Nashville was the market for cotton and other produce. At one time the Nashville merchants, realizing that most frontier farmers had little cash on hand, offered to take "cash or cotton" in payment for all purchases.[8] The price offered by the average wholesale merchant in 1804 was fifteen cents per pound for loose cotton, and seventeen cents for baled lint.⁹ The price of cotton varied from time to time, but there was a general upward trend. In 1807 Nashville merchants attempted to stabilize prices and, over the vehement protests of the cotton growers, agreed among themselves to pay only twelve and fourteen cents.¹⁰ They were unsuccessful, however, and the price of cotton in Nashville rose to twenty and twenty-one cents per pound. Cotton in Tennessee and indeed throughout the South was now well on its way toward a comfortable seat on a throne erected by and to be constantly buttressed by Southern planters and Northern and foreign markets. Cotton in Dickson County never proved overly successful, however. By the beginning of the second quarter of the century production was declining rapidly, and by 1850 only nineteen bales weighing four hundred pounds each were produced in the entire county.¹¹

Practically all of the settlers owned stock, because beasts of burden were very necessary for plowing. Cattle, swine, and poultry, which provided a ready meat supply, were raised in abundance. Too, wild game roamed the hills and valleys and supplemented the diet of the pioneers. The milch cows usually were belled, for there were few enclosures to keep the cattle within a reasonable distance of the home, but beef cattle were permitted to roam the pastures unhampered, in frontier fashion. One author has included the cowbell among the five most essential things on the frontier. The other four were rifles, cows, houses, and axes.¹² The abundance of land and pasture made cattle raising profitable, for they could be turned on the open range and rounded up at market time. The large number of "ear marks" recorded in the Minutes of the county court testifies to the extensive nature of the cattle business in the early years of Dickson County. Successful corn crops meant large numbers of corn-fed poultry and swine, although many hogs were raised on the open range in the same manner as cattle.

By 1810 over 4,500 people had settled in Dickson County. In Middle Tennessee the population of this county was exceeded only by that of Davidson and Montgomery. The basic structure of the economy was agriculture, but by 1810 the economy had expanded in such a manner that craftsmen of all types were present, and stores and small industries were being established. Professional men, too—doctors, lawyers, ministers, and teachers—were finding their way into the county, and Charlotte was becoming an enterprising frontier town. The Indian was no longer the menace he once was, and while a party did go on the warpath in 1809 in the present area of Garner's Creek and kill Colonel William Garner (for whom that creek was named) and wreak much destruction, no longer did the farmer feel the necessity of taking his trusty rifle each time he went into his fields of corn and cotton.¹³

While many of those who followed agricultural pursuits made a good living, others experienced difficulty in paying taxes. As early as March 1, 1805, Sheriff Robert Weakley found a number of settlers delinquent and advertised in a Nashville paper the sale of their land in order that their tax bills might be met. For example, Thomas Hogg's heirs had nearly 2,000 acres on Yellow Creek on which no taxes had been paid.

William P. Lewis had over 700 acres on the same creek, and John Dickson had 600 acres on Barton's Creek, all of which was to be put up for sale.[14] By December of the same year David Hogan, who had replaced Weakley as sheriff, announced through a Nashville paper that the property of the following would be sold at the front door of Molton Dickson's store in Charlotte in order to satisfy delinquent taxes: Hezekiah Barnes, 333 acres; John Dickson, 600 acres; Thomas Hamilton, 640 acres; and Samuel Jackson, 1,068 acres.[15] Other notices appeared from time to time announcing other people to be delinquent. In 1814, former Sheriff Robert Weakley was behind in his tax payments, and 640 acres of his land on Yellow Creek, and other property on Barton's Creek and at the mouth of Harpeth River, was to be sold for taxes. Ben Harris on Turnbull likewise was delinquent at the time, and Hugh Dickson's lot number 53 in Charlotte was to be sold.[16]

The tax rate during the first few decades of the county's history was quite low when compared to modern standards. An early meeting of the county court established the following tax rate:
County Tax—6¼ cents on each white poll, 6¼ cents on each 100 acres of land, 12½ cents on each black poll, 12½ cents on each town lot, and 5 dollars on each store.
Jail Tax—25 cents on each white poll, 12½ cents on each 100 acres of land, 25 cents on each black poll, 25 cents on each town lot, and 10 dollars on each store.
Poor Tax—6¼ cents on each white poll, 5 cents on each 100 acres of land, 10 cents on each black poll, 12½ cents on each town lot, and 2½ dollars on each store.[16]

It is interesting to observe that the tax on Negro slaves was about twice that of the levy on whites.

Public gatherings for political rallies and for sales such as described above generally took place in front of Molton Dickson's store until about 1810, when the courthouse was completed. As mentioned, some people believed that the sale of town lots in Charlotte would bring in sufficient revenue to construct public buildings. The lots did not sell as rapidly as some had hoped, however, and by 1806 new building commissioners had been appointed. In May, 1806, they advertised that a contract would be let for the construction of a courthouse and other public buildings. The temple of justice was to be twenty-four by thirty-two feet in size, and to be partitioned into four or more offices. At the time of the announcement it was undetermined whether it would be of frame or brick, but the commissioners specified that it was to be done "in an elegant manner." They further stipulated that all lots in Charlotte which were not sold by the time of the letting of the contract would be sold "on a credit of four and nine months." The commissioners who signed the announcement were Sterling Brewer, George Clark, Robert Dunning, and John Davidson.[17]

Work on the buildings apparently was begun immediately, but the completion date cannot be ascertained because some of the county records of the period have been destroyed. Financial difficulty must have

Montgomery Bell (1769-1855)

This portrait was made late in Bell's life, and shows a determined but perhaps disillusioned man.

Bell's Monument

The monument over the grave of Montgomery Bell is located in what is now Cheatham County. At the time of Bell's death and burial, however, the burial plot was in Dickson County. The stone shows a furnace in operation, under which appears:
"Montgomery Bell, born Jan. 3rd, 1769, in Chester Co., Pa. Died April 1st, 1855, in Dickson County. He was one of the earliest and most successful iron masters in the state. This monument is erected by his executors. W. C. Watkins, J. L. Bell, O. P. Roberts, 1855."

"Uncle Harry" Primm was born in slavery

"Uncle" Harry Primm was born in slavery. Until his death in the early 1940's he could recall vividly stirring scenes of the ante-bellum and Civil War days. His home was at Promised Land.

Cumberland Furnace

been encountered from the beginning, however, for in the following year the legislature passed an act giving to the county court the right to levy an additional tax "for the purpose of completing the public buildings."[18] In the same legislative session Hickman County was carved from Dickson, and the present boundary between the counties was established.[19]

By the time the buildings were completed, many business and professional men had established themselves in the county. Thomas Overton and a man named Barr were among the first to be admitted to the bar, and they, like many others, practiced in the courts of several counties. Thomas Claiborne, Jr., for example, who was to distinguish himself in law and politics, announced in a Nashville paper in 1807 that he was available for practice in the courts of Dickson, Davidson, Wilson, Rutherford, and Williamson counties. The young lawyer pledged himself "that no exertion shall be wanting . . . to execute with the most prompt and unremitting zeal such business as a generous public may confide to his management."[20] Thomas Hart Benton, later to distinguish himself on the national level, also practiced in Dickson County before 1812. Benton came to Tennessee from North Carolina when only nineteen, and soon began law practice in Franklin. The proximity of that town to Charlotte made it inevitable that he would come before the Charlotte bar on many occasions.[21] To a Dickson County client he at one time advised that a land entry should set forth complete boundary lines, including the nearest streams, the nearest mountains, any places of note nearby, and the natural boundaries which might divide it from other lands.[22] Cave Johnson, who studied law in the office of Parry W. Humphreys on Yellow Creek and later set up offices in Clarksville, practiced at the Dickson County bar. In 1817 he was elected solicitor-general for the Tenth District, which included Dickson, Stewart, Humphreys, Robertson, and Montgomery counties.[23] Eleven years later he was elected to Congress from the Tenth Congressional district, of which Dickson was a part. William Collier, of Charlotte, and many other men of lesser note, practiced law at the Dickson County bar.

Molton Dickson established what was probably the first general store in Charlotte and, as mentioned earlier, it played an important part in the lives of the early settlers. Dickson was an able man and had many other interests besides the mercantile business. A cousin of William Dickson, the merchant held several public offices in the county, including that of county surveyor, state senator, and county register. Just when he went to Dickson County is not known; perhaps he and his brother David, who later became county court clerk, were in the vicinity by the time the town of Charlotte was laid out. By 1805 his store was established on the public square. The Nashville *Impartial Review and Cumberland Repository* announced in its columns July 23, 1807, that Molton Dickson had been authorized to receive and solicit subscriptions to that newspaper in Charlotte and Dickson County, and invited all to visit Dickson's store and subscribe to the paper. Probably the second to engage in the mercantile business was John Holland, who in 1806 obtained a license to keep a general store and to sell a variety of groceries, dry goods, and whiskey. In the same year John Spencer was granted a license to keep an "ordinary," or saloon, in his new residence in the town of Charlotte.[24] Various others were granted similar licenses from time to time.

In case supplies of alcoholic beverages ran low merchants and dealers had little difficulty in replenishing their stock. Many farmers operated stills on their farms and converted their surplus grain into a liquid for which they found a ready market. Several large distilleries were maintained, and Christopher Strong and Daniel Leech owned one of the largest ones on Johnson's Creek.[25] Samuel Croft and Nathan Peeples operated one of equal size on Yellow Creek, and by 1820 their business was thriving to such an extent that they advertised through a Clarksville paper for a "first rate distiller."[26] In the same year, Sheriff Rich Batson advertised land for sale on the east fork of Yellow Creek which, he pointed out, was "an excellent seat for a distillery."[27]

By 1808 Joseph Wingate, a hat maker, was in business on the public square of Charlotte. On April 27 of that year he advertised in the Nashville *Impartial Review and Cumberland Repository* for "one or two apprentices who would come recommended" to aid him in his newly formed hatter's shop. He promised that the boys would be well cared for and that they would be given a good education and good training. He also advertised for "three or four journeymen" whose wages he promised would be "the highest" in the country. The custom of apprenticing youths to a master craftsman has a flavor of medievalism, but it was practiced extensively on the frontier. A youth would be apprenticed to a craftsman who would keep the boy for a period of time and teach him a trade. Sometimes the craftsman was paid by the boy's parents or guardian, and in other cases he received only the products of the youth's labor for his compensation. When the youth felt that he had learned the trade sufficiently well, he submitted his masterpiece to several craftsmen who examined it thoroughly and, if they believed it met proper standards, conferred upon the youth the full privileges and responsibilities of a master craftsman.

By the 1820's many business establishments were prospering, despite the panic of 1819 and 1820. Minor Bibb, Thomas Pannell, Christopher Robertson, and Jacob Voorhies had established stores in the county. Voorhies, in addition to his mercantile establishment, also operated a school. Licenses to establish ordinaries were issued at almost every court meeting, and court records of "ear marks" indicate a rapid growth of the cattle business.

As mentioned in another chapter, by the 1820's the iron industry was being expanded by Montgomery Bell, various members of the Napier family, and others. James Robertson was the first to see the potentialities of iron in Dickson County, however, and it is Robertson who deserves credit for the discovery of the rich ore fields in the county. While his production never approached that of Bell's, Robertson did make a successful operation of the business. One of his customers was James Winchester, who operated a large store in Sumner County. In 1803 he ordered from Robertson "about a ton of large castings, say pots and kettles from ten to twenty gallons," and also some of the "smallest kind of hand ware, such as skillets, and so forth." The Sumner County merchant apparently made purchases from the Dickson iron works not infrequently, for he complained that the last castings he had bought were too high and that he would expect lower prices in the future. He also stated that in an earlier order too many "small ovens" were received and that "there is more than a ton of them yet on hand at this time." He also ordered bar iron at twelve cents per pound, if Robertson would guarantee that it was of good quality, and offered to pay in either cash or salt.[28]

Another business in which Dickson Countians engaged on a limited scale was traffic in slaves. Montgomery Bell was probably the first to bring blacks in large numbers in to the county. Anthony Vanleer, the Napiers, and other iron masters also had many Negroes. During the slaveholding period the iron masters of the county held approximately one-fourth of the slaves. The typical farmer of Dickson County, however, held very few or perhaps no slaves. Of those who did own Negroes, all held only a few, and more held one slave than any other number. Like most farmers of the South who held few slaves, the Dickson County yeomen tended to keep their Negroes until they died and to treat them with kindness. It was required by law that bills of sale of slaves were to be filed with the county court, and the first recorded sale was for "one Negro boy" purchased by Sterling Brewer.[29] At the first meeting of the court in 1805 John Turner sold to Nathan Nesbitt "a negro Man slave named Bill," and William Teas purchased of Joseph Teas "a negro."[30] Some slaves indicated a great deal of natural ability, while others were surly and lazy. The subject of slavery in Dickson County is treated more fully in a later chapter.

The expansion of the county's economy was facilitated greatly by the building of roads. Within a few years after the county was established roads leading to Charlotte from the Cumberland furnace, Yellow Creek, and Weakley's Ferry had been constructed, and more were in the process of being built. By 1806 a dirt road had been constructed between Nashville and Charlotte.[31] By that year a post office had been established at the county seat, and Richard Waugh was the first postmaster. In the summer of 1806 the Postmaster-General issued a statement calling for bids to take mail from Nashville to Charlotte once each week. The run was made each Friday and the round trip was to be accomplished in one day. The mail left Nashville at 6:00 A. M. and would arrive at Charlotte by noon. It would leave Charlotte one hour later and arrive in Nashville at 8:00 P. M. This, of course, would require traveling at a rapid pace, for the rider must cover about seven miles per hour on the Nashville to Charlotte trip, but could travel a bit more slowly on the more difficult afternoon leg of the journey. A few years later the county court appointed a thirteen-man committee to study the conditions of the roads and make a report at the next meeting of the court. The magistrates were particularly interested in a road from Charlotte to Dover, and the committee was authorized to make a study and to recommend the nearest and best route to the Stewart County seat. By 1824, in addition to the roads mentioned, pikes stretched from Charlotte to Columbia, Charlotte to Franklin, and Charlotte to Clarksville. Columbia and Clarksville early became tobacco centers, and the farmers of Dickson County probably carried their crops to these markets in addition to Nashville. All of the early lines of transportation were dirt roads, of course, which meant that frequently they were muddy in the winter and dusty in the summer.[32]

The population grew as the economy expanded. In 1795 Tennessee County, which included the area later to become Dickson, Robertson, Montgomery, and parts of other counties, had a population of only 1,941 whites and 398 slaves. Fifteen years later, however, in 1810, Dickson alone had 4,516 inhabitants, of whom nearly 1,000 were Negroes. The census for the same year indicated that the surrounding counties of Humphreys, Hickman, Stewart, and Montgomery had, respectively, populations of 1511, 2583, 4262 and 8021. Davidson was the state's largest with 15,608, surpassing even the counties of East Tennessee. By 1810 twenty-six counties were in central Tennessee with a population of 287,501, while the twenty-two counties of East Tennessee had only 135,312. One of the chief reasons for this great influx was the negotiation of treaties (made by 1806) between the United States and the Cherokees, whereby the Indians relinquished their claims to most of central Tennessee.[33]

During the next decade the population growth declined somewhat, inasmuch as the area west of the Tennessee River was being opened for settlement. While many people came into Dickson County, few remained. Most pushed westward to settle in the fertile river bottoms of the Tennessee and the Mississippi rivers. Andrew Jackson made a huge purchase from the Chickasaws in 1818, and this newly acquired land acted as a magnet in drawing people into the West. The result was that the population of Dickson and other Middle Tennessee counties grew much less rapidly during the decade prior to 1820 than in the preceding decade. The 1820 count showed an increase of only 674, or a total of 5,184.[34]

While economic pursuits were of great importance to the frontiersman, they did not dominate his life exclusively. Religious services and camp meetings played an important part in his life and, as will be noted in a later chapter, became of paramount concern to the people in every community of Dickson County. The Presbyterians, Methodists, and Baptists were in Middle Tennessee as soon as settlements were established, and they did much for the spiritual and educational advancement of the people. All-day singings, weddings, dances, and parties were a source of entertainment, although excessive merrymaking sometimes brought the participant condemnation by his more puritanical associates. Dancing often resulted in expulsion from a religious body.[35] Court sessions always brought large crowds to Charlotte, giving those who assembled ample opportunity to swap horses and yarns, or just to visit old friends. The large number of saloons and distilleries indicate that for those who needed occasional snorts of "good cheer" there was always a large quantity of "redeye" handy, which flowed freely at elections and court sessions. Such prominent citizens from the Turnbull neighborhood as John Gray, William Terman, and Beedy White imbibed quite freely while in Charlotte on more than one occasion, but unlike most, they repented and promised to drink no more.[36]

Grown-ups got together at corn-huskings, quilting parties, house-raisings, log-rollings, communal ground clearings, and other activities, while the young folk always could find excuse to stage a party or a frolic at which they found opportunity to spend hours in "heavy" courting. When a new settler came into a frontier community his immediate need was shelter, and the men of the neighborhood generally would pitch in and help him build a cabin. Most of the log structures were large one-room buildings with a fire place on one side, and it was in this room that the entire family—often consisting of ten or more children—slept, ate, and lived. The frontiersmen usually built a kitchen in the rear, sometimes attached to his house, but occasionally several feet from it. The log cabin which housed Samuel McAdow and family in 1810 was more elaborate than most. McAdow, who came to Dickson County as a Presbyterian preacher and settled some ten miles southeast of Charlotte, constructed a two-room cabin with a wide passageway, or hall, between the rooms. His chimney, like most of them, was made of sticks, dirt, and stone, and the fireplace was entirely of stone. His logs for constructing the house had been squared with a broad-axe, had been notched on each end and carefully laid in place, and the cracks had been daubed with mud. Several small windows had no glass but were equipped with clap-board shutters which hung on wooden hinges.[37]

Once the home of the pioneer was built, a log-rolling was next in order. The large trees, once felled and stripped of their branches, would be rolled into a common pile and burned. The light from the fire would supply sufficient illumination for an all-night dance or frolic, and the blaze, ever shooting skyward as more fuel was piled on, could be seen for miles around. The ground now cleared, except for the stumps which in most cases were too difficult to dig out, was ready for the frontiersman's first crop.

As mentioned, the holding of court in Charlotte was always a signal for a gathering, and court weeks were the busiest of all for the Charlotte merchants. The stagecoach brought lawyers and businessmen from Nashville, Clarksville, and other surrounding towns, and the villagers were usually on hand to observe the stage coaches, as indeed they were three-quarters of a century later to watch the locomotives as they chugged in and out of Dickson. One arrival in Charlotte was scheduled for 6:00 P.M., and when the coach reached Petersburg hill, just outside of town, the coachman would sound a number of blasts on his horn equal to the number of his passengers so that the operator of the Charlotte Hotel would know how many places to set at the table. The blasts on the horn, of course, likewise would inform the citizenry of the approaching coach, and by the time it arrived on the public square they were assembled to welcome the guests.

The county court met quarterly, and around that body centered much of the political, social, and economic life of the people. Magistrates were apportioned according to the militia districts, or "Captains' Companies," in the county. The district containing the county seat was allowed three justices, and the others two. There were nine members in the original court, but the number increased with the influx of population. The early justices were appointed by legislative act, and were guaranteed their offices for life upon good behavior. The very fact that they held their offices for life, that they usually were men of considerable wealth and prestige, and that the court had sweeping legislative powers, meant that the "Squires" of the early 1800's held a position of respect in their communities comparable to that of the English squire in the days of Addison's and Steele's mythical Sir Roger de Coverly. They tried cases, settled disputes out of court, gave advice on matters of all sorts to their neighbors, led the church services, directed community affairs, and in a host of other ways set the pattern of life in their surroundings and acted as a kind of father-confessor to ignorant and unfortunate ones who sought their assistance. As an official body the magistrates levied taxes, elected county officials, approved or disapproved sales of slaves, recorded stock marks, appropriated money for the support of paupers, established county roads, issued licenses, approved or rejected the contruction of dams on streams, and attended to many other duties, all of which made them powerful men within their county. The early court records found in the office of the county court clerk testify to their manifold duties. In 1805, for example, the court took note of the illegitimacy of a three-year-old child named Thomas McGammon and that his mother had no visible means of support. She had prayed the court for relief, and that body authorized Matthew Gilmore, a blacksmith, to take custody of the child, keep him until he reached the age of 21, and teach him the trade of blacksmith.[38] In the days when labor was scarce and slaves were high, Gilmore probably felt that he had made a good bargain, because support would cost him little while the products of the youth's labor, until he reached his majority, would go to Gilmore. At the same meeting the court observed that wolves roamed the hillsides and caused farmers and stock raisers considerable trouble by their depredations. The court offered an unstipulated reward to all who would slay one or more of these marauders and present the scalp to the court. This measure was in keeping with an act of the legislature which had authorized the court to pay as high as two dollars for each wolf scalp, and smaller amounts for crow's and squirrel's scalps. As late as 1846 the court continued the practice, for in that year Davis E. England, Mark Harris, and others produced wolf scalps in open court and were rewarded.[39] An important part of almost every court session was to register individual stock marks, for stock was permitted to run loose in open range style.

Other courts met in Charlotte besides the county court. A court of law and equity is said to have been held in Charlotte in the early 1800's and attended and presided over by Andrew Jackson, but no record of this court now exists. In 1817 the place for holding the Supreme Court of Errors and Appeals for the Fifth Judicial Circuit was removed from Clarksville to Charlotte, and the clerk of that court was authorized to establish his office in Charlotte by December 20, 1817.[40] This court met quarterly, and brought outstanding attorneys to Dickson County.

The musters and militia elections always drew crowds. State law provided that all "free men and indentured servants" between the ages of 18 and 45 were to enroll in the militia.[41] The militia of each county composed a regiment, and within the county there were districts from which came a company. The militia divisions served as civil districts and, as noted, two justices of the peace resided in each except the one which included the county seat, and that district was allowed three justices. The legislative act which provided for the county organization also provided for the county militia. The general musters were held where the county court convened.[42]

In the early wills may be found much about the way the people lived and about their economic and social well-being. A person after writing his will usually had two or more friends to sign as witnesses. At his death it would be filed with the county court, probated, and recorded in the Will Books. For many people their wills were the only documents they ever wrote, and some are filled with amusement and others with pathos. Some were in essence personal letters written to survivors admonishing them to take care of the widow or younger children. Others were sermons in loving devotion and tender affection. Still others would say to an enemy what the testator could never find the courage to say while living, or insult a relative by eliminating him entirely from the bequests. The economic fruits of their entire lives often were listed.

The will of Joseph Dickson was the first to be recorded in the county court records. Dickson, an uncle of William Dickson, had lived most of his life in North Carolina, but late in life he had moved into the Cumberland country. He had served as a captain in the Revolutionary War, and was the father of nine children, several of whom, also, migrated to Dickson County. His will, written in grandiose manner, is typical of those of the time. Practically all began by acknowledging the frailties of the body, but faith in God and the hope of an everlasting reward, was the faith of all, and Dickson's will set the pattern. It began:

> In the name of God, Amen! I, Joseph Dickson, of the state of Tennessee and the county of Dickon, being sick of body but of perfect mind and memory, [do say] thanks be to God for his mercies, but calling to mind the frailty of man and knowing that it is appointed for

men to die, have thought proper to constitute, appoint, make and ordain this to be my last Will and Testament, Viz.,

First, I deliver up my soul to Almighty God who gave it to me and my Will and desire is that my body be interred in a gentle and decent manner ...

From there Dickson went on to more mundane matters, and proceeded to parcel out his real estate and personal property among his children. Each male child, including Hugh, David, Joseph, Molton, Abner, William, and Robert, was bequeathed one slave. Among his Negroes Dickson had two for whom he apparently had real affection. His "old Negro woman, Phillis" he left to his wife with the instructions that she was not to be sold, but was to be permitted to live for the rest of her days on the plantation and to be supported when she got too old to work. His "old Negro fellow called Harry" who had been with the family practically all of his life, was too old to work and was to be given his choice as to with which of Dickson's sons—Hugh, David, or Molton—he should live his remaining days. He was to be accorded the privilege of refraining from work and was to be maintained in comfort.[43]

Many wrote of love for their family. William Norris, who died in 1807, was a devoted husband, and indicated in his will (recorded February 3, 1807), that his greatest concern was for the care and maintenance of his "loving wife." To her he willed most of his property, including several slaves.[44] James Goodrich likewise wrote of "my beloved wife," and left her and his children over thirty slaves and much real and personal property. Goodrich apparently had so many slaves that he ran out of names for them. One child he called simply "Newborn," another "Roccolina," and still another "Big Peter."[45] John Humphries, likewise a man of means, used one paragraph of his will to brand a no-good son-in-law a thief. Probably never summoning the courage while living to tell the young man exactly what he thought of him, Humphries decribed his in-law as being one who would steal if he had the opportunity, and who had "feloniously" stolen from him.[46]

Opportunities for formal schooling were rare on the frontier, but were not entirely absent. Religious leaders often conducted schools, which probably were more like Sunday Schools of today. Alexander Campbell conducted one at the forks of the Piney River shortly after the county was established, and Jacob Voorhies and others became associated with educational developments early in the county's history. Here again the recorded wills mutely speak forth, in this case of the educational interests of the people. Joseph Dickson, indicated great concern about his children's education. Fearing there might not be sufficient money in the estate to provide for their training, he commanded that his "young negro fellow called Virgil" be hired out for ten years and the money received therefrom be used to educate his children.[47] William Norris, Joseph Davidson, Jacob Lampley, and many others wrote of a growing concern for the education of their children.[48]

As indicated earlier, economic pursuits were never sufficiently strong to crowd from the minds of the people an interest in politics, although not a great deal of political fervor was shown in Tennessee until the 1830's. The justices of the peace were not elected but appointed by the legislature to hold office for life, and most of the other county officials were selected not by the people but by the county court. This held true until the revision of the constitution in 1834. Tennessee came into the union as a Jeffersonian Republican state, and since there were few Federalists (and probably none in Dickson County) there was little interest in national elections. It was during the three decades preceding the Civil War that political enthusiasm reached fever heat in the state, and this period will be discussed in another chapter. The act creating the county provided that in all elections for governor, representatives to Congress, and members of the general assembly, Dickson County should be considered a part of the "electoral district" of what was then Robertson and Montgomery counties, and elections should "be conducted under the same rules . . . as by law established. . . ."[49] The sheriff of Dickson County was authorized after an election to take the ballots to Clarksville and deposit them with the sheriff of Montgomery County, who would certify the poll to the general assembly.[50] In the state elections Dickson Countians usually followed the lead of the people of Davidson, and always voted for Middle Tennessee candidates rather than for those from the East. One election is sufficient to show this. In 1817 Governor Joseph McMinn, a native of Rogersville, in East Tennessee, was candidate for re-election. McMinn, although a man of mediocre ability, had had a successful first term and witnessed considerable prosperity in the state. Many believed that this should entitle him to a second term. He had been opposed in 1815 by a Nashvillian, Robert Weakley, but had defeated him handily. In his race in 1817 McMinn was opposed by Robert Foster, also of Nashville. Although McMinn was reelected by better than a two-to-one majority, Dickson and Davidson went strongly for Foster, Dickson by a 520 to 198 majority.[51]

By 1820 Charlotte was no longer a frontier town nor was Dickson a frontier county; the ever-moving line of settlement had shifted westward. Material advancement and diversified economic activity had gone hand in hand and social activities were ever expanding.

CHAPTER IV

Early Religious Development

By the time Dickson County was formed ministers of three major religious denominations, Presbyterians, Baptists, and Methodists, had been preaching for several years to the frontiersmen of the Cumberland country. The Presbyterians were the first to bring the gospel to the settlers of Kentucky and Tennessee, but the Baptists and Methodists were not far behind. By 1785 Thomas B. Craighead had established a Presbyterian church and school in Nashville, and William McGee was preaching to saints and sinners alike throughout central Tennessee. Other ministers of this denomination followed, and soon other churches and schools were established in the frontier country. The Presbyterians more than any other group were instrumental in furthering a cultural influence in Middle Tennessee, but they were unable to maintain a dominant position as the frontier expanded and matured. The inelastic Calvinistic theology came into conflict with the frontier philosophy, and this, coupled with internal dissension, caused the Presbyterian group soon to lag behind the Methodists, Baptists, and later the Christians (Disciples), who had a more informal doctrine and liturgy.[1] Baptist ministers came into Tennessee not long after the Presbyterians. Led by Tidence Lane, Joshua Kelly, and others, they appealed to the frontiersmen in such a way that within a few years their number of converts far exceeded that of the Presbyterians. The Methodists, too, grew rapidly, and by 1787 they had organized the Cumberland circuit and by 1789 had erected a small chapel in Nashville.[2] As was true of the Baptists, the educational qualifications for Methodist ministers were not high, and soon circuit riders covered Middle Tennessee from one extremity to the other as they sought to bring the gospel to the frontiersmen.

The majority of the people of the Kentucky-Tennessee area manifested no great degree of religious fervor in the closing years of the eighteenth century. Their thought and attention were primarily upon clearing forests, fighting Indians, and building cabins, rather than upon spiritual matters. Bishop Francis Asbury, who traveled throughout Middle Tennessee, once expressed fear for the salvation of the souls of the frontiersmen whom he noted "frequented poisonous liquor shops" and neither prayed nor feared God.[3] Many of the leaders showed no inclination toward religion. Andrew Jackson had objected vehemently at the Constitutional Convention of 1796 to the inclusion of a provision which would require all office holders to believe in God and in a future state of rewards. A brother of James Robertson, Elijah, a known drunkard, was indicted on several occasions for public drunkenness.[4] Montgomery Bell was a ruthless slavedriver who made hard bargains. Although in his later years after he had become wealthy from exploiting Dickson County soil for iron ore and human beings for labor he became imbued with a philanthropic spirit and emancipated slaves and gave money for the establishment of a school for boys, it is easy to believe that his hundreds of employees and slaves were not encouraged in religious precept and example. It is always difficult for a people to rise above its leaders, and by 1800 when the great revival came, the hearts and minds of the people of Tennessee and Kentucky were in great need of religious conversion. One author described the people of this area as having "lived for generations out of touch with civilization."

> They were impoverished and ignorant [he wrote], and religion had ceased to be a vital force in their lives. Only an emotional appeal could move them and there was, up to this time, no organization in America with sufficient missionary zeal and power to penetrate the wilderness and reach them in large numbers.[5]

The religious movement known as the Great Revival of 1800 began in Logan County, Kentucky, which lies northeast of Dickson County.[6] Its effects were far reaching and were felt throughout Middle Tennessee. At the beginning of the movement the Presbyterians, Baptists, and Methodists all participated, but the Presbyterians, with James McGready as the central figure, apparently initiated it. As the revival progressed and became dominated by more and more emotional upheavals and demonstrations, however, many of the Presbyterian ministers withdrew on the grounds that the emotional contortions to which many people were subjected were not indicative of true religion. Too, they accused McGready of sensationalism, for he, being an emotional person, often would leave the pulpit and promenade up and down the aisles of the church or the tent in his efforts to arouse enthusiasm and to exhort sinners to come to the mourners' bench. After a few months of the revival only five Presbyterian ministers, including McGready and Samuel McAdow, were in favor of continuing it.

The coolness with which the Presbyterians viewed the revival alarmed McGready and his supporters. While the Methodists and Baptists were doing their part in spreading the gospel, the Presbyterians refused on what seemed to some people very shallow grounds. At some of the camp meetings hundreds of people would assemble with no minister to preach to them. On other occasions laymen, with inadequate preparation, would lead the services. This led the five ministers favoring the revival to insist that the Cumberland Presbytery should grant temporary authority to preach to certain men who did not have the full formal educational requirements to enter the ministry, but who were adjudged by their brethren to be "sound" men in doctrinal matters. The highest body of the Presbyterian Church, however, objected to this on the grounds that it violated rules of the church and would place among the people an inferior ministry. Considering the pressing need for ministers, the Cumberland Presbytery ordained men to preach despite the order of the General Assembly to the contrary, and this resulted in strife between that Presbytery and the mother church which lasted for several years.

By 1810 the years of argument between the ministers favoring participation in the revival and those who did not had resulted in no amicable settlement, and some in the Cumberland Presbytery considered separating from the mother church. Those favoring a separation were few. McGready, while supporting the things for which the ministers in the Cumberland Presbytery stood, had retired from the controversy rather than be a party to the prolonged bickering. By 1810 only William McGee, Finis Ewing, Samuel King, and Samuel McAdow favored a division in the church if such appeared necessary as a last resort.

McAdow had come to Tennessee in 1799 and had preached in much of Tennessee and Kentucky; he vigorously supported the Great Revival until his health failed in about 1807 or 1808. In 1808 he came to Dickson County to live near the home of his niece, Mrs. Mary Larkins. In that year he built a frontier log cabin near Acorn Creek, a few miles from the home of his niece. It was to this log cabin that Finis Ewing, Samuel King, and Ephraim McLean came on the evening of February 3, 1810, to discuss the advisability of constituting a presbytery separate and distinct from the main Presbyterian body. Here they found McAdow living in a state of semi-retirement, but still very much interested in all matters pertaining to spreading the gospel. After a lengthy discussion the men decided that they should go out in the crisp winter night to pray. According to legend, they prayed for the entire night until the dawn began to break. It was with the break of day that a decision to separate from the Presbytery was reached. According to one historian it was McAdow who first "saw the light," and as he did his "face was all aglow with light" as the morning dawned. "With a cheerful and heavenly countenance" he informed his friends that God had heard and answered his prayer, and that "God had given him clear assurance that the proposed step was approved of Heaven."[7] Returning to McAdow's cabin, the group then drew up a statement which they proposed to give wide circulation, as follows:[8]

> In Dickson County, Tennessee state, at the Rev. Samuel McAdow's, this fourth day of February 1810, We, Samuel McAdow, Samuel King, and Finis Ewing, regularly ordained ministers in the Presbyterian church, against whom no charge either of immorality or heresy has ever been exhibited before any of the church judicatures, having waited in vain more than four years; in the meantime petitioning the General Assembly for a redress of grievances and a restoration of violated rights, have constituted, and do hereby agree and determine to constitute into, a Presbytery, known by the name of Cumberland Presbytery.

They also renounced completely the doctrine of predestination, but retained a belief in "the perseverance of the saints." McLean was then ordained, and Samuel Nelson McAdow, three-year-old son of Hannah Cope and Samuel McAdow, was baptized, being the first person to be baptized into the new faith.

The Cumberland Presbyterian faith spread like wildfire among the frontiersmen of Dickson County, and indeed throughout the South and West. Within a short while a sanctuary had been established about four miles northwest of Charlotte and named "New Hope." During the 1820's Cumberland Presbyterian churches, were built throughout the county. One was located on Johnson's Creek about five miles northeast of Charlotte, Bethel was organized on Yellow Creek, Bethlehem on Jones' Creek, and Mount Liberty in the present vicinity of Bellsburg.[9] During the 1830's a congregation was organized in the town of Charlotte. Inasmuch as there were so many other churches within the immediate vicinity of the town the people probably did not feel the necessity of establishing one until that time. In December, 1837, however, a Cumberland Presbyterian congregation consisting of forty members was organized. A board of Elders was chosen, among whom was a merchant named Christopher Dickson. The people manifested much interest in the plans for a church. A Miss Sally Walker was among the first to join on profession of faith.[10]

The spiritual enthusiasm of the people of Charlotte was not matched by their material generosity, however, for little money was contributed to the building of the new church. The fund drive began in 1837 immediately after the organization of the congregation, and $500 was raised,[11] but by the following year the effects of the great depression of 1837 were being felt in Dickson County just as they were over the entire nation. This caused the matter to languish for well over a decade until the mid-1850's when three men—Leonard Lane Leech, Benjamin Corlew, and Clark Larkins—contributed most of the necessary funds for the building of the edifice. Bricks used were manufactured within the town limits of Charlotte, at a kiln owned by James Dickson. Carpenters were aided by slaves, of which both Leech and Corlew had an ample supply. The church was practically complete by 1861, but Charlotte was invaded in 1863 and taken by the Federal troops who proceeded to convert the newly finished church into a hospital.

While the Presbyterian Church experienced internal difficulty, another group of Presbyterians, descendants of the Secessionists and Covenanters of Scotland, established a short-lived church in Dickson County. By 1804 they had built a small log meeting-house on the western outskirts of Charlotte. Remembered for the fact that they sung only hymns with words directly from the Psalms, the group sometimes were called "Psalm Singers." The Dickson County group was led by a minister named Samuel Brown, who did not long remain in the county. They were unsuccessful in their bid to gain followers and soon disbanded.[12]

Methodism, as noted earlier, reached Middle Tennessee by 1787. In that year a Conference was organized and Benjamin Ogden came into the Cumberland settlements to preach.[13] A sanctuary was built near the present public square in Nashville, but the movement did not make much headway until the advent of the Great Revival. It was that movement which acted as a catalyst in boosting the waning hopes of Bishop Asbury, who in 1797 had expressed a fear that many of the Westerners would lose their souls.

By 1808 the Western Conference with five large districts had been formed, and nearly twenty thousand people had joined the church. In the following year a famous Methodist evangelist, generally referred to as "the Rev. Mr. Bascom," appeared in Nashville and the surrounding area, smoking cigars and wearing a frock-tailed coat, but electrifying congregations with his dynamic style of delivery.[14] In the same year a log building was erected on Sulphur Fork Creek, a few miles east of Charlotte, and named Smyrna Church. Shortly thereafter Mount Lebanon Methodist Church was founded in the same vicinity. By 1840 a sanctuary called Mount Carmel had been built at the head of Barton's Creek, Soule's Chapel on Horse Branch of Barton's Creek, and Bethany Church on Harpeth River. Some of the early ministers who served this denomination were Michael Berry (who allegedly preached for sixty-two consecutive years), James Sizemore, Henry Hutton, and Caleb Rucker.[15]

As mentioned earlier, the Baptists had been pioneer workers in the early religious work of the Cumberland country. With the Methodists and Presbyterians, they had played a prominent part in the Great Revival of 1800 and had won many converts. Within Dickson County the Baptists formed a church on Turnbull Creek, about twenty miles southeast of Charlotte, in 1805. This church has continued down to the present time, and it is the oldest one in the county. Of much interest is the fact that the church members have preserved faithfully and completely records of every meeting.

The first recorded meeting of the Turnbull Baptist Church took place on "Saturday before the 2nd Lord's day in September," 1805, when a small group met at the home of John Parker to discuss the formation of a church in that locality.[16] Monthly meetings were held thereafter until February, 1806, when the small group decided to "send to our Sister Churches for help to look unto our standing and ability." Men were dispatched to the nearby Big Harpeth Church in Williamson County and other nearby churches to seek aid. On May 28, 1806, the congregation was organized officially, and it was inscribed in the records that ". . . We the Church of Christ on Turnbull Creek holding Believers Baptism by immersion eternal and particular Election of Grace and final perserverance of the Saints in Grace to Glory, have set apart this day . . . for a time of fasting and prayer. . . ." On the same day Parker's brother, Daniel Parker, was ordained a minister in the Baptist Church. John Parker, the organizer of the church, was born in Culpeper County, Virginia but spent his childhood in Georgia. He was reared in poverty and received few of the educational advantages which children of the more well-to-do parents received. Describing himself as "a man of war," Parker vigorously defended his church doctrine, and fought many doctrinal battles with the Methodists and other non-immersing groups. His forceful opposition to formal education, benevolent societies, foreign and home missions, and schools of theology, made a lasting impression upon many of the backwoodsmen in Kentucky and Tennessee and wherever he preached. According to one source he was in Dickson County as early as 1803, but within a few years thereafter moved to Sumner County where he continued his gospel ministry in vigorous fashion.[17] Much of the success of the church on Turnbull must have been due to the dynamic leadership of the Parkers. After preaching in Sumner County and in parts of Kentucky, John Parker returned to Dickson County for a short while, but he soon continued his westward journey. After leaving Dickson County he preached in Arkansas for a few years, and then went to Texas along with hundreds of other Tennesseans who rushed to take advantage of the cheap land. Once in Texas Parker organized another church and settlement called "Fort Parker" and supplied the same vigorous leadership. His small congregation, subjected to frequent Indian raids, failed to withstand an onslaught made by Comanches during the mid-1830's. The blood-thirsty savages massacred all the men, including Parker, and carried away the women and children and held them in slavery. Cynthia Ann Parker, a nine-year-old granddaughter of John, was among the group. She later married a Comanche, and her son, Quanah, was the last chief of his tribe.

Hard work and perseverance on the part of the membership made the Turnbull Church grow and prosper. Careful and close discipline was preserved at all times and persons who failed to live up to the standards of the church and the Christian faith found themselves excommunicated. To everyone this meant social and spiritual ostracism, and to the more pious it meant that the sinful ones' chances of entering the pearly gates were indeed slim.

At the October, 1806, meeting certain rules of order were adopted which illustrate the democratic spirit that pervaded the entire West. Each person was to be given the right to speak, and even the Moderator could not interrupt him unless he broke a rule of the decorum. Among the twelve rules of order are to be found the following which are representative of the twelve:

1. The Church members shall take their seats on order and Church meeting shall be opened and closed by prayer.
4. A door shall be opened for the reception of members.
6. Only one person shall speak at a time, who shall rise from his seat and address the Moderator when he is about to make his speech.
7. The person speaking shall not be interrupted in his speech by any except the Moderator till he is done speaking.
8. He shall strictly adhere to the subject and in no wise, reflect on the person who spoke before, so as to make remarks on his slips, failing, or imperfections but shall fairly state the case and matter as nearly as he can so as to convey his light or idea.

9. No person shall abruptly break off, or absent himself from the church without Liberty obtained from it.
10. No person shall rise and speak more than three times to one subject without leave from the church.
11. No member of this church shall have liberty to interrupt by ... whispering or otherwise in time of public speech.
12. The moderator shall not interrupt any member till he gives his light on the subject except he broke the rules of this Decorum.

As mentioned, those who strayed from the straight and narrow paths sometimes were turned out of the church. A very important part of the church's program, therefore, was the meetings of the session in which a small body of deacons assembled with the pastor and sat in judgment of the conduct of the other members. This body was not only in charge of the temporal affairs of the church, but it also judged the spiritual life of the members. Any person accused of wrong-doing usually was brought before the session, and the accused and the aggrieved were summoned to answer charges before this church court. As in a court of law, the plaintiff and defendant could bring witnesses, and in some cases the result would be a conviction and in others an acquittal. A conviction sometimes resulted in the accused's being given another chance, but more often in excommunication.

Among the many cases to come before the church session was one in 1812 in which Edmund Russell accused William Burnet of using profanity. Russell and another member named John Magee were appointed to cite Burnet to trial at the next session meeting. When the court convened in September Burnet appeared, and the session clerk noted in the records that "satisfaction took place between the church and Brother William Burnet." In the same year John Hammon presented to the church court a report that Isaac Tomkins and Sister Jenny Turman were not on speaking terms, and that the cause thereof should be removed. Both Tomkins and Miss Turman were required to attend the next church session, and at this meeting a reconciliation was established, and all were at peace again.

Jeremiah Bugg did not escape so lightly. He was accused of "telling a ly" [sic] and was excommunicated. In February, 1813, William Terman, who had been quite active in reporting the sins of others, was found to have inbibed too freely in spirituous liquors and to have become intoxicated. For this he was turned out of the church. Late in the same year two others were brought before the session for drunkenness. Joshua James and Beedy White had been seen together in an intoxicated condition, and for this they were ordered to appear before the church court. White made no defense and was excommunicated, but James had his wife and other friends and relatives to appear as character witnesses, and they persuaded the court to give James another chance. He was retained. Giving a man another chance did not always work, the session members discovered, and after a man had committed an offense repeatedly his name was striken from the rolls of the church. This was true of William Burnet who, as mentioned above, was cited in 1812

Church Marker at Montgomery Bell Park Entrance

This picture of a log cabin was drawn by an artist from a description given him by relatives and friends of the Reverend Samuel McAdow, a founder of the Cumberland Presbyterian Church. It is supposed to be an exact replica of McAdow's cabin wherein the first Cumberland Presbyterian congregation was organized.

THE OLD LOG HOUSE.

Residence of Rev. Samuel McAdow. The house in which the Cumberland Presbyterian Church was organized February 4, 1810

Main building of Ruskin Cave College (1911)

Cannon balls molded at Montgomery Bell's Cumberland furnace

for use of profanity. Burnet was excused after his first trial, but a year later he was discovered to have fallen again into the habit of cursing, so in February, 1813, he again was brought to the church session. The members apparently saw much good in Burnet and hesitated to see him go, but duty came first. After deliberating upon the case for two months they excommunicated him.

The church generally was lenient with one who confessed his own sins and pledged himself to a change of ways. For example, in April, 1820, Thomas Gray stood before the entire congregation and stated publicly that recently while in Charlotte he had "made use of too much wine." While no church member saw him and reported him, Gray made his confession, stating that such conduct was not a part of his character and that he was sorry for his sin. Gray, a prominent citizen, was given the right hand of fellowship, and no action was lodged against him. In the same year Minor Bibb, a prominent farmer and merchant of the neighborhood, stated publicly that "a report had creep [sic] out into the world" apropos to his having purchased cattle on the Sabbath day. The rumor had been misleading, Bibb reported, as he fervently pleaded his case before the entire church. After hearing Bibb's side of the issue the entire congregation appeared satisfied and agreed to give Bibb "the right hand in token of fellowship." Two years earlier a Brother Gentry appeared before the church session to state that "a difficulty" for sometime had existed between himself, his wife, and a woman designated as Sister Harding. Although Gentry claimed that they all "had pursued the gospel steeps," still no satisfaction had been attained. Gentry then prayed the session that it take his case under advisement and assist him in solving the problem which weighed heavily upon the consciences of them all. The session agreed to appoint a committee of seven prominent members to investigate the case and "by the help of Almighty God to try to bring about a reconciliation of the parties. . . ." After several weeks of deliberation the committee was able to report that all was well again with the Gentrys and the Hardings.

Many women were cited to appear before the church session. Their sins were often dancing and card playing. A Sister Barfoot, however, in 1816 was excluded for "taking up with a married man." Some years later a Sister Hutchenson was excommunicated for "not being obedient to her husband as directed by Saint Peter, and 2nd, for not attending to the calls of the church." A Sister Brown was cited to appear before the session for "speaking harsh words" of a Brother Thomas, particularly, by "saying he was a lyer" [sic]. Daniel Parker found that being the minister's brother did not prevent his being called before the church session. In November of 1808, Parker allegedly sold to a neighbor a sick cow while representing the cow as being in sound condition. He was brought to trial before the session, which body appointed a committee consisting of Murriel F. Brown, Aldin Beaver, Thomas Sherly, Daniel White, Levi Murphey, and Elisha Parker to study the case and report their findings to the session. After investigating the details of the case they agreed that Parker had no intention to deceive, and ruled, "We do not believe Brother Parker sinned in selling the cow because we believe that he did not know at the time she was sick."

Judging the conduct of church members was the main function of the session, but not the only one. The body acted as a sort of protecting earthly father over the flock. Members went to the session for advice on many matters. For example, in August, 1816, the Reverend Parker asked the session to set a correct price for corn. After conferring with various farmers of the community they set the price at seven shillings and six pence per barrel.

The Turnbull church grew rapidly. In the year 1812, for example, 22 members were added. Soon after the initial organization a large church building was erected. The structure had a spacious balcony where the Negroes, both free and slave, sat during the worship services. In the early days of the church no separate services were provided for the blacks, but later services came to be held on Sunday afternoons, usually under the supervision of a white minister or a white deacon. Still, however, many continued to meet with the whites until a separate church was built for them in the 1850's.

Negroes were received into membership in the same manner as the whites were at the Turnbull church and were considered to have the same spiritual status. There were two methods whereby one might be received into full fellowship of the denomination—by profession of faith, and by transfer of a letter from the church of last membership indicating that the person was in good standing. Negroes were admitted in both ways, the same as whites were. For example, in September, 1828, the congregation received one Carrel Milley "by the information of her master letting us know that she was a member in the state of Virginia and baptized by a worthy Baptist." Several years later the minister baptized and received into membership "Elias Napier's negro woman by religious experience."

Negroes were subjected to trial before the church session just as the whites were. While churches might draw a color line in the seating arrangements, there was no segregation when the Lord administered justice through the church session. One of the first blacks to face the church court was "Minor Bibb's negro woman" who was not named specifically in the lengthy proceedings, but was referred to on each occasion simply as "Minor Bibb's negro woman." This slave, according to her accusers, was guilty of three offenses—drinking excessively, dancing, and "keeping bad hours." In June, 1816, the session propounded some preliminary questions, but bound the slave over to the next meeting. Minor Bibb, her owner, failed to appear at the July meeting, and it was finally October before a decision was reached. The slave was found to be guilty on all three counts. The final decree was terse and to the point: "The church then considers her no more with us." In January, 1850, Moses Parker's slave Eveline was accused of "a wicked crime," the details of which were not given in the records. At her trial, however, she denied the accusation, and for lack of convincing testimony and evidence she was acquitted. In August of that year, however, another trial was held inasmuch as new evidence had been uncovered. Still again she denied knowledge of the offense, but circumstantial evidence pointed the finger of guilt at her to such a degree that the group decided to turn her out of the church.

The Negroes and whites worshipped together in the same building in the Turnbull church, with the two races sitting in different parts of the church, or with the Negroes in the balcony. This practice continued with apparent success until the 1850's, when a slave by the name of Moriah Sellars bumped against the wife of Levi Tidwell in an accident which most of the whites thought could have been avoided. Friction resulted, the whites thinking the Negroes to be getting a bit too "uppity," and a separate building for the blacks was erected on a nearby lot.[18]

It can be observed readily that religion to the people at Turnbull was a thing which was very real within their hearts and minds. So it was with the Presbyterian camp meetings, and with all the religious movements of the ante-bellum days. For example, in 1838, C. D. Bell of near Charlotte wrote to Anne Jane Bell of Pennsylvania for the purpose of informing her that Margaret Dunaway had professed faith before a Presbyterian session. This, Bell wrote, "created great excitement among her friends." Benjamin Robertson, a prominent businessman, "shed tears freely" and "observed to someone that he liked her a great deal better now."[19] At about the same time Sarah Bell wrote to Anne Jane Bell to inform her that "there is still a warm interest expressed among the people" of Charlotte on the subject of religion.[20] Several months later Sarah wrote to Anne Jane to describe a scene which took place at a Presbyterian camp meeting held near Charlotte. Two young ladies were visited by the Holy Spirit, she wrote, and went to the altar. The minister knelt by them and "prayed more fervently than I ever heard any person." Sarah Bell herself was deeply affected and continued:

> I was sitting by them and became deeply interested in them and prayed that they might be converted. That night I received a stronger manifestation of my being forgiven than I ever had before.[21]

By 1860 there were sixteen Methodist and an even dozen Presbyterian churches in the county. There were nine Baptist, five of which were Primitive Baptist, and one Christian (Disciple of Christ) church. The Methodists had erected buildings with greater seating capacity, but the Presbyterians had spent more money on architecture. The sixteen Methodist churches had a total seating capacity of over 4,000 and had an assessed valuation of $4,600, while the twelve Presbyterian churches seating a little over 3,000 had about the same assessed valuation. Eight Baptist churches with a seating capacity of over 2,500 were valued at about $2,000 and the one Christian church was listed at $150.[22]

Religious activities during the Civil War came to a virtual standstill, except for the fervent prayers of parents and others who had loved ones on the battlefield. It has been mentioned earlier that the Federal forces which invaded Charlotte in 1863 occupied the newly erected Cumberland Presbyterian Church and converted it into a hospital. After the war organized religious activities resumed and expanded greatly, owing partly to the growth of the town of Dickson. The influx of Pennsylvanians of German origin in the years immediately following the war resulted in the organization of a Lutheran Church. The sanctuary was a well-built and well-planned structure and continued in existence for over a half century, until it was disbanded recently because of lack of membership. Other religious activities and plant expansion in the post-Civil War days are discussed in succeeding chapters.

CHAPTER V

Two Decades of Growth and Development, 1820–1840

THE period 1820–1840 was one of growth and expansion, not only for Dickson County, but for Middle Tennessee in general. Every county experienced growth in population, and in agricultural and business activity. During the twenty year period the people of Dickson County participated actively in the affairs of the state. One citizen became speaker of the state senate and, interestingly enough, a few years later lost the wealth he had accumulated in a foolish get-rich-quick scheme. The county became an area of state-wide interest when in 1830 the county seat was visited by a tornado which wreaked destruction in its path, and again three years later when an incensed slave murdered a white man. Business operations, especially the iron furnaces, increased tremendously and there was widespread talk that business operations would expand considerably after the laying of a railroad through the heart of the county.

The United States Census for 1820 indicates that the population of Dickson County had increased by that time to 5,184. Of this number, 1,976 were white males and 1,879 were white females; 1,305 were slaves, and twenty-four were free Negroes. The vast rank and file were born and reared in Dickson County, and only two were classified as "foreigners not naturalized."[1] The exact population figures for Charlotte are not available for 1820, but the county seat was a growing community of a hundred or more people. Roads had been opened between it and other Middle Tennessee towns, and lawyers and businessmen were in and out quite frequently. It had been designated a few years earlier as the location for the holding of the supreme court of errors and appeals for the fifth Judicial District, and the clerk's office had been moved there from Clarksville.[2] A dozen people had built homes and places of business around the square. Interestingly enough, in 1821, a legislative act gave such persons permission to build in front of their buildings "porticoes or piazzas" for "their own and public convenience." These porticoes jutted out upon the public square, and some which had been built apparently were being criticized as nuisances, for the act also provided that those already in use and those which in the future might be built would be considered as private property, "without being viewed as nuisances in said town."[3]

It was in this same legislative session that Sterling Brewer, prominent Dickson County farmer and businessman, was elected speaker of the state senate.[4] Brewer's career rivals that of Montgomery Bell in point of interest. He was one of the county's earliest settlers. In 1795 he purchased from William Lane of Nashville 640 acres on Jones' Creek and by 1803, when the county was officially formed, he was a highly respected citizen. He was named one of the first justices of the peace, and also was a commissioner to establish and lay out the town of Charlotte. In 1804, however, an event occurred which threatened to wreck his budding political career. In a race for the position of commander of the Dickson County militia in which Brewer was an unsuccessful candidate, Sheriff Robert Weakley accused him of having been tried for a criminal offense in North Carolina before he came to Middle Tennessee. Brewer hotly denied the accusation, and sued Weakley for slander. After considerable litigation Brewer was awarded $200 damages and his name was cleared.[5]

Over half a decade elapsed before Brewer again ventured into politics. In the meantime he farmed extensively, acquired more slaves, and became more prosperous. In 1810 he announced his candidacy for representative to the state legislature from Dickson County, and was elected. He served for only one term and returned to his Dickson County farm after the legislative session. By 1817 he had accumulated considerable real and personal property, was a prominent churchman, and had been elected to the state senate from a district composed of Dickson, Hickman, and Robertson counties. Two years later he was chosen for a second term, but resigned for reasons undisclosed. In 1821 he was elected for a third term, and by this time he was a familiar figure among legislators in Knoxville and Murfreesboro where the legislative sessions then were held. He had been a staunch supporter of one of Tennessee's greatest governors, William Carroll, and he became Carroll's choice for speaker of the senate.

Of the many important matters which came before the Tennessee legislature of 1821, the numerous petitions for divorce, then granted by the legislature, attracted the speaker's attention. Even former Governor Joseph McMinn was among those who filed a petition for legal separation. Brewer was a staunch Methodist who took his religion seriously and who believed divorce was wrong. He therefore requested the Reverend Robert Paine, later to become a bishop in the Methodist Episcopal church, to preach a sermon to the legislators on the topic. Paine declined, but secured from Brewer permission to invite the Reverend Valentine Cook, a Methodist minister and president of a Methodist college in Kentucky, to deliver the sermon, and the legislature met in joint session to hear him. "Never did that singularly powerful preacher appear to greater advantage," Bishop Paine was later to write, and he convinced the legislators that from a New Testament point of view divorce was wrong. The result was that many petitions for divorce, including McMinn's, were turned down.[6]

At the end of the legislative session Brewer, then in his mid-fifties, decided to retire from politics and to devote the rest of his life to farming and retirement in Dickson County. These years should have been filled with joy and satisfaction instead of grief and despair. But Brewer was a man of wealth—and he wanted more. At this point in his life he was visited by a charlatan from an eastern city who represented himself as being a scientist and an expert in mineralogy. The ingratiating stranger told Brewer that he believed that underneath Brewer's farm there converged several salt-water streams which, if tapped, would yield considerable wealth. Salt was scarce indeed at that time, and brought a good price on all markets. Most Nashville merchants advertised daily that they would pay for farm produce in "either cash or salt," which indicates the position the mineral held in the business transactions of the day.[7] Brewer appeared quite interested, and permitted the stranger to make a survey. The latter took from his coat his "divining rod"—a sturdy peach tree fork which, it was claimed, would quiver and pull downward when over a salt stream provided it was in the hands of one gifted with the art of locating such streams—and began. Brewer, with apparently more knowledge of law and politics than of science, watched with amazement while the rod, time after time, appeared to quiver and pull downward as the stranger walked over the farm. Brewer, now believing he had a "gold mine" in salt, agreed to pay the stranger a handsome price to make an extensive survey on his land and to draw maps locating spots where wells should be drilled. The stranger made the survey, took Brewer's money, and disappeared. Drilling was expensive, and Brewer, being a man of caution, decided to employ other "scientists" before spending money on drilling equipment. A second, and then a third, was called in, and each confirmed the findings of the first. The third to come was Valentine Cook, the same college president and Methodist minister who had addressed the legislature several years before when Brewer was Speaker of the senate, and whose moving eloquence had won Brewer's utmost respect. He brought from his Kentucky home his "divining rod," proceeded with a survey and, amazingly enough, confirmed the findings of the other "mineralogists" before him. If Brewer had consulted with Bishop Paine about Cook's reliability he no doubt would have received the utmost encouragement, for Paine soon was to write of Cook (divining rod and all) that he was a man "distinguished for learning, piety, and usefulness . . . an expert in chemistry, electricity, and kindred subjects. . . ."[8] Convinced beyond a doubt now, the well-to-do Dickson County farmer ordered expensive machinery and hired a crew of workmen to begin drilling at a place recommended by Cook and the others. For three years Brewer let his farm go to ruin while his slaves and other workmen drilled wells on the farm. At one place after drilling several score feet Brewer struck a hard crystalline limestone bed which made operations slow and difficult, but at 300 feet he reached water which had "a brackish taste." This encouraged him to drill farther, although by this time he had poured thousands of dollars into the operations. Finally at a depth of one thousand feet the auger broke. With heavy heart and anguish of spirit Sterling Brewer now was forced to turn aside from his pipe dream. Most of his slaves and personal property had been sold, and much of his real property had been mortgaged. Disappointed, discouraged, and disillusioned, the former legislator, having aged a score of years during the three-year period, wanted to see no more of his Dickson County land. He moved to Nashville where he lived a few more years in very modest circumstances. George Frederick Mellon, a Nashville newspaperman, wrote of him as a "man who died in poverty," and Bishop Paine, his close friend who conducted his funeral, stated that he "buried him from a humble rented house in Nashville."[9] Census records for 1830 indicate that he did own eight slaves, but he owned no real property, and the number of slaves owned was less than half the number he had owned ten years previously.[10]

While Brewer was fruitlessly searching for salt-streams, others successfully took from Dickson County soil iron ore and transformed it into pig iron. By 1820 Bell had disposed of his interest in Cumberland furnace to devote more time to expanding his other interests, and Anthony W. Vanleer and Bernard Vanleer now operated it under the name of "Anthony W. Vanleer and Company."[11] Anthony Vanleer, like Bell, became highly successful in the iron business in Dickson County, and a town in the county was named for him. At the time of his death he owned some twenty thousand acres surrounding the furnace and persued extensive argricultural operations in addition to iron exploits.[12] In 1820 he announced through the Nashville press that he had taken in as a partner Robert Baxter, a young man who later became well known as an iron manufacturer of Dickson County and Middle Tennessee. Vanleer, like many other iron masters, owned and operated an "iron store" in Nashville, where he sold "castings, stoves, machinery, steam boat machinery, and so forth."[13] Throughout the period before the Civil War, Vanleer operated the furnace and expanded his land holdings. By 1850 he held 12,500 acres of Dickson County land, and by the end of the following decade his holdings had expanded to nearly 14,000 acres.[14] By 1870 Vanleer had passed away, and his vast domain was inherited by a granddaughter, Florence Kirkman. She, in the meantime, had married a Federal officer named J. P. Drouillard. This enterprising young man organized the J. P. Drouillard Iron Company, which operated the furnace until about 1889. It is not known just how efficiently or extensively Vanleer operated, but in 1873 Drouillard was producing 360 tons per month during the summer months, and a little over 3,000 tons per year.[15] Vanleer's slaveholdings were just as extensive as his landholdings. In 1820 he owned forty-three slaves and by 1840 had increased the number to 114. A majority of them were under thirty-six years of age, and over one hundred were employed in the iron works.[16] The days of slavery came to an end with the Civil War, of course, but most of the blacks remained in the vicinity of the furnace after the war and worked for Drouillard.

Dickson County was in the heart of the Western Iron Belt, and it is natural that others interested in iron would not permit Vanleer, Bell, and Robertson to monopolize the ore. The Western Iron Belt, whose exact center lies in Dickson County, is about fifty miles wide and embraces an area of more than 5,400 square miles.[17] In addition to Dickson, it includes all or parts of Hickman, Humphreys, Montgomery, Lewis, and Stewart counties. The ore was of the brown hematite variety, and the banks varied greatly in the richness of the ore. In some places it was mixed with a hard cemented cherty mass which yielded a poor return, while in others it was compartively free from impurities and yielded a return of better than fifty per cent.[18] This brought to Dickson County others interested in iron, among whom were the Napiers, who, in the 1820's began to rival Bell and Vanleer. George F. Napier, Richard C. Napier, and perhaps others of that name settled in the part of Robertson County which later became Dickson. If either was interested in iron before 1820 he was not pursuing the interest to the extent that other iron masters were. In 1820 George F. owned only fifteen slaves, compared to eighty-three held by Montgomery Bell and forty-three held by Anthony Vanleer, which indicates that if he had secured iron interests by that time, he was not engaged in the operation very extensively with the use of slave labor. Richard C. was not in the county in 1820, but by 1830, he, Henry A. C. Napier, and John W. Napier were county residents in addition to George F. Napier. All were large slaveholders. Richard C., who married a daughter of James and Charlotte Robertson, and by 1830 had inherited property from the estate of his father-in-law, owned eighty-six slaves of whom seventy-one were men and boys between the ages of ten and thirty-six, and only four of whom were women.[19] Collectively the Napiers owned over 125 slaves, whom they worked extensively in their plants on Turnbull Creek. These captains of industry did not restrict their operations to pig iron alone, but they also made kettles, stoves, and similar utensils. Some of their best slaves were molders, who shaped the iron "pigs" into kettles, pots, and pans. Advertising their wares regularly in the Nashville newspapers, the iron masters also operated an "iron store" in Nashville on Union Street, which served as an outlet for their finished products. An advertisement which was published over a period of several months or longer praised the Napier products and quoted a testimonial from "a high official in the War Department" of the United States government. This official had purchased quantities of the Napier iron and had submitted it, along with iron produced by others, to grueling tests. Upon completion of the tests the Napier iron was found "to be equal in quality to any that is found in commerce." Their best produce was known as "Turnbull Iron," and a large quantity usually was available at the store on Union Street.[20]

By the early 1830's George F. Napier had become interested in iron ore in Lewis County. In 1833 he and Felix Catron purchased of George H. Catron the Buffalo Iron Works in that county for $18,000. For nearly four years they operated the furnace under the name of "Napier and Catron," but the venture did not prosper. By the summer of 1838 they were indebted to a Nashville bank for the sum of nearly $7,000.[21] It was at this point that Elias W. Napier, an uncle of George, entered the

Lewis county venture and assumed the bank note and took over his nephew's note. Elias Napier and Catron continued to operate the business for a few months, but by 1838 the partnership was wholly insolvent, and Elias was compelled to make the note good. After several years of litigation Napier acquired full possession and in 1845 conveyed by deed a half interest to his nephew, W. C. Napier, and agreed to accept reimbursement from the profits of the operation. Napier died three years later, however, and bequeathed to his nephew the entire enterprise, which remained in Napier hands for several decades thereafter.[22]

By 1840 Elias Napier, now an elderly man in his sixties, had entered extensively into the Dickson County operation. His ready supply of cash no doubt served as a catalyst to the established Napier interests. In 1840 he held seventy-one slaves, fifty of whom he used at the iron works and ten in agriculture. A retired physician, in addition to being a shrewd businessman, he was probably more successful in his iron operations than other members of his family.

Another firm which operated one furnace and two forges in the county during the 1830's was known as Tennessee Iron Works, operated by Robert Baxter and W. R. Hicks. It is not known just when the concern was organized, but quite probably in the late 1820's.

By 1830 Hicks and Baxter were operating Carroll Furnace, which had been established earlier by Montgomery Bell and which was located near Bettstown on the Cumberland River. Baxter, a young man in his thirties with ten years' experience in Vanleer's works, apparently applied all the vigor of his youth and experience to the enterprise. In close competition with the Napiers and Vanleer, Baxter and Hicks advertised through the Nashville papers that their products were "not inferior to any in the United States."[23] In 1830 nearly one hundred slaves were listed in Baxter's name, practically all of whom worked at the furnace. Ninety-four of them were under the age thirty-six, and eighty of them were men.[24] They included forgemen, waggoners, molders, and common laborers. In June, 1830, the firm advertised for additional Negro labor; they wished to purchase "twenty likely young negro fellows" who were between the ages of eighteen and twenty-four. Vigorous, healthy blacks between these ages were those most sought after in both agriculture and industry and always brought fancy prices. The fact that Baxter and Hicks would advertise for twenty men of this age indicated that their operations were expanding and that they were making money, for such a purchase would require an outlay of at least $10,000 and probably more. In the same advertisement the iron masters offered employment to several good blacksmiths, and to "two or three" women for "light duties" around the furnace.[25] Earlier they had announced that they maintained a store in Nashville, where they always kept on hand a ready supply of iron products.[26] The Baxter family continued in the iron business for many years, and in 1850 Theodore Baxter and G. H. Baxter were owners of a furnace, with Howard Mockbee as manager, but the census records no longer listed the name of Robert Baxter.[27]

Isaac H. Lanier is another who was associated with the iron business of Dickson County, but little is known about him or his operations. It is quite probable that he was associated with Anthony Vanleer at the Cumberland furnace. At any rate he was in the county by 1830 and in that year held fifty-one slaves. His name did not appear in the census records thereafter. In 1828 he joined Vanleer and Wall Dixon to warn the public against taking by assignment a note issued by Montgomery Bell. The three had given Bell a four-year note for ten thousand dollars in July, 1825, but three years later Bell had not complied with the terms of the agreement. Apparently the crafty Bell once again had betrayed the confidence of his associates and Lanier was one of them.[28]

In addition to the iron works other businesses expanded during the 1830's and 1840's, and mercantile establishments were among them. During the 1820's Minor Bibb, Thomas Pannell, Jacob Voorhies, and Christopher Robertson established places of business in the county. Bibb, a man in his forties at this time, lived in the Turnbull Creek neighborhood. In 1830 he had twelve slaves in addition to extensive real property holdings. Jacob Voorhies, a young man in his thirties, had come to the county from New Jersey several years before as a poor man. He had received a good education and by 1840 established a school in addition to his place of business and also owned seven slaves.[29] During the following decade John Ward, Benjamin A. and Theodore M. Collier, and others founded businesses, the Collier family setting up an enterprise on the public square. The latter family had come some years earlier from Virginia and had become quite prosperous in Middle Tennessee. Thomas Collier, probably a relative of Benjamin and Theodore, was in the county by 1820 and owned twenty-three slaves at the time.[30]

As the county grew and as new enterprises were formed, better means of transportation developed. By 1824 stage coaches were running regularly across the state from Knoxville to Memphis, and Charlotte was on the main route. In that year the stage from Nashville to Memphis ran once each week, and made six major stops before arriving in Memphis. The first stop was at Chestnut Grove, eighteen miles west of Nashville; the next was at Charlotte, forty miles from Nashville. After leaving Charlotte the stage traveled thirty-eight miles west to Reynoldsburg, thence thirty-one miles to Huntingdon, and then to Jackson, thirty-eight miles from Huntingdon. The coach made a final stop at Bolivar, twenty-eight miles from Jackson, before going the last lap of the journey into Memphis.[31] By this time there were other roads leading out of Charlotte to practically all of the surrounding county seats, including Dover, Clarksville, and Franklin.

The road from Nashville to Charlotte apparently did not stand up well under the traffic, for in 1838 an act was passed chartering the Charlotte and Harpeth Turnpike Company. This company, to be headed by three Davidson Countians and Epps Jackson, James Larkins, Jr., Benjamin C. Robertson, Thomas W. Overton, Joab Hardin, James Christian, and John James Hardwicke, was to construct a road from "the top of the hill about one mile from Elijah Robertson's" (probably the present Nine Mile Hill), to Charlotte. The corporation members were authorized to sell shares of stock for fifty dollars each in order to raise $130,000. To realize returns from their investment, the shareholders were authorized to erect toll gates for each five miles of macadamized road, and for each ten miles of graded or sanded surface, but not more than five on the entire route. In order to prevent people from going around the toll gate, the corporation was given the right to purchase one hundred acres adjacent to the gates.[32] The same legislature also chartered a company to construct a road from Charlotte to Reynoldsburg, the latter town being located in the western part of Humphreys County. This corporation included these officials: John Eubank, Humphreys and Augustin Roberts, J. P. Hardwicke, Henry A. C. Napier, William Norsworty, Absalom Massie, and eight men from Humphreys County. The corporation, like the Charlotte and Harpeth, could sell stock at fifty dollars a share in order to raise the necessary capital. The turnpike was to be thirty feet wide except in "mountainous areas," where it could be as narrow as fifteen feet. Ditches for drainage had to be dug on each side, and not more than seven toll gates could be maintained. No gates were allowed within two and one-half miles of Charlotte, Waverly, or Reynoldsburg.[33]

During the late 1830's considerable interest was manifested by Tennesseans in a railroad which would run east to west across the state. By 1837 a preliminary survey was completed and submitted to the state legislature, and for awhile many people believed that Tennessee would become the gateway to the west through the use of this rail system. Much interest was shown in the proposal in Dickson County, for it was thought that the line would run through Charlotte. Public addresses and solicitations for stock purchases were made in the county and many people there and throughout the state bought stock, but the entire project failed.[34]

No banks were established in the county during this period, but in 1833 interest was shown in one which was to be begun in Nashville with a capital stock of two million dollars. Dickson Countians interested in the project were John Montgomery, George Smith, John C. Collier, John C. Napier, Benjamin A. Collier, and William Hightower. These men were authorized to "open the books" and sell stock to all Dickson County subscribers who wished to purchase it at one hundred dollars per share.[35]

In the midst of the peace and prosperity of the twenties and thirties occurred two events which made lasting impressions upon the people of the county, and upon their off-springs for generations to come. The first was the tornado of 1830, which almost destroyed Charlotte and the surrounding area; the second, occurring three years later, was the brutal murder of a white man by an enraged slave. The destructive tornado struck the county seat on the night of May 30, and although the violent winds swept through Middle Tennessee, only the towns of Charlotte and Shelbyville sustained serious damage. In the Bedford County seat the courthouse and several other public buildings were destroyed, but in Charlotte the destruction was even greater.[36] Appeals for help for the unfortunate victims appeared in two Nashville papers, and in papers of Sparta, Jackson, and probably other surrounding towns. All insisted that those who had been blessed with an abundance should share with the less fortunate people of Charlotte and Shelbyville, with all convenient haste.

The first report of the destruction to reach the Nashville papers was one which stated that many people had lost their lives and that every building except two was leveled. This report came to the Nashville *Republican and Gazette* by a traveler who had spent the night in Charlotte, but who had hastened unhurt toward Nashville in the early morning following the windstorm. The next account published in the paper (June 5) indicated that there was no loss of life, but that several people had been injured critically and were not expected to live. Among these was Mrs. John Eubank, first wife of the man who represented Dickson County in the state legislature for a decade before the Civil War. Also, a Mrs. Coffee allegedly was blown into the forks of a tree on Petersburg hill and remained there throughout the night until rescued by friends on the following morning. Both women were badly mangled, and died within a few days.

Several days after the storm William Williams of Dover described the damage to his brother Samuel in Cincinnati. The winds, rains, and thunderstorms were some of "the most powerful" he had ever seen, he wrote, and his own home in Dover had been struck by lightning. According to information received in Dover, the towns of Charlotte and Shelbyville had been completely destroyed by wind.[37] Although Williams' report was not far from correct, the town was not completely destroyed. Property damage was extensive, however. The two-story courthouse and the jail, both of which had been constructed of brick a score of years earlier, were demolished. A man, probably William Collier, was in the courthouse at the time of the storm and was buried in the rubbish, but miraculously escaped serious injury. No prisoners were incarcerated at the time, and the jailor escaped without sustaining serious injury. The following list of property damage not only provides a conception of the extent of the damage, but also gives some idea of the property then held in the county seat. Business places destroyed or damaged were: a store operated by B. A. Collier, a tailor's shop managed by a man named Glasgow, a store owned by a firm known as Voorhies and Smith, the saddle shop of Thomas Palmer, a grocery opperated by a man named Massey, the post office, a grocery owned by a man named Smith, James Nesbit's cotton gin and tavern, Robert Livingston's hat shop, and a general merchandise store operated under the name of James Steele and Company. In addition to the places of business, many dwelling houses were demolished or partly destroyed. Those suffering property loss were forced to endure the additional handicap of having their clothing, bedding, and furniture scattered for miles. Among those losing dwellings were: a Mrs. Clinton, Dr. B. M. Carter, Thomas Palmer, Thomas Epps, John Eubank, Jacob Voorhies, Robert Livingston, James Gould, S. Bowker, and B. C. Robertson.

The graphic portrayal of the tornado as recorded in the Nashville *Republican and Gazette* is of interest. The reporter stated that

> About half past ten o'clock last night, our village was visited with a tornado, the violent and destructive effects of whch no pen can describe nor can they be adequately conceived except by those who were witnesses to the awful and terrific scene. Our little town is now, literally, a heap of ruins. Many, who but yesterday had a comfortable home, are now without a place even to shelter themselves, while their clothing and provisions have been swept away in the general wreck. The wind approached the village from the southwest, and although the appearance was frightful, and one constant glare of lightning inspired awe and alarm, yet no one anticipated, none could anticipate, and even now it is difficult to realize, what the ravages of 5 minutes have produced. But yesterday we were at ease, and comfortably situated; today many are wandering about the streets, not knowing where to go, or how to procure the means of suppling their necessities. Many, who but yesterday were blessed with health and the full enjoyments of the comforts of life, are now languishing on their beds, with broken limbs and mangled bodies, and some with scarce a hope of recovery. But amidst all these calamities, the hand of a protecting Providence has been displayed in the almost miraculous preservation of many of our citizens.

In 1830 there was no Red Cross or other relief agency to care for those who suffered such calamities, and the fear and distress experienced by the people must have been heart rending. The *Republican and Gazette* and other Middle Tennessee newspapers published appeals for aid. The June 9 issue of that paper announced that a committee composed of John Montgomery, James Gould, and W. R. Hicks had been appointed to apportion gifts of clothing, money, bedding and furniture among the needy people. All citizens of Nashville and the surrounding area were invited to come forward and deposit at the store of Baxter and Hicks, located on College Street in Nashville, anything which they could share with their Dickson neighbors. "These people are now hungry, and naked and houseless wanderers," the newspaper pointed out and urged those blessed with material gain to come forward and share it with the less fortunate.

Added to the distress of physical discomfiture was the fact that the public records deposited in the courthouse and in other buildings which housed law offices were blown over the countryside. Fortunately, many of them were recovered but some never were. The legislature of 1837 took official notice of the destruction of the records and provided that, inasmuch as many of the records of Dickson County had been destroyed in the tornado—including judgments and executions—any and all persons who had received land from a Sheriff's execution could, upon obtaining a court judgment, establish title and secure deeds if they were able to produce the sheriff's receipts.[38]

One hundred years after the destructive windstom had visited the county the editor of the *Dickson County Herald* published a lengthy account written by Dorsey L. Castleman, Charlotte native and correspondent for the paper, in which the author vividly portrayed the sufferings of the Charlotte residents of a hundred years earlier. "I hope," he wrote, a memorial will, at some future time, be erected to commemorate the sufferings and hardships experienced by our pioneer inhabitants during the storm of a century ago.... So, also we must not forget the misery and suffering underwent by our predecessors—limbs broken, bodies mangled, with devastation over every inch of our county, let us recall the holocaust of 1830 and with much reverence bless the years that have brought us through unharmed from devastation, which the Supreme Ruler of the universe has so graciously ordained for all.

The second event of significance mentioned above was the murder of a white officer named William C. Bird by a recalcitrant slave named Wiley. The fearful deed was accomplished in November, 1833—less than three years after the launching of the abolitionist newspaper, *The Liberator,* and the fearful Virginia debacle by Nat Turner. Abolitionist tracts and pamphlets were circulated throughout the country by 1833, but it is unknown whether Wiley had had access to such inflammatory material. Just why Wiley went into a fit of rage on November 25, 1833 and pounded Bird's head to a pulp with a club will never be known, but his deed created fear throughout the county and surrounding territory. The Negro was arrested immediately and incarcerated to await trial. The county court which tried him convened in special session on December 19. After a trial lasting three days the jury rendered a verdict of guilty and recommended death by hanging. Not wishing to have the blood of the Negro on their hands during the Christmas holidays, the magistrates set the execution date for December 28, and Wiley spent the Christmas season in the Charlotte jail.

On the day set for his execution, Wiley was taken from the jail, his hands tied, and he was placed in a cart and carried about a half mile east of Charlotte. There two upright posts had been planted between which a cross-piece with a rope dangling had been secured firmly. Whether intentionally or not, the officers had located the place of execution in a natural ampitheatre, and hundreds of people congregated upon the surrounding hills to watch the public hanging. Slaveowners were invited to bring their slaves, so that all might see the dreadful fate which awaited a murderer. Finally, without giving the convict an opportunity for a last word, the officials had the cart driven between the uprights, while they placed the noose around the neck of the unfortunate black. The cart then was driven out from under the Negro and (as one account stated) he was "jerked into eternity." A Negro minister was on the scene to preach a funeral oration in which he "delivered a solemn warning" to the other slaves who congregated around in fear and trembling.[39]

Except for these two events, little occurred to disturb the peaceful scene other than an occasional fire or robbery. Of the latter, one which was featured in the Nashville press was the robbery of William B. Davis, a prominent businessman of Dyer County. On the night of November 24, 1833, while spending the evening at the home of Robert Collier, Davis was relieved of seventy-one dollars. Although his saddlebags had been securely locked in one of Collier's rooms, they had been rifled and relieved of their contents after the burglars broke a window and entered Collier's dwelling.[40] It is safe to say that this event, which ordinarily would have been a major topic of conversation, was crowded off the conversational carpet by the Wiley affair.

Scarcely a legislative session was held during this period but that an act was passed affecting Dickson County. For example, in 1833, amid the usual matrimonial peace and harmony, Gilly Harmon petitioned the state legislature to grant her a divorce from her husband, Lewis Harmon. Divorce was a legal process rarely resorted to in those days, for it placed a stigma upon the persons involved which only death could remove. The state legislature granted divorces then and not infrequently refused the petitioner, as mentioned earlier in the chapter. In this case, however, the legislature carefully considered the plea and then passed an act which declared that "the bonds of matrimony heretofore entered into, and now existing, between Gilley Harmon . . . and . . . Lewis Harmon, be, and the same are hereby, dissolved, and the said Gilley restored to all privileges of a *feme sole*."[41] In the same year the legislature befriended a poor man named Richard Cook of Dickson County, by giving him the right to "hawk and peddle goods, wares, and merchandise" within his native county and also in Hickman without a license.[42]

In the next session of the legislature, an act was passed authorizing the laying off of civil districts in Dickson County for the purpose of electing justices of the peace and constables. Two justices and one constable were to be elected in each district except the one which included Charlotte. That district would have three justices and two constables, inasmuch as it included within its bounds the county seat. William Hightower, Joseph Kimble, William Hogins, James W. Christian, and Minor Bibb were first appointed to make the survey, but when Kimble and Bibb announced that they could not serve, Thomas Jarnagin and James Pullin were appointed in their places.[43] The same legislature created the twelfth Chancery District, to consist of Dickson, Hickman, and Humphreys counties, and court for these three counties was to be held at Charlotte on the fourth Mondays of March and September.[44] Two years later Charlotte was incorporated "under the name and style" of mayor and alderman. One mayor and five aldermen were to be selected to administer the affairs of the town.[45]

Recorded wills and bequests written during the period indicate that the people of the county enjoyed far greater prosperity than they had twenty years earlier when Dickson was still a frontier settlement. Moses Easley, for example, had farm implements of various descriptions and also a loom and other personal property which he willed to his wife. His possessions indicate that he patronized the iron works of the county, inasmuch as he had two pots, two ovens, two skillets, one pair of dog irons, and one pot rack—all of which he bequeathed to his wife. John Humphreys owned a "stand of curtains of mixed colors with coverlet" which apparently he valued highly and which he bequeathed to his daughter Sophia. To all his children he left featherbeds, and to each of his sons he left a saddle and bridle. Practically all wills continued to be written in a very reverent manner as they had been written for many years before. For example, the will of James Goodrich, written in 1818 and probated in 1824, began:[46]

> In the name of God, Amen. I, James Goodrich of the State of Tennessee and the County of Dickson, being of sound sense and mind and memory, thanks be to God, do this 29th day of August in the year of our Lord one thousand eight hundred and eighteen make this to be my last Will and Testament, that is to say, I give my soul to Almighty God and by the merits of Jesus Christ I trust and believe to be saved; and my body to be buried in such decent manner and Christianlike manner as my executor hereafter named may think proper.

In the midst of the economic turmoil the people of Dickson County did not neglect the education of their children. While public education in Tennessee and the South was never emphasized in the antebellum days as it was in some of the Northern states, it is interesting to note that there were thirteen "common schools" in Dickson County in 1840, in addition to Tracy Academy and the Charlotte Female Academy. Attending these schools, exclusive of the last two named, were 444 students who came from homes where nearly 14 per cent of the parents were unable to read or write.[47] Parents who had been denied the opportunity of an education apparently wanted to make sure that their children did not mature to the same fate. In 1840 schools were located in all of the ten civil districts with the exception of the third, fourth, and fifth. In the first district a school was maintained by Andrew Dunnigan, with 49 pupils, and in the second district, Lucretia Horner taught 55.

In the sixth district there were two schools in addition to Tracy and the Charlotte Female Academy. Thirty-five pupils attended a school taught by John Porter and 16 attended another headed by Isaac Hill. In the remaining districts, the teachers and numbers of pupils were as follows: seventh district, Daniel Moore with 11 and James Trotter with 19; eighth district, Soloman J. Reynolds with 55 and Christopher Meek, 26; ninth district, George C. Dotson, 30, and Peter Jackson, 50; and tenth district, Reuben Shadowen, 36, William J. Knight, 27, and Howard W. Turner, 35. Most of the teachers were young men without much property and most of them boarded in the community in which they taught. Reynolds and Meek were in their twenties, and nearly all of the others were in their thirties, except Shadowen and Trotter, who were slightly over sixty years of age. None held slaves except Moore, who owned four, and Trotter, who possessed one.[48]

While the people of Dickson County actively engaged in politics during the decades of the twenties and thirties, partisan politics did not become a burning issue in Tennessee until the late thirties and early forties, when the Whigs and Democrats locked horns in many a partisan battle. Political events, therefore, other than those already discussed, will be reserved for a succeeding chapter.

CHAPTER VI

The Expansion of Slavery

ALONG with their religious faith the pioneers brought a belief in the institution of slavery, a thing which some spiritual leaders later condemned. The earliest settlers brought their slaves with them as they pushed through the wilderness to establish homes on the Cumberland. When James Robertson and his party returned to the bluffs on that river in 1779, Robertson brought a Negro man with him. Also, in the following year slaves accompanied the Donelson party, which took a circuitous water route from Fort Patrick Henry in East Tennessee to the fort established by Robertson on the Cumberland.[1] During the next two decades more slaves were brought in, and by the time Dickson County was created the institution of slavery had become firmly entrenched in Middle Tennessee.

As mentioned earlier, it was the iron furnaces which brought the first great influx of slaves into the county. Robertson, Bell, Anthony Vanleer, John Fentress, and the Napier brothers found slave labor quite profitable in the accomplishment of all work requiring manual labor and in some work requiring a degree of skill. Bell, for example, ran his furnaces almost exclusively with Negroes, some of whom demonstrated a considerable degree of technical knowledge. All of the iron masters held large numbers of slaves, but often they found that during rush seasons they were obliged to comb the countryside for slave labor which might be hired by the day, or by the week, or month. Montgomery Bell even resorted to Nashville newspapers to publish advertisements soliciting hired labor.[2] Second to the operators of furnaces and forges, farmers employed more slaves than any other group. Men like Christopher Strong, Spencer T. Hunt, Minor Bibb, Thomas Collier, Daniel Leech, and Sterling Brewer, all owned fifteen or more blacks during the slaveholding period and employed them on farms.

The majority of the people in Dickson County, however, did not own slaves. For example, in 1820 there were only 205 families which held slaves out of a total of 638 families and a total population of 5,190. This same ratio, about one slaveholding family out of every three, existed to the outbreak of the Civil War.[3] It is also interesting to note that of those who held slaves in the county, more held one slave than any other number. For example, in 1820, fifty-seven of the 205 slaveholding families held only one slave, while only 26 held two, 19 held three, and 16 held five. In that year there were only 16 who held more

70

than 15 slaves, and only eight with more than 25. This approximate ratio continued through 1860.⁴ The main reason why people of Dickson County did not hold large numbers of slaves was that the soil and the climate were unfit for agricultural pursuits of the plantation variety. As mentioned earlier, the growing season was too short for cotton to be grown with the same degree of profit as it was in some of the West Tennessee counties. Too, rural families tended to be large, and both boys and girls learned early in life to do their share of the chores about the farms. While Dickson County families were no larger than those of other counties, many had homes full of children. John Sowell, for example, by 1820 had 18 children, and six of them were under 10 years of age. Willie Balthrop had 14 children, and Robert West had 10, by the same year. Monroe Corlew, born in 1852, was the nineteenth and last child of Benjamin and Phoebe Harris Corlew. Randolph Harris and Abraham Harris had only seven children each, but each had five sons under ten years of age. This no doubt assured them an ample labor supply for years to come.⁵

The fact that the great majority of the people of the county who held slaves were small slaveholders meant that they would take an attitude toward the institution of slavery different from that which was taken by some owners and overseers in the Deep South. In Dickson County as indeed in the great majority of Southern states in the pre-Civil War days, the landholdings and slaveholdings were relatively small, which gave the owner ample opportunity to appreciate well the abilities and limitations of the Negroes. Many of the whites loved their slaves as they did members of the family, and gave them the same medical attention and the same food that their families enjoyed, and buried them in the same cemeteries. Many likewise provided educational opportunities for the blacks and not infrequently remembered them in their wills by distributing items of personal property and sometimes real property.

Typical of those who showed consideration for slaves of honesty and ability was Montgomery Bell. A bachelor who was said to have had many children both black and white, Bell readily associated with his slaves although he owned so many that it was impossible for him to know them all. One old Negro, James Worley, was an especial favorite of Bell. Worley had become the property of his master while Bell was in business in Lexington, Kentucky, and came with the iron master to Dickson County in the early 1800's. The Negro was highly trusted by his master and often was placed in charge of large shipments of iron products to Cincinnati, New Orleans, and other river ports. He would collect for the products and safely carry the money or produce received in exchange to his master. Bell once was said to have exclaimed that in all his business dealings Worley "was never a dollar short." Merchants of Nashville, Cincinnati, and New Orleans allegedly offered Bell fabulous sums for the slave, but the iron master replied on at least one occasion, "I would not take all of New Orleans for him."⁶

As a crowning reward for Worley's services, Bell named one of his furnaces for the Negro. Worley Furnace, one of the smaller Bell establishments, was located just south of the present city of Dickson. Bell owned 83 slaves in 1820, 97 in 1830, and by 1850—five years before he died—he had accumulated 332.[7]

Many were far more humane in their everyday treatment of their blacks than was Bell. Elias W. Napier was one of them. In his will, probated in 1848, Napier emancipated over 30 slaves and was as lavish in praise of each as he was also lavish in providing them with personal property. His slave called Ephraigm was an object of special affection. The Negro had lost an eye in service for his master, but despite this, had continued to work faithfully and honestly. Napier stated that "in consequence of Ephraigm's faithfulness, honesty, and industry in attending to my business" he was to be granted his complete freedom, and also, in partnership with a slave named Tom, was to be given Napier's "best wagon and eight of . . . the best mules and gear."[8] To many others he gave cash. For the "yellow boy, Soloman," whom he set free, Napier ordered his executors to provide him with "fifty dollars per annum for his schooling and other expenses, until he be put to some trade . . . ," and to pay him upon his reaching 21 years of age "the sum of Five Hundred Dollars to begin his trade on. . . ." For all emancipated he provided enough "bacon, corn or meal, sugar, coffee, and salt to last them for a year after emancipation."[9]

The will of Joseph Dickson carried provisions for the slaves similar to those in Napier's will. Dickson provided that his "old Negro woman, Phillis," should be permitted to live on his farm all of her life, and that she was to be supported by his sons.[10] John Humphries, a justice of the peace and owner of fifteen slaves, in 1826 provided in his will that his "old negro woman Amy," should receive her freedom and should have the right to live with his heirs for the rest of her life. In order for his sons to receive their portion of the bequeathed property, they were commanded to maintain Amy as long as she lived.[11] Moses Fussell gave his "slave Man Ben" his freedom and, as did Humphries, provided that the slave could live his remaining days with the master's children.[12] George Tubb and Mary Woodward, while not emancipating their slaves, provided that those blacks who had served faithfully for so long should never be sold out of the family. Mary Woodward provided also that her slave named Moses must be supported in his old age by her children in order that Moses' declining years might be free from pain and worry. Moses was given the right to choose with which of Mrs. Woodward's children he desired to spend his remaining days.[13] Joab Hardin did not provide for the emancipation of his slaves in his will, probated in 1852. The reason, probably, was that by that time it was a violation of Tennessee law to give a slave his freedom unless the owner removed him, or provided for his removal, from the state. Hardin, then, perhaps in view of this legal provision, did not emancipate any slaves, but he took great pains to assure them a satisfactory existence. Five of his slaves, including a mother and her infant daughter, were willed to

Hardin's minor daughter, Sarah Ann. As guardian for Sarah Ann, Hardin appointed E. E. Larkins, who in such capacity was to supervise her property until she reached maturity. Larkins was commanded not to hire out the five slaves indiscriminately, nor any others which might go to his ward through a division of the estate, but was directed, "as far as might be in his power," to "hire them out at private hiring to humane and just persons, although in doing so he may receive a smaller amount of hire." In his will Hardin further stipulated that when the guardian hired the slaves, he should reserve the right to resume possession of them in case he thought the slaves were mistreated. Finally, Larkins was directed to pay Hardin's "old man Sawney" seven dollars annually and to pay a similar sum to each of the other slaves. The daughter was directed to continue these payments after she became of age throughout the lifetime of the slaves. Two others were to be sold and each was to receive five dollars upon completion of the sale. In another item of the will the testator appointed his father-in-law, Daniel Leech, guardian of his two youngest daughters, Faustina and Lorena, and directed that Leech be governed in hiring out slaves willed to those wards by the same stipulations set forth regarding slaves belonging to his oldest daughter.[14]

The first recorded sale of a slave in Dickson County came in December, 1804, when Ross Brewer sold to Sterling Brewer "one Negro boy."[15] By the time of the next meeting of the county court Joseph Turner had sold to Nathan Nesbitt "a negro man slave named Billy," and Joseph Teas reported that he had sold to William Teas "a Negro."[16] Sales of slaves were required to be approved by the county court, and to be recorded in the Minutes of that court, and throughout the slaveholding period there was hardly a quarterly session but that the sale of a slave was recorded.

The price which a slave would bring varied considerably throughout the period, for there were many factors involved in determining a fair value. During hard times the average price would decline, but in days of prosperity it would advance. The age, size, and physical condition of the Negro were major factors in determining his price. The "prime field hand"—the young Negro man between the approximate ages of 16 and 35—always brought a greater price than did any other. For an older slave to bring an equivalent amount he would have had to have some type of skill which would make him especially valuable. As a slave grew older his value declined, until in his old age he became a liability, and owners sometimes paid other slave owners to take the aged ones off their hands. As mentioned earlier, the great majority of slaveholders of the entire South felt bound by a strong moral obligation to care for an old or diseased slave. This, together with the spirit of affection most owners held for the slaves, caused slaveowners to maintain many blacks who actually had a negative value. Most references to the sale of slaves in Dickson County did not include the price of the slaves, but occasionally such a reference may be found. In 1831, for example, Joel R. Taylor of Davidson County sold to Joab Hardin a 21-year-old Negro boy for

$450.[17] In 1837 George Clark sued William Cox for the value of two slaves, a woman and her female infant, which Cox was alleged to have stolen. The jury set the value of the two slaves at $1,078, which was perhaps the highest price brought for female slaves during the period. Two years later another jury adjudged a Negro man to be worth $1,000.[18] The values set by the juries are higher than average for the time and is considerably more than such slaves would bring at public auction. Negroes sold on the block in liquidation of an estate seldom brought what they would at private sale. Some of the lowest priced blacks were sold at auction in 1843, and belonged to the Joseph Larkins estate. A "boy named Sam," for example, brought only $200; a "man named John" brought $275, a "woman named Ginsey" $300, and a "boy named Bill" only $300.[19] Reas Bowen sold a slave in 1842 to Epps Jackson for $1,287.50, which was probably the highest price brought by any Dickson County slave up to that time. The slave was warranted to be a skilled forgeman and refiner and to be "sound, healthy, and sensible." Bowen agreed forever to defend the title, age, and health of the Negro.[20] Bowen died in 1846 and all of his slaves sold at public auction brought over $600 each.[21]

A report of the assessed evaluation of slaves, found in the state comptroller's reports, affords an idea of the average price of the blacks. These figures of course take in consideration all slaves—those of the "prime field hand" variety as well as those having no value at all. The evaluation in Dickson County compares favorably with that of other counties in the immediate vicinity. It is somewhat lower, however, than that of most of the West Tennessee counties and higher than that of the counties of East Tennessee. For example, in 1838 the average value of all slaves in Dickson County was $540, in Hickman $578, in Davidson $578, in Rutherford $598, and in Williamson $614. In the rich farming land of West Tennessee where cotton was grown at good profits, the average price was much higher. The lowest evaluation in 1838 of all was in Johnson County in East Tennessee, which was $368. The following table presents the average value of slaves in Dickson County, and also in the state as a whole, for comparative purposes.[22]

Year	Dickson County (average value)	Tennessee (average value)
1838	$561	$540
1840	571	543
1842		509
1844	454	420
1846	448	414
1848	474	467
1850	477	507
1852		547
1854	554	606
1856	720	689
1859	1100	855

Runaway slaves created many problems. Occasionally blacks would leave Montgomery Bell's iron works, as mentioned in a previous chapter, and Bell advertised through the Nashville papers for their return.

Not infrequently would runaway slaves from other areas make their way into Dickson County. The appearance of one in Charlotte in September, 1814, created quite a stir. The Negro appeared in the town wearing large blue beads about his neck and carrying a large clubaxe. Joseph Wingate, sheriff, immediately took him into custody, and upon questioning him found that he could speak very few words of English. His threatening manner caused Wingate to believe that he was little beyond the cannibalistic stage of civilization, and that he had not been in this country long. Wingate advertised in the Nashville *Whig* for the owner, urging him to come to Charlotte with haste and take the Negro away.[23] A few years later a runaway slave from Natchez appeared in Charlotte and was arrested by Sheriff Clark Spencer. The sheriff had just taken him into custody, however, when he broke loose and made his escape. He was believed to have belonged to Walter Irvin of Natchez, who was requested to come to Charlotte and help in the search for him as soon as possible.[24]

As mentioned, a frequent practice in Dickson County (as throughout the entire South) was that of hiring slaves. If an owner did not intend to plant as extensive a crop as his slaveholdings would justify, he might hire out some of the slaves to someone who needed additional labor. Furthermore, many farmers who were not able to buy slaves would hire one or more during a busy season. The slave usually received the same treatment and care while hired out as he did when worked by the owner, and the owner usually stiplated good care and treatment in the agreement. William Corlew, for example, in 1839, put some of his slaves out for hire and stipulated in the contract that the renters were "to agree to furnish the slaves with one summer and two winter suits of clothes, one wool hat, and blanket," in addition to other necessities of life.[25] The owners of the iron furnaces rented more slaves than any others, and they usually supplied slaves with two or three suits of clothes each, and hats, shoes, blankets, and overcoats if the Negroes were to work during the winter. Work on Sunday and beyond the regular hours during the week generally brought to the slaveowner additional remuneration. A weekly ration for the hired slaves generally consisted of seven pounds of bacon, a peck of meal, and a quantity of molasses. Often the slaves hired at Cumberland Furnace traded their rations for produce of all sorts to whites living in the area.[26]

Although there may have been a tendency on the part of some people to abuse hired slaves, the thought of the bond and financial responsibility for the health and welfare of the hired blacks was generally sufficient to restrain a renter from inflicting undue abuse. If a slave became sick and died, or if he ran away, the person who had hired his labor was personally responsible. State Representative John Eubank, who had rented a slave from Joab Hardin in 1846, on one occasion expressed concern to Hardin since the slave had run away twice within a few weeks. He wrote Hardin, "On my return home yesterday Evening from Town to my astonishment your Boy Jack had left .... you had better take him back...."[27]

The usual price paid in Tennessee for hired slave labor was $80 to $100 per year, in addition to the necessities of life which were provided the Negro.[28] The price of course varied considerably with the skill, age, and sex of the slave. At the iron furnaces slave labor often brought more, because the work was more difficult and often required use of certain skills and techniques. The furnace owners in Dickson County paid from $100 to $200 at one period during the development of the iron works, and the labor of a few of the skilled workers brought even more.[29]

The recorded wills sometimes stipulated that certain slaves were to be hired for specific purposes, and many specified that the money received was to be used for the education of the slaveowner's children. Other owners stipulated that their slaves should be hired only in the types of labor to which they had been accustomed, and still others specified that the blacks should be hired only to just and humane persons. Hiring slaves sometimes created problems. In 1839 William Corlew was forced to sue the operators of an iron furnace on Yellow Creek for his rent money.[30] In the same year Richard Napier brought suit against George F. Napier to recover $51 "for the hire of Negro Man Jim...."[31] In some cases the slaves did not like the new temporary master and ran away, while in other cases they liked their new surroundings so well that they wanted to stay once the period of hire was over.

The people of Dickson County apparently looked upon the institution of slavery as being one in which there was no great inherent evil but which, like the poor, was with them always. Ministers like Samuel McAdow held no slaves but did not condemn slaveholding, and other ministers like Garner McConnico actually owned slaves.[32] During the 1820's a great deal of emancipationist sentiment was found throughout the state, and by 1830 there were 25 emancipation societies with a membership of over 1,500. By the mid-1830's, however, emancipationist sentiment began to decline throughout the South. A major factor was the beginning of the abolition attack in the North which was waged with increasing bitterness as the years passed. Other reasons why such sentiment should wane were that the Nat Turner insurrection of 1831 in Virginia implanted fear in the hearts of many slaveholders throughout the South, that the center of population in Tennessee began to shift to an area where slavery was more profitable, and that many men began to recognize the necessity for a defense of slavery, which defense was already in a formative stage throughout the slave states. In addition to these general causes, there were other factors of a more localized nature which occurred during the 1830's and thereafter which caused more and more Dickson County slaveowners to think twice before freeing their slaves. In a previous chapter the murder of a slaveholder by a slave named Wiley has been discussed. The recalcitrant Negro, who may have been familiar with the Nat Turner insurrection and the growing abolitionist activity, on November 25, 1833, assaulted William Bird of near Charlotte, and killed him. One month later

Wiley was hanged.³³ Two other factors were the proposed slave insurrections of 1835 and of 1856, in which Dickson County slaves were involved.

The first of the proposed insurrections was of minor consequence, and did not get beyond the rumor stage. Wild reports were circulated, however, that the slaves at all the Middle Tennessee furnaces planned to join together for a revolt against the whites. Probably some of the more intelligent ones among them had received quantities of incendiary literature from Northern abolitionists in which slaves of the South were encouraged to lead revolts against their masters. In nearby Montgomery County the fear was so great that weapons were procured from the state armory in Nashville in order that the revolt might be crushed in the beginning.³⁴ Nothing came of this insurrection scare, but the following year the general assembly of Tennessee passed an act making it an offense punishable by law to circulate printed matter, make addresses, or preach sermons which fostered discontent or insubordination among slaves.³⁵

The second of the proposed insurrections came in 1856, by which time the 75-year-old spirit of comity between the North and South was rapidly fading away. After the scare of 1835 the Negroes at the Middle Tennessee furnaces worked peaceably for two decades without manifestation of revolutionary ideas. By 1856, however, an insurrectionary spirit was growing throughout the South, and the proposed revolt of that year caused panic among the whites far and near. The proposed insurrection embraced states from Delaware to Texas, and received considerable publicity in the Southern press and such Northern newspapers as the New York *Journal*, the New York *Tribune*, and the Evansville *Journal*.³⁶ The entire iron district on the Cumberland and Tennessee rivers received a scare at the time, and one writer has referred to this area as being "perhaps the most terror-stricken community of the entire South. . . ."³⁷ There were many furnaces in Middle Tennessee, and in some areas the Negro population in the vicinity of the furnaces outnumbered the whites. This was true in the neighborhood of Louisa Furnace in Montgomery County, where a keg of powder was found under a Negro church—put there, presumably, by blacks intent upon insurrection. A 24-hour patrol was set up in the area, and when a Negro named Britton was heard haranguing a group of slaves—presumably inciting them to insurrection—he was shot on the spot after he refused to obey an order to cease and desist.³⁸ According to a Nashville newspaper the slaves were being organized as "generals" and "captains" and were planning a movement for Christmas day, at which time they were to march on the city of Clarksville and capture the town, plunder its banks, and then flee to free territory in the North where they had been assured that they would be safe.³⁹ The patrol throughout Middle Tennessee was strengthened, and it was reported that in Clarksville every household had ample arms and ammunition for any emergency. Iron furnace owners and operators were notified by the Clarksville city council on December 17 that no visiting slaves would be permitted to remain in the town for more than two hours unless accompanied by "a responsible white person." In case of violation of this ordinance the slave was to be taken into custody and given twenty lashes.[40]

At nearby Dover the people were in a state of panic and reportedly were well armed. Just north, in Christian County, Kentucky, a committee of citizens appealed for help, stating that "From reliable information we expect an attack from the negroes of the Iron Works on our town tomorrow morning, perhaps tonight. Please come to our assistance."[41] They stated that from "reliable information" they had learned that Negroes of Eclipse, Clark, and Lagrange furnaces had united and "were marching from Dover and were within eight miles of that place when last heard from." In Nashville the city council increased the slave patrol for both night and day duty. Negro schools and churches were forbidden temporarily to operate, and all Negro assemblages after sundown were prohibited by city ordinance.[42] Interestingly enough, it was the confession of a Dickson County slave which enabled the law enforcement officers to disrupt the plans before the proposed revolt had got underway. A Negro at Cumberland Furnace who had been taken in by the plotters learned of the plans and then escaped from the furnace and reported to the authorities. His revelations were such as to cause the immediate arrest of nearly 80 slaves, "most of whom confessed their complicity in the plot and gave precise details as to the manner of execution of their project."[43] Jails of all the Middle Tennessee counties were filled immediately, as whites now in a state of panic imprisoned all blacks upon the slightest suspicion. In Dover nineteen Negroes were hanged, and in Dickson County several dozen were implicated and some probably were hanged.[44] The panic resulted in a serious financial loss for the furnace owners and operators, and 25 furnaces were forced to cease operation temporarily because of the widespread paralysis.[45]

The ruthless manner in which the proposed insurrection was put down well indicates the extent to which fear gripped the minds of the people of Dickson County and of the South in general by 1856. The fact that the Northern newspaper editors, with few exceptions, viewed the proposed insurrection with great rejoicing, sorrowing only that it had not been successful, made increasingly wider the breach between the people of the North and South. It is significant that during the 1830's stipulations in recorded wills began to appear in which the testator expressed fear that his slaves might become dangerous and unruly. As early as 1838 William Morrison provided in his will that if two slaves which he bequeathed to his wife "should prove to be refractory or disobedient, my Executors are requested to sell such negroes . . . and to use their own discretion and make such disposition of a refractory or disobedient servant as they may think best for the benefit of my wife."[46] Several years later Hartwell U. Slayden, a farmer and small slaveowner, wrote in his will that if "any of the negroes become contrary and ungovernable by my companion Jane or by any of my children . . . who are of age to govern and manage slaves, such of the negroes shall be put up and sold to the highest bidder."⁴⁷ William Adams wrote in 1849, "I authorize my Executor that in case my negro man Toby should become contrary or ungovernable to hire and sell him as he may think best, . . ." and in 1860 John May who held over 20 slaves wrote, "in case any negro I have left to my wife should become unmanageable or unrully [sic] my said wife shall have the power to sell or exchange any such negro. . . ."⁴⁸

It has been mentioned earlier that masters not infrequently would free their slaves. This practice, however, was followed rarely after the mid-1830's. Occasionally an owner provided for a form of compensated emancipation;—that the slave should be free when he had worked out his cost and maintenance. Such was the case of a slaveowner named Mary Yarrell, who in 1831 provided:

> I give and bequeath my negro woman named Matilda her freedom at my death when the said Matilda pays over to my Executors the sum of One Hundred Dollars for the express use of my nieces. . . . Then the said negro woman is to be free the residue of her days.⁴⁹

By the 1850's emancipation sentiment resided in the minds of few, if any, so far as the small slaveholder was concerned, and the days of voluntary emancipation were virtually at an end. Tennessee law provided that if a slave was emancipated he must be removed from the state. Christopher Strong and Montgomery Bell were the only Dickson County slaveholders who attempted emancipation after 1850, and both sent slaves to Liberia. They indicated a belief that gradual emancipation and deportation of the slaves was the best method whereby the United States might be relieved of a most pressing problem, and they sought to inform each slave of the advantages and disadvantages of remaining a slave in this country and of obtaining his freedom in the African republic of Liberia. Strong, who owned considerably fewer slaves than did Bell, provided in his will that all of his slaves should be given a choice of remaining in slavery or going to the African colony.⁵⁰ He further provided that those who wished to be free were to be placed in the hands of the American Colonization Society and taken to Liberia. At Strong's death, for some unexplained reason his executor did not place the slaves in the hands of the Society, but instead hired Robert McNeilly, prominent Dickson County lawyer, to accompany the blacks and place them safely on the Liberian shores. McNeilly, with his strange cargo, sailed from New Orleans and, after a few weeks on the Atlantic, deposited the slaves near a colony where other former American Negro slaves resided. After about three years, McNeilly began to receive "the most pitiful appeals" from members of the group pleading for goods and supplies, but most of all, for McNeilly to come for them and take them back to America.⁵¹ Information was not clear on the subject, but from the letters McNeilly understood that two or three of the more intelligent of the freedmen had appropriated the entire colony and were ruling as an oligarchy. Many had died and most of them seemed on the verge of starvation. Shortly before the Civil War the letters came no more.[52]

Several years before his death Montgomery Bell became imbued with a philanthropic spirit, and offered freedom to all his slaves who would agree to go to Liberia. He proposed to them that if they wished their freedom he would pay their transportation and furnish them with enough provisions and food to last for six months.[53] About 90 slaves accepted the offer and assembled in the winter of 1853 in Nashville, where they were joined by others from Middle Tennessee, and transported to Savannah, Georgia. From there, on December 16, 1853, they sailed for Liberia on the *General Pierce*.[54] Aboard the ship were some of Bell's best slaves. When they reached Liberia they expressed great joy at the sight of the surroundings, and instructed the ship captain to write Bell "a most loving letter ... and tell him how much we love him, and will never stop thanking to the Lord for his goodness to us."[55]

One other topic should be discussed briefly in connection with slaveholding in Dickson County. Many Northern writers, both before the Civil War and after, sought to leave the impression that in the South there was a wide social gap between those who held slaves and those who did not, and that jealousy and ill will existed between the two groups.[56] In the early 1920's, John Trotwood Moore, then State Librarian of Tennessee, in an effort to obtain firsthand information on slavery in the ante-bellum South, sent questionnaires to hundreds of Civil War veterans who had lived during the days of slavery. Thirty Confederate veterans from Dickson County answered the questionnaires, and the conditions which they revealed are the basis for the following discussion. Although these questionnaires, deposited in the State Library, must be used with care since they were returned by old men 50 to 75 years after the time of the events described, many students have found them to be fairly reliable sources for the study of general conditions of the ante-bellum South.

The answers to the questionnaires sent in by Dickson County veterans show that there was no feeling of superiority on the part of the slaveholder in the county, and that there appeared to be no social line drawn between those who held slaves and those who did not. If a farmer had been reasonably successful and desired to spend part of his savings on slaves, he made the purchase with no apparent thought of putting himself in a higher social class. The acquisition of a new slave seemed to be similar to purchasing a new mule or building a new barn, and if any feeling of superiority existed, it was perhaps because of the economic superiority rather than because of the mere fact that one had slaves and the other did not.

In reply to the query, "Did the men who owned slaves mingle freely with those who did not own slaves, or did slaveholders in any way show by their actions that they felt themselves better than respectable, honorable, men who did not own slaves?" most gave an emphatic answer quite like that of Moses Garton, who replied, "There was no difference made between the men who owned slaves and those who did not." A few gave qualified answers such as that given by Elias N. Cathey, who replied, "In most cases slaveholders mingled freely with non-slaveholders but in rare instances a slaveholder seemed to think himself above a non-slaveholder."

To the question, "At the churches, at the schools, at public gatherings in general, did slaveholders and non-slaveholders mingle on a footing of equality?" all answered in the same vein as did G. H. Cline: "Slaveholders and non-slaveholders mingled freely. There was a general good feeling between non-slaveholders and slaveholders." A similar response was given in answer to the question, "Was there a friendly feeling between slaveholders and non-slaveholders in your community, or were they antagonistic to each other?" All of the replies indicate that if a candidate for public office in the county owned slaves, it made little or no difference one way or another so far as his vote-getting power was concerned.

Those who held slaves worked by the side of the Negroes and everyone had to work for a living, the questionnaires indicate. To the question, "How was honest toil as plowing, hauling, and other sorts of honest work of this class regarded in your community?" all replied that it was regarded as honorable. To the question, "To what extent were there white men in your community leading lives of idleness and having others do work for them?" most answered "none," while a few offered a brief explanation, as did James K. Clifton, who wrote, "Then as now there were idlers, who expected others to work for them. These idlers were not confined entirely to slaveholders or non-slaveholders. There were some worthless nobodies in both classes, but none seemed to feel themselves better simply because they owned slaves."

Thus the questionnaires indicate that there was little or no class distinction in Dickson County based solely on the ownership of slaves. This does not mean, of course, that there were no social distinctions among these people. Economic differences invariably cause social differences, and Dickson County was not immune to such custom. But the Moore Questionnaires do reveal that feelings of superiority were generally based upon economic status and not upon mere ownership of slaves.

Slavery ended, of course, with the Civil War. This affected the economy of Dickson County very little, however, for the livelihood of the people had never been based to any considerable degree upon the institution of slavery.

CHAPTER VII

The Coming of the Civil War, 1840-1860

During the several decades preceding the Civil War, Tennessee played a most important part in the political affairs of the nation. In many other ways the state held a superior position. Governor James C. Jones, elected governor in 1841, reported to the legislature that the state was fifth in the nation in population and that it ranked almost as high in its economic possibilities.[1] By 1837 Andrew Jackson had served for eight years as President of the United States, and had been largely responsible for Van Buren's election. James Knox Polk, later to become President, was speaker of the House of Representatives, and Felix Grundy had served with distinction in both houses of Congress. During this time the state was the scene of a vigorous two-party system in which Democrats and Whigs fought each other tooth and nail and virtually alternated in the governorship. Tennessee, also experienced economic growth and witnessed an agricultural awakening during the 1840's. Iron works in Middle Tennessee were expanding, business was growing, and people enjoyed a standard of living never dreamed of by their pioneer ancestors of a generation before. In the midst of this expansion and development, to be sure, there could be heard an occasional discordant note of the slavery controversy and sectional animosity, but Tennesseans were loyal to the union which they had helped establish. This loyalty continued until action by the federal government forced them to join the states of the Deep South. In all of these events, Dickson County played an important part. It grew and developed and was an integral part of the state.

The people of Dickson County were a homogeneous group, who pursued many fields of endeavor. The census records for 1850 and after reveal a great deal about the American people which is not to be found in the earlier census records. It shows, for example, that the majority of the Dickson County population was Tennessee born and bred, but also that there were many who had come from other states and a few from other countries. Of those not born in Tennessee, more came from North Carolina and Virginia than from any other states. More than 250 hailed from North Carolina, and over half that many had been born in Virginia. There were twenty or more who were natives of Pennsylvania, South Carolina, Kentucky, Georgia, and Alabama. The states of New York, New Jersey, Maryland, Louisiana, Missouri, Massachusetts, Indiana, Illinois, Mississippi, and Ohio were represented by at least one each.

A half-dozen or more were born in Ireland, England and Scotland, and at least one each in Wales, Prussia, and Bermuda. Several, unable to read and write, indicated only "Europe" as their place of birth. William and Mary Lewis came in this category. Not only could they neither read nor write, but they had five sons, all of whom were classified as idiots in the 1850 United States census.[2]

Of those who designated North Carolina as the place of birth, some no doubt, were born in the Tennessee territory while that area was still a part of North Carolina. Of those born in other states, many had lived still elsewhere before coming into Dickson County. As mentioned previously, Montgomery Bell had lived for awhile in Pennsylvania, had worked as a hatter in Kentucky, and then had come into Tennessee. James and Elizabeth Woodward were born in Virginia as was their son, John. John, however, had come to Tennessee, married a Tennessee wife, and reared four children all of whom were born in this state. In 1850 his parents were living in Dickson County with him. John Hutton, a 34-year-old school teacher born in Virginia, had married a Tennessee wife, and they had had a Mississippi-born child, aged 7, and another child, aged 5, born in Tennessee. John and Mary Roach, Irish natives, apparently wasted little time in getting to Dickson County, once they arrived on American shores. They had two children, one a three-year-old daughter born in Ireland and the other a one-year-old son born in Tennessee. William and Bridget Busk, another Irish couple both aged 25, had a four-year-old son born in Ireland and a two-year-old child and a one-year-old child born in Ohio, which indicated that they had been in Dickson County for less than a year when the census taker visited their home in 1850.

The people followed many different occupations, but the vast majority were farmers. Of those who tilled the soil, the majority owned their land, but there were also many who were not landowners, but who worked as day laborers. There were many trades and several different professions represented in the county in 1850. Felix Courfman was a tinner, John Eubank and William Dickson were tailors, D. W. Adcock was a shoemaker, Burrell Hunter a steamboat pilot, Isaac Groves a forgeman, and George Southerland a blacksmith. H. A. Bibbs, a tailor, and his wife Milbrey ran a boarding house, and among those living with them were a law student named R. B. Cox, James L. Butler, a sadler, Courfman the tinner, and Dickson the tailor. W. J. Mathis was sheriff, Cyrus Chichester was jailor, Thomas Murrell was trustee, and Thomas McNeilly was county court clerk. Charlotte and the surrounding territory had an abundance of doctors, lawyers, and merchants. Among the lawyers were S. L. Finley, aged 28, who lived with the sheriff; John W. May, 24, who boarded with E. E. Larkins, a school teacher and businessman; John C. Collier, 60, and others. Among the physicians in 1850 was a Prussian native, Francis Schmittou; Augustine Roberts, a Virginian, and his son Willis; D. C. Chamberlain and son Franklin, James M. Larkins, George H. Swift, W. B. Joslin, A. G. Parish, Aaron James, E. W. Ellis, and W. A. Moody. Among those classified by the census taker as merchants were James W. Dickson, Joab Hardin, William Collier, H. W. Allen, Thomas Overton (of Virginia), T. H. Grigsby (from Alabama), Jonathan Ward, William Anderson, and a host of others. Henry Goodrich, 69, Massachusetts-born, was a hatter, and E. N. Phillips (a North Carolina native), and his son Napoleon, ran a distillery.

Over a dozen Methodist, Baptist, and Presbyterian clergyman were preaching in the county in 1850. In addition to the trades and professions mentioned above, there were at least the following represented in 1850: wheelwright, carpenter, sawyer, ditcher, brick layer, woodchopper, molder, salesman, clerk, engineer, miller, waggoner, revenue collector, collier, fisherman, overseer, cabinet maker, cooper, tanner, stage driver, stone mason, and wagon maker.

Many of the residences housed two or more families, but were not classified as inns. In the home of A. D. Ramey, for example, there lived William Laird, a sadler, and a family of three headed by a stagedriver named Thornton Hendrick. W. R. V. Schmittou and wife had been given a contract by the county court to house and care for the paupers of the county, and in 1850 four were under their care. They were Peter Seals, 60, from North Carolina; Isaac Stone, 39, of Tennessee; Tabitha Shearod, 49, of North Carolina; and Elizabeth Crogard, 48, a native of Virginia. The practice in many of the counties at this time was to let the contract for the keeping of paupers to the person who would make the lowest bid, rather than to erect a separate poor house or maintain a county farm. Perhaps Dickson County followed that procedure.

Among the oldest citizens of the county in 1850 were Gustavus Rape and Christopher Strong. Rape, 94, had come to Dickson County from North Carolina, and his 78-year-old wife, Barbary, was a South Carolina native. He had fought in the Revolutionary War and in 1850 was still drawing a pension for his military service. Strong was 90 and had come from Ireland into Pennsylvania and had moved southward to Tennessee. His wife Rosanna was 66, and she, like Barbary Rape, was a South Carolina native. When young, he had settled several miles southeast of Charlotte and owned thousands of acres on Jones' Creek. The road from Nashville to Charlotte ran through his farm, and one of the more difficult parts of the journey was "Strong's hill" (on which the county poor house today is situated). A branch, found at the foot of the hill and flowing into Jones' Creek near the present county farm, is known today as Strong's Branch.

As mentioned, more people of Dickson County tilled the soil for a living than pursued any other occupation. By the 1840's farmers of Tennessee experienced an agricultural awakening in which more emphasis was placed upon crop rotation, scientific analysis of the soil, and the use of better and more efficient farm implements.[3] The early emphasis in the state had been upon corn, tobacco, and cotton—crops which took fertility from the soil but replaced none and which led to erosion in hilly land. By 1850, however, farmers of Dickson County and many other surrounding rural counties had begun to place more emphasis upon crop diversification. The raising of wheat, rye, and oats was practiced to a greater extent in the forties and fifties, and cattle grazing became increasingly important. Wheat was urged upon the farmers of the state as a money crop by such outstanding farm publications as the *Agriculturalist*, and the editor lamented the fact that the people of the state bought wheat elsewhere when they could raise it in the state at a profit. In 1857 the state agriculture bureau offered a premium of $100 for the best ten acres of wheat produced in the state to be accompanied by a statement concerning the best mode of cultivation.[4] In Dickson County many farmers by 1850 had turned from the production of cotton and were experimenting with wheat. In that year only two farmers, Sam Bowen and William Studdard, produced cotton for the market, and their total production consisted of only eighteen bales weighing 400 pounds each.[5] Most of the farmers in counties as far north as Dickson had given up hopes some years before of making a fortune from cotton, and had turned to other crops. In 1850 Dickson farmers produced 3,789 bushels of wheat, but ten years later raised 22,722 bushels, which indicated a growing interest in the production of the grain. In 1850 over 60,000 bushels of oats and several hundred bushels of rye were produced. Over 11,000 bushels of Irish potatoes and over 26,000 bushels of sweet potatoes were grown. Indian corn was the standby, however, and every farmer had a crop of that grain. In 1850 nearly 390,000 bushels were grown on Dickson County soil, and ten years later, over a half million bushels. In 1850 over 8,000 bushels of corn was produced on the farms of Anthony W. Vanleer alone, while William H. Nichols produced 4,500, Gustavus Rape 1,000, Milton Loftis 1,200, and William Garrett 1,250.[6]

Although critics of tobacco culture continued to point to the destructive effect the plant had upon the fertility of the soil, farmers of the middle and northern counties increased the acreage of the crop during the 1840's and 1850's, and the ready markets at Springfield and Clarksville served as an impetus to greater production. One correspondent of a prominent agricultural paper, *The Southern Cultivator*, urged that more attention should be given to tobacco, for the counties in which the weed was cultivated were more prosperous than others in the same vicinity, he said.[7] In Dickson the interest in tobacco increased tremendously as more land was cleared and less emphasis was placed upon cotton. In 1850 James Dickson produced for the market over 7,000 pounds of tobacco, Christopher Meek and William Coleman produced 1,000, John Yates 3,000, and George Cooksey and James James over 800 each. In the following decade more farmers increased their production and some doubled and tripled the amount of land devoted to tobacco.[8] The total amount produced in 1850 and in 1860 readily shows the increased interest. In 1850 a little over 25,000 pounds of tobacco was placed on the market, while ten years later well over a half million pounds was sold from Dickson County.[9]

Livestock husbandry was a thing to which many Tennessee farmers turned their attention during the several decades immediately preceding the Civil War. In the early days not a great deal of attention had been placed upon cattle, which were permitted to graze upon the open range. Indiscriminate methods gradually gave way to more ample provisions for livestock, however, and by 1840 more attention was being given to fences and barns. By this time it was well known that cattle needed shelter in the winter and that an adequate supply of hay was a very necessary item. Too, farmers knew that careful attention to breeding would produce a superior herd of bovine. Some of the finest cattle of the entire South were found in nearby Davidson County, and some of these no doubt were brought into Dickson. Men like B. A. and T. L. Collier, William H. and John Napier, G. W. Hiland, and John Corlew had livestock valued in the thousands of dollars, and hundreds of other Dickson farmers had smaller herds.[10] In 1850 farmers of the county owned less than 2,500 head, exclusive of milch cows and working oxen, while by 1860 the figure had been doubled. Increasing attention also was given to sheep, horses, and milch cows, and the number of each doubled between 1850 and 1860.[11]

The large production of corn meant a similarly large production of swine. Nearly every citizen, whether he lived in town or in the rural areas, had a few hogs. In 1850 Christopher Strong, although a man of ninety summers, had on his farm over fifty hogs. In 1860 Jacob Leech practiced law in Charlotte and owned only eight acres, yet he had twenty hogs and produced a small quantity of corn on his land. William H. Nichols in 1850 raised over 200 head of swine, and B. A. and T. L. Collier, A. W. Vanleer, William C. Napier, and G. W. Hiland, all numbered theirs in the hundreds.[12] The number of hogs raised in Dickson County in 1850 was a little over twenty thousand, while in 1860 the number had increased to nearly twenty-five thousand.[13]

Sheep raising of course meant wool production, and some of the finest wool of the nation was produced in Middle Tennessee. Mark Cockrill, for example, a Davidson County farmer who owned over five thousand acres located in the western part of the county on the Nashville to Charlotte Pike, won international fame for his wool. In 1850 he challenged anyone to show him finer wool, and in the World's Fair of 1854 in London he was awarded first prize, and thus could boast rightly that his was the finest wool in the world. In Dickson County farm owners like Vanleer produced wool in large quantities. George Luther and John Eubank typified the small farmer of the county in wool production. Luther owned scarcely two hundred acres, yet produced in 1850 thirty pounds of wool for the market, while Eubank in the same year produced twenty-five pounds from a farm of a little over three hundred acres. In 1860 over 17,000 pounds of wool was produced in the entire county. In annual wool production the farmers of Dickson County exceeded the production of farmers of Hickman, Humphreys, Stewart, and other rural Middle Tennessee counties from a few pounds to several hundred.[14]

In addition to the crops mentioned, most householders had good-sized gardens in which they raised a large variety of vegetables for their own consumption and sometimes for the market. They produced such farm commodities as butter and cheese for the market, although in relatively small quantities. Rice was grown with only a fair degree of success, but every farmer produced large quantities of hay, peas and beans, clover, and orchard products. Around nearly every home there were chickens and turkeys in abundance, and most people produced sufficient poultry for an abundant supply of meat and eggs. Whether families owned farms or not, they usually had at least one milch cow, fifty or more fowls, and half dozen or more swine.

The amount of land in cultivation in 1850 and in 1860 is perhaps the best indication of the increasing interest in farming. In 1850 only 31,000 acres were in cultivation, while in 1860 over 55,000 acres are recorded in the census as being "improved land." Too, there was an increasing interest, not only in Dickson County, but all over the state and the South, in better farm implements. At the beginning of the nineteenth century among the common farm implements were some which had been in use since the days of Moses. Clumsy wooden plows, scythes and cradles, harrows consisting of nothing more than a heavily weighted log, and an occasional crude threshing machine, were all in wide use.[15] In the few decades to follow, however, farmers witnessed a revolution in farm implements, as men like Cyrus McCormick and others turned their attention to perfecting better farming tools. By 1840 a state farm publication had advertised at least the following for farm use: the cultivator, straw cutter, horse rake, corn crusher, threshing machine, roller, drill harrow, and improved harrow.[16] In the ten year period from 1850 to 1860 the value of farm implements increased considerably in every rural county of Middle Tennessee. In the urban counties like Davidson where many such implements were already in use the increase was relatively small. In Dickson, however, the value tripled from 1850 to 1860. In nearby Humphreys the value doubled, and in Hickman it increased by about one-half.[17]

While more people of Dickson County followed agricultural pursuits than any other occupation, others made a living in the mercantile business or, as mentioned earlier, from professions, skills, or trades. The iron industry, discussed in preceding chapters, reached its height in the two decades preceding the Civil War, under the capable management of such men as Anthony Vanleer, W. A. Fentress, Theodore Baxter, and others. By 1840 more young men who had learned the iron business in Pennsylvania and on the British Isles came into Tennessee and gave the state the benefit of what they had learned in the East. As early as the 1820's Vanleer had become associated with Robert Baxter, of English ancestry, and by 1850 the Baxter family was well entrenched in the iron business of the county. Theodore Baxter in that year was operating a furnace near Cumberland Furnace and had as his business manager Maryland-born Howard Mockbee (sometimes spelled Mockba). A. Musgroves, William Mulberry, Washington Mulberry, and Joseph Mulberry were Kentucky-born forgemen and woodhaulers, and Dave

Lot and Thomas Murphy were Pennsylvania-born forgemen. Thomas Overton operated a store worth $2,600 in the community. W. B. Joslin was the physician, and J. R. Riddle and Jesse Daniel were school teachers. South Carolina-born M. Berry was a Methodist clergyman with a family approximating a dozen children.[18] Anthony Vanleer, sixty years of age, was still the owner of the Cumberland Furnace in 1850, in addition to thousands of acres of real estate which stretched from the present town of Vanleer to the furnace. He estimated for the census officials in 1850 that his real estate alone was worth over $60,000, which was indeed a conservative estimate. Men born in Tennessee, Maryland, Ohio, and Virginia worked at the furnace. William C. Napier, a young man of 30, operated Carroll furnace nearby, which he valued at $15,000, but which he sold shortly thereafter to Robert Baxter, Jr. He had in his employ John Huckharkan, a Scottish ore digger, Thomas Walker, a Maryland-born furnace manager, and many others who were wheelrights, coopers, and molders. Professional and business men were always necessary at the furnaces, and living near the Napier furnace were William Anderson, grocer; W. A. Williams, Cumberland Presbyterian preacher; A. G. Parish, physician; and James Adkins and Alston Myatt, school teachers. By 1860 Hugh Kirkman, Vanleer's son-in-law, had assumed the management of Cumberland furnace and operated it on a charcoal hot and cold blast basis with a capacity of twelve tons per day. By this time Daniel, George, and James Hillman of New Jersey had given their lives toward the development of Cumberland Furnace, and James Hillman today lies buried in a small cemetery near where the furnace once was. John Stacker of Pennsylvania was another who had given much to the development of Dickson County iron ore.[19]

A first-hand account of iron works in Dickson County was written in 1915 by the son of John H. B. Mockbee and nephew of Robert Baxter, who served as a captain in the Civil War and who visited Dickson County occasionally from time to time until his death several decades ago.

> My earliest recollection [he wrote], goes back into the forties [1840's]. I became familiar in my youth and early manhood with the iron business in consequence of a close kinship with several iron men. You will doubtless be surprised when you consider the number of these enterprises and the vast capital required to build and successfully operate them. There were thousands of men employed at the iron works, most of them slaves, but many white men were also given employment at remunerative wages, especially skilled workmen in the forges, and as founders and moulders. Moulders made pots, skillets, ovens, and irons....
> The management of the works had to use system in the employment of their labor. As early after Christmas as possible they would start out on horseback visiting all the slave owners for miles around in order to secure labor to carry on the work for the next year.... In addition to clothing and food the employer contracted to supply medical aid and medicine throughout the period of the contract.
> My uncle on my mother's side, Robert Baxter, owned and operated

several furnaces in Montgomery and Dickson counties. Sometime in the early fifties my cousin, Robert Baxter, Jr., bought Carroll Furnace from William Napier, and upon his taking charge of it I went there to live with him remaining until I was fifteen years old. While there I attended Tracy Academy, the school kept by Professor Larkins, a splendid man and fine teacher. It was in his school and under his tutorage that I obtained all the training in books that I ever received.[20]

Although economic pursuits must of necessity occupy a paramount place in the lives of people, the Dickson County citizenry did not permit them to interfere with their participation in political activity. Tennessee had been admitted to the union under the administration of Thomas Jefferson and had been known as a Jeffersonian Republican state until the emergence of Old Hickory in 1824. Although in that election Jackson had not been the victor, he had won a decisive majority in Tennessee and continued to do so in the two elections which followed. By the mid-thirties, however, opposition to Jackson led by Hugh Lawson White and John Bell, the latter a Stewart County land owner, began to crystalize, and by 1836 it was sufficiently strong to defeat within the state the old Indian fighter's choice for a White House successor. Jackson's opponents described him as one lustful for power whose tactics were not dissimilar to those employed by King George III of Great Britain in the days when the American colonies were seeking their independence. To indicate that they were fighting against dictatorship, the opponents of Jackson began to call themselves "Whigs," and by 1835 two parties had evolved in the state.[21] During the next two decades "partisan fury" characterized Tennessee politics.

Although the Whig element was reasonably strong in Dickson County from the beginning, it was never sufficient to overcome the Democratic strength in this nor in various other rural counties of Middle Tennessee. The first test of strength for national candidates came in 1836 when Jackson's man, Martin Van Buren, was pitted against several Whig candidates for the Presidency, including Hugh Lawson White of Tennessee. While White carried the state by a substantial majority, in Dickson the vote was Democratic by better than a two-to-one majority and was even greater than two to one in the nearby counties of Hickman, Stewart, and Humphreys. Of those counties in the immediate vicinity of Dickson, only the urban centers of Davidson and Montgomery gave White a majority.[22] In the meantime the Whigs handed the Democrats repeated setbacks on the state level, but there, too, the Dickson County Democrats remained adamant. In 1837 Governor Newton Cannon, a Whig, won a sweeping victory over his Democratic opponent and in the legislature the Whigs gained a 49 to 26 majority in the house and an 18 to 7 plurality in the senate. Nevertheless, in that year the people of Dickson refused to support Cannon. To the house they elected a staunch Democrat named John Eubank, who was to hold the office for the next decade, and to the senate they reelected Thomas Shaw, who had served two earlier terms as a Jacksonian Democrat and who was to serve two more as a defender of Democratic principles.

During the forties and early fifties interest in political contests permeated even the most backwoods communities. During that time elections took on a uniform and sometimes entertaining pattern as rival candidates toured the state and spoke from the same platform. Some of the state's outstanding orators lived at the time, and the people gathered from miles around to cheer their candidate as he poked fun and ridicule at his opponent, and to claim their "share" of free barbecue and liquor, which generally were present in abundant quantities. The gubernatorial election of 1839 and the presidential election of 1840 brought to the people of the state fifteen months or more of continuous political activity, the like of which they had never seen before. On the state level the Whigs had been in control for four years with Newton Cannon as governor. The domination by the Whigs had been galling to Andrew Jackson and other state Democrats, and they mustered all available strength for the election of 1839. Their ace proved to be James Knox Polk, at that time Speaker of the House of Representatives of the United States. First, last, and always a loyal Democrat, Polk resigned his seat in the House and returned to Tennessee to run for governor. In Dickson, as in all Tennessee counties, partisan politics was at its worst and much bitterness ensued. John C. Collier and his brothers led the Whig campaign, while John Eubank, the McNeilly men, Major V. F. Bibb, and others led the attack of the Democrats. The campaign became so bitter that one Charlotte observer wrote to a Pennsylvania relative that "John C. Collier and brothers have injured themselves by interfering in the elections too much. . . ."[23] Just after the election the same observer wrote that "we have heard nothing else except the election for the last three months."[24] Dickson County delivered her usual majority to the Democrats, who won handily, and James Knox Polk became governor.

On the national level in 1840, the Democrats found Martin Van Buren and the panic of 1837 to be major liabilities, and that party lost to the Whigs when William Henry Harrison became President. No major speaking engagement was held in Dickson County in 1840, but many local Whigs no doubt attended the great mid-state Whig gathering at Clarksville on May 29 of that year. Seven to eight thousand people jammed the streets of the Montgomery county seat, as good weather accompanied the meeting. Music and marching were the order of the day, as "bands, military companies, and cavalry were spaced among the marching delegates." Many horse-drawn floats passed in review, one in particular catching the eyes of the loyal Whigs. It was of a log cabin on wheels, which advertised the fact that the Whig presidential candidate was born and reared in such a cabin and thus was one of the common people. Coon skins were nailed to the door and a caged coon ran to-and-fro inside. Free barbecue and hard cider were avaliable in large quantities for everyone.[25]

Whatever inspiration Dickson County Whigs might have gained from the Clarksville rally was not sufficient for the party to carry the county, however, for the majority of the folk remained loyal to the party of the Old Hero. Although the Whigs were able to elect the President by a good majority, in Dickson County the Democrats won by a vote of 653 to 396. Dickson was in the Ninth Congressional District along with Montgomery, Robertson, Benton, Henry, Humphreys, and Stewart, and every county except Montgomery and Robertson gave Van Buren sufficient majority to enable him to carry the district by a small vote.[26] In the following year the Whigs elected the governor, as the people of the state were lulled by the skillful oratory of James C. Jones into such lethargy that they chose the youthful Whig over the experienced and stable Democrat, James Knox Polk. The latter attempted a political comeback two years later, and again the persuasive oratory of Jones was too much for him. In each election the people of Dickson County remained loyal to Polk, although his majority in 1843 was not so large as in former years. The rural counties surrounding Dickson again voted Democratic. In 1843, for example, Hickman gave Polk a majority of 913 to 277, Stewart gave him a 662 to 470 plurality, and Humphreys he carried by better than 150 votes. In the same year Cave Johnson of Montgomery County, a regular practitioner before the Montgomery and Dickson county bars and a man who was fast becoming a national figure, was elected to Congress by the small margin of 228 votes. Dickson County gave him a 602 to 342 majority, without which he would have been unable to win.[27]

By 1844 four years of Whiggery had brought Democrats to their best efforts and they nominated for the Presidency a dark horse from Tennessee, James K. Polk, and began a thorough organization and campaign for political support in every state down to the county and town level. Polk's opponent was Henry Clay, a man well known throughout Tennessee and Kentucky and indeed throughout the entire nation. As time for the election approached feeling ran high—so high, said one Dickson County contemporary, that "the farmers and everybody quit work and went about boosting their candidate, yelling and hooping and giving barbecues and having a high old time generally."[28] Both Whigs and Democrats staged rallies in Charlotte with "brass bands, songs and cheers." Enthusiasm reached such fever heat in the county that many of the more ardent proponents of their party adopted and wore special uniforms during the numerous rallies. The Democrats wore white trousers with red stripes down the sides and small figured callico coats and white caps. The Whigs donned nankeen suits and wore coat-like blouses with ruffles in front.[29] The preceding legislature had passed a reapportionment bill placing Dickson in the Eighth Congressional District along with Davidson, Montgomery, Robertson, and Stewart—a thing which must have been wormwood and gall to Democratic Dickson and Stewart. Not to be fazed by the preponderance of Whigs in the District, however, the Dickson Democrats organized thoroughly in every precinct and voting place, and in Charlotte on election day they rolled out several barrels of whiskey, knocked out the heads, and hung dippers on the sides of each. All who came were "welcome to help themselves."[30] The district was lost to the Whigs by over five hundred votes because of the preponderance of Whigs in the large counties of Davidson, Montgomery, and Robertson, but Dickson County went Democratic by a vote of 706 to 339.[31]

A few weeks after Polk's inauguration the Dickson County Democrats held a meeting in Charlotte for the purpose of rejoicing generally and also for nominating a candidate to represent the county in the next session of the legislature. Every civil district sent delegates to the place of meeting, and Sellman Edwards, farmer, was made chairman, and Thomas Murrell, secretary. Robert McNeilly, a prominent attorney and political leader, made the opening address in which he pleaded for a continuation of unity and asked that all aspirants for representative be given the opportunity of addressing the assemblage. At the end of his speech he nominated Major V. F. Bibb for the position. William A. Moody, a 28-year-old Charlotte physician who was later to make a small fortune in Dickson County, addressed the group and stated that he had announced as a candidate at a time when he thought the incumbent, John Eubank, would not seek the position. Having heard on that day that the able Eubank wanted to return for another term, Moody announced his withdrawal in favor of the incumbent. Eubank then was called upon to speak, at which time he asserted his "availability" should the Democrats desire his continued services. Eubank was a highly respected and well-to-do farmer who had lived in the county all his life. He had witnessed the tornado of 1830 and had lost his wife and much property in that catastrophe. By 1845 he had accumulated some property, had represented Dickson in the legislature since 1837, and had been a loyal Democrat. Before Major Bibb had an opportunity to speak, McNeilly had withdrawn his name and the group then elected Eubank by acclamation.[32]

Within a month after this meeting in Charlotte the idol of the Democrats, Andrew Jackson, had succumbed at the Hermitage. For days after his death on June 8, the columns of the Nashville *Union*, leading Democratic organ in Middle Tennessee, were encased in black, and county courts and Democratic committees throughout the state had adopted resolutions of respect. Assemblies were held in most of the cities and towns at which orators vied with one another in their efforts to heap praise upon the memory of the old warrior. One of the largest of the gatherings was held at Charlotte on July 17, and hundreds of people came from miles around. Charlotte was centrally located, had always been a Democratic stronghold, and proved a suitable place for a midstate assembly of that kind. The speaker for the occasion was George Jeremiah Harris, editor and publisher of the Nashville *Union*, and one of the ablest Democratic orators of the state. In a two hour address on the overflowing courthouse lawn, Harris told his audience that Jackson was one of the greatest leaders the country had known and that only George Washington was to be compared with him. Typical of the orators of the day, Harris said in part:

> He is gone. He sleeps with the fathers. His name is registered high

among the highest, upon the scroll of fame.... Some of you have been his compatriots in arms—others have enjoyed his acquaintance, his friendship—the aged are well informed of his history, and the youth have doubtless heard their fathers and mothers describe his deeds of greatness.

Harris then proceeded to describe the lowly conditions of his birth, his lack of formal education, and his early life. For over two hours the hills and valleys of Charlotte echoed with the thunderous oratory of the Nashville editor as he told of Jackson's "inflexible" integrity and his "undisputed" patriotism as he fought Homeric political and military battles. The emotion of the hour must have swelled as he said,

> Andrew Jackson was to the American people as the sun to the mariner. When our old ship of state was lashed by the surging billows of popular opinion dangerously excited—when the political storm threatened to strand her upon the sterile beach of despotism—when the blindness of partisan zeal had so far affected the public mind as to obscure the light of reason, when we had lost our reckoning, and the national craft was in a condition which made the wisest of all parties shudder for the result—where did we turn for advice, for counsel?

The flowing peroration must have excited even greater emotion when the accomplishments of George Washington, still within the memory of many, were compared with those of Jackson.

> Like the father of his country, [Harris concluded] he descended to the grave loaded with all the civil and military honors of his countrymen .... His memory will bloom upon our altars for ages and ages with perennial freshness. The mother shall teach her infant to lisp their names in unison—the father shall teach him to emulate their sterling virtues. An admiring posterity shall make frequent pilgrimages to Mount Vernon in the East, and the Hermitage in the West, to linger around the mounds which contain the ashes of the illustrious dead, to commune with the spirits of the immortal Washington and Jackson.[33]

The people of Tennessee were so nearly evenly divided between the Whigs and the Democrats during the next decade that each party alternately supplied the state's governor. Aaron Brown, Democrat from Giles County, was elected governor in 1845, but his Whig opponent, Neill S. Brown, defeated him two years later. In both of these elections Dickson County gave the Democratic candidate a two-to-one majority.[34] As the Presidential election of 1848 approached, election fervor equal to that of 1844 was engendered. The Democrats had nominated Lewis Cass of Michigan and the Whigs had chosen a Mexican War hero from Louisiana, Zachary Taylor, and both developed able campaigners and followers within their parties. "A Democrat" from Charlotte several weeks before the election wrote the editor of the Nashville *National Union*, a strong Democratic and state rights paper, to assure him that "Dickson will do at least as well as in 1844 and 1847."[35]

Cass and Taylor could not visit every hamlet and town in the interest of their campaigns, but their causes did not suffer. In every community across the state supporters extolled the virtues of their candidate. In Charlotte on September 24 former Democratic Governor Aaron V. Brown was scheduled to meet former Whig Governor James C. Jones on the platform, and they were to discuss the relative merits of Cass and Taylor. On the appointed day, however, Jones could not appear but sent Robertson Topp, a staunch Whig from Memphis, to appear in his place. Topp was not an orator, and appeared unprepared, nervous, and listless, a Nashville newspaper reported.[36] "At an early hour this morning the yeomanry of Dickson began pouring into Charlotte . . . to hear Governors Brown and Jones," the correspondent reported. Brown was "in all his majesty of intellect" and for "an hour and a half he kept the crowd spell-bound . . . by the eloquent and moving appeals to the reason and good sense of his hearers." Topp, however, speaking for Jones, proved a disappointment to the Whigs and was described as one who was offensive and dull and who "spent most of his time apologizing for not being prepared." Both stuck mainly to the issues, however, discussing the Wilmot Proviso, the lack of civil experience of Taylor, and the lack of Whig support of the Mexican War. Brown's mention of the war, just ended, brought among the throng "a silence . . . that was almost felt—not a sound save . . . the breathings of some, whose relatives had bled and died in the war. . . ."[37]

Dickson County delivered to Cass the usual two-to-one majority given all Democratic candidates, but to no avail, for the war career of Taylor ushered him into office by a good majority. Hickman County gave Cass better than a three-to-one majority, and Stewart and Humphreys were safely in the Democrat fold, although the state as a whole went Whig.[38] Whig leaders were jubilant, but already the party was showing signs of disintegration as the Northern wing began to indicate a strong antislavery position. This was their last successful Presidential victory. Colonel William B. Campbell, elected governor of Tennessee in 1853, became the last Whig to hold that office.

During the 1850's the increase in the number of voters reflected the growing population and the increasing interest in politics. In the Presidential election of 1852, for example, 930 votes were cast, over 600 going to Franklin Pierce the Democrat. In the gubernatorial race of 1855, however, 1,133 voted, with 745 expressing a choice of Andrew Johnson and the remaining voting for the Know-Nothing Party candidate, Meredith Gentry. In 1856 nearly 1,200 voted, and over 800 of them for Democrat James Buchanan. By this time the adherence of the Northern Whigs to an antislavery position had driven many Southern Whigs into Democratic camps and the Whig Party may be said to have disintegrated. The short-lived Know-Nothing Party was losing what little strength it had, and the newly-organized "Black Republican" Party appeared to be the formidable foe of the future. John C. Fremont, the Republican candidate, received virtually no votes in Middle and West Tennessee, and Know-Nothing Millard Fillmore received a smattering of votes, but Buchanan carried the state by a seven thousand majority. The increase in voting strength found in Dickson County was also reflected in other rural counties of Middle Tennessee. In Hickman in 1852 the total vote was 1,090 while four years later it was 1,324. The total vote in Humphreys increased from 734 in 1852 to 975 in 1856, and in Stewart the increase was from 1,263 to 1,501.[39]

Throughout the forties and fifties Dickson County sent to the state legislature a steady supply of able law makers. John Eubank served in the house for a decade between 1837 and 1847 and staunchly supported the Democratic Party. A yeoman farmer, part-time tailor, and small slaveholder, Eubank was a man of moderate means whose forebears had come to Tennessee from Virginia and had settled near Charlotte. In 1843 he caused no small degree of excitement among the homefolk by proposing an amendment to the capitol location bill to erect the state capitol at Charlotte. Although he had the support of others from small counties in Middle Tennessee, the measure was defeated by a sizable majority.[40] Eubank was succeeded by William A. Moody, who served for the next eight years. Moody, a physician, had sought the office in 1845, but had withdrawn before the election in favor of Eubank. A survey of the legislative journals of the time he served indicates that he, like Eubank, voted straight down the Democratic line. His medical practice was such that he could not devote full time and attention to legislative duties, however. By 1860 Moody had accumulated $18,000 in real property and $15,000 in personal property, and also owned a few slaves.[41] W. J. Mathis, who had served as sheriff for several years, was in the house from 1855 to 1857, and was succeeded by F. T. von Schmittou, who served one term. The Schmittou family had come to this country from Prussia years earlier, and F. T. was of the second or third generation of this family in America. By 1860 there were at least half a dozen families by this name, all indicating a high degree of agricultural skill, all owning a small amount of property, and all able to read and write.[42] The ability to read and write represented a great accomplishment and often was considered sufficient qualification within itself for the legislative halls. Many in Dickson County of English, Scotch, and Irish background could neither read nor write. In 1850 from a population of 8,404 there were over 1,000 adults who were illiterate.[43]

Dickson County was in a senatorial district with several other counties, and therefore did not have a senator who was a county resident every term. Two of the ablest men representing the district which included Dickson were Jacob Voorhies and Thomas McNeilly. Voorhies, a well educated man, had come to the county from New Jersey as a school teacher, but by the time of his election to the senate in 1841, had become a successful merchant and property owner.[44] He served two terms, retiring in 1845. Thomas McNeilly was elected in 1857 and served until Tennessee seceded from the Union. He was a well-to-do lawyer and had been circuit court clerk before his election to the senate. There were several McNeilly families in the county before the Civil War, all of which distinguished themselves before the bar, in business, and in the Presbyterian ministry.

By 1860 the country was on the brink of a national catastrophe. Dickson County and Dickson Countians were to play an important part in the War for Southern Independence, which is recounted in the next chapter.

CHAPTER VIII

Civil War and Readjustment, 1861-1870

THE DECADE of the 1860's was a most disastrous one for the people of Dickson County, as indeed it was for the people of the entire South. A clear and peaceful scene became clouded with the terrors of war, and Dickson County parents watched their sons march away in five companies in 1861 to participate in a needless and fratricidal war in which many were to make the supreme sacrifice. The people witnessed the closing down of the thriving iron industry which had brought to the county its biggest payroll. They saw Federal troops march into the county as early as 1862, strip the citizenry of the bare necessities of life, by 1864 establish a Federal camp at Charlotte, and there take over the Cumberland Presbyterian Church—then in the final stages of being completed—and convert it into a hospital. The sufferings of the people did not terminate in 1865 when the firing ceased. The Brownlow regime in leech-like fashion fastened itself upon the people of the state for the four years following the war and was a destructive force the like of which has never been witnessed or recorded in the pages of Tennessee history. Those who had fought for or sympathized with the North and those opportunists whose loyalties changed with each chance for personal profit fared quite well in Tennessee under the Brownlow regime, but those whose sympathies had been with the South—as was true of practically all the people of Dickson County—were kept in the political background by the vindictive governor. A. T. Nicks was one of those few who did cooperate with Brownlow and was rewarded with a position which bore the title "Assistant Superintendent of the Freedman's Bureau," but few other Dickson Countians were willing to do what many considered was equivalent to selling one's political birthright for a mess of pottage. By 1870 war and reconstruction had wrought their worst in Tennessee, and the people of the county looked with hope to the prospects of the future. The population was growing rapidly as immigrants from Northern states poured into Sneedsville [1] and the surrounding territory and began to build homes. Sneedsville, White Bluff, and Gillam [2] gave promise of urbanization to a county which, except for the county seat, had been predominantly rural before the Civil War.

The decade of the 1860's dawned upon a people who had few apparent worries of a local nature other than a drought which curtailed crop production. While the impending castastrophe of sectional bitterness hung like a threatening cloud over the North and the South, the people continued their economic pursuits uninterrupted. The great majority of people tilled the soil for a living. Farmers indicated that the wheat and oat crops might be cut by as much as two thirds and that the corn crop would be cut by one half, but despite the drought the soil yielded abundantly. Dickson County land in 1860 yielded about thirty bushels of corn per acre, and about ten bushels of both wheat and oats.[3]

Professional men were numerous in the county at the time, and there were probably more ministers represented than any other profession.[4] Among the leading ministers of the time were George Staley, S. A. Ellis, and Gusten Jamison, Methodists; A. J. Parish, J. H. McNeilly, and A. N. Larkins, Presbyterians; and Empson Bishop, David Gray, and John S. Reynolds, Baptists.[5] At least a dozen physicians were scattered throughout the county in 1860, and most were relatively young. W. T. Crockett and J. W. Paine were still in their twenties, and all of the others except W. A. Moody and Sam James had not reached forty. The prosperity of the physicians is indicated by the assessed evaluation of their real and personal property. Crockett was only 25, yet he had property assessed at over $12,000, and Moody, some years older, had real and personal property valued at nearly $35,000.[6] In addition to these, there were at least the following practicing medicine in the county in 1860: R. H. Sizemore, J. L. Davis, J. M. Larkins, E. W. Ellis, W. H. Daniel, C. Slayden, D. R. Dickson, and A. R. Griffith, the last of whom was an Englishman by birth. A host of lawyers practiced before the Dickson County bar in 1860, many of whom did not reside in the county but who would ride in from Nashville and Clarksville on court day to plead the causes of their clients. Thomas McNeilly and Robert McNeilly were probably two of the ablest lawyers residing in the county. Thomas was 51, had practiced in the county since a youth, and in 1860 was worth over $25,000. Robert, with whom he was associated, was two years his senior and was worth nearly $20,000 in real and personal property. Robert had six children, one of whom was a Presbyterian minister. Tom C. Morris, who was to represent Dickson County in the Constitutional Convention of 1870, was a practicing attorney in addition to holding the office of circuit court clerk. W. J. McClelland and W. Shaw, the latter of whom was only 20, had offices on the public square, as also did Henry Collier and Jacob Leech, the latter of whom was known throughout the state for his ability to stamp and shout his way through any criminal case regardless of its relative merits, and to come out victorious. Leonard Lane Leech was licensed to practice law, but he devoted most of his time to his extensive land and mercantile interests.[7]

Many others had extensive mercantile pursuits. A Scotsman named George Hutcheson, who had married a Tennessee girl by whom he had four children, operated a store in Charlotte and had property valued at nearly $12,000. Elta Carr, another native of Scotland, had mercantile interests valued at over $16,000, and an Alabaman named T. K. Grigsby valued his property at nearly $60,000. Other merchants and their property valuations were: J. W. Dickson, a Tennessean, $78,000; L. L.

Leech, Tennessee-born, $81,000; W. James, North Carolinian, $16,000; and W. C. Collier, a Tennessee native, $55,000. R. J. Grymes, G. L. Nolen, and A. J. Allen specialized in staple and fancy groceries, and James Mathis kept a tavern. B. E. Freshorn was a tobacco manufacturer, and made cigars, smoking tobacco, and chewing tobacco. W. E. Hicks, 25, kept the home for paupers. In addition to his wife and two children, Hicks had under his care in 1860 five men and four women, one of whom was a native of Ireland, two of whom were Virginia-born, and two of whom were born in North Carolina. J. N. H. Kirfman, 35, worked as a tinner; P. A. Miller, A. O. Johnson, William Kelley and others, as cabinet makers; J. C. Butler, J. D. Dodson, R. N. P. Hurt, and others as saddlers; and W. A. Scruggs, Henry Stuart, Oliver Spicer, J. J. Burgie, D. Burgie, and many others as carpenters and brick layers. Along with these occupations there were at least the following to be found in Dickson County in 1860: stone mason, wheel wright, stage agent, wood corder, molder, waggoner, boatman, chair maker, stage driver, gunsmith, collier, peddler, railroad hand, tailor, wagon maker, shoe maker, and blacksmith.[8]

Wages appear to have been good for that day and time. An average farmhand in Dickson County could earn with board about $12 per month. A day laborer, whether on the farm, on the railroad, or in industrial pursuits, could earn about a dollar per day without board or about seventy-five cents with board. Carpenters and brick layers fared better. They could earn up to $2.50 per day without board, and about $2.00 to $2.25 per day with board. Female domestic servants were paid about a dollar per week and were given room and board.[9]

An enterprise which in 1860 employed many people in addition to bringing new residents to the county was the construction of the Nashville and Northwestern Railroad. The war temporarily interrupted the construction work, but in 1860 nearly two hundred Irishmen had been brought into the county and they, in addition to many who were natives of the county, built road beds and laid track. Some years earlier railroads had been started in Tennessee, but Middle Tennessee lagged behind the other two sections of the state largely because of the excellent river transportation system.[10] The Tennessee Central Railroad Company had been formed in 1848 to construct a road from Fulton, Kentucky, on the Mississippi, to Nashville. Public addresses and solicitations were made in Dickson and other counties, and in 1853 work was actually begun. Lack of funds, however, prevented completion of the project. The construction of the Nashville and Northwestern was interrupted with the coming of the war, but in 1864 General Grant, in laying plans for the final drive on the Confederacy, decided that the line should be completed, at least as far as Johnsonville in Humphreys County. He therefore sent the Twelfth and Thirteenth United States Infantry, Colored, into White Bluff and in a relatively short time the Negro troops completed the stretch from White Bluff to the indicated termination point.[11]

The railroad workers of Irish descent are easily determined by their names which appear in the census records of 1860. For example, there were several families of Fitzpatricks, Badgers, Bodkins, Scanlons, and Heallens. A typical Irish railroad worker and his family was that of Michael Heallen. His wife was named Bridget, two sons bore the names of Patrick and Michael, and two daughters were named Buley and Mary. More than a dozen of the women were named Bridget, and nearly every family had sons with one or more named Pat or Patrick, Michael, or Barney. Many of them came directly from Ireland to Dickson County. Two families had children under one year of age born in Ireland. William and Bridget Busk, both 25, had a four-year-old son born in Ireland, and two-year-old and one-year-old children born in Ohio, which would indicate a brief sojourn elsewhere between the time they left Ireland and the time of their arrival in Dickson County. Many of the Irish remained in the county and participated in the Civil War, while others followed railroad construction into other counties.

The census records of 1860 indicate that the great majority of Dickson County residents came into Tennessee from Pennsylvania, Virginia, and North Carolina. In addition to those from these states and Ireland, there were in 1860 Dickson Countians born in South Carolina, Kentucky, Missouri, Georgia, New York, Alabama, Ohio, Mississippi, Illinois, Connecticut, Maryland, Vermont, Texas, Massachusetts, Scotland and Canada. Many of those from Virginia and Pennsylvania stopped in North Carolina or Kentucky long enough to marry, or to engage in business for a few years. Typical of those in this category was A. W. Roberts, a Virginia-born farmer worth nearly $25,000 in 1860, who went from Virginia to Kentucky, where he remained long enough to court and marry a wife, and then came to Tennessee, where he fathered the first of several children. John Swinney, born in Virginia, left his native state for Ohio where he worked for awhile, married, and then headed southward. They stopped in Kentucky long enough to have their first child, Alice, and the following year moved to Tennessee. Their second child, a son named D. J., was born shortly after their arrival and was seven months old when the census enumerator visited their home in June, 1860. Others like B. A. Collier and wife, and also T. L. Collier, all of whom were born in Virginia, apparently came straight to Dickson County from Virginia. Mrs. Anne Jane Bell, a widow in 1860, had come to Virginia from Ireland where her son, W. B. Bell, was born. They had come some years earlier to Dickson County where Bell had accumulated considerable property.[12]

Regardless of from whence the people came, all must have been aware of the impending catastrophe which for years had hung like a Damoclean sword over their heads. The people of the North and the South for years had been growing apart, and William H. Seward and Abraham Lincoln had spoken of an "irrepressible conflict" and of a "house divided" which could not stand. By early 1860 the impending division along sectional lines was a topic widely discussed in every newspaper and public gathering. The people of Tennessee beyond any question favored remaining a part of the Union so long as they could do so peacefully and honorably. The editor of the Nashville *Banner*, leading Whig organ of Middle Tennessee, in January of 1860 spoke of secession as being "the vilest, most damnable, deep laid and treacherous conspiracy that was ever concocted."[13] Many joined in the condemnation of secession, and others argued from the practical side that Tennessee was in no position to secede because of its dependence upon Northern goods.[14] By mid-summer however, it became apparent that the ardent opposition to secession was breaking down in some quarters. The newly-formed Constitutional Union Party, advocating compromise between the two sections, picked John Bell of Tennessee as its Presidential candidate. Bell, who was interested in extensive iron works in Stewart and Dickson counties, believed that if both sections adhered strictly to the Constitution the Union might be preserved, but that compromise on both sides would be necessary. Tennesseans, indicating a desire for compromise, voted for Bell by a sizable majority. Abraham Lincoln won, however, although he received less than forty per cent of the popular vote and scarcely a vote below the Mason-Dixon line and the Ohio River. Lincoln, a Kentucky-born Whig, had ridden into power on the Black Republican ticket—a party which was the avowed enemy of slavery and the South, and whose success now forced South Carolina into secession. While Tennessee and the other border states hesitated, the states of the Deep South plunged headlong into secession as a last resort to retain their rights under the Constitution as they construed them. South Carolina seceded on December 20, 1860, and by February 4, 1861 six other states of the Deep South had joined the Palmetto state and sent delegates to Montgomery, Alabama, to form the Confederate States of America. The people of Tennessee still demurred, determined to remain within the Union so long as they could do so honorably and so long as no act of hostility should be committed against them. Horace Greeley, editor of the New York *Tribune*, advised that the "erring sisters" should be permitted to depart in peace, but John Bell and many others hoped that through compromise the rent in the national structure might be repaired. They constantly worked toward that goal. President Buchanan had taken the position that secession was illegal, but that the Federal government had no power to force a state to remain in the Union against its will. Like Robert E. Lee, he looked upon the union as a spiritual entity which could be held together only so long as a spirit of love and forbearance was manifested by both sides. When such ceased to exist the final "divorce decree"—secession—was the only answer. On this basis the people of Dickson County and of Tennessee could have remained a part of the Union, and they cautiously awaited the inauguration of Lincoln, scheduled for March 4, 1861, to determine his attitude. The editor of the Nashville *Republican Banner*, no longer ardently pro-union, announced in February that "Tennessee will stand ... in favor of the Union as long as there is a hope for its preservation upon the basis of equal rights to all sections."[15]

In the meantime Governor Isham G. Harris, an ardent secessionist, issued a call to the general assembly to convene in extra session on January 7 to consider the impending dangers. Upon assembling, the legislature passed an act which provided for a referendum on February 9 to determine whether the people wanted to call a convention at which the secession question would be discussed. In order to avoid calling another plebiscite in the event the convention move carried, the people also were asked to select delegates to the convention, should the move for such a convention receive a majority of votes. A slate of Union and secession candidates hastily was filled. When the referendum was held, the people voted 68,282 to 59,449 against even calling a convention, and 91,803 to 24,749 for the Union candidates. This indicated that three fourths of the people of Tennessee favored remaining with the Union, and that the majority of them favored it so strongly that they did not even believe it was necessary to call a convention to discuss the matter. The people of Dickson County voted by a majority of nine for the convention but by a three-to-one majority in favor of Union delegates. The following table of Middle Tennessee counties is given for purposes of comparison:[16]

County	For Convention	Against Convention	For Union	For Disunion
Hickman	755	298	646	603
Montgomery	1611	389	1852	62
DICKSON	499	490	813	278
Davidson	2626	3100	4887	769
Humphreys	385	327	544	279

All eyes now turned to the inauguration of Lincoln to learn the policy the new President would pursue. Men saw in the inaugural address what they desired to see depending upon their secession or Union leanings, but Lincoln did not continue long with double talk. Determined to force the issue before the Confederates could become well organized, he dispatched a vessel to relieve the United States troops at Fort Sumter, South Carolina—an act which the Confederates earlier had warned would bring their fire upon the fort. Despite the warning the ship was dispatched, and on April 12 the Confederates fired upon Fort Sumter, and gave Lincoln adequate cause to herald to the nation that the South had committed an overt act of war. He then called for 75,000 volunteers to "suppress rebellion," and in this one act swept the people of Tennessee and thousands of others into the arms of the Confederacy. Governor Harris' reply to Lincoln was succinct and to the point. He telegraphed: "Tennessee will not furnish a single man for purposes of coercion, but 50,000 if necessary for the defense of our rights and those of our Southern brothers." Announcing to the world that "in such an unholy crusade no gallant son of Tennessee will ever draw his sword," Gov. Harris issued a call for a second extra session of the legislature to meet in Nashville on April 25.[17] Upon convening, the group heard Harris urge the immediate framing of an ordinance of secession to be given to the people immediately for acceptance or rejection. Consequently, on May 6 "A Declaration of Independence... Dissolving the Federal Relation between the State of Tennessee and the

United States" was drawn up and a referendum was set for June 8. The change which had come over the people of Tennessee was amazing, but it was such a change which ever makes the study of human affairs fascinating. Despite the fact that a few months previously they had voted overwhelmingly against secession, now on June 8, 1861, the people voted 108,399 to 47,233 in favor of leaving the Union and joining the Confederacy. The people of Dickson County voted better than sixteen to one for separation. The following table indicates the vote of selected Middle Tennessee counties:[18]

County	For Union	For Separation From Union
Hickman	3	1400
Stewart	99	1839
DICKSON	71	1141
Davidson	403	5638
Humphreys	0	1042

As the time of the referendum had approached, the newspapers of Middle Tennessee constantly urged separation. The Nashville *Republican Banner*, like the people of the state, had turned about face in its attitude toward secession and now strongly urged it. With the election four weeks off, the editor urged the people to vote for "the best interests of the state" in strong terms:

> ... the rapidly developing policy [of the North] of ... subjugation of the South, so clearly and unquestionably determined upon by the Federal administration, ... must serve to speedily convince every patriotic and fair-minded man in the South that all hopes of a reconstruction of the Union, or of averting the impending conflict, must be abandoned, or our people must bow the knee in abject submission to the arrogant and tyrannous majority....[19]

One week later the editor, irate at what the northern "war journals" printed, addressed the people of the state:

> *People of Tennessee!* If you could sit here in our offices and read all the journals of the North as we do, there would be little Northern sentiment left.

He quoted from many Northern journals, particularly the Chicago *Democrat*, which urged the President to call out one and one-half million soldiers and make short work of the whole thing, and the New York *Times*, which called for a "warrior, not a philosopher—a Cromwell, not a Bacon or a Locke."[20] On voting day the editor had only contempt for those few who wanted a "union with a people thus dead to all moral and consitutional obligations!"[21]

By the time Tennessee seceded the war had begun and hundreds of men had marched off to battle. During the first of May, three companies of infantry were formed and equipped in Dickson County and sent to Nashville to join other troops. There they were placed in the Eleventh Tennessee Regiment and designated Company H, under the command of Captain W. J. Mallory, who had fought in the Mexican

War; Company C, commanded by Captain William Green; and Company K, commanded by Captain William Thedford. All three companies were sent to Camp Cheatham, in Robertson County, for further training. Before the year was over, two more companies were formed and assigned to the Forty-ninth Tennessee Regiment. Company B was under the command of Captain Thomas K. Grigsby, Charlotte merchant, and Company D was commanded by J. B. Cording, a well-to-do farmer of the county. They were sent immediately to the defense of Fort Donelson, a most strategic fortification where it was feared that the Federals would launch an early attack.

The Eleventh Tennessee Regiment, which included three Dickson County companies and others from Davidson, Humphreys, Robertson, and Hickman, was placed under the command of General Felix Zollicoffer and sent into East Tennessee to guard railroads and bridges. They fought in several battles in East Tennessee and southern Kentucky, but the end of the year 1862 found them back in Middle Tennessee and under the command of General Braxton Bragg at Stone's River near Murfreesboro. Bragg's mistakes, for which he became well known and which were condoned only by Jefferson Davis, lost for the Confederates their grip on the fortifications at Murfreesboro, and by the conclusion of the first week of January, 1863, Bragg and the men were trudging wearily eastward. Upon reaching the Shelbyville-Wartrace-Tullahoma area they went into winter quarters but were harrassed by the Federals again in late spring and driven toward Chattanooga. Bragg decided not to make a stand at that city, but pushed on into northern Georgia near the Chickamauga River. There he met the Federals in one of the bloodiest battles of the war which, had it not been for his dilatory nature, could have resulted in a great victory for the Confederates. Companies C, H, and K, ragged from participation in these and other battles, were also at the great Confederate defeat and slaughter of Franklin and Nashville in 1864. Those still alive and able to fight were then assigned to General Joseph E. Johnston, and the surrender of Lee at Appomattox found them at Bentonville, North Carolina. They were surrendered to General William T. Sherman on April 26, 1865, at Greensboro.[22]

As mentioned, the other two Dickson County companies, B and D, were assigned to the Forty-ninth Regiment, which was under the command of Colonel James E. Bailey and which included men from Dickson, Robertson, Benton, Cheatham, and Montgomey counties. Shortly after their formation they were dispatched to the defense of Fort Donelson in Stewart County, for it was believed that part of the Federal strategy was to take the Mississippi River and the nearby strongholds of Fort Henry, which guarded the Tennessee, and Fort Donelson, which guarded the Cumberland, and then cut the South in two. Confederate errors and lack of nerve lost for the South another important battle at Fort Donelson, and thousands of Confederate troops were surrendered in February, 1862, including the Dickson County men. They were then taken to Alton, Illinois, where the officers and enlisted men were separated, the officers being taken to St. Louis and thence to Camp Chase, Ohio, and finally to Johnson's Island. The enlisted men were sent to Camp Douglas near Chicago, but were exchanged several months later. They joined the group which Bragg had commanded shortly after the encounter at Chickamauga and were consolidated with the Forty-second Regiment in 1864, inasmuch as the Forty-first and Forty-second had lost many men and had just enough remaining to make one regiment. The end of the war found them with Johnston in North Carolina, and they were surrendered to Sherman. The end of the war found only one survivor of Company B, William Taylor.[23]

While hundreds of Dickson County men were in other states fighting the Federals, war came to their homes. The first glimpse of actual war conditions came quite unexpectedly when Fort Donelson fell in mid-February, 1862, and Nathan Bedford Forrest moved his men through Cumberland Furnace and Charlotte en route to Nashville. Lieutenant-Colonel Forrest (later General) had come to the Stewart County fort early in February where he came under the command of a triumvirate of military mediocrities, Brigadier Generals John B. Floyd, Gideon Pillow, and Simon Bolivar Buckner. Floyd, a one-time Virginia governor who had served in President Buchanan's cabinet; Pillow, a Mexican War hero who was in command of Tennessee's provisional army; and Buckner, Mexican War veteran and commander of the Kentucky State Guard; all, had become convinced that the Confederates were demoralized. Floyd and Buckner attempted to convince Pillow that they could not hold the important Stewart County entrenchment and that to attempt it would be suicide. They believed that the only avenue of retreat was across the icy Cumberland and that to try it would bring untold death and disease from exposure. Floyd and Pillow decided to attempt an escape—which they executed successfully—and left to Buckner the unsavory task of meeting U. S. Grant's terms of unconditional surrender. Forrest, however, refused to let his men be included in the surrender, and advised Pillow of his intentions. The latter, probably never fully convinced that surrender was the only alternative, advised Forrest to "cut his way out" if the men were willing. Forrest found that every man of his daring cavalry preferred to follow him rather than surrender to the Federals, and on Sunday, February 16, he began his trek southeastward toward Nashville over frozen roads almost entirely ignored by the enemy.

By nightfall of the sixteenth the men reached Cumberland Furnace, and there they remained overnight. A heavy snow had fallen throughout the day and stood ten inches deep as Forrest and his men rode into the iron manufacturing community in sub-zero weather. The people of Cumberland Furnace were found to be most hospitable, and many opened their homes to the shivering men. The sick and wounded were left behind when Forrest proceeded toward Charlotte on the next morning, and were cared for by the people of the community. Many of them died and were buried on a hillside just north of the town.

Stones were erected for some, but many today lie buried in unmarked graves. One stone bears the inscription, "James C. Peacher, 2d Ky. Cav. CSA, born December 31, 1844; died April 14, 1863." His home was only about twenty miles north of the Kentucky-Tennessee line.

Proceeding at daybreak to Charlotte, Forrest found the county seat in a "state of wild alarm and agitation" over a report that Nashville had fallen into the hands of the Federals. The information had been brought to Charlotte by "a local legislator" (probably Thomas McNeilly) who had ridden hard from Nashville—his horse on arrival was "white with sweat-foam"—where the report had been circulated that the Federals were at the gates of the city. Forrest devoted his best efforts to quieting the fears of the populace, assured them that the rumor was a false one, and threatened the legislator with arrest and punishment. All blacksmiths were pressed into service to shoe the horses most in need, while the men filled the saloons and held the civilians spellbound with tales of war. Forrest lost little time in Charlotte, however, and by nightfall he had proceeded toward Nashville as far as the valley of the Harpeth where he made camp for the night.[24]

Another Confederate cavalry regiment rode through Charlotte several days before on the way to Fort Donelson. Among the men in the regiment was John H. Wharton of Cannon County, who recorded in his diary that he had passed through some "new" towns, one of which was Charlotte, whose population he estimated to be about 300. Wharton's cohorts were turned back before reaching Fort Donelson, however, as they received information that the fort had fallen. They had retraced their steps and had marched through the outskirts of Charlotte on their way to Nashville several hours before Forrest arrived. When Forrest, in keeping with his policy of readiness for combat, halted his men about a mile out of Charlotte and had them discharge their pieces and reload, the Wharton regiment, thinking that the Federals were on their heels, abandoned their wagons and supplies and fled in disorderly retreat. Forrest, later coming upon the abandoned supplies, retrieved them and replenished his depleted stock of goods.[25]

From that time to the end of the war the people of Dickson County caught glimpses of military activity. Some weeks after the battle of Fort Donelson and the resulting Forrest march through the county, a group of about sixty Federals visited the county on a raiding party, and encountered a band of guerrillas a few miles from Charlotte. There they engaged in a bitter hand-to-hand encounter. By the summer of 1862 guerrilla warfare was at its peak in Dickson and the surrounding counties, and a prison was established by the Federals on the public square of Clarksville, which lay some thirty miles north of Charlotte. By the fall of 1862 there were seven guerrillas from Dickson County in the prison facing charges such as "Rebel agent" and "spy." In nearby Humphreys County considerably more guerrilla activity was transpiring, and several men were shot and others were hanged by the vengeful Federals.[26]

By March, 1863, Colonel Sanders D. Bruce, who was in command of the Twentieth Kentucky Infantry, United States Infantry, was in complete control of Clarksville, and his men visited Charlotte not infrequently. On March 13, he wrote his commanding officer of a foray in that vicinity. "My cavalry found another party of rebel cavalry yesterday near Charlotte," he wrote, "capturing 13 prisoners with horses. Five are new conscripts who claim to be Union men, and desire to take the oath. Instruct me."[27] In the late fall or early winter of 1863 a portion of two Federal regiments numbering around four hundred took Charlotte and remained there until March, 1864. They established headquarters in the courthouse, pitched tents in the courtyard, and built makeshift barracks. The Cumberland Presbyterian Church was taken over and used as a hospital. Much damage was done to the public buildings, and some of the public records were destroyed. Smokehouses were raided, stores were taken over, and much property was destroyed in a wanton manner. To combat this activity the people of Dickson County went underground and engaged the invader in guerrilla warfare. According to one source, "A continuous fight was kept up between the Federals and the guerrillas, and not a few lives were sacrificed as a result." Several weeks before they broke camp, the Federals captured a Charlotte citizen named William D. Willey and shot him as a guerrilla. He allegedly killed John Lindsey, a Dickson Countian who cooperated with the Federals. Another citizen named Demps Dobson was shot about the same time by the Federals, who placed a scrap of paper in the dead man's hand on which had been written "Shot in retaliation for the killing of John Lindsey."[28] This Federal contingent was under the command of a Major Kirwine and a Lieutenant Donnehue.

After Kirwine's men evacuated Charlotte another group of Federals passed through the town in going from Johnsonville to Nashville. They had been led to believe that General Forrest was on his way to Johnsonville intent upon wiping out the Federals, and they were said to have reached Charlotte "in a state of demoralization, having left behind them a trail marked by guns, ammunition, blankets, flour, meal, meat, and in fact everything they found unhandy to carry in their flight." Upon reaching Charlotte they learned that the crafty Forrest had shifted his command in such a manner as to block their flight from Charlotte to Nashville. At Charlotte the Federals decided to join other Federals at Clarksville rather than to risk an encounter with Forrest.[29]

As in every war, news from the fighting front was anxiously awaited by the folk back home, just as the men in uniform eagerly sought news of the folk they had left behind. Calvin F. Austin and M. V. Adcock were two Dickson County boys at the front who tried to keep the homefolk informed. In November, 1861, they were in East Tennessee under the command of General Zollicoffer. Austin, writing at that time to friends and relatives near Burns, penned:

> "... all the boys is better sadisfied than they have been since we left .... I reckon we will take winter quarters heare. We are at Cumberland Gaps.

I believe all the boys is getting well but Wm. Tatum, he has the mumps very bad. Burell Clifton is mending very slow, him and Tatum expect they will get furlows home. J. J. Brown says he don't want to go home. Silas Tidwell is pestered with rhumatis.... was very sick... The first that I got that I could eat was sum soup of that Jack made of an old hen he got hold of on the road, he made the best soup that I ever eat... but it would have been a heep better if that bug hadent droped in it.... I think you would be delited to be heare a day or too, and as boys is scearce theare you had as well come out and take Christmas with us.

...I want you all to write as often as you can and give me all the newse you can...."

Adcock, a drummer in the regimental band, was a close friend of Austin's, and placed in Austin's letter a communication of his own addressed to Kisiah Adcock, his mother, who also lived near Burns.

"Dear mother, sisters, and brothers and also all inquiring friends [he wrote]:
I drop you a few lines in C. F. Auston's letter to let you know that I am well at this time, and do cincurly hope when theas few lines come to hand they may find you all well and doing well.
Big Albert, I want you to set under that old crib shelter every rainey day tell you get your corn all shucked out...."

Both Austin and Adcock lived through the war and returned to their homes near Burns where they spent their declining years.[30]

William B. Bell of Cloverdale was a Dickson County officer who languished in a Northern prison for several years and who wrote to his wife each week. His many letters show a great anxiety for the health and welfare of his wife and children, and an ever present yearning to return to the state of his nativity. In one letter he asked for a pair of "James' pants and a frock coat of common grey."[31]

While many made the supreme sacrifice on the field of battle, others returned to their surroundings of pre-war days to begin life anew. Thomas K. Grigsby came back to a mercantile business which he had established in Charlotte in 1848. He had marched off at the head of Company B in 1861, had been captured by the Federals at Fort Donelson, and held prisoner for nine months, but later had rejoined his old regiment in which he rose to the rank of Colonel. In 1870 he was elected to the office of county court clerk, a position he held for some twenty years thereafter. Christopher C. Collier served with Company C, and in 1865 returned to Charlotte to resume mercantile activity with his brother William C. Collier. R. D. Eubank, son of John Eubank, who had represented Dickson County in the legislature for so long, served from 1861 to 1865. He returned to the county in 1865 and began farming. He was elected trustee for Dickson County in 1880, a position which he held for some time thereafter. Colonel George H. Morton, a native of Scotland, had served with the First Battalion of Tennessee Cavalry, and was wounded six times. In 1865 he came to White Bluff, which by the end of the war was a growing urban center with a railroad, and established a mercantile business. Isaac M. Bowers was another prominent citizen who took up abode in Dickson County after the war.

He was a native of Wilson County but was in business in Kentucky shortly before the war. With the outbreak of the war he enlisted in Company K of the First Kentucky Cavalry, and in 1863 became a scout for General Forrest. After the war he came to Charlotte for a short while, married, but returned within a few months to Kentucky. In 1866 he was in Alabama operating a farm, but by 1869 he had returned to Charlotte where he sold general merchandise. Many others, too numerous to mention, and some whose names appear in the chapter on slavery, answered the call of their state when war broke out, and then returned to peaceful pursuits after the war.[32]

Most of the furnaces and forges which had done much to raise the standards of living of the people of Dickson County before the war did not reopen. Cumberland Furnace, which came into the hands of a Federal soldier named Drouillard who had married the granddaughter of Anthony Vanleer, reopened after the war and prospered for some years thereafter. Perhaps the biggest development after the war was the rapid expansion and growth of a railroad stop, Sneedsville, established during the war and named for a railroad engineer named Sneed. General Grant was interested in completing the strip of railroad leading from Nashville to Johnsonville, and by late 1864 the road through the

---

Office Ass't Sup't Freedmen's Bureau,
COUNTY OF *Dickson Tenn*

TO ALL WHOM IT MAY CONCERN: *Charlotte Feby 26–*

This is to Certify, That *Daniel Dadsen* and *Nancy Fitzgerel* of the County of *Dickson* State of *Tennessee,* have been living together as husband and wife, for the space of *25* years, and are regarded as such by the Supreme law of the land, which establishes this Bureau, and, as such, are entitled to all the rights and privileges, and subject to all the pains and penalties; as others who have been legally married by the laws of the State.

A. T. Nicks
Assistant Sup't Freedmen's Bureau.

FREEDMEN'S BUREAU DOCUMENT

Before the Civil War slaves were not married in the modern legal sense of the word, but many lived together as common law husbands and wives. This certificate, dated February 23, 1866, signed by A. T. Nicks, Assistant Superintendent of Freedmen's Bureau, certifies that two Negroes, who had been living together for 25 years, are now regarded as legally married.

county had been completed. In that year W. H. Crutcher erected the first building in Sneedsville, now Dickson. Crutcher's building, erected on what is now Main Street just north of the railroad, was taken over by the Federal soldiers, and torn down after they left. Crutcher rebuilt in 1865—a small log store sixteen feet square—and sold general merchandise. By 1866 and 1867 other log houses were built, and by 1870 the village gave promise of surpassing both Charlotte and White Bluff in growth possibilities.[33]

Inasmuch as most of the people of Dickson County had been Confederate sympathizers, very few were permitted to vote or participate in state government immediately after the war. The vindictive William G. Brownlow became governor in 1865, and the Reconstruction government which dominated the state for the next four years was made up largely of a minority of native citizens who had remained loyal to the Union cause during the war. They were not "scalawags" in the sense of the term as used in the Deep South, nor were they carpetbaggers, but most had conscientiously supported the Union cause. Only Albert Nicks and a small group of Union supporters were willing to go along with Brownlow, and in the election of 1865 when the governor was selected, the number voting in Dickson County was only four per cent of the number which had voted in 1861.[34] By 1867 a few more people had been enfranchised, but Brownlow had been careful to make sure that they were "loyal" Republicans whose votes could be counted on. In that year about five times as many voted as in the preceding election. The following table of selected Middle Tennessee counties illustrates the fact that enfranchisement came slowly.[35]

Per Cent voting in given elections based on number voting in June, 1861

County	For Governor 1865	For Governor 1867	For Governor 1869
Montgomery	4	40	76
Cheatham	9	18	44
DICKSON	4	20	63
Davidson	17	43	70
Humphreys	4	20	57

Perhaps the most disconcerting thing was the great amount of lawlessness throughout the county, as indeed throughout the entire South. Bushwhackers circulated freely after the war, the Ku Klux Klan operated in the county, and hunger drove both blacks and whites to thievery and pillage. Any public gathering was a signal for an altercation, and voting precincts on election days were usually scenes of bitter strife. General Hugh Kirkman, who married the daughter of Anthony Vanleer and operated Cumberland Furnace before the war, was one who was visited just after the war by a lawless, thieving pair of bushwhackers. Kirkman related that when the two toughs rode up and announced that they had come to steal his saddle and anything else they could take, fortunately for him a small party of the home guard, or guerrillas, came to his assistance and fired on the bushwhackers, killing one and driving the other into Kirkman's home for cover. The home guard leader then announced that they would burn the house in order to drive out the armed bushwhacker. The latter, knowing that men of his category were always killed on sight by the home guard, then agreed to come out of the house if the leader would agree to shoot him rather than burn him, and to shoot him through the heart rather than through the face and head. This was agreed upon, but as the depraved creature emerged from his place of hiding he was seized, several muzzles pressed harshly to his head, and his brains were scattered over the surrounding area.[36]

Altercations between blacks and whites were common during the period just after the war. The native Southern whites resented the efforts of those who tried to place the Negro in places of political responsibility for which he was not equipped by training to handle. Over the state of Tennessee and throughout the South violence erupted on numerous occasions in which both blacks and whites were slaughtered.[37] A number of fracases occurred between Negroes and whites in connection with the elections of March, 1868. Clarksville, Murfreesboro, Pulaski, Marshall County, Williamson County, and Maury County, in addition to Dickson County, witnessed altercations between the races during this month of the elections.[38] In the March 31st issue of a Nashville paper, a conspicuous place was given to an article which began, "There are in Dickson County a class of colored men who stand up for their rights. . . ." The article referred to an altercation at the Cumberland Furnace precinct where members of the Conservative group had tried to compel several scores of blacks to vote against the Brownlow regime. The Negroes refused to vote at all until they had returned home and procured loaded muskets. These they shouldered, and marched defiantly back to the polls. The Conservatives, also armed but outnumbered, engaged the blacks in an interchange of firing in which a few on both sides were wounded. They were forced to retreat, after which the Negroes were said to have voted as they pleased.[39]

Another cause for violence and strained race relations was the educational system. Much emphasis was placed upon education of Negroes by the Educational Division of the Freedmen's Bureau, which began to operate in the South immediately following the war.[40] The whites did not object to the education of the blacks and, in fact, began the educational process for them long before the Civil War. The objectionable item was the agitation to educate blacks and whites in the same schools. Another thing equally objectionable was the subject matter taught the blacks, which many whites had reason to believe tended to foment discontent and dissatisfaction among the Negroes.

In general, the people of Dickson County raised little objection to Negro schools. J. H. Barnum, Assistant Superintendent of the Education Division of the Freedmen's Bureau, toured Dickson and other Middle Tennessee counties in 1868 to procure for the Bureau a true picture of Negro education. His first stop was at White Bluff, where he called a meeting of all interested white citizens. There he found many people who "manifested a great interest in the subject of schools."[41] T. T. Thompson had been selected as chairman of a committee to further the education of blacks and whites alike, and was doing much for the betterment of his community. On the matter of Negro schools, Barnum found that there were not enough Negro children at that time to form a colored school, but that the whites indicated no objection to the formation of such schools when a need for them appeared. Traveling by horse and buggy, Barnum next visited Charlotte, where he found a Miss Winchester in charge of a colored school. This school, which had been in session for several months, was conducted in a house belonging to a white person. Miss Winchester had rented the building for $4 per month, but the colored people of the area were interested in buying it and were in the process of raising $300. They had petitioned the Freedmen's Bureau to aid them in the purchase, and Barnum expressed the belief that such a purchase would be a good investment. The Bureau agent also visited Sneedsville, which he found to be "a growing place . . . largely settled by northern people." All in all, Barnum found few colored people in the county, but where they did live he found no opposition to their being educated.[42] In the same year a reporter for a Nashville paper surveyed the educational picture of the state, and made special mention of the efforts of a white minister, the Reverend H. Duncan, to educate the Negroes at Cumberland Furnace. The school at Charlotte was aided by funds from the Freedmen's Bureau, but the Cumberland Furnace school was a private affair held together largely by the sacrificial efforts of Duncan. Barnum further observed that there were only thirty-five colored teachers in the state in 1868, and three of these were in Dickson County.[43]

T. F. McCreary, superintendent of public schools of the county, and M. M. Hiland, teacher of a Negro school in the vicinity of Jackson's Chapel, did not paint so rosy a picture in their reports to the state department. McCreary, in his report of 1869, indicated that there was a Negro scholastic population of 521 as compared with 2,693 whites. While there were 35 white schools with 35 teachers, there were only three Negro schools with three teachers. Out of this scholastic population, which included all persons between the ages of six and twenty, only 700 whites and 60 Negroes attended school regularly. He had observed that there was "so much distrust" among the people of the county that they "hang back" from the organization and opening of more schools. For the year 1868, he reported that he had been paid nothing for his services, and that 38 teachers had been paid a total of only $869.06 for the year.[44] M. M. Hiland, who lived in Cheatham but who taught in Dickson County, reported that for two months during the year 1868 he had conducted a Negro school in the vicinity of Jackson's Chapel. Admitting that he should have been "hanged for it," but probably greatly needing the small amount of money paid for his services, Hiland had conducted the school against the wishes and in spite of the threats of the whites of the community. Finally, however, he received a note which perhaps caused him to disband the school. Signed "By order of the Grand Cyclops," the note stated:

> M. M. Hiland, alias Nigro Hiland:—
> You are hereby notified to disband the school of which you are in charge at Jackson Chapel as it is contrary to the wishes of every respectable man in the vicinity and an insult to the refinement of the community. If this notice fails to effect its purpose, you may expect to find yourself suspended by a rope with your feet about six feet from terra firma. We hope you will give the same consideration: and in case of failure on your part, we intend to carry into execution the above mentioned plan.
> BEWARE! BEWARE!! BEWARE!!! [45]

A large population movement took place over the country during the war and the years which followed. Dickson County was no exception. Of a population of 9,340 in 1870, nearly twelve hundred were born in states other than Tennessee. Large numbers came into the county from North Carolina, Virginia, Georgia, Alabama, Kentucky, Pennsylvania, and Ohio. There were ten or more whose land of birth was England, Wales, Ireland, Scotland, or Germany.[46] Proponents for an industrialization of the South literally begged for immigrants from the North and from foreign countries to come into the South and develop the natural resources and raw materials. Proponents of the "New South" philosophy saw in the agrarian system of the Old South an incubus which had prevented their section from progressing and taking its rightful place. The leading Nashville papers, the *Republican Banner* and the *Daily Press and Times*, daily propounded the philosophy of industrialization and solicited immigration from the Northern states.[47] The state legislature, too, joined in the move to acquire capital and immigrants. Hermann Bokum was named Commissioner of Immigration for the State of Tennessee shortly after the war, and took an extensive tour of many of the Northern states in an effort to arouse interest among prospective emigrants to Tennessee. He reported to the state legislature in 1868 that the people of Tennessee were greatly interested in the development of its natural resources, water power, and other resources, "and that to attain this end she needs capital and the intelligent labor of the North and of Europe."[48] He reported that already many immigrants had come into Dickson, Coffee, Bedford, Franklin, and other counties. For this he claimed part credit because of his extensive appearances before groups in Chicago and other Northern cities. He also noted that some were leaving Prussia for the United States, and he expressed a "sincere hope" that "a portion of this valuable immigration" should be secured for his state.[49] He was especially interested in German settlers, and had appeared before a German Society in Chicago to interest them in emigration. He observed that those of that national group were industrious and thrifty, often saving enough money to purchase a farm after they had been in the country for only a year. Too, they frequently brought capital with them, Bokum stated. Many had come into Dickson County, bringing an average of between $1,500 and $2,000 per head of family.[50]

William Darby's *The Emigrant's Guide* gave an extensive and exaggerated account of the advantages which Tennessee had to offer immigrants. Dickson County was very desirable, Darby stated, because of the large number of rivers and creeks and because it was on the Nashville and Northwestern Railroad. Four towns were located on the line, including Hutton, just over the Dickson-Cheatham line; White Bluff, three miles farther; Sneedsville, ten miles from White Bluff; and Gillam, eight miles from Sneedsville. Immigrants were especially advised to investigate Sneedsville, where one "C. Beringer, of Allegheny City, Pennsylvania, is establishing a colony of farmers and merchants who, like himself, are immigrants from Pennsylvania." Those interested in receiving further information were advised to contact M. J. J. Cagle of Charlotte.[51]

Generally over the South the immigrants tended to come in groups and sometimes settle in colonies. In the summer of 1867, a large contingent from Pennsylvania purchased 40,000 acres of iron lands in Hickman County and proposed to manufacture iron. This action the Nashville *Daily Press and Times* hailed as the "harbinger of better days" for the entire South. A short time later the newspaper reported that over thirty "thrifty and independent" families had come from Pennsylvania and had settled within the last few weeks at Sneedsville.[52] In March of 1868 the same paper ran a lengthy article in which it pointed out that Dickson, among other counties, had been benefited greatly by the immigration from the North.

The census records of 1870 tell the story of the national and state origin of the settlers in the various counties.[53] In Dickson County more came from the states of Pennsylvania and Ohio than any other Northern state, although many Northern and Southern states were represented. Within the first five districts—the southern side of the county— people from the Northern states tended to settle in large numbers. In the first district over a dozen Pennsylvania families came in, and there were also families from Illionis, Indiana, and Ohio. In districts two, three, four, and five, these same Northern states were represented in addition to New York, Wisconsin, Connecticut, and Delaware. People also had come from Prussia, Scotland, England, and Ireland, and from the Southern states of Kentucky, Georgia, Missouri, Louisiana, North Carolina, South Carolina, Virginia, Alabama, and Mississippi, but the majority of the newcomers hailed from Northern states or foreign countries. Out of a population of about 3,000 whites living in the first five districts, nearly one third of them were natives of areas other than the Southern states. About ten Pennsylvania families settled in the sixth district, in which was located the county seat, and one family came from Indiana and one from Ohio. The sixth, seventh, ninth, tenth, and eleventh districts received relatively few immigrants and of those who came, far more were from the Southern states of Alabama, Georgia, Kentucky, Mississippi, and North Carolina than from any other states.

The eighth district, wherein was located Cumberland Furnace, also received many immigrants from Pennsylvania, who came to work in the manufacture of iron. There were in 1870 over one hundred Pennsylvania natives alone who worked at the furnace, and others were from Ohio, Ireland, Scotland, Germany, and various Southern states. The district had a larger population than any other, which was due largely to employment afforded by the furnace. Seven hundred thirty-eight whites and 371 Negroes found homes in that district. Not all of the immigrants of the district worked at the furnace, however. The family of A. E. C. Miller tilled the soil and Miller's descendants and other relatives have been some of the best farmers and citizens Dickson County has had. Miller was born in Gotha, Saxony in 1824, but came to America in 1837 where he married a Pennsylvania wife, Eliza Jane Goan.[54] Six of their children, Pasevent, Augustus, Lincoln, Elmer E., Virgil, Idilla, and Lawrence Edgar, were born in Pennsylvania. They had moved to Dickson County in 1869 or early 1870, and in 1870 owned property worth over $7,000. By 1886 they owned over twice that much. The twelfth district had a few immigrants from New York, New Jersey, Pennsylvania, and Canada, and several from Alabama, Florida, Kentucky, and Georgia.

Many of the families did not come directly to Dickson County from the place of their birth. Henry Bluecock and wife were natives of Prussia, but had lived in Pennsylvania before coming to the first district. George Carrey, an engineer born in Vermont, lived in Indiana long enough to marry, then moved to Pennsylvania where two children were born, and thence to the first district of Dickson County. His close neighbor was Pennsylvania-born John McElhany who had married and settled in Ohio. McElhany's two-year-old child, Mary, was born in Ohio, but Samuel, aged 3 months, was born in Dickson County. Edward Mason and wife were born in England, but lived in South America for a few years before coming to Tennessee. Most of the immigrants were farmers but not all. Levi Shawl, of the fifth district, was a blacksmith, Sam Thompson was a merchant, and L. T. McCreary a physician. All were Pennsylvania natives. Many of the families named their children for Civil War heroes. Mark Garton of the third district had one child named Beauregard, which indicates that he was quite familiar with the exploits of that able Southern general. Other families had children named Robert, Thomas, and Joseph, probably for Lee, "Stonewall" Jackson, and Johnston. Despite the fact that there were hundreds from the Northern states, not one Ulysses, or William Tecumseh, can be found.

While after the war the majority of the people of Dickson County appear to have been born and reared in the county, the fact that many newcomers were arriving, principally from Northern states, was to modify somewhat the thinking of the people politically, and was also to affect adversely the close unity which once was existent over the whole county.

CHAPTER IX

Growth and Development, 1870–1900

THE POPULATION of Dickson County more than doubled during the thirty year period of 1870–1900. Paced by the rapid growth of the town of Dickson, the county increased from a population of 9,280 in 1870 to 18,635 thirty years later. People from the North, particularly Pennsylvania, Indiana, and Ohio, continued to pour in to the county in large numbers of both blacks and whites emigrated from the surrounding Southern states. The Negro population, included in the above figures, increased from 1,677 in 1870 to 2,919 in 1900. The number of people born in states other than Tennessee increased from 1,200 at the beginning of the period to well over two thousand in 1900.[1] The foreign born increased from 84 in 1880 to 107 in 1900. Nearly 300 additional people in the latter year were native born but of foreign parents. People of German origin predominated, with an ample sprinkling of Canadians, Irish, Swiss, and Austrians.[2]

Dickson County was featured by the press as an area of "Southern clime" where cheap, fertile land could be purchased, and the publicity must have reached the eyes of many. Men like J. Franck Rumsey of Chicago, W. A. Scheonfeld of Chicago, and various others bought thousands of acres in the county for speculative purposes. "No part of the state offers better advantages to the colonist than our neighboring county of Dickson," the editor of the Clarksville *Semi-Weekly Tobacco Leaf* wrote in 1885. "Her lands are rich in mineral resources, while for agricultural pursuits they are very productive. . . . Her forests of the finest hardwoods are inexhaustible, while she has the advantage of railroad and river communication with the markets of the world."[3] At approximately the same time the editor of the Nashville *Banner* reported that a Nashville attorney had been employed by a New York land syndicate to examine title to 40,000 acres of land below Charlotte. A "northern gentleman" at the same time was in the vicinity of Gillam for the purpose of purchasing land for the formation of a colony of people from the North. Some 15,000 acres had been purchased in the neighborhood of Gillam, for a price ranging from $2.50 to $6 per acre. "A fine forest of timber" was on the land purchased.[4] The following year a prominent Charlotte attorney pointed to the great supply of iron ore which he claimed was "simply inexhaustible" and believed that it should interest many emigrants in coming to Dickson County.[5] James B. Killebrew in an address in Nashville in 1890 paid tribute to the people of Dickson County and their development of iron, and proclaimed the county an area sure to experience growth and expansion in the years to come. He praised the immigrants who had aided in the material development, and especially "that great Pennsylvanian," Montgomery Bell, "bold of heart and broad in intellect," whose "patriotic cannon balls were sent hurtling through the ranks of the enemies of his country at New Orleans."[6] Even as late as at the turn of the century small colonies of immigrants were still coming. A Nashville paper reported in the spring of 1898 that one hundred families, "tobacco raisers from Montgomery County," had purchased land in the vicinity of Dickson and were planning to move immediately. They had been attracted by "the low price [of land] and superior tobacco soil of this locality."[7]

The chief occupation of most of the people continued to be farming. Farm censuses were taken every ten years, and for this period of 1870 to 1900 the census for the year 1880 is chosen for a close examination of agriculture in the county. In that year there were 1,766 farms, consisting of over two hundred thousand acres. Most of the land was in forest, and about one third was cleared. The average size of the farms was 123 acres, although there were five with over one thousand acres. Two thirds of the farms were between fifty and 500 acres. Of the 1,766 farms, 1,250 were cultivated by the owners. One hundred fifty-four farms were leased for a fixed money rental, and 362 for a share of the products. Livestock was produced on a larger scale than ever before. In 1880 there were nearly 2,000 horses and about the same number of mules, asses, and working oxen. There were over 3,000 head of cattle, and 22,670 hogs. Over 12,000 pounds of wool had been clipped in the spring of that year. Corn was still the chief grain crop, and each year nearly half of the cleared land was planted in corn. Over six hundred thousand bushels of corn were produced during the year 1879. In the same year over fifty thousand bushels of oats and over forty-five thousand bushels of wheat were produced. Barley, rye, buckwheat, and sorghum cane were produced in smaller quantities. Tobacco was becoming more and more an important crop, and in 1879 seven hundred fifty-five acres produced 494,428 pounds. Some was marketed in Nashville, but many farmers sold their tobacco on the Clarksville loose leaf floors. Poultry, eggs, and honey, were produced in moderate quantities. In general, in agricultural pursuits Dickson County compared favorably with other nearby counties of comparable size, as is indicated in the following table:[8]

	Cheatham	Hickman	DICKSON	Humphreys	Montgomery
Number of farms	1,054	1,549	1,766	1,348	2,241
Farms cultivated by owner	654	1,165	1,250	993	1,530
Number of cattle	4,135	7,653	7,586	7,218	8,319
Number of sheep	3,107	8,568	5,640	6,980	7,518
Number of swine	14,514	25,464	22,670	22,062	40,393
Number bushels corn	457,189	828,117	616,422	826,941	1,236,561
Number bushels wheat	18,036	37,491	45,318	25,371	148,534
Number pounds tobacco	950,352	21,858	494,428	21,326	8,266,461
Number bushels sweet potatoes	17,099	22,311	22,181	29,386	47,540
Number bushels Irish potatoes	8,009	13,305	24,435	9,000	28,182

While the great majority of people, regardless of whether they were natives or newcomers, continued to follow agricultural pursuits for a livelihood, many were turning to industry and mercantile activity. Iron manufacturing continued to be the leading industrial activity for awhile, as before the war. Not all of the iron forges and furnaces re-opened after the Civil War but, as mentioned in the preceding chapter, Cumberland Furnace did re-open under the management of J. P. Drouillard, a Northern soldier who had married Florence Kirkman, a granddaughter of Anthony Vanleer. Although the panics of 1873 and of 1893 slowed down operations considerably, it may be said for the entire thirty year period that the operation of the furnace approached the scale on which it was operated in the ante-bellum period. The editor of the *Dickson County Press* noted in 1886 that the furnace was then making twenty tons of "superior iron" per day. "The iron ore of this section of the county is simply inexhaustible, . . . and no man or company that has ever operated those works has ever failed," it was said of the Cumberland furnace. Lack of adequate transportation facilities was claimed to be the main reason why production had not increased considerably more, and the construction of a railroad to join the furnace with Dickson and Clarksville was believed to be the only obstacle in the way of great industrial advancement for Dickson County. Once such a road was built it was claimed that "the hills all along the different prongs of the creek will willingly give up their millions of hidden wealth in iron, and the fertile fields will part with their abundance of grain and tobacco, and every stick of its valuable timber will be brought into demand."[9] In 1889 the Southern Iron Company of Nashville purchased the interest of Drouillard, but retained Colonel Robert B. Stone as manager and continued to reap profits.

Census records for 1870 and 1880[10] indicate that well over a hundred men—black and white—found employment at the furnace. As mentioned, many of them were from Pennsylvania where they had worked in furnaces and forges before coming to Tennessee.[11] Their skill and experience added much to the development of the industry.

The workday at the furnace during the summer months sometimes was sixteen hours or longer, and the men accomplished a large number of tasks. Many were axemen and waggoners who went into the countryside round about to bring fuel for the hungry fires. William Loch Cook, who became a justice of the state supreme court, spent some of his boyhood days in the vicinity of the furnace, and described a typical workday as follows:[12]

In the early 1880's I occasionally saw the commencement of the workday at Cumberland Furnace, near my home. At the beginning of the day the sunrise whistle blew and the sleeping day seemed to spring to life and action. The farm hands started from their quarters, the coal teams left the barns for the coaling grounds; the iron wagons drew toward the pig yards to get their load for the river. The farm hands went away whistling, singing and hallowing; the teamsters were popping their long whips with short handles and geeing and hawing their teams, and the old furnace heaving and sighing, for me, from the dormant life of the back woods, all that was an oasis of noise and activity in a vast desert of silence and rest.

An industry new to the county after the war and which offered great promise for several years was crude oil production. As early as June, 1865, several oil men from Pennsylvania had surveyed Dickson County lands and had announced their belief in oil potentialities. They had formed a company which included two local men, George H. Hudson and John C. Hogan, and leased land on a farm belonging to George W. Brown on Jones' Creek, about seven miles east of Charlotte. Soon the entire county became fair prey for oil prospectors, much to the delight of the local citizenry. This company struck gas at 57 feet, but had struck nothing else when at 187 feet their auger and bit broke. They procured new tools and again struck gas at 57 feet, and finally oil at 295 feet. Transportation and refining difficulties caused them to halt operations, but not until some 300 barrels had been shipped to a Nashville refinery. From 1865 to the turn of the century (and even after) others tried it intermittently. L. H. Gomley from Pennsylvania drilled to 630 feet in 1878, and two years later a company composed of James Howell, James Graham, J. M. Crumpler, and a Dr. Shacklett drilled several wells, but no attempt proved profitable. In the fall of 1885 the "Dickson Oil Company" was formed, and exhibited high hopes for success. Its stockholders were prominent citizens, including Dr. J. T. Henslee, Henry Smith, Dr. C. M. Lovell, J. R. Bryan, and W. S. Coleman, of Dickson; N. B. Lipe of McKenzie, E. B. Teachout of Huntingdon, and several others from Carroll County. Announcing that they planned to go 1,000 feet or more "if oil can be mined in paying quantities," the stockholders leased land on the farm of George W. Brown, and told of plans to construct a refinery on the railroad. By the following spring much heavy machinery had been brought to the farm, and the editor of a Clarksville paper announced that "They are fully equipped to go any requisite depth, . . . and if oil is there they will get it."[13] The *Dickson County Press* observed that "just a few weeks ago they were offered by a Northern Company $500 for a sublease," and the Dickson *Democrat* christened the spot on Jones' Creek "Oildorado."[14] High hopes alone were not sufficient, however, and, although this concern operated on a larger scale than any heretofore, it met the same fate as the others. In 1899 the Dickson *Home Enterprise* observed that another oil boom was engulfing the county. "All necessary papers have been signed, machinery purchased and work is ready to begin," it was reported. "Should it prove successful, the possibilities it means for Dickson and Dickson County would be untold," the editor hopefully wrote.[15]

There was at least one report during the period that Mother Earth was not only ready to yield crude oil in abundance, but large quantities of silver ore as well. A Nashville paper observed in 1880 that a vein of silver ore had been found on the Nashville, Chattanooga, and St. Louis Railroad near White Bluff. The ore was assayed by a mineralogist who found it to be "very rich." "A company with capital of $25,000 is soon to be organized," it was reported.[16]

Toward the end of the century many business establishments and industries of a more successful nature were formed. Practically every farmer had timber on his place and sold a considerable amount to saw mills, planing mills, and stave factories. Dickson became the state headquarters for the lumber firm of Tuthill and Pattison of Cincinnati, described by a Dickson paper as "one of the largest lumber dealers of the country." L. S. Tuthill, senior member of the firm, established an office in the Anderson Hotel, where he paid "the most liberal prices for lumber," and was "always in the market to buy." The Dickson Stave Factory, operated by two Missouri men, S. G. and George Holland, was another manufacturing establishment which employed several men. It was located in east Dickson, and manufactured hoops and staves in large quantites, and employed "many men." The owners operated other stave mills in the states of Kentucky and Alabama under the name of Holland Brothers. Perhaps the largest user of timber products, however, was the Dickson Planing Mill, operated by Crosby and McFarland. Located in west Dickson along the main line of the Nashville, Chattanooga and St. Louis Railway, the establishment was described by the editor of the *Home Enterprise* as "the chief manufacturing plant of Dickson." Organized in 1887, the plant by 1900 covered two acres in lumber yards and buildings. Crosby, the senior member of the firm, was a native of Wisconsin and had come to Tennessee in 1884 with a small amount of capital. In 1888 he became associated with McFarland, a Pennsylvania native, and formed the partnership. The plant was 40 by 120 feet and two stories high. The planing and dressing machinery was located on the first floor, while on the second floor lumber for inside finishings and cabinets was prepared. In addition to preparing the lumber, the firm made counters, casings, book cases, and office fixtures.[17]

The Dickson Roller Mills, owned and operated by Myers Brothers of Kentucky and W. T. Rogers of Dickson, was the largest firm of its kind in the county. Located in the northern part of Dickson, the mill had a capacity of 70 barrels of flour per ten-hour day and 180 bushels of meal for the same period. A sixty horsepower engine supplied the motive force which turned a "giant array" of machinery.

The "greatest manufacturing plant in Dickson and the largest brick making concern in this section of the state" was the Dickson Brick Company, established in 1893. It was owned and operated by W. R. Boyte, assistant cashier of the Dickson Bank and Trust Company, and Dr. C. M. Lovell, a practicing physician and vice-president of the bank, and was managed by Will Dull. Employing "a great army of men," the plant had a capacity of 50,000 bricks per day, and furnished building material for cities over a wide radius.

The Dickson Photo Copying Company was established during the nineties, and built up a mail order business from over the entire country. It employed several workers, whose work was "perfect in detail." Frames were constructed and picture work completed on a large scale, and it was predicted that the company soon would excel all other similar business establishments in the South. C. E. Noyes, an Indiana native, and J. J. Kistler of Ohio established a marble cutting and tombstone works in Dickson during the late eighties. Their work was of "excellent quality," yet "at prices that make it possible for those in every station of life to procure head stones for friends."[18] There were many other manufacturing establishments besides these, such as Bryan, Coleman, and Company of Burns, which manufactured staves and lime; the Waverly Stave Company, of Dickson; and probably a dozen or so more which dealt in lumber, grain, and other products.[19]

There were numerous grocery, hardware, furniture, dry goods, boots and shoes, and general merchandise stores scattered throughout the county. Several restaurants were maintained in the towns where a traveller could secure a full-course meal for twenty-five cents. Board and lodging could be had at the hotels and boarding houses for seventy-five cents per day or ten dollars per month. Those buying groceries could purchase hens for twenty cents per pound, eggs for eight cents a dozen, and butter for as little as ten cents per pound. Country hams could be bought for nine cents per pound, with shoulders two cents cheaper. Meal sold for fifty cents per bushel, and flour for three cents per pound.[20] Saloons and liquor stores were located in Charlotte and Dickson. W. H. Butler, described as an "artistic mixer of fancy and wholesome drinks," ran the Red Rover Saloon, described in the *Press* as the "Palace of Happiness." Located on the public square of Charlotte, Butler's place sold "the finest drinks, good whiskey, brandy, and wines," and also "fresh groceries," which were marketed "day and night." W. R. and D. F. Hudson were proprietors of the "Climax Sample Rooms," located on the southside of the public square, and sold not only "the finest wines and liquors," but also cigars and tobaccos. Not only did they mix "every kind of drink in the latest and most approved style," but also kept a full stock of groceries which they advertised at "rock-bottom prices." Oscar R. Leech, not to be outdone by Butler and the Hudson brothers, operated the "White Elephant," where he sold drinks and general merchandise. Court week in Charlotte often would result in near depletion of their liquid stock; therefore, the proprietors generally visited the Nashville wholesale dealers several days before the opening of the judicial hearings. In 1891 the *Dickson County Press* noted in a routine manner that[21]

> Oscar R. Leech, the polite and attentive bar tender at the "White Elephant," William H. Butler, the artistic and fancy drink mixer in the "Palace of Happiness," and the "Red Rover," and William R. Hudson, of Hudson Brothers, who will be found behind the bar at the "Blue Tiger," and "Climax Sample Rooms," ready to make you feel rich, were all in Nashville the first of the week replenishing their stock for court week.

The prohibition movement in the state which gained headway during the late eighties and early nineties, and resulted in the formation of the Prohibition Party in 1887 in Tennessee, probably did not cramp the style of the saloon keepers. In the early nineties, however, when in Dickson an intoxicated man was killed by a train, a group of citizens forcibly closed the saloons temporarily and confiscated the whiskey.[22]

Of the many other businesses which flourished during the thirty year period here under discussion, newspapers were published in the major towns. A thorough search has failed to uncover any evidence which might point toward the publication of a paper within the county in the days before the Civil War. Perhaps the first was *The Independent*, established in 1878 by N. B. Morton. Morton was of a distinguished Dickson County family, of which Lieutenant Colonel George H. Morton, Civil War soldier who settled in White Bluff after the war, was the most outstanding. The Mortons were of Scottish extraction, the first member of the family coming to New York from Scotland in 1836.[23] *The Independent* was published for three years and was supplanted in 1881 by N. B. Conant and Samuel C. Freeman's *Dickson County Press*.[24] The *Press* was a seven-column, four-page paper, published every Thursday, and it carried a variety of news items and advertisements. It was the only paper in the county until 1886, when Samuel C. Freeman began publication of the Dickson *Democrat*. It was somewhat similar to the *Press* in make-up. The first issue was published May 20, 1886, and Ralph A. Freeman, Dickson resident and son of the publisher, today owns the only copy of the first edition. Several weeks before the first issue appeared, the Clarksville *Semi-Weekly Tobacco Leaf* noted with some degree of alarm the plans to publish a second paper in Dickson County. Asserting that much of the prosperity then being enjoyed by the county was due to the *Press*, the editor expressed the opinion that the county was too small and too sparsely populated to support two papers and predicted that "the venture will prove disastrous" and would "result in the publication of two nondescripts without the force or influence that is now wielded by the one newspaper."[25] Although the paper apparently did well, the death of Samuel Freeman, which occurred only a few years after the paper was established, resulted in the suspension of its operation. In 1890 the *Democrat* was revived by W. T. Crotzer and Graham Edgerton, who changed the name to the Dickson *Advance*. The first issue appeared in August, and a Clarksville paper observed that it "gives promise of a live, readable county paper."[26] This paper was published only for a short time, and merged with the *Home Enterprise* in August, 1891.[27] The *Home Enterprise* had been established in Dickson in 1890, and it was published through the turn of the century. R. H. and S. C. Hicks were the editors and general managers. Through their paper they ardently sought the advancement of the city of Dickson which they believed to be "one of the revelations in Tennessee development" and "one of the star towns on the N. C. & St. L."[28] Two years later two more newspapers were launched. They were *The Critic* which was published in Dickson, and the *Dickson County Independent* published in Charlotte. Neither probably was published for very long. The first issue of *The Critic* came off the press on February 2, 1893, and was published by W. T. Loggins and Company. It consisted of eight pages of five columns each, and was printed on a good grade of rag content paper. The editors promised in the first issue to make it "one of the best family newspapers in the State," and advised their readers that

> It will be our aim to make it a clean, pure paper, giving all the local news obtainable and selecting such matter from our exchanges as we think will best suit our readers. The weekly sermons of the great divine, T. DeWitt Talmage, will be one of our special features; . . . We shall endeavor to make it a newspaper, not a sensational sheet. True it will claim Dickson as its home, but will fairly and honestly represent every portion of Dickson County. It is of as much important to the people to have Charlotte, White Bluff, Tennessee City, or other neighborhood, grow and prosper....[29]

The first issue of the *Independent* came off the press March 2, 1893. It consisted of four pages of seven columns each. Victor A. Doughty, editor and publisher, called upon his friends to help him make a success of his new venture. "We have invested our all in this printing outfit," he wrote in the first issue. Doughty carried a wide variety of news items and advertisements. Charlotte saloons bought much advertising space. "The eighth wonder of the world" were the words used to describe W. H. Butler's "faculty to make men feel rich—the Palace of Happiness."

The *Dickson County Press* was moved from Dickson to Charlotte in 1886 and was published by the Charlotte Publishing Company. This company consisted of prominent men of Charlotte, including I. M. Bowers, W. Blake Leech, R. L. Leech, R. B. Stone, and others. It remained the owner until 1891 when the paper was moved back to Dickson under the proprietorship of a firm known as Smith and Talley. In 1892 it was acquired by B. F. Harris who moved it back to Charlotte, but Will J. Conant acquired it again in 1893 and moved it to Dickson. In approximately 1898 it was again brought to Charlotte, and was published for several years by Thomas Hill. Three years later it was being edited by Henry C. Leech and G. C. Dismukes, and published by R. L. Leech. It was continued on into the twentieth century for an indeterminate period.

In August, 1894, the first issue of *The Coming Nation* published in Dickson County rolled off the press. It was the chief organ of the Ruskin socialists who moved from Greensburg, Indiana, and formed a colony near Tennessee City. It carried virtually no Dickson County news, but was concerned almost entirely with propagandizing the doctrines of socialism and the happenings at the Ruskin colony. The character of *The Coming Nation* and the Ruskin colony is discussed in detail in another chapter.

Just after the turn of the century Charles and Harry Bevan, brothers-in-law of J. A. Wayland who had established the Ruskin settlement and published *The Coming Nation*, founded the Dickson *Verdict*, which they published until the fire of 1905 destroyed their plant. W. L. Pinkerton of Hickman County established the Dickson County *Herald* at Dickson in November, 1907. Ralph A. Freeman, who had been with Bevan's *The Verdict*, became associated with him. In 1910 Pitt Henslee, Dickson banker, and Freeman bought the *Herald* from Pinkerton, and Freeman took over the editorship. After Henslee's death in the early 1920's his son, Lipe, together with Freeman, operated the paper until 1927 when Freeman gained full possession. For a decade and a half Freeman was sole owner, editor, and publisher, but in 1942 he sold half interest to Leland G. Ishmael. Seven years later Ishmael acquired full interest, and today is the owner and publisher. Bob Hickerson is the present editor. Other papers flourished in the twentieth century, including R. E. Reeder's *New Idea* at Burns and Brice Thompson's *Charlotte News Banner*, but only the *Herald* has continued uninterrupted publication. Today it remains Dickson County's only newspaper.

The county papers of this period were not greatly different from their counterparts of today. One major difference lay in the fact that advertisements dominated the first page, and another in that professional men advertised their services freely. The county paper of that day and time, just as today, was the chief means through which news of county happenings was disseminated. The court sessions and church meetings, the visitings of community friends, the crimes and misfortunes, and the joys and sorrows, all, were shared by everyone through the weekly editions of the county newspapers. Advertisements of business establishments, doctors, dentists, and lawyers appeared side by side. Dr. L. D. Wright advertised his possession of a "mad stone" which, it was claimed, when applied to a rabid animal's bite would cause immediate healing. An itinerant "doctor" caused much disturbance in the early 1880's by gaining the confidence of the people of the county and then deserting his patients after swindling them on many occasions. "It is not a good plan to put too much confidence in a traveling doctor," the editor of a paper advised.[30] Several years later much publicity was given to happenings which rocked the Edgewood community. A Methodist minister of that area deserted his family and his congregation—reportedly for "another woman." He had come to Dickson County during the 1880's, had "walked blameless, keeping himself unspotted from the world, discharging his pastoral and Christian duties efficiently," and had married a Dickson County woman. On March 9, 1891, he disappeared and was not heard from until several weeks later. Upon his return to Edgewood he gave no information as to his whereabouts since March 9. The Edgewood people accused him of having another wife and family in another state, but he denied their accusation.[31]

Much publicity was given to the murder in 1886 of a man named Rayburn. J. E. Neblett and a man named Wilmuth were indicted for the offense, but were not convicted.[32] Several years later Luman Moore, described in the press as a "quiet fellow" was shot in the chest by Sam Work, who was described as "a dissipated character." Attempted manslaughter charges were preferred against Work.[33]

The discovery of Jewel Cave, now operated commercially by Elzevir Lawson, occurred in 1885 when Thomas Rogers and his daughter, Fannie, were exploring the foot of a wooded hill near the banks of Yellow Creek. News of the discovery caused a mild sensation. Rogers and daughter had crawled into the cave where they found a large room opening into other rooms. As they explored they "marked their way with shavings whittled from a pine board with a pocketknife," the newspaper reporter stated.[34]

The editors were usually at their best when they wrote obituaries, especially if the deceased had died when young. The death of James R. Thompson, sixteen-year-old son of T. D. and Anna Thompson, became the subject for a lengthy and flowing obituary in March, 1882.

> He was so young [the editor wrote]; life was just unfolding its fairest phases; just developing in dim outlines its most wonderful possibilities. Hope waved high her brilliant ensign and pointed on to bright years to come, and every circumstance of his being, youth, health, intellect, and kindly heart, lent confirmation to the fair promises. But when his life seemed most strongly fortified by every requirement for safety and continuance, the sable banner of death was planted on its citadel and all his unfolding faculties of mind, body, and soul were sadly gathered into the small compass of the grave.[35]

The death of William W. Leech, who was killed in a fracas in Texas in October, 1882, became the subject for a beautifully written obituary appearing in the *Press* November 23, 1882.

> He was far from home [the writer said], surrounded by strange faces, which rendered his situation sad indeed. To linger day and night in a contest with the destroyer, and look in vain for the familiar faces gazed upon in childhood, or the yearning look of life, that bent over our cradle in watchful solicitude in the helplessness and innocence of infancy, to hear no brother's voice, or sister's tones, breaking with hope and encouragement upon the dull ear, as death gradually seals it to all earthly sounds; to have nothing but visions of home and its loved ones, its remembered spots and unforgotten things passing before us, without hope of ever again mingling with them in the social circle, or at the altar of prayer, is truly appalling. If his father had been at his death couch to console him, or the beloved mother of his infancy administering to his wants . . . to wipe from his brow the grave-cold clammy dew, it would have been a comfort and solace in his last moments, and would have mitigated the surroundings of his death.... He now sleeps in the suburbs of the town [Charlotte] in a lot rendered sacred by the interment of his great grandparents and other near relatives.
>
> > There he will lie and sweetly sleep,
> > His deeds all done but not forgot
> > While all his early doom shall weep
> > And parents idolize the spot.

Most of the county papers carried editorials. Practically any development was fair prey as a subject. For example, in 1888 the editor of the *Press* condemned the federal government for not recognizing properly the deeds of valor of the men who fought in the Mexican War. He wrote:

> The country has never been engaged in a war in which so much wealth and territory was acquired by the powers of our soldiers as that of the Mexican war, and yet these gallant men have been almost wholly ignored until very recently, and even now a very small per cent of them are allowed pensions from the government. This shameful neglect . . . will ever remain a blot upon her ... name. It is to be hoped that the incoming Congress

while it is dealing out pensions with such lavish hands [to Northern Civil War veterans] will remember even at this late day to do these faithful soldiers and their aged widows at least simple justice.[36]

The editors of the time frequently clamored for new industry. This they believed would come only after adequate transportation facilities were established, and they therefore sought railroads first. As mentioned in a previous chapter, by the end of the Civil War a track had been laid through the county, stretching from Nashville westward through White Bluff, Dickson, and Tennessee City, and into West Tennessee. At the beginning of the period, 1870–1900, this was the only line through the county. By the end of the period, however, a branch of the Louisville and Nashville had been built from this line at Pond Switch (commonly referred to then as Contrary Pond), in a northerly direction through Sylvia, Vanleer, and Slayden, and on to Montgomery County and Clarksville. A spur was built at Vanleer leading through the Dry Hollow community, and to Cumberland Furnace, which gave the iron industry of that area adequate transportation facilities. Also, by the end of the period the Centerville branch of the Nashville, Chattanooga, and St. Louis Railroad had been constructed. This began at Centerville and terminated at Colesburg where it joined the main N.,C., and St. L. line through the county. By the end of the century railroad fervor had quieted considerably, for many no doubt realized that railroad construction in the county had reached its saturation point. The preceding thirty years, however, were years of railroad fever in which people from all over the county sought a railroad through their farms and communities.

The people of Charlotte and Cumberland Furnace had watched with envy the construction of the line through White Bluff, Dickson, and Tennessee City. Charlotte wanted to participate in the growth which usually accompanied the building of good transportation facilities, and the iron manufacturers at Cumberland Furnace wanted a less expensive means of getting their produce to market. Soon after the war there was considerable talk of a line from Dickson to Clarksville, which would go through Charlotte and Cumberland Furnace. In the early 1880's the editor of the *Dickson County Press* announced with enthusiasm the arrival of two railroad men who came to make surveys and determine the proper route for a road connecting Dickson with Clarksville. The men proposed two routes; one which would go through Charlotte and Cumberland Furnace, and the other (called the ridge route) would go through Pond, Vanleer, and Slayden. After making the survey they were to confer with leading citizens along both routes to ascertain the amount of money and land which would be subscribed.[37] Interest lagged for several years but was renewed in 1888 when the Louisville and Nashville line announced a policy of devoting more earnings for the next three years to the construction of more branch lines. The prospect of extending the Princeton-Clarksville branch of that line to Dickson again appeared very bright. Montgomery County citizens were especially interested, and believed that if such a road were constructed to serve the "richest and most valuable ore banks known," Clarksville soon would rival Birmingham as an iron center.[38] Early in January of 1888 a railroad meeting was held at Charlotte, and was presided over by Major I. M. Bowers, a leading citizen of the county. Bowers recommended the appointment of committees to publicize the needs and advantages of a line through the town. A citizen wrote to the editor of the *Dickson County Press* to state his ideas of how the line should run.

Look at a map of Tennessee. Look at Dickson County. Thirteen furnaces in blast at one time . . . right along the iron belt that continues out of our county into Montgomery County.... If built the road should be named Dickson and Montgomery County Iron Road.... A project is on foot to run a feeder from Pond on the Northwestern to Cumberland Furnace. This won't work . . . because a road from the Pond to Cumberland Furnace would not touch the ore belt until it reached the latter place. But suppose the road would leave the Northwestern at Dickson and strike the ore belt within a few miles, then proceed near the Laurel Furnace and on by Belleview and Charlotte to Cumberland Furnace and the immense fields of ore just north of there, and you have a tributary or feeder to the Northwestern that would give an average of 500 tons of freight per day of iron alone.[39]

Late in February the presses of Charlotte and Clarksville heralded the "glorious news" that the line soon would be started. The *Press* stated that it was "no longer a matter of speculation" but that the connecting link between Clarksville and Dickson soon would be made, providing the peoples of Dickson and Montgomery counties "come up to the rack" and display their interest in a financial manner. In Dickson County alone, the *Press* stated, one hundred thousand dollars would be spent in construction, and a taxable wealth of three hundred dollars would be secured by the road.[40] Things continued to progress slowly, however, due in part to the lack of interest shown in Charlotte. In the following spring a Clarksville paper announced that subscription books had been opened, and urged all in Dickson and Montgomery who planned to pledge to come forth immediately and do so.[41] Spring and summer passed, and fall came, but still subscriptions lagged. The *Dickson County Press* urged the people of Charlotte to contribute—"eight or ten thousand would insure us the road," the editor explained. "What can we do or say to arouse the people of Charlotte to the necessity of prompt action in this matter?" the editor asked. "This is the chance of a lifetime and if we let it escape WE ARE DOOMED."[42] With prophetic insight the editor had spoken! Six months later the Louisville and Nashville Railroad Company sent a force of twenty surveyors to Pond to begin a survey via the ridge route through Vanleer and Slayden to the Montgomery County line. A spur track was to extend westward from Vanleer to Cumberland Furnace, and it was understood that the spur would be completed before the part of the main track to Clarksville.[43] By fall over 250 teams of horses and mules and over twice that many men were employed in grading which, it was claimed, would be completed by the last of November. Ties and rails were to be laid immediately, and it was predicted that Cumberland Furnace would be connected with the Nashville, Chattanooga, and St. Louis track by the first of the following year.⁴⁴ The financial failure of contractors Mundy, McTighe, and Company, however, caused a delay of several months, and it was not until May, 1891, that the strip between Cumberland Furnace and Pond was opened. Six months later the main line from Pond to the Montgomery County line was completed.⁴⁵ Thus ended the railroad boom for Dickson County. The panic of 1893 soon struck with all its fury, and with it went many of the dreams of a great iron center in Dickson and Montgomery counties. The furnace closed temporarily, but later re-opened on a somewhat modified scale. In the twentieth century the people were to witness the closing and dismantling of all iron works in the county, and the taking up of much of the railroad track built to serve the iron ore area.

The interest in politics which had been manifested by the people of Dickson County in the earlier days was matched or even exceeded by similar enthusiasm during the period of 1870–1900. From the earliest times the people had taken pride in the fact that they could be counted in the ranks of the Jeffersonian-Jacksonian Democrats, but with the influx of people from Northern states after the Civil War, some persons feared that the Republican Party might successfully rival the Democrats. In 1870, however, which was the first election year after the war in which the great majority of the populace could vote, the Democratic gubernatorial candidate, John C. Brown, received 852 votes in the county while his Republican opponent received less than half that number.⁴⁶ Two years later when it became apparent that the diverse elements in the Democratic Party might have difficulty in agreeing upon a candidate, the Dickson County Democrats led by Tom Morris and Jacob Leech endorsed Brown for a second term as early as April.⁴⁷ In 1874 they swelled the Democratic majority four-to-one, as Democratic Governor James D. Porter received 903 votes to Horace Maynard's 224. "The Republican heads are hanging low," a Dickson reporter telegraphed the editor of the Nashville *Union and American* after the election of 1872.⁴⁸

During the 1870's Dickson County had able Democratic representation in the legislature. Of those who served during this decade, two of the more outstanding were Jacob Leech in the house and W. A. Moody in the senate. Moody had served in the house before the war, had practiced medicine in Charlotte, and after the war had moved to Tennessee City where he continued his medical practice and his interest in politics. He died in 1885.⁴⁹ Leech had a varied career, and of the dozen or so Leech lawyers who have practiced before the Dickson County bar, if Blake and Herbert have topped all others in learning and understanding of the law, certainly Jacob must stand forth as the most spectacular and colorful. Born and reared in Dickson County, Jacob Leech studied for the ministry at Cumberland University and served as a chaplain with the Forty-ninth Regiment during the Civil War. Immediately after cessation of hostilities he returned to Cumberland to study law, and after graduation from the law school he began practice in Charlotte, where he remained until his death in 1898. While never an outstanding legislator, he did meet with success before the bar. His success, however, appears to have been due largely to his ability to pick a sympathetic jury and then to play upon the sympathies of that jury until the real issues were clouded, rather than to any profound knowledge of the law. Thus he became an outstanding lawyer in the field of criminal practice. His usual tactics in cases before juries seem to have been those of "softening up" the jury with a series of tales and jokes until it was entirely friendly to him and his client, after which he would display his uncanny skill of making each juror feel that he was in the same place and predicament as the accused, and the common decency and honesty demanded a decision for his client.

An article appearing in the *Tennessee Law Review* several years ago recounted some of Leech's antics.[50] In a case tried soon after the Civil War, Leech was called to defend a son of a deceased veteran of that war. The son, whose father the attorney had served with during the war, was accused of murder. At the trial Leech recognized among the veniremen several Civil War veterans, and he knew that the fires of that disastrous struggle still burned brightly in the hearts of every Confederate veteran. Therefore, in his speech before the jury he soft-pedaled the atrocity for which the youth was being tried, but graphically portrayed many Civil War scenes in which the father of the accused had fought and suffered until, almost to a man, the jurors stood with tears streaming from their eyes muttering protests against the hanging of the accused. Knowing that an open manifestation of grief and sorrow nearly always is contagious, Leech often was able to shed copious tears before juries if such seemed necessary to impress them. For fear lest he could not keep the supply of tears coming at a time most needed, he allegedly took to each criminal case a newly cut onion, the juice from which he would rub in his eyes at a propitious moment. Judge John A. Pitts, a Nashville lawyer, told of hearing Leech plead for a continuance for one of his clients, in which he stated the following grounds for seeking to postpone the trial until the next term:

> Well, yo' honor, please, [he began], in the first place, if the defendant goes to trial now, I'm afeared he'll be convicted and sent to the penitentiary. The State has got a whole raft of witnesses here and the defendant ain't got nary one. In the next place, if the case is continued the defendant will have a chance to break jail and git away. An' then agin, it's fo' months till the next term, and in the meantime the woods might ketch afire and burn up the jail, or the state's witnesses might die or move away, or the defendant hisself might die. And so, yo' Honor, please, we ain't ready, and on these grounds we ask yo' Honor to continue the case.

The judge, taken aback by the boldness, yet frankness, of the plea, granted a continuance.[51]

Leech served in the house from 1871 to 1875 and from 1877 to 1879, and in the state senate from 1887 to 1889. While a sturdy Democrat and, as described by a Nashville newspaper, "an affable gentlemen, generous and courteous," he left no outstanding legislative record. He introduced many bills in each session, but few got beyond the second reading. In the session of 1873 he was one of a small minority which voted against the important school bill which set up a workable public school system for the state. It was during this session that he and a few others of his temperament decided to monopolize the floor of the house for several hours by telling jokes and introducing "nonsensical" resolutions. While to some the antics no doubt were amusing, to many legislators of serious temperament it was an unnecessary waste of time, and to such an extent that a group led by Representative Houk presented a protest against "the disrespectful and nonsensical . . . resolutions which have been presented here. . . ."[52] On his third trip to the legislature, in 1877, Leech soundly championed the cause of creditors in the very important issue of the state debt. While others argued that the state should repay on the basis of fifty cents or less on the dollar, Leech argued that the bondholders had loaned the state their money with no other thought than that they would receive payment at par. Therefore, in order to maintain the state's goodwill and credit, the bonds should be paid off at par or at least at more than fifty cents on the dollar.[53]

Although in 1880 the Republicans rode into power with Governor Alvin Hawkins, the people of Dickson County remained within the Democratic fold throughout the eighties and nineties. In 1880 the Democrats split in Dickson County, as they did over the entire state. Jacob Leech, regular Democrat, was defeated for the Senate by Vernon F. Bibb, described as a "Bolter" Democrat. The Republican candidates for senate, house, and governor were within less than 200 votes of the Democrats, because of the division in the ranks of the latter.[54] In the same year the Dickson Democrats elected the following leading party men as delegates to a state Democratic convention, called in the interest of party harmony:[55]

District	Delegates
1	J. M. Moody, N. R. Sugg
2	J. C. Buford, R. G. Work
3	H. A. Spencer, Moses Tidwell
4	J. M. Stuart, S. C. Galloway
5	A. Myatt, E. W. Andrews
6	W. L. Grigsby, T. C. Morris, Jacob Leech, Carroll Leech (colored)
7	Benjamin Turner, Milton Mitchell
8	T. B. McCaslin, J. T. Cunningham
9	James Schmittou, John Shelton
10	A. J. Cooksey, S. H. Reynolds
11	Jesse Daniel, W. A. Moody
12	W. G. McMillan, G. H. Morton, and W. C. Charlton

These men must have been effective, for by 1882 the Bolters were fading and harmony was restored throughout the state. In that year the Democrats nominated William B. Bate as their gubernatorial candidate, and in October he addressed nearly 900 people assembled on the courthouse lawn at Charlotte. Two hundred fifty men on horseback met him, and escorted him from Dickson to Charlotte for the occasion. His speech aroused the Dickson Democrats to unity and to action. "There are not a dozen Bolters in the County," a reporter for the Nashville *Daily American* wrote after Bate's visit.[56]

Of the many state and county elections held during this period, perhaps more interest was engendered in the election of 1890 than in any other. Three strong factions in the Democratic Party existed at the time. The Farmers' Alliance group desired the nomination of John Buchanan of Rutherford County, the Bourbon element sought the selection of Josiah Patterson of Memphis, and the Industrialist faction espoused the cause of Jere Baxter. Baxter, while not a Dickson Countian, had blood ties in the area through Robert Baxter and others who had helped to develop the county's iron works. Too, he was a powerful railroad man, and the county ardently sought better transportation facilities at this time. Therefore, the newspapers of Dickson County backed Baxter, much to the distress of the editors of the Clarksville and Columbia papers who sought the election of Buchanan and who apparently read every weekly paper in Middle Tennessee in an effort to gain a consensus of political opinion.[57] In the county Senator John D. Sensing championed the cause of Buchanan, while Jacob Leech led the Baxter forces.[58] Buchanan received the nomination and went on to defeat his Republican and Prohibitionist opponents by sound majorities. Dickson County gave Buchanan a four-to-one majority over his Republican opponent, and a ten-to-one majority over the Prohibitionist candidate.[59] The Democratic candidate for Congress, N. N. Cox, carried the county by about the same majority, as did G. M. Tubbs, candidate for the state senate. W. Blake Leech, a young man of twenty years then making his first political bid, was defeated by another Democrat, R. J. Work, for representative.[60] That the people of Dickson County were loyal to the Democratic Party rather than to Sensing and Buchanan was apparent two years later when Buchanan, with Alliance backing, ran against Peter Turney, the regular Democratic nominee. Dickson County gave Turney 1,275 votes to 397 for Buchanan, while the Republican candidate polled 471.[61]

In each of the national elections Dickson County went safely into the Democratic fold. This was apparent from the Grant-Greeley contest of 1872 (when the American people sought in vain to pick the lesser of two evils), to the McKinley-Bryan affair of 1900. In 1880 the Democrats of Dickson endorsed Hancock and English, candidates for President and Vice President, and "great enthusiasm" for these men prevailed. "In W. S. Hancock we recognize all the good elements of a military man, combined with statesmanship of the first order," they announced. After a Democratic assemblage near Ruskin was held in the same year, a reporter wrote that he had not seen such political enthusiasm since 1840. Barbecue and a "flying genny" were no doubt partly responsible for part of the large and enthusiastic crowd.[63] In 1884 they participated in the Democratic victory by giving Grover Cleveland 1,339 votes, which was nearly three times the number mustered by the supporters of Blaine.⁶⁴ Practically all of the lawyers, prominent businessmen, and newspaper men were strong adherents to the Democratic party.

During the eighties and nineties the people of Dickson County were represented ably in the house and senate by such staunch Democrats as Civil War veteran W. J. Mallory, N. B. Sugg, H. C. Richardson, and Pitt Henslee. There were many other prominent political leaders. Looming high among the influencial lawyers was Thomas C. Morris, a Charlotte native who was reared in Humphreys County, but who returned to begin the practice of law in Charlotte at the age of 21. An able lawyer under whom Governor Tom Rye and many others studied, Morris was elected county court clerk in 1859 and held the position through the war. In 1870 he was elected delegate to the Constitutional Convention which was called for the purpose of revising the state Constitution. There he played an important part in the proceedings and voted against the levying of a poll tax upon the people of Tennessee.⁶⁵ While he held no other political office during his lifetime, he was at all times an outstanding Democratic leader.⁶⁶ Another who studied law under Morris and who became an able Dickson lawyer was W. E. Cullum. Born in the Beaver Dam community, Cullum was admitted to the bar in 1883 at the age of 19. Described as one who exhibited "rare tact in handling the most delicate intricacies of cases," Cullum, in addition to his successful legal practice, headed the "Bryan for President" movements in the county in 1896 and 1900.⁶⁷

Several members of the Grigsby family played prominent roles in the political and legal affairs of the county. Colonel Thomas K. Grigsby, an Alabama native who engaged in mercantile pursuits in Charlotte before the war, was elected county court clerk in 1870 and held the office for more than two decades. His son, William L., born in 1854, became clerk and master of the county, and later was circuit judge of the Tenth Judicial District which then embraced Dickson County. In 1894 he was a delegate to the national Democratic convention. His brother, Samuel, served as justice of the peace for the sixth civil district for twelve years, and in 1884 was elected sheriff.⁶⁸

Another family which contributed much to the legal and political leadership of the county was the Leech family. In addition to Jacob Leech, already mentioned, Hardin, Blake, Ransom, Herbert, and Henry C. were prominent in law and politics. Leonard Lane Leech, father of Hardin and Blake, was licensed to practice but devoted his time to farming and to mercantile pursuits. Perhaps the most prominent of them all was Blake, who was graduated from Cumberland University in 1890, and who later became a professor of law at Dickson Normal College. In 1890 he was defeated by 15 votes for state representative but was elected to that office two years later. In 1894 he was a successful candidate for attorney-general of the Tenth Judicial District. Shortly after completing the law course at Cumberland, he made an extensive tour of Europe and observed judicial procedure in many countries of that continent. A Dickson newspaperman, writing of him at the turn of the century, said:[69]

> ... he is an unassuming, courteous gentleman, with a kind word and hearty handshake for all. He is a Democrat of the Jeffersonian type, tenaciously clinging to the fundamental law of Democracy: majority rule. In the office of Attorney General, this district has never had a representative to serve it better, and is highly commended by all classes, regardless of party affiliations. As a citizen he is very public spirited and contributes his full share to any cause having for its aim the pushing forward of Dickson County.

R. D. Eubank, Civil War veteran and county trustee; J. A. Dodson, Civil War veteran and circuit court clerk for several terms; Pitt Henslee, banker and state representative; W. L. Cook, lawyer and state representative, and many others, were leaders in political activities for thirty years before the turn of the twentieth century. A. L. Scott and C. M. Lovell were also outstanding during the period, Scott being a Republican. Lovell was appointed postmaster of Dickson in 1897.[70]

The twentieth century dawned upon a prosperous people in Dickson County. The basic economy remained agricultural, but industry and merchandising were expanding. The population had increased to well over 18,000, and some men predicted that if the growth of the next thirty years should compare favorably with the growth of the period 1870-1900, the population by 1930 might well exceed 30,000. Wars and emigration to cities, however, caused the population to stagnate, and a half century later it was little greater than it was in 1900.

Judge Joe B. Weems

County judge of Dickson County, 1918 to 1934.

H. T. V. Miller

A one-time mayor of Dickson, Mr. Miller was otherwise prominent in city and county affairs.

W. J. Sugg

Dr. Sugg for many years has been among the best known and beloved physicians.

Some of the charter members of the Dickson County Historical Society organized in January, 1956.

Members of the Dickson County Historical Society, which was organized in January, 1956. Front row, right to left: J. B. White, President; Robert E. Corlew, Vice-President; Mrs. Floyd Williams, Secretary-Treasurer; Miss Willie G. McMillan, Mrs. Joe B. Weems, and Hartwell Gentry, members of the Advisory Council. Second row, left to right: Miss Bessie Greer, Mrs. J. B. White, Mrs. Ray Stuart, Miss Lola Miller, Mrs. Minor Stuart, Miss Jamey Weems, Miss Eleanora Miller, Mrs. Hartwell Gentry, Mrs. Grace H. Still, Mrs. Ann Smith, Mrs. Vina Mitchell, Mrs. Lester McCaslin. Third row, left to right: William Sugg, Wiley Russell, J. Minor Stuart, James A. Weems, T. H. Richardson, Kenneth Mitchell, D. L. Castleman, Clifton Goodlett, Wilbur F. Marsh. Charter are: H. O. Anderson, Randall Clayburn, Ray Stuart, Robert Harrington, Edward Sugg, Mrs. Edward Sugg, Mrs. Robert Harrington, Mrs. Clifton Goodlett, Roy Gentry, Mrs. Mary Scott Corlew, Mrs. R. E. Corlew, Sr., Henry Collier Leech, Slayden Weaver, Patty Wright Speight, Mrs. Olin Wright, Mrs. Olin Wright, Billy Raymond, Jimmy Clemmer, J. M. Clement, Larry Jobe, Neil Jobe, Mrs. Garner Harris, Miss Mable Miller, Mrs. Sara Wishart, Mrs. Elizabeth Chapman, Mrs. Albert Hines; Miss Anna Belle Clement, Mrs. Wayne Radford, Wayne Radford, Mrs. Eddie Swank, Floyd Williams; Dr. Mary Baxter Cook, Gertrude Borchert, Emmett Bibb, A. H. Bibb, Stanley Martin, Mrs. Stanley Martin, Miss Mary Ella Sensing, J. B. Worthy, Bob Hickerson, Iris H. McClain, Jill Knight Garrett

Robert E. Corlew, Sr. (1873-1930)

Mr. Corlew was born near Charlotte in 1873 and was educated in the public schools of the county and at Dickson Normal. He received the degree of Bachelor of Laws at Cumberland University. He was superintendent of public schools for over a quarter of a century, and died in office in 1930. He also practiced law at Charlotte.

L. J. Browning (1865—)

Mr. Browning, well over ninety years of age, has been a prominent figure in Dickson County for nearly three quarters of a century. He has held various county political positions, and for many years was cashier of the Dickson County Banking Company.

William Loch Cook

Mr. Cook, who died in 1941, was a circuit judge and later, a member of the state supreme court.

Directors of First National Bank, Dickson

One of the largest banks of the county is the First National, of Dickson. Directors pictured here are, seated, left to right: Graham Robertson, President; D. E. Beasley (deceased), J. B. White, Clerk and Master of Chancery Court; Gordon Mitchell, Assistant Cashier; E. H. Meeks, Jr., Cashier. Standing, left to right: W. M. Rutledge, owner of Rutledge Chevrolet Company; B. F. Nesbitt, optometrist; William T. Stewart, Manager, Stewart Lumber Company; R. A. Freeman, former owner and publisher of the *Dickson County Herald*; W. A. Parker, distributor of Pan-Am products; L. E. Buttrey, merchant; and F. S. Bright.

Manager and office force of Dickson Manufacturing Company

The Dickson Manufacturing Company is one of several industrial establishments in the county. Pictured are, left to right: J. M. Hayes, Manager; Hauty Burch, Forelady; Winifred Shelton, Stenographer; Evelyn Martin, Forelady; Mildred Hutcheson, Head Forelady; Delma Harden, Bookkeeper; Bertha Buttrey, Forelady; Ruby Jordan, Forelady; Bessie Beasley, Forelady; Mary Hall, Forelady; and Lucille Kelly, Forelady.

CHAPTER X

A Socialist Colony Comes and Goes

THE SOCIALIST tradition had been known to the American people for over a half century when in July, 1894, Julius Augustus Wayland led a small band of followers into a thousand acre tract in Dickson County and established the Ruskin Cooperative Association. Of the eighteen thousand people then living in Dickson County, however, the number familiar with the writings of Marx or Fourier or Ruskin probably was quite small, and those familiar with the work and activities of DeLeon, Wayland, and the Americans of kindred spirit probably could have been counted on the fingers of one hand. It is not to be thought strange, therefore, that when the Ruskin colony was established the native Dickson Countians tended to regard it with an air of skepticism. Communal living and unorthodox religious views were things which few if any of them could accept. There was, consequently, little integration between the natives and the followers of Wayland and his interpretations of the writings of John Ruskin, but nevertheless the socialistic experiment remains an important chapter in the history of Dickson County.

The plans for the colony originated in the fertile brain of Wayland completely divorced from any connection with or knowledge of Dickson County. As a matter of fact the sandy-haired, stoop-shouldered newspaper man probably had never heard of the county nor of Yellow Creek when he conceived the adventure.[1] Described by one Marxian historian as "the greatest propagandist of Socialism that has ever lived,"[2] Wayland turned out the first issue of his chief propaganda instrument, *The Coming Nation*, at Greensburg, Indiana, in April, 1893.[3] This paper was to make him and the Dickson County settlement famous.

Wayland was born an Indianian in 1854 and experienced a youth of privation. His father died when he was only three months old and had left his mother penniless. He was apprenticed at an early age to a publisher and while thus serving, his eager mind devoured all printed matter within its grasp. His ambition to become an editor was gratified when at the age of nineteen he became a partner in a printing business.[4] He made money in both real estate and printing and was considered "comfortably fixed" at the age of thirty-nine. He became a close adherent to the Republican Party and was rewarded with a postmastership during the administration of Rutherford B. Hayes. Happiest when in the role of newspaper writer and editor, Wayland devoted most of his time to publishing even though his caustic pen oftentimes got him into trouble and necessitated his moving about not infrequently. The early 1890's found him in Colorado, and during that time he became converted from a "hard-headed Republican" captalist to an ardent Socialist.[5] He plunged wholeheartedly into the Populist campaign of 1892 and published a paper, *The Coming Crisis*, in the interest of the Populist cause. On the eve of the depression of 1893 he disposed of his interests in the West and returned to his native state of Indiana, and to the little town of Greensburg. There on April 28, 1893, he published the first issue of *The Coming Nation* which was to make him known throughout the United States as a "grass roots Socialist." The growth and success of the paper was phenomenal. Six months later it had a paid subscription of 14,000, with new subscriptions pouring in daily.[6] Several new staff members were added from time to time among whom was Rousseau Hess of Akron, Ohio, who became Wayland's business manager and his advance agent into Dickson County to prospect for more favorable quarters.

The citizens of the small town of Greensburg never accepted Wayland and his followers and, according to one authority, avoided "Wayland and his family . . . like the plague. . . ."[7] This was ever galling to the Socialist leader to whom socialism was becoming more and more a god. After publishing sixty-four weekly issues in the small Indiana city, Wayland announced on July 21, 1894, that "The next issue will be published from Tennessee City."[8] In the second week of August, 1894, came the publication of the first issue of the paper from Dickson County. Before this, however, Wayland had publicized the idea of a colony founded upon socialist principles where its members would have peaceful homes, an assured living, and a place for the more ardent to preach the gospel of socialism unhampered by the sneers and jeers of the people like those of Greensburg. To the many people distressed by the panic of 1893 this must have appeared to offer a haven of rest unsurpassed in any other economic system. Proposing to finance it largely by money made from his newspaper, Wayland announced that when the subscription list reached one hundred thousand, by which time the new profits should amount to about $23,000, he would be ready to proceed in earnest. He thought of buying from 3,000 to 4,000 acres in an area where there was plenty of fertile soil and easy accessibility to a railroad. Any person of good moral character who would send to him two hundred subscriptions for his newspaper, or an equal amount in cash, would become a charter member of the colony.[9] He emphasized that one might thus become a member without any expenditure of money.

The subscription list mounted rapidly almost entirely because of the able pen and propaganda methods of Wayland. When capitalists sought to buy advertising space in the paper, which no doubt would have swelled the intake of cash considerably, Wayland would reply proudly that he did not wish to enrich himself at the expense of others while so many of his brothers lay in poverty, hunger, and filth, but that he only desired to make enough to establish his colony successfully, and that this amount could be procured through subscriptions. More and more he advised the reading and careful study of the writings of the English socialist, John Ruskin, who had become his patron saint, and upon whose philosophy he believed the near perfect life might be achieved on this earth.[10] When the subscription list reached 60,000 Wayland announced that he was ready to proceed with his plans for establishing a colony. Cheapness of land in a sparsely populated area where there was plenty of timber and limestone to be worked was of a paramount consideration, and Wayland dispatched his business manager, Hess, in search of such property.

Immediately after the Civil War, as mentioned earlier, many people of the North went to Dickson County and to the South in general in search of cheap land. J. Franck Rumsey of Cook County, Illinois, probably connected with a Chicago Land Company, had bought considerable land in Dickson County with hopes of making profits on speculation if and when an increase in population should make it more valuable. Hess met with Rumsey and others, who proceeded to show him various tracts including the Dickson County property. In early June, 1894, Wayland announced to his readers that Hess had spent several weeks in the South in search of land which would meet the requirements he had stipulated. "He has been in many sections of Tennessee," Wayland advised, "and so far favors the Tullahoma site more than any other."[11] Just why in making the final decision Hess found the Dickson County site more appealing than the Coffee County property is not known, but six days after this announcement, June 15, 1894, Hess closed the deal by which he purchased two tracts of 500 acres each for $2,500.[12] Wayland began immediate plans to shake the dust of Greensburg from his feet and to proceed southward to an area which he hoped would become for him a modern utopia.

The land Hess purchased lay about two miles north of Tennessee City and about forty miles west of Nashville. The Nashville, Chattanooga, and St. Louis Railroad ran through Tennessee City, which was most pleasing to Wayland, who probably believed he was getting a bargain in the land for which he paid Rumsey $2.50 per acre. On July 21, 1894, Wayland and *The Coming Nation* bade farewell to Greensburg and by two weeks later W. H. Lawson, "Pressman and stereotyper," had arrived at the colony site and had set up the press. Wayland, at the head of a small group of disciples, followed immediately. He had given detailed directions for others throughout the country who might desire to join him, and three days after his arrival workmen from diverse areas representing different trades were congregating. At least "one carpenter, one machinist, one barber, one shoemaker, one baker, one blacksmith, . . . one butcher, one cooper, and one laborer" had arrived and others were on their way.[13] Wayland was not overly pleased with the land in general but the fact that it was away from the industrial centers was greatly in its favor. He had much less regard for the "few natives" of the area whom one colonist described as "long, lank, lean Micawbers who had been waiting over forty years for the ground to turn itself up and raise its own crop."[14] A joint stock company was formed with all but six of the male members contributing $500 for which they received one share of stock. Each wife also was granted a share of stock in order to place her on a footing equal to her husband. The corporate name "Ruskin Cooperative Association" was adopted, and a charter was granted by the state.

The colonists found that although they worked hard, the infertile soil yielded little. Too, there was small demand for lumber products or limestone which they hoped to develop. After less than a year in their location they decided to look for more fertile soil which would meet Wayland's other requirements. The nearby bottoms of Yellow Creek appeared to meet their demands, and the creek itself appeared to them as a "small rippling stream of pure crystal-clear water"—something which they did not have at their first settlement.[15] Here they purchased from three Dickson County farmers four tracts of land, which came to be known as the Rogers tracts, the Smith tract, and the Adams tract (taking the names from the men from whom they were purchased), for a total of $16,000. The Rogers land consisted of two fertile tracts of 321 and 62 acres, the Smith tract of 130 acres, and the Adams tract of 284 acres, which made a total of over 800 acres.[16] With renewed hope the Ruskinites now plunged headlong into the task of clearing the land. Especially were they pleased with the two large caves on the property. Not only would they serve as refrigeration for milk, meat, and vegetables, but also as a resort from the summer heat which many of the people from cooler Northern climates found unbearable. The editor of *The Coming Nation* quoted one of the physicians of the colony, Dr. W. H. Charlesworth, as recommending the cave on hot summer afternoons as the best means of avoiding heat prostration. "To go into the big cave out of the hot sunshine, is like stepping at one stride from the Sahara to Siberia," he wrote. "In the roomy entrance . . . you may find just the right temperature in which you can be comfortably cool. . . ."[17] The larger cave had an entrance of 69 feet which opened into a main room of 90 by 250 feet with a ceiling whose lowest point was 40 feet. "The wealth of its myriads of dazzling white stalactites and stalagmites . . . cannot be adequately described by words . . . . Mammoth Cave, of Kentucky . . . does not contain anything like the profusion and delicacy of stalactite formations for which the Ruskin Cave is becoming justly famous," J. K. Calkins wrote in the same issue.

Much of the land hastily was cleared and the colonists went to work with renewed strength in the Yellow Creek bottom land. Although the leaders claimed at all times that there should be adequate time for leisure and contemplation and that the members "are supposed to take time to be human," which the "wage slaves" of the capitalistic system were alleged not to be,[18] the many needs of the association caused them to work long hours each day. Herbert N. Casson who later became editor of *The Coming Nation* described the average workday as follows:

At 5:30 every weekday morning the steam whistle blows three blasts to awaken the sleepers, at 6 it calls them to breakfast, and at 7 it bids everyone go to work. From 12 to 1 is the dinner hour, and at 5 the day's work is over.[19]

According to the editor of *The Coming Nation* the farm yielded abundantly and the settlement became known for farm and garden produce from "Nashville to Memphis."[20] By 1896 the colonists were manufacturing many items which they sold over the nation and even in Europe. The newspaper ran standing advertisements of Ruskin Ready Remedy, "especially recommended and used for years as a certain cure for flesh wounds, cuts, burns, bruises, bites, and an invaluable preparation for throat troubles," which sold for twenty-five cents per bottle. Ruskin suspenders, "durable, comfortable, scientific, economical," were sold for forty and fifty cents, and chewing gum known as "Ruskin Tolu" was sold six packages for twenty-five cents, "postage paid." Apparently the sale of books from a stock which was said to have consisted of thousands of volumes was fairly successful. Bellamy's *Looking Backward*, George's *Progress and Poverty* and *Social Problems*, and Brice's *A Financial Catachism* could be purchased for fifty cents each, while small pamphlets, some of which were written by Ruskin members with titles such as "Coxey's Cause and Cure," "The Cooperative Commonwealth," and "The Class Struggle," could be bought for five cents or less.[21] When it was intimated by critics that things might not be going so well financially at Ruskin the editor of *The Coming Nation* countered with the claim that more was manufactured and sold at Ruskin than at any other community of its size in the country. "Ruskin Tolu, Ruskin Store, Ruskin Caves, Ruskin Hotels, Ruskin Bakery, Ruskin Schools, Ruskin Smithy, Ruskin Library, Ruskin Printery, Ruskin Knittery, Ruskin Sawmill, Ruskin Flour mill, Ruskin Suspenders, Ruskin Shingle mill, Ruskin Ready Remedy—We're getting on fine," he wrote.[22]

A special "Ruskin script" was used in the colony instead of money, the unit being an "hour" rather than a "dollar."[23] Men and women unable to work drew script valued at twenty-five hours per week and children at ten hours per week, but a good worker in robust health might draw several times that amount depending on the number of hours he spent at work. Items in the community store bore a price of "hours" rather than money. A price list published in 1897 reveals the set value of articles in terms of hours of work:[24]

One pound of tea	1 hour	One pair of woman's shoes, best	52½ hours
Three sticks of candy	½ hour	One gallon coal oil	6½ hours
One cut of tobacco	2 hours	One quart peanuts	1 hour
One pair of pants	37 hours	One gallon gasoline	6 hours
One lemon	½ hour		
One pound of coffee	7 hours		

The wants of the people were few and many of the above items were classified as luxuries. Most of the members ate at the community dining hall which encompassed the entire third floor of the Ruskin Association Hall, near the large cave.[25] Food was prepared and served by members to whom this task had been assigned so that the vast majority had no culinary tasks to perform. The individual members had no rent to pay, no taxes, no doctor's bills since doctors lived in and were a part of the colony, and no general household expenditures unless one chose to eat in his own cabin instead of in the community messhall. One member remarked, "The great fear of want for his family does not haunt [us] . . . ."[26] A visitor observed, "The settlement lives as one great family. . . ."[27]

At all times the editors of *The Coming Nation* glorified the common man. ". . . *The Coming Nation* . . . is for the common people first, last, and always," Wayland wrote.[28] Always referring to himself as the "one-hoss editor," Wayland explained that such a title was to indicate that he himself was a laboring man. "I am one of them and proud of that. . . . They are the salt of the earth, and any reform that ever comes must come through them," he wrote.[29] Yet between the individual colonist and the leaders who controlled the colony and the newspaper there appears to have been a great gulf. The ordinary colonist seldom if ever contributed to the paper and apparently had no part in the formulation of an editorial policy for it. Observing that there were not even assemblies to discuss the operation of the colony on the local level, one member noted after the downfall of the colony that "the only forum we had in Ruskin was the Lyceum. All other meetings were forbidden . . . except once a year to elect officers."[30] While the colonists rose early and labored long, it was the printing press which earned the money necessary to keep the colony alive. As long as Wayland remained at the head it seemed to bring in cash in abundance. Financially successful weeks or months would be announced through the press frequently. During the second week of October, 1894, for example, Wayland proudly wrote that the total receipts from the press were $576.80, and boasted, "Who says cooperation is a failure?" The gulf further was apparent in that those who did write for *The Coming Nation* constantly heralded the dawn of a new day erected upon the philosophy of John Ruskin and Edward Bellamy—a thing which probably was not fully understood by the average worker in the colony who toiled from sunup to sundown.

Through their schools, lyceums, newspaper, and tracts and pamphlets which flowed from the printing presses, the leaders spread their gospel of socialism and agnosticism. Never did an issue of *The Coming Nation* appear without one or more references to the social injustices of the day, the blame for which often was heaped upon the shoulders of the religious denominations and ministers. In news items and cartoons the sufferings of the poor were contrasted with the sybaritic existence of the opulent who generally were pictured as fat, lazy men who violated all accepted standards of decency and morality. Typical of the references to social injustices, which appeared as "one-hossisms" as long as Wayland was editor, are:

A Chicago saloon keeper kicked a man to death for refusing to pay for a drink of whiskey—ten cents. Human life is getting pretty cheap when a man is killed for ten cents.

The small storekeeper is doomed. The big stores, handling everything, can and will push him out of the trade and reduce him to beggary.

Ninety suicides in Pittsburg last year. If the desire of people to get out of the world is an indication of the success of this so-called civilization, then it is a howling success. How wise people are to vote for a system of government so beastly that people will kill themselves to get rid of its horrors!

The poor man will not always be willing to fight the rich men's war, or vote the rich men's tickets.

Every strike has been met with military force by the corporations.... The men [should] quit striking and go to voting. By their ballots cast for men who hate private monopolies, the men can control every court and soldiers and militia and use them against the corporations.[31]

Wayland saw a close parallel between conditions in ante-bellum days and his own day and time. The slaves, according to Wayland, had merely changed the color of their skins while the monopolists had shifted from chattel slavery to wage slavery. Although once a member of the Republican Party, Wayland now castigated its leaders for departing from the principles of Abraham Lincoln while at the same time paying lip service to the Great Emancipator. "Chattel slavery debauched the nation . . . but wage slavery has . . . debauched everything. Great corporations buy and sell Congress as so many slaves. They pile up wealth unheard of under wage slavery . . . they defy the constitution, courts, or any other power. . . . They debauch every legislature to elect to the United States Senate members of their corporations. . . . Millions are annually taxed from our people. . . . The rich don't care—they can reduce wages to pay taxes. . . . Will another Lincoln rise up to lead the people to the abolition of wage slavery? I think the time will produce the man."[32] The times indeed were out of joint and the sham and hypocrisy which made the rich richer and the poor poorer seemed to the editors of *The Coming Nation* to be the order of the day.

Schools were not neglected in the colony but it was a socialistic education to which the boys and girls were subjected. An eight-grade day school was maintained. According to W. H. Lawson, the pressman who came with Wayland and who remained in Dickson County after the dissolution of the colony, the teachers were quite competent and tended to emphasize the importance of practical trades in addition to classical education. Especially was this true of Isaac Broome, nationally known sculptor; Dr. W. H. Charlesworth who practiced medicine in Charlotte and Nashville for several decades after the close of the colony; and Dr. Walter Van Fleet, who taught agriculture.[33] In addition to the schools where reading, writing, and arithmetic were taught, there was an art studio, a music studio, an extensive library where most works on socialism could be found, and a lyceum.[34] One of the dreams of the colonists was to establish a college in which to teach their economic doctrines. Such a school they would call "The College of the New Economy." For months announcements were made in *The Coming Nation* accompanied by solicitations for funds and a list of those who already had contributed and offered words of encouragement. In the May 15, 1897, issue appeared the widely heralded announcement that the foundation of the main building was being laid, and the extensive floor plans were spread across the paper. Much publicity was given to a letter from Frank Parsons, a professor at Boston University, who offered to come to Ruskin and teach when the plans were completed. Henry Demarest Lloyd, the crusading muckraker, was called upon to make the main address at the exercises attending the laying of the cornerstone, and this address was published in booklet form and advertised for months afterwards in *The Coming Nation*. "Comrades" everywhere were asked to give according to their ability so that the school might be established without delay. In one accounting much was said of the contribution of one socialist from Topeka, Kansas, who had mailed in a check for $100, and also of eight contributions of twenty-five cents each from eight laborers in Dayton, Ohio.[35] The closing of the colony in 1899 found the "College of the New Economy" far from completion and with little more than a foundation and a cornerstone.

The people of the colony were completely indifferent to organized and formal religious services, and according to one who visited the colony, the great majority were agnostics. No church was maintained, but a few did attend a Methodist church at Edgewood two miles away.[36] The colony leaders were said to have discouraged religious services and denominationalism because, they contended, it would have been impossible to establish a commonwealth of equality where people were divided along theological lines.[37] The editors of *The Coming Nation* periodically condemned organized religion as a tool of the wealthy employed to keep the laborer satisfied with his lowly state in life. In one issue Wayland accused the churches of serving the wealthy while letting the poor starve, and argued that a person cannot worship properly when hungry. "Man can approach Christ—can realize the Christian ideal only through his spiritual nature after his material nature is satisfied," he wrote. Always seeking reform at the ballot box, Wayland urged the ministers of the land to enter politics if they wanted to serve mankind. "The minister does not relieve himself of responsibility when he wraps his clerical robes around himself and cries 'politics,'" he argued. Hinting that theologians taught immortality so that wage slaves would not revolt, Wayland urged more of them to be like Moses who, he argued, did not waste time preaching immortality but preached deliverance from poverty, bondage, and the Egyptian oppressors.[38] He was a natural critic of missionary societies. On one occasion, after noting that money was being sent by churches to Christianize the Africans, he called upon the religious groups to "divert their funds from the well-fed heathens of Africa" and distribute them among the "starving working people of America." "Our own churches have no sympathy for the down-trodden," he moaned, "but sustain a system that makes paupers of millions."[39] The contempt with which he held the ministry, however, is best illustrated by his comment shortly before he departed the colony: "When you hear a minister exhorting his congregation to 'lay up treasures in heaven,'" he wrote, "you can bet he is pretty slick and is doing his utmost to lay up treasures on earth. He is always willing to hear a call to some other point at a greater salary."[40] On the other hand there were times when he indicated that he was not far from the ideal of the golden rule. In an address to the colonists delivered several months after their arrival in Dickson County, Wayland said:

> As you treat others, so will you be treated. If you are kind to them, they will be kind to you. If you care for them in their sickness and distress, they will watch over you in your time of need. But if you have no care for them, if you do not brighten the sick chamber, if you do not share their burdens, no charter, no by-laws, will guarantee you or yours these flowers of life when you are old, or sick or distressed.[41]

Wayland's departure in the summer of 1895 was followed by a lessening of derogatory remarks regarding the ministry, but more emphasis upon a social gospel. Sermons of Herbert N. Casson, a preacher who had left the Methodist church to establish a "Labor church" in Lynn, Massachusetts, came weekly to occupy two columns on the front page of *The Coming Nation*. Casson's usual theme was the evil accompanying the unequal distribution of wealth. "The United States is rich," he would say, but "the poor are everywhere." "If Uncle Sam were to die he could bequeath 164 acres of land and $5,000 to every family," he advised his listeners and readers on one occasion. The "poor ye have always with you" was true only so long as rich men were permitted to monopolize the wealth of the land at the expense of wage slaves.[42] Casson, who left Lynn in 1899 to join the group at Ruskin as editor of *The Coming Nation*, described the religious sentiment of the people, in an article written shortly after his arrival and appearing in a magazine of nationwide circulation, as one of "indifferentism." "The majority of the colonists are indifferent in religion," he wrote. "They call themselves neither orthodox nor infidel. They feel, nevertheless, that their brotherly cooperative life is in perfect harmony with the teachings of Christ."[43]

The people as a whole were a heterogeneous group representing all sections of the country and having diverse backgrounds and inclinations. All were American citizens, but by 1899 twelve different nationalities were represented. Some were little more than bums and hobos, as was Allen Field who became one of the chief trouble makers in the months before the final dissolution of the colony.[44] Others were well educated and cultured people, as was the family of Dr. W. H. Charlesworth, who joined the colony shortly after its organization. Charlesworth was a physician and his wife taught music. Mrs. Irene Charlesworth Johnson, daughter of Dr. Charlesworth, recently recalled that colony life was "pleasant enough." Her mother was required to teach music only in the mornings, and her afternoons were free to devote to practice, her children, or other tasks. She of course had few household duties inasmuch as meals were taken at the community dining hall. To Mrs. Johnson the colony was

> interesting in many ways. For one thing, there were some quite unusual people who joined the colony, which would be natural since it took unusual

and venturesome people to join a venture such as that. Dr. Vanfleet, who originated the famous Vanfleet rose, was a member and I remember him well. He played the clarinet and he and the violinist used to come to our house and my mother would accompany them on the piano.

Another man, a Mr. Edwards, was a Welshman, an editor, and a born actor. We never knew when he was Mr. Edwards and when he was acting the part of someone else, like a little boy goes around playing that he is a tractor, or an Indian. I remember a group of people gathering one evening to hear him read Shakespeare. The meaning was, for the most part, over my head but I remember enjoying the sonance of his reading, and I guess that is part of the enjoyment people get from poetry as well as the meaning.[45]

A series of quarrels culminating in the dissolution of the colony began soon after the colony was established. The "one-hoss editor" must have sensed the impending crisis long before it broke, for he wrote only a few months after the colony was established:

There is no danger to our colony from the outside. If our members have sense enough to hold together, not to allow trifling, petty matters to create dissension, this colony will grow to rival other corporations and all its members will be rich in all the opportunities of life. I have no fear of outside interference, nor quarrels over weighty matters. It is only the meanest, smallest matters that can create dissension and I believe some members of every family is [sic] well enough posted to avoid these little clashes.[46]

A series of quarrels began in the spring of 1895, however, and resulted in Wayland's quitting in disgust before the colony was a year old. The quarrels continued to plague the colony until its close in 1899. When the smoke of battle cleared from every dispute there were two conflicting accounts. The first major rift was between Wayland and other stockholders over the possession of *The Coming Nation*, the paper Wayland had claimed as the "child of my brain and heart."[47] Wayland's opponents termed him an "individualist" who had never surrendered full and complete title of the paper or the presses, but who sought to retain them for himself in order that he might fill his own coffers. Wayland, however, claimed that at the very outset he had deeded to the Ruskin Cooperative Association full title to *The Coming Nation*, but that the bare pittance allowed him by the Association was insufficient to cover full costs. The complete story probably was never printed, but Wayland departed the colony at the end of July, 1895, and shortly thereafter established an even more successful socialist paper which he called *The Appeal to Reason*. Claiming that Wayland had left behind a debt of $3,500, the victorious "loyalists" were able to write that "... when the smoke of battle cleared away there were no individualists left on the grounds to tell the story of their defeat."[48] The "one-hoss editor" left Dickson County never to return. He went first to Kansas City and thence to Girard, Kansas, where he published his *Appeal to Reason* with the same phenomenal success that he had published *The Coming Nation*. Here he continued as an exponent of grass roots socialism until his death by suicide in 1912.[49]

The remaining members of the Association continued to carry on, although they were forced to admit that the "contest between individualism and cooperation shook the very foundations of the Colony." An editorial board temporarily assumed the editorship of the paper in Wayland's place, and repeatedly assured its readers that the stability and future of Ruskin had not been damaged, but that the people were "united and happy." Claiming that Wayland had offered them the choice "of tolerating . . . the private ownership of the means of production or losing Brother Wayland," they had been forced to sever Wayland's connections.[50] What they actually had done, however, had been to open a Pandora's box of troubles which haunted them to the very end. It was another case of Jerusalem stoning her prophets.

The editorship of the paper was assumed for a short while by A. S. Edwards, who earlier had been closely associated with Wayland but who became his bitter enemy. In early 1899 Herbert N. Casson, the Socialist minister who had formed a "Labor church" in Massachusetts, became editor. He had been expelled from the Socialist Labor Party in 1896 for certain irregularities, and two years later had wandered southward to join the Ruskin Association. For quite some time he had kept in close contact with Ruskin, and his sermons had appeared weekly on the front page of *The Coming Nation*. In the fall of 1897 he went to England and there had observed that "in all the large towns in Great Britain . . . [were] readers and admirers of *The Coming Nation*. Many told me it was the ablest Socialist paper they had ever seen."[51]

The Coming Nation and the colony appear never to have been the same after Wayland's departure, although they remained in their Dickson County location for three more years. During this period the colony continued to be wracked with dissension and unrest. Factions soon developed and each group vied with the other in heaping violent criticisms upon one another. One faction led by a colonist named Cowell was accused of seeking to dispense with the institution of marriage in order to employ practices of "free love" and "sexual promiscuity." Cowell admitted only that he had been interested in a paper called *The Fire Brand* which had advocated anarchism and free love. The paper had been forbidden the use of the mails, and had against it at that time a large number of suits by offended parties. Cowell had sought to raise money within the colony to aid in the defense of the paper, and was said to have had a small group of followers at Ruskin.[52] The Cowell group failed to make much headway but did arouse some indignation among the non-colony people of the area. Soon thereafter a strike among the pressmen occurred which was settled only when the foreman was removed.

The dissension, termed the "straw which broke the camel's back" and which resulted in the dissolution of the colony, began late in 1898 or early in 1899. It was said to have been caused by Allen Field, whom Charter Member W. H. Lawson described as a hobo. Field had come to the colony with nothing more than his carpenter's tools, but he had been a close friend of Wayland, who had taken him in and given him a share of stock. The charter members had conferred upon their wives a share of stock also, but wives of later joiners had not received this benefit, and Field's wife was in the latter category. Believing that they had been discriminated against, Field and a sizable group led a movement to issue more shares of stock so that each wife might own one regardless of when her husband joined the colony. This was opposed by the charter members, who sought court injunctions to prevent additional shares of stock from being issued, and they became known as the "injunctionists" in the bitter quarrel. Finally, seeing that they would be unable to depose the Field group, they brought action seeking the dissolution of the colony and were joined by various creditors of the Association.[53]

In the meantime there were those who tried to stem the tide of destruction which slowly was creeping over the settlement. The teacher and sculptor, Isaac Broome, addressed the Association on May 10, 1899, and he called for a "return" to a spirit of cooperation. "What ability and good judgment there may be existing among us cannot be brought forward because the principle of cooperation does not exist in Ruskin," he said. "Everything seems to be decided on and done by a few men, or one man. The Association is practically a despotism."[54] Herbert N. Casson, now editor of *The Coming Nation*, sought to represent to the world outside that all was going well in Ruskin. Writing in *The Independent* in January, 1899, he described Ruskin as being "one of the most unique and influential communities in America." Boasting that it then consisted of 250 colonists and was "steadily increasing," Casson pointed to the "great" material wealth of the colony. There were 22 mules and horses, 45 cattle, 12 sheep, 18 hives of bees, 150 pigs, and 1,000 chickens, he advised, and the total possessions he claimed to have a value of $78,000. The free love group and anarchist faction had been weeded out, he indicated, for he pointed to the fact that before one could become a member he must be a Socialist and be opposed to anarchy and free love.[55] Late in July, 1899, however, the dissenters who were now called the "Injunctionists" and among whom were the few remaining charter members, succeeded in having the assets of the colony placed in the hands of a receiver and the property sold and divided among the stockholders. The result was a legal battle which monopolized the Chancery Court of Dickson County for several years. It ended in financial disaster for both parties but financial victory for the lawyers and court officials and for some Dickson Countians who were able to purchase the land and farm equipment for a fraction of its cost and worth. By this time the Ruskin group had invested over $18,500 in real estate alone, and had improved much of the land. Several score buildings had been erected, and the property had been stocked with cattle, sheep, and hogs. Herbert Casson, the newspaper editor, had estimated the total value of the real estate and personal property at nearly $100,000. The Association at that time consisted of approximately 138 members each of whom had invested $500.

H. J. Bowers, Charlotte lawyer, was named receiver in June, 1899, but his ill health made necessary the appointment of W. Blake Leech, young Charlotte lawyer, as special receiver. The parties decided upon

July 27 as the date for the sale of the property, and by sunrise of that day hundreds of curiosity seekers and farmers seeking bargains had congregated in the Ruskin property. Sheriff W. R. Hudson cried off the sale, at which fine horses were sold for as little as $9, and hogs which on the market would have brought $20 to $30 per head went for $5 to $10.[56] The rest of the personal property was sold and likewise brought only a fraction of its worth. The real property sold even more poorly. The receiver showed that the Rogers tracts were encumbered with a mortgage of $3,000 held by Jacob Leoffel, and the Smith tract by a mortgage of $2,000 held by Henry Jacobs, and the Adams tract by a mortgage of $900, but nevertheless the sales on the first day were not overly disappointing. Ransom Leech, as trustee for the minority group, or "Injunctionists," bid $11,000 for the Rogers, Smith, and Adams tracts (now known collectively as "New Ruskin"), and George Wright bid $1,458 for the thousand acres of the area of the first settlement, now known as "Old Ruskin." By August 24, J. R. McClelland had advanced Wright's bid to $2,300, and W. A. Bell had raised the price of a small shack in Hortense from $20 to $26. The sad part for the Ruskinites, however, was that those who bid did not comply with their terms, and the Chancellor was forced to reopen the sale and call for new bids. Finally Thomas Rogers was permitted to purchase the four tracts for $1,505—a small fraction of the original cost and the many improvements—although the attorneys excepted and argued vigorously that the amount was inadequate. The final report of the receiver filed in chancery court in March, 1901, indicated that $10,529.39 was the total sum collected by him from all sales. This would mean that the property which Casson had estimated to be worth near $100,000 brought little over $17,000 when the value of the mortgages is included. As the colony's creditors over the nation learned of the suit they, too, filed suits in order to become parties and to participate in the assets. The receiver's report showed that less than $5,000 went to the stockholders of the colony, although they had claims amounting to nearly $70,000. This amount was prorated among them and the share of each approximated $36. Some stockholders had borrowed on their shares, and many had assigned them to H. C. McDill, W. H. Charlesworth, and others. When the division was made some of the stockholders received as little as one dollar since they had borrowed on their shares. The creditors received $1,276.06, and the court costs amounted to $388.16. It was the lawyers who walked off with the lion's share from the long and involved litigation. Bowers was allowed a fee of $700 as receiver, and Blake Leech $275 as special receiver. The Charlotte law firm of T. C. Morris and W. L. Cook received a fee of $150, while Ransom L. Leech, Hardin Leech, and John A. Pitts collectively received the fat sum of $1,400.[57]

The majority group bought *The Coming Nation*, and this remnant of the badly torn Ruskin Cooperation Association moved with the newspaper which they hoped would continue to be their meal ticket to Ware County, Georgia, where they sought to reestablish a socialist colony on the Ruskin principle. They claimed that they had received offers on "very favorable terms" from the commissioners of immigration of Virginia, Georgia, and Alabama, but believed that the Georgia site offered the most advantages.[58]

Believing that they had contributed much to the world despite their apparent lack of success, the Ruskinites heralded that the Dickson County settlement, even in failure, "may be a valuable contribution to the lesson of the great reform movement shaking the world to its very center."[59]

In one of the last issues of *The Coming Nation* published in Dickson County, the editors continued to pay lip service to the ideals of cooperation. "In the spirit of brotherhood, let us reason and plan together for the future," they editorialized. "Ruskin says, 'It is useless to put your heads together if you cannot put your hearts together. Shoulder to shoulder . . . and you'll win the world yet.' "[60]

Many of those who had been associated with the colony did not follow the leaders to Georgia, but remained in Dickson County. W. H. Lawson was one of these, and in 1932 he was operating Jewell Cave, a scenic spot not far from Ruskin where picnics and dances were held periodically.[61] Many were able to find work at Cumberland Furnace. Tents hastily were set up for those wanting to work, and R. H. Stone no doubt considered that he had gotten a bargain in labor from the disillusioned and defeated Ruskin group. One of their number who went North and secured employment with Peoples' Institute Settlement of Chicago, wrote of the unhappy furnace workers as follows: "they are to become the wage slaves of a contractor to the furnace company. Their job is getting out wood for charcoal. . . . Many of these men have never done hard manual labor before. . . . Not a professional axeman [among them]. . . . The great, proud, cooperators of Ruskin [are] rushing for a miserable chance to slave."[62]

Several appraisals were made of the colony after its downfall. One of the most critical was that of Professor Broome who had taught school at the settlement. In a small book published in 1903 Broome presented a brief history of the colony and pointed to some of its defects. He believed too much emphasis had been placed upon the gaining of material things, that there had been too much extravagance, too little knowledge of business procedure and practicality, too much reliance upon mendacity, and too little of a spirit of cooperation. The financial situation became such that on several occasions the colony was on the verge of dissolution when a new colonist would appear with a $500 membership fee. "Here comes another $500. Thank God, Ruskin is saved," the president was alleged to have exclaimed on more than one occasion.[63] Broome presented figures to show that the large claims of membership were grossly exaggerated. Ruskin had hundreds of visitors from time to time but not many fee-paying members. At the time of dissolution in 1899 Broome claimed that there were only 85 shareholders, but chancery court records indicate that there were more. The following table taken from Broome's book is helpful, although it is probably not entire accurate:[64]:

Year	Number Admitted	Number who withdrew	Died	Members remaining on June 22, 1899 from those who had joined in given years
1894	26	21	2	3
1895	33	29	0	4
1896	30	14	0	16
1897	30	14	0	16
1898	37	7	0	31
1899	15	0	0	15

Broome insisted that although the membership continued to increase slightly, the circulation of *The Coming Nation* and the spirit and interest of the people of the colony steadily declined.

J. W. Braam made a more objective appraisal in the same year in an article appearing in the *American Journal of Sociology*.[65] Braam and Broome were in agreement in that they believed that one important cause of the downfall was the utter lack of experience in business matters and the gross extravagance of the colony leaders. Hess had paid too much for the land in the beginning, Braam alleged, when he paid $2.50 an acre for land which any Dickson County farmer could have told him was worth only the timber, since the hard-pan soil would produce very little. Braam pointed to many other mistakes, such as the purchase of $2,000 worth of woodworking machinery which no colonist could effectively operate. There was always a distorted picture presented by the leaders of the colony, Braam argued, which exaggerated the conditions in an effort to obtain more contributions and more members.[66]

The Nashville *Banner* and the Nashville *American* passed judgment at the time of dissolution, although both papers had ignored the colony heretofore. "It is certain that the experiment being tried . . . in the name of socialism must have written over its grave the one-word epitaph—'failure,' " a reporter for the *American* wrote. But yet a lesson had been learned. "More good will come to the cause of socialism by a new effort, in which the defects which worked the ruin of the former experiment may be avoided," it was stated.[67] The *Banner* expressed regrets but no surprise at the failure of the colony. The editor of that paper saw in the colony

a commendable and harmless enterprise, which, however, lacked the substantial conditions for success. The socialistic cooperative community plan may be pretty enough in theory to satisfy the minds of some people of its practicality but there are inherent defects that cannot fail of operating disadvantageously. One defect in the system is the disregarding of the relative values of labor and of service. If the contributions of all the members of the socialist community were of like value in the development of the general interests the plan might be made practicable, but any system which ignores the gradations of talent and skill and the comparative worth of labor is essentially unjust and cannot be made the basis of a successful permanent social order.[68]

Mrs. Irene Charlesworth Johnson who as a child lived with her parents at the colony saw as the basic cause for the dissolution a people living under two irreconcilable laws at the same time. Like Abraham Lincoln in the pre-Civil War days, she would argue that "a house divided against itself cannot stand."

Whatever the ostensible cause of the break-up of the colony, [she wrote] in my opinion it bore the seeds of its dissolution in its very being. It was an attempt at carrying out one economic order in a limited sphere, surrounded by, and under the general laws of, an entirely different economic order. It was not basically a question of the right or wrong of either order. It was a matter of the impossibility of any community living under two irreconcilable laws at the same time. To expect that is as naive as to think the free world can ever be "buddies" with the men of the Kremlin.[69]

Within a few weeks after the sale of the property the remnant of the group moved to Ware County, Georgia, where they pledged to engage more in manufacturing and less in agriculture. They met with even less success in Georgia, however, than they did in Dickson County. On June 13, 1902, *The Coming Nation*, the newspaper which for so long had been the meal ticket of the colony, was moved to Rich Hill, Missouri, and by early 1903 the Ruskin group in Ware County, Georgia, had disintegrated. *The Coming Nation* was unsuccessful at Rich Hill and on January 1, 1904, it came to rest with its founder and creator, Julius Augustus Wayland, who merged it with his *Appeal to Reason*, then being published in Kansas.[70]

After the Ruskin Cooperative Association left Dickson County a college was established on the grounds, and remained until the early 1920's. In more recent times the grounds have been operated as a picnic and resort area with only small success.

CHAPTER XI

Educational Development

ONE OF THE most interesting and important subjects in the history of any county is education. Enlightened people, knowing the advantages which accrue to those having a knowledge of the rudiments, have sought to procure for their children an acquaintance with at least the fundamentals of reading, writing, and arithmetic. Such was true of the people of Dickson County from the earliest days. Although it is to be admitted that public education in Tennessee and throughout the South has lagged behind that of some other states and sections of the country, that point has been highly exaggerated. Although all efforts before the Civil War to establish a permanent public school system in Tennessee accomplished little, private schools and academies did much toward educating the people. No satisfactory public educational system was established in the state until after the conclusion of the Brownlow regime, but the matter had not gone unnoticed. As early as 1815 the legislature had passed an act which provided for the free education of orphans without means. Seven years later an act was passed looking toward the establishment of a public school system, and providing that such would be financed from the revenues and taxes accruing from public lands. Supplementary acts were passed by the legislatures of 1825 and 1827, but unfortunately they were worded in such a manner as to impress upon the citizenry that a public school was a pauper's school, and no one wanted to be tagged with the stigma of poverty. These acts were never carried out to any extent, and in 1838 another bill was passed which established a public school system. Nine hundred eighty-seven school districts were established in the state, and a census was taken of boys and girls between the ages of six and twenty-one and indicated a school population of 185,432. The state was to provide 62½ cents per student, and the county was to provide the rest of the necessary revenue. Although the aims of the legislators were laudatory, such hindrances as lacks of experience, differences of opinions, and ignorance in general caused few tangible results to accrue for the next two decades. Nothing was done during the Civil War, and in the bitterness and confusion of the immediate postwar years public education was permitted to languish, until the passage of the public school law of 1873.

In the meantime preachers and teachers continued to establish private schools. Many of them maintained an excellent faculty, offered a variety of subjects, and had a most salutary effect upon the people of the communities in which they were located. Probably the first school to be established in Dickson County, private in nature, was organized by Alexander Campbell on the forks of Piney River in the southwestern part of the county. Campbell taught his twenty-five pupils the fundamentals of reading, writing, and arithmetic. Several other schools were established contemporaneously. An Englishman named James Scott, a thorough scholar and competent teacher, conducted one near Campbell's school. Two others, taught by Jesse Ross and John Donnegan, stood somewhere in the Piney River-Turkey Creek vicinity. The date of the operation of these schools is not known, but probably was during the first two decades of the nineteenth century.[1] Schools and libraries went hand in hand, and it is interesting to note that the first library in the state to be established in a rural county was founded at Charlotte in 1815. In that year a legislative act was passed incorporating the "Dickson Library Company," and designating the third Monday in December, 1815, as the date for the organizational meeting. Five directors were to be elected at the meeting. Two years later the company was still functioning and electing officers.[2]

It was not until the 1820's that schools were operating in Charlotte. An academy was authorized for the town as early as 1806, and in 1807 a board of trustees, consisting of Michael Molton, Richard C. Napier, Christopher Strong, Molton Dickson, William Stone, Montgomery Bell, and Robert Jarman, was appointed. Clearing the wilderness and establishing homes came first, however, and nearly two decades elapsed before the school functioned successfully. It was in the early 1820's that construction of a school plant was begun on East Street just north of what would have been the intersection of East and Brewer Streets had the latter street been made to intersect with East as originally planned. There the school remained as a bulwark of education for over a century.

Jacob Voorhies, mentioned in an earlier chapter, came to the county from New Jersey around 1820, and was instrumental in the establishment of a classical school in Charlotte. In 1823 an announcement signed by P. W. Humphrey, John C. Collier, Sterling Brewer, and C. Robertson, trustees, appeared in a Nashville paper stating that an academy had been "lately established" in Charlotte. Its course of study was largely classical, with emphasis upon Latin, Greek, French, and English. A "Mr. Caleb" had been employed to teach students desiring courses in English, the announcement stated, while Voorhies was to conduct all other courses. Costs were moderate. A student might enroll in the "higher branches" for thirty dollars per academic year, while courses in reading and writing would be only ten dollars. The price of board and maintenance ranged from sixty to eighty dollars for the school year. The trustees described the institution as being one of the best of its type in the country, and invited "persons residing at a distance" to send their children to the school where they would be given a "liberal education" at "very moderate terms." Many advantages of life in Charlotte were pointed out. The town was described as being

> situated in the state of Tennessee, about forty miles distant from the Cumberland, and the same distance from Harpeth river; in a high, dry country, the atmosphere pure and serene, free from fogs and other noxious vapours. The town is abundantly supplied with the purest spring water; and if health depends upon local situation, it may be reasonably presumed to exist at Charlotte. During the last two or three years past, when disease in various forms has pervaded most of the towns in the United States, the people of this place have enjoyed good health.... The Supreme, Circuit, and Equity courts, which are held here, bring to the place men of learning and talents from other parts of the state, whose conversation and investigation of causes in court, may add to the sources of mental improvement.[4]

The school which came to better known than any other in the county was Tracy Academy. The plant was constructed of brick and was one of the best in Middle Tennessee. Valentine S. Allen owned the land upon which the building stood until 1842, at which time he deeded it to the board of trustees which then included John C. Collier, Theodore L. Collier, and William Balthrop.[5] Many courses were offered. In addition to the basic subjects of reading, writing, arithmetic, and English grammar, studies in the classical languages and higher mathematics were available for those with the necessary backgrounds. The names of many of the early teachers are not known, and for some only the last names are remembered. Among the first were a Professor McGuiggan, a Mrs. Richardson, and a Miss Farley. Professor Ebenezer Erskine Larkins, who devoted nearly a half century to teaching in public and private institutions of Middle Tennessee, was one of the best known of the early faculty members. Born and reared in what is now Houston County, Larkins came as a young man during the 1830's to take charge of Tracy, and for most of the next half century served either as teacher or principal. The Academy continued into the twentieth century. It was not until 1907 that Trustees C. H. Underhill, J. A. Hickerson, and A. G. Castleman conveyed Tracy to the county board of education, then composed of S. E. Hunt, J. D. Smith, E. H. Stone, T. M. Harper, and E. H. Tidwell. The building was used for educational purposes until the early 1920's, when the property was sold and another school building was built a quarter of a mile north of the original location.[6] The quality of work done at Tracy was comparable to that done today in senior high schools and junior colleges, and many no doubt graduated with a better knowledge of the English language and English literature than do many college graduates of today.

Another well-known private school was established on Barton's Creek in 1843. It was known as "Cloverdale," and was founded by W. B. Bell. Bell's father had come to America from Ireland in the 1700's, after having participated in an Irish rebellion against the oppression of the English. Some members of the Bell family went to Cornplanter, Pennsylvania, some to Virginia, while others came to Dickson County. Bell was well educated, and established at Cloverdale a first-class school.

He was assisted by his sister, Anne Jane, who had studied in England before coming to America. Cloverdale operated continously from its formation until 1899, except for a brief period during the Civil War. It ranked with Tracy in the quality of work done, and offered a variety of courses. A gradebook for 1884 indicates that students were enrolled in many courses, including Latin, Greek, French, German, philosophy, surveying, geology, higher mathematics including calculus, and a variety of music courses including piano, organ, guitar, and mandolin. A reporter from the Nashville *Union and American* visited the graduation exercises in 1872 and expressed amazement at the proficiency of the students. D. R. Leech delivered the graduation address, after which

Professor J. C. Armstrong with his classes in lingual lore entertained us in such a manner that we don't wonder at his being sent to expound the good book to the Grand Turk [the reporter wrote]. Miss Nancy Coldwell, of Shelbyville, presided over the musical department . . . [which rendered selections that would] vie with ye grand coming jubilee.[7]

In all of his statements to students Bell was careful to point out that his institution was "not simply a finishing school," but also "taught that there is no excellence without labor."[8]

Tuition was sufficiently low at the private schools for almost anyone who wanted an education to attend in comfort. In 1876 it was reported that tuition averaged $1.33 per month at most of the schools in the county. Board and room were equally inexpensive. As late as 1897 a student could obtain board and room, which included washing, lights, fuel, and so forth, for as little as $10 per month at Cloverdale.[9]

For a few years after the public school law of 1838, public, or "common," schools tended to flourish. The census of 1840 indicates that in the preceding year 444 students attended a dozen schools scattered throughout the area. In these schools the state bore part of the expense, but not all except in cases where the child was an orphan without support or the child of a pauper. The county was divided into ten districts, and one or more schools were operated in all the districts except three.[10] After state support was curtailed several years later, many of the schools continued to exist as private institutions.

The recorded wills of the ante-bellum period mutely testify to the interest in education of a people among whom nearly one fifth were illiterate. Christopher Strong bequeathed thousands for educational purposes. He willed $7,400 to Clark and Erskine College (now Erskine College) in South Carolina, part of which was to be invested and to "serve as a perpetual fund for the education of indigent young men who are preparing for the Gospel Ministry in the Associated Reform Church." To his great-grandsons, Charles Betts and Joseph Dickson, he willed his extensive library and provided that each should receive a "liberal education . . . at the preparatory schools and colleges under the care of the Associated Reform Church" if either or both carried out their expressed desire to enter the ministry of that church.[11] William Matlock, after directing that his funeral expenses be paid, commanded that the rest of his property should go to his wife for the purpose of enabling her "to raise and school [his] younger children who have but little education. . . ." Jacob Lampley directed his executor to sell all property of which his wife had no immediate need, and "to put that money to the use of schooling my children. . . ."[12] These wills, written during the 1850's, and many others written before and after that date, testify to the interest of the Dickson County people in education. A will benefiting public education more than any other in the early years was that of Spencer T. Hunt, written in 1843. Hunt owned extensive properties in Dickson and Humphreys counties, and had lived in both counties. In December, 1843, several weeks before his death, he wrote a will in which he provided:

> After the death of my said wife, Mary, I hereby devise and bequeath the whole of my estate, both real and personal, to the Comptroller of the Treasury of the State of Tennessee and his successors in office to the use and benefit of the common school fund of the Counties of Dickson and Humphreys to be applied to the benefit of common schools in said counties as the law may allow other school funds to be applied; that is to say that my desire is . . . funds arising from the sale of my estate in the Bank of Tennessee to be loaned as other funds in said Bank are loaned out and the interest arising thereon to be annually paid over to the common school Commissioners for the counties of Dickson and Humphreys to be applied provided it be practicable. . . .[13]

Hunt's wife apparently did not live long thereafter, for in 1848 a resolution was passed in the state legislature directing the comptroller of the treasury to proceed as early as practicable in collecting the money designated, and in investing it in bonds of the state of Tennessee for the use of the schools of the two counties.[14] The money proved of great value through the years in the educational program of Dickson County.

The Civil War caused the closing of the schools, since all who could shoulder a musket marched off to war and those who could not did necessary work at home, as all of the people steeled themselves to resist the invader. The stress and strain of the post-Civil War period made the re-opening of schools most difficult. Even by 1869, four years after the rigors of war had ceased, only about forty per cent of the people of school age were enrolled in schools of Dickson County. Being enrolled did not mean that they were regular in attendance. The fact that the government was in the hands of the Brownlow regime from 1865 to 1869 caused much discontent and lack of interest in almost everything the state attempted, including even the school program. This was due in some measure to the fact that the program was headed by John Eaton, Jr., a Federal military officer, who advocated the education of the blacks and whites together in the same schools. Eaton, while well educated and able, never gained the confidence of the people of the state. T. F. McCreary, superintendent of schools in Dickson County in 1869, reported to the state superintendent that "our people have . . . much distrust about the state officers doing their legal duty in the matter of paying over to the schools the tax which was levied and collected for schools. . . ."[15] The overthrow of the Republicans and the election of Democratic Governor Brown and a strong Democratic house and senate in 1871 restored the confidence of the people in their state government, and plans looking toward the establishment of a public school system were begun at once. In 1873 the legislature passed a law which became the basis for the present system of public education. It provided for a permanent school fund of over two million dollars, the interest from which was to go for school purposes. An enabling act assessing a poll tax was passed, and although it was inoperative for some years thereafter, the proceeds from it were earmarked for educational purposes. The law further provided that school districts be set up in each county, and that directors for them be appointed. By 1876 County Superintendent Leonard L. Leech was able to present a picture radically different from the one McCreary had presented a few years before. Leech, who according to his own testimony had "devoted the best years of ... [his] life to teaching," noted with pride the great amount of interest in public education which had developed within the past few years. He also ponited with pride to marked improvements in attendance, observing that the average daily attendance was the highest he had ever known in the county. He paid especial tribute to the public interest in education. "No one ... has opposed the increase in taxes purely for school purposes," he reported. He stated that all districts except one were completely out of debt. This he partly attributed to the funds made available to the county by the will of Spencer T. Hunt. "The children of Dickson and Humphreys counties are erecting a monument to the memory of Spencer T. Hunt that will be perpetuated, I trust, for generations to come," he wrote. Many improvements of a material nature had been accomplished. Ten new school buildings had been erected during the past year, bringing the total to 24 log structures and 16 frame ones. Thirty-seven white teachers of which 30 were men, and eight Negroes of which six were men, composed the corps of teachers of the county. During the year each had taught sixty days, and collectively they had received salaries amounting to $2,226.65. Leech was paid $250 per annum for his services. There were then in existence, the superintendent observed, twenty private schools having an enrollment in 1875 of nearly 500 pupils, who paid an average of $1.33 per month tuition. Many of the private schools were in the process of consolidating or ceasing operation entirely in order to make room for the public schools, but their principals indicated no malice against the public schools. "If any collision has ever occurred between the academies and the public schools, I do not remember it," the superintendent reported.[16]

Ten years later Superintendent B. F. Harris observed many additional improvements. The school year had been increased to four months, most of the teachers' salaries were increased to $20 per month, and the county had levied a tax of $1.75 per $100 of assessed property valuation for school purposes. "We are making some progress in our schools," Harris reported. Although some of the teachers were incompetent, the majority of them were "first-class teachers, both ladies and gentlemen ... and they are doing some good work for the cause of education," he said. The number of private schools had then dwindled to four, while the number of public schools had swelled to ninety. One brick, 30 frame, and 59 log plants had been constructed, and collectively were valued at $4,000. Two frame buildings had been built during the past year, each at a cost of $100. Over $600 worth of equipment was provided the schools. Ninety teachers, including fifty white and ten Negro males, and twenty-five white and five Negro women, were paid a total of $5,840 during the year. The superintendent's salary was now $200 per year.[17] Superintendent W. G. McMillan protested against the low salary during his term in 1882, and believed it should be such that one could devote his full time to the duties of office. He had found much public spirit in 1882, and believed that "many of our best citizens and largest taxpayers are desirous of increasing the taxes sufficient to extend them to five months." He probably believed that out of such interest should come sufficient funds for a salary increase, but none did, as Harris in 1886 was being paid less than was Leech in 1876. Harris noted in 1887 that each year brought increasingly less dissatisfaction among the patrons of the schools. This he attributed largely to the quality of teachers in Dickson County, whom he believed ranked "with the best in the state."[18]

In April, 1895, one of the first teachers' institutes to be held in the county convened in Dickson for a two-day session. It was conducted by T. B. Loggins and W. T. Wade, about whom more will be said presently.[19] The institutes for that day and time, while primarily for the instruction of the teachers, were really neighborhood mass meetings at which leaders from various fields of endeavor were called upon to make speeches on educational subjects. The speeches were intended to arouse interest among the teachers and such patrons who might attend. The following year Superintendent Agnes Shipp, the only woman ever to serve in this position in the county, reported that county institutes were being held monthly. The school term now extended to four and one-half months, and teachers were paid $25 per month. The superintendent's salary had been raised to $225 per year. A variety of subjects were taught in the schools, including spelling, reading, writing, arithmetic, English grammar, geography, United States history, Tennessee history, vocal music, elocution, geology, agriculture, algebra, plane geometry, natural philosophy, bookkeeping, hygiene, civics, and higher English. Some new schools had been established, while others had been consolidated. Of the 89 school buildings, 52 were log, 36 were frame, and one was brick. By 1896 a tendency can be observed, which was to continue to the present, for more women to enter the teaching profession and for more men to leave it. In 1896 there were 55 men and 45 women, while ten years earlier the number had been 60 men and 30 women. Also a decline in the number of log structures and an increase in frame buildings may be seen by that year.[20]

At the turn of the century, by which time S. E. Hunt was superintendent, the school population and average daily attendance had increased tremendously from what it had been ten years previously. "I will say that the outlook for the schools of Dickson County is favorable," Hunt wrote. In the preceding year a uniform text-book law had been passed, which proved to be of great assistance to school administrators and patrons over the state. Hunt was succeeded in office by B. C. Gilbert of White Bluff, who was replaced by R. E. Corlew. He served from 1903 to 1905, and again from 1907 to the time of his death in 1930. His quarter century in office was a fruitful one marked with much improvement in the public school system of the county.

As has been mentioned, the establishment of a public school system caused many of the private schools to consolidate or cease to operate altogether. Among the last to succumb was Cloverdale, which closed its doors in 1899. Perhaps more attention centered around a private school which was established toward the beginning of the public school program than any others. This was Edgewood, established on Yellow Creek in 1885 by Professor W. T. Wade and certain interested citizens of the Yellow Creek community. Five years later it was moved to Dickson where, as Dickson Normal College, it became one of the outstanding institutions of the state in the preparation of teachers for the public schools.

The Edgewood Normal originated in the minds of a dozen prominent families living in the Yellow Creek neighborhood. Realizing the need for education above the elementary level, they decided to establish a school of their own provided it could be staffed with competent men. W. T. Wade, a Virginia native then teaching in Humphreys County, had been recommended by some to be a proper individual to head the school, and J. C. Hunt and others hastened to Waverly to meet him. To their delight he agreed to come, and in 1885 the school began in a one-room building. Wade had among his first forty pupils several who later gained prominence, among whom were Dr. W. W. Slayden, S. E. Hunt, Walter Guerin of Los Angeles, and Dr. Claud Guerin of Nashville. Community interest mounted considerably after the first year, and sufficient money was pledged for the construction of a large two-story building. It then became a boarding school, as the entire second floor came to be used as a girls' dormitory and the first floor as classrooms and library. Also at the beginning of the second year Professor T. B. Loggins was added to the staff, and he came to acquire a half interest in the school shortly after he joined the faculty. By 1890 the fame of the institution was being spread abroad, and the original number of students, forty, had been increased to over 400. Boys and girls came from over the entire South, and in 1890 twenty-three states were represented. Many people moved into the community for the purpose of educating their children. The chief feature of attraction appeared to be Professors Wade and Loggins. Well educated men whose hearts were in their work, these personable educators exhibited great skill in business matters and in the art of instruction. Neither was a Dickson County native. Wade was born and reared in Lynchburg, Virginia, and was educated at the National Normal University, Lebanon, Ohio. Loggins was a Mississippi native and a graduate of the Glasgow (Kentucky)

Normal College. He did additional work at the National Normal University. The latter school conferred upon both Wade and Loggins honorary Master of Arts degrees as an award for their distinct contribution to education in Dickson County.

In the midst of the educational prosperity, gloom came to Edgewood. The great interest manifested in the school began to cause Professors Wade and Loggins to look for a more favorable location. In the course of their search they were visited by representatives from the town of Dickson, who sought to impress upon them the possibilities afforded by the rapidly growing town, which lay some 16 miles southeast of Edgewood. A school known as Dickson Academy had been established there several years before under a Professor Johns and a Professor Osborne, but it showed none of the promise of success which the Edgewood school had indicated. The citizens of Dickson were willing to pledge more in a material way than could the people of the Yellow Creek community. Furthermore, Dickson offered transportation facilities that Edgewood could not match. Wade and Loggins were convinced of the advantages of a move and made plans to establish a school in Dickson in time to open for the September, 1891, term. Their decision caused considerable distress among the people of Yellow Creek, many of whom had moved near the school solely for the purpose of educating their children. In an open letter published in the *Dickson County Press* in April, 1891, J. C. Hunt accused the schoolmen of bad faith. They had given every indication that the institution would have its permanent location at Edgewood, Hunt alleged, but at the same time they had "been carrying on their negotiations with Dickson in a secret and surreptitious manner." In doing so Hunt charged, they had violated "every principle of honor and fair dealing."[21]

The allegations and bitterness did not deter Wade and Loggins, however, who proceeded with plans for moving to Dickson. In September of 1891 they opened the first session of Dickson Normal College. Twelve acres in east Dickson had been purchased for a thousand dollars an acre, and five buildings had been erected. Several of the building were dormitories, for some of the boys and most of the girls were "boarding school students." Professor Loggins and family lived in one of the dormitories, and several of the members of the faculty also lived on the campus. Most of the classes met in Girls' Hall, which offered additional classroom facilities. A variety of subjects, including English, Latin, Greek, mathematics, bookkeeping, commercial subjects, elocution, music, penmanship, and telegraphy, composed the curriculum. The number of applications for admission far exceeded the facilities even at the beginning, and plans hastily were made for expanding the plant before the beginning of the next session. In the summer of 1892 a large brick building was erected, the faculty was expanded, and the Dickson Normal school was well on its way toward becoming one of the best in the state.

In the meantime the citizens of Edgewood were not idle. They had spent thousands of dollars and countless hours in the establishing of a school in their community, and while they could not compel Wade and Loggins to return, they could and did continue operation of the school as best they could under the old name of Edgewood Normal. The institution was placed in the hands of Professors Hunt and Tubb, men whom the editor of the *Dickson County Press* described as "Young gentlemen of a high order of talent, large experience as teachers and [who] will beyond doubt maintain the high character of Edgewood Normal College as a first-class institution of learning."[22] Although most of the students went with Wade and Loggins, Tubb and Hunt were able to open in the fall of 1891 with over one hundred students. A Clarksville paper paid tribute to the Edgewood people who were attempting to continue. They had "an ideal school," the editor wrote, which "is away from all the vices and temptations to which cities and towns are subject. . . ." The town was inhabited by "the best families of the county . . . [who] have a single interest and that is for the advancement of the school," he wrote. The faculty, in addition to Hunt and Tubb, consisted of Ida Stone, a daughter of Colonel Robert B. Stone, who taught music; Professor R. R. Smith who taught band and music, and Professors R. V. Pollard and B. F. Walker, who headed the commercial department. "All the houses are now occupied and a cry for more are causing new ones to be constructed. I predict for it a brilliant future," the editor concluded.[23] Some growth came to Edgewood, but not a sufficient amount to continue the operation of the school. Shortly after the turn of the century its interests became merged with those of Ruskin-Cave College, which was established on the grounds where Wayland and the Ruskin Cooperative Association had built their temporary utopia.

From the end of the nineteenth century to the time of the passage of the general education bill in 1909 the Dickson Normal College experienced its decade of greatest growth and development. At the close of the nineteenth century a Dickson newspaper paid special tribute to the school: "During its fourteen years existence it has turned out thousands of young men and young ladies, representing middle, southern, and western states, and filling every walk of life from preaching the gospel to presiding over banking institutions." The faculty at that time included Professor Wade who taught mathematics and metaphysics; Loggins who taught Latin and natural sciences; W. J. Davies, Greek and mathematics; Mrs. Lucia A. Wade, German and bookkeeping; Flavia Gaines, elocution and physical culture; A. C. Hughes, preparatory mathematics, history and geography; G. H. East, penmanship; J. L. Wyman, piano, organ and voice; Idella Ottenville, mandolin, violin and guitar; Lula Hughes, librarian; J. T. Fulgum, telegraphy; and Mrs. Annie Garner, matron. The number of students at the time approximated 700. Tuition varied with the courses taken, and board, room, laundry, and fuel could be had at $7 per month.[24]

In 1904 the officials prepared a 32-page booklet giving a full description of the many advantages offered by the college. They indicated that although Professor Wade had been forced to retire to a farm in his native Virginia because of ill health, Loggins was doing an excellent job at the helm. The faculty now consisted of Loggins, E. B. Wilson, Mrs. Addie C. Loggins, Mrs. Alice Evans Hickman, Miss Gertrude Rogers, R. E. Corlew, Russell O. Dufour, and Miss Birdie Hopson. The board of trustees included Dr. C. M. Lovell, Dr. T. F. McCreary, W. H. McMurray, all of Dickson; Norman M. Byars of Brownsville, and Dr. Dorsey T. Gould of Nashville. "Unusual care has been taken this year in the selection of our faculty," Loggins announced. "All ... are active Christian men and women, in the prime of life, and each has a successful experience in his line of work, ... and all are fully abreast with the most advanced thought and most modern methods of teaching. ..."[25] In 1906 Loggins announced that the enrollment for the preceding year was approximately 800 students. "Every room in our seven large buildings has been literally *full*, and provisions had to be made for other rooms to accommodate our unusually large boarding patronage," he said. Thousands of young men and women have been provided "the greatest boon of the age," he wrote, and pointed to the fact that

We have taken hundreds of poor boys from the plow and poor girls from the profitless routine of the kitchen, and, by helping and encouraging them, have placed them on the road to success. Wherever we go through our Southland we meet the old boys and girls, joyously pursuing their chosen professions, and as ever, full of life and enthusiasm.... It does not matter what you expect to pursue as a lifework, you will find here just such advantages as will furnish you a safe foundation on which to build and to succeed.[26]

Loggins seldom missed an opportunity to explain that the school was not for training teachers only, but was equipped to give one a broad general education and to prepare one for any of the professions. This he carefully stated in the Bulletin of 1906. He wrote:

Some have thought because ours is a "Normal school" that it is an institution for teachers only. There was never a greater mistake. It is true that training teachers for the public schools, Normal schools, and colleges of this and other Southern states is an important part of our work ... but this is by no means our only or greatest work. We endeavor to give the best general education and furnish the best equipment for any business or profession. To this end we give thorough instruction in all the common-school branches, Latin, Greek, German, English, mathematics, sciences, history, commercial branches, shorthand, music, elocution, and so forth. Many of our pupils have never taught and never expect to teach. We fit them well for the duties of life—for any calling or profession. Among our former pupils are judges, senators, legislators, lawyers, doctors, merchants, preachers, teachers, bookkeepers, stenographers, and so forth.[27]

The Bulletin for 1909 told of a dozen or more medals and prizes awarded by various citizens of Dickson to students who excelled. W. H. McMurray, for example, had pledged a ten dollar gold medal to the most outstanding student in writing and speech making; W. T. Rogers awarded a ten dollar prize to the pupil most proficient in music; and A. H. Leathers presented a similar award to the music student with the best all-around record. Scholars honored during the preceding term included Bessie Smith, Lucile Ridings, Donald Sensing, Arthur Miller, Lida Rogers, Dockie Shipp, Wilson Sharp, and many others.[28]

The general education bill of 1909, while providing a great boon to the youth of the state, spelled doom for institutions such as the Dickson Normal. The law provided for the establishment of three normal schools for the preparation of white teachers, one to be located in each of the three grand divisions of the state and supported by state funds. By 1911 institutions at Memphis, Murfreesboro, and Johnson City were being made ready to serve the public at a much smaller cost to the student than schools like Loggins' could do. In anticipation of the establishment of these schools, students began to withdraw from the semi-private schools to await the opening of the state schools. Loggins' enrollment dropped considerably after 1909. In the Bulletin of 1910 he announced that he would now concentrate on quality more than ever, and had decided to limit the number of students to 250. The decision was not made by choice, of course, but by circumstance. "With this number we shall be able to select our pupils from moral, honest, and upright young men and women, boys and girls, and thus throw around those who come to us the very best influences," he wrote. But Loggins could see the handwriting on the wall, for he knew that he could not operate with such a small number, nor compete with schools maintained with public funds. The school year 1911-1912 was the last one for him, but just before that school year began he decided to make one final effort to stem the rising tide of the state institutions. He printed many testimonials from men like Semour A. Mynders, former state superintendent of public instruction, William H. Johnston, presiding elder of the Fayetteville district of the Methodist church, and various others who told of the excellent educational advantages which only Loggins at Dickson could offer. Other testimonials were offered by men like Benton McMillan, and Robert L. Taylor. He conceived the idea of stressing the point that a year at Dickson would equip one well for entrance into one of the state normals, and he called especial attention to the "very strong" faculty there. To prospective students of West Tennessee he addressed this message:

> Do you expect to attend the West Tennessee State Normal School at Memphis . . . ? Then come to Dickson . . . and we will prepare you for that work and care for you as no other school can. . . . Dickson College has been indorsed by more State Superintendents and school officials than any other school in the state.[29]

To the down and out he extended a special appeal and offered them the magic wand of education if they would but come to Dickson. He wrote:

> Young man, young woman, toiling in obscurity, yet with a laudable ambition, sometimes disheartened and almost ready to give up, surrender should be the last resort, the last thing thought of. To give up, to complain at your lot or growl at your luck . . . is not the thing . . . to do. Often a determined purpose, a holy ambition to succeed, is all that is needed. Just say you will, and you will. There is always a way for the one who is

brave and courageous. Wind up your affairs at home, break away from the surroundings that hinder you, leave the associates and the associations that would hold you back, come to Dickson College, the practical school that makes practical men and women overcome obstacles and do things in the world in spite of lot or luck, and you will be placed in the highway that leads surely to success and, if you will do your share, perhaps to fame and fortune.[30]

At the conclusion of the 1911-1912 term, Loggins departed, but turned the affairs of the school over to E. B. Wilson who had taught mathematics and science there before; and Wilson operated the institution for several years. In 1919 the state legislature passed a law requiring every county to maintain at least one high school. At that time the county had several two-year high schools, but no four-year schools. Negotiations were begun with T. B. Loggins for his property on which the Wilson school was then operating, and culminated in the purchase of the property for $16,500, this amount to be shared equally by the county and the town of Dickson. The first term opened in 1919 with W. M. Bratton, who had headed the Wilson School, as principal. Among his first pupils were Walter Erranton, Mary Allen, Frank Gatewood, Kate McMurry, Lipe Henslee, Albert Wilson, James Bryan, and many others. Students from all parts of the county and also some adjoining counties attended, and paid $20 per month for board and room.[31] The rapid growth of the town of Dickson necessitated the erection of larger quarters by 1930, and at that time a new and larger building was constructed. The plant has been expanded several times during the past 25 years, until now it is one of the best in the county.

Under the guidance of R. E. Corlew much educational progress was made during the decade following the establishment of Dickson High School. A junior high school was begun at Charlotte in 1921, but the rapidly increasing enrollment necessitated the expansion into a four-year school by 1927. Since that time the original building has been doubled in size, and a new gymnasium and football field have been constructed. A two-year high school opened at White Bluff in 1923, and was located on land donated by Colonel William James, whose body now lies buried on a plot adjacent to the school property. In 1927 additional buildings were erected and William James High School began as a four year school. Several junior high schools were established throughout the county during the 1920's, but have now disappeared with the advent of better transportation facilities. Among those two-year schools were Woods Valley in the ninth district, Eastside in the fourth district, Vanleer at the town of Vanleer, and Glenwylde in the eighth district. The latter school was established on the grounds of the old "Glenwylde High School," which had opened on Horse Branch August 17, 1891. It was under the direction of H. H. Marshall of Goodlettsville and Dr. W. H. Crouch of Beefrange.[32] The Vanleer school was the last to close, its students being transported to Charlotte for the first time in 1955. The Dickson Training School for Negroes began as a two-year school during the 1920's, but expanded into a four-year school in 1936. Today it is known as Hampton High, and is one of the best Negro high schools among the rural counties of Middle Tennessee.

The last college to be operated in Dickson County was a private institution called Ruskin-Cave College. It began in 1904 and closed during the early 1920's. The school was headed by R. E. Smith and Colonel R. J. Kelly, and was operated by a board of trustees of which Jerry Nesbitt and W. T. Nesbitt were members. Smith, in 1956 a resident of Shreveport, Louisiana, had taught at McEwen and also in Meridian, Mississippi, before coming to Dickson County to head the school. As has been mentioned earlier, the property settled in the 1890's by the Ruskin Cooperative Association, was put on the auction block in 1899 and was purchased by Thomas Rogers. The land was encumbered with mortgages amounting to $3,900, and Rogers sold it almost immediately to the Cumberland Valley Land and Improvement Company for $1,505. The Company, composed entirely of Dickson County men such as W. G. McMillan, president, S. E. Hunt, secretary, W. L. Cook, H. J. Bowers, W. R. Hudson, W. H. McMurry, H. J. Larkins, J. M. Hicks, W. M. Diamond, J. R. Neblett, and R. D. Eubank, made some improvements on the land, cleared it of part of the mortgages, and sold it the following year to W. A. Bell for $6,875. In 1904 the board of trustees of Ruskin-Cave College purchased part of the land from Bell for educational purposes.

Smith proved to be a puritanical administrator, but a thorough one. He operated the school on the Biblical principle, "The fear of the Lord is the beginning of wisdom," and ardently sought to accomplish his aim. His college was a "safe place for boys and girls," even though some church schools were not. In the College *Bulletin* for 1911 he described the school as a place where there were

no railroad evils [?], no tobacco or whisky sold in the village, no football or brutal games! Yet there is ample opportunity for physical development —fine rowing and swimming pools, tennis, field drills, etc.

No young man could bestow a gift upon a young lady or even write to her unless the gift or letter had first been inspected by the president. No young ladies were to be on the campus after sundown unless properly chaperoned, and none were to wear low-necked dresses or appear in classes or on the campus without hose. When accused of being too strict, Smith replied that his staff did not consist of "old fogies," but of "consecrated . . . , practical, Christian educators, with the courage of our convictions." He concluded

with hopeful hearts and willing hands, we fling to the breeze our banner of "Holiness unto the Lord," and invite all true lovers of home, humanity and heaven to rally to our standard, and assist us in the greatest work of today—training men and women for tomorrow.

The giant cave, which had been the pride and joy of the Ruskinites of a decade earlier, was used in many ways by the college. It alone probably drew many students. Smith described it as among the natural wonders of America.... Back two hundred feet from the entrance is a lake, from whose unfathomable depths comes the purest, coldest, clearest water this side the sparkling fountains of Switzerland. Peering into this limpid flood, we flatter ourselves that we see the bottom, only to find that this bottom is the mirrored ceiling. Aside from its purity, this water possesses rare medicinal properties.

... we follow a long, winding passage for several hundred feet to the second hall.... The passage branches off into numberless smaller passages, which, in turn, lead into other chambers and as we wander where no ray of light has pierced the darkness for—lo!—these thousand years, a strange feeling of awe comes over us, and a profound sense of our nothingness and God's omnipotence creeps into our minds and hearts.[34]

The school began to decline after the United States entered the World War in 1917. Most of the male students were mustered into service, and Smith and Kelly left soon thereafter. During the early 1920's the school closed its doors never to open again. It had graduated many outstanding men in its few years of operation, among whom are the Honorable Q. M. Smith, prominent educator, and the Reverend Earl Hamlett, a high official in the Methodist Church. D. E. Ray of Jackson, Guy Stephenson of Dyersburg, and R. B. Stone of Pulaski, and hundreds of others likewise are graduates who have made outstanding contributions to the state and nation.

A brief look at statistics for three selected years during the last half century reveals a story of educational progress within the county. In 1915 over one thousand boys and girls of school age could neither read nor write. This was over one fifth, or twenty per cent, of the total number. By 1930 that number had decreased to less than 700, and the percentage to about fourteen. By 1956 illiteracy rapidly was becoming a thing of the past.

Teachers salaries have increased consistently. In 1915 teachers were paid an average monthly salary of $60, while in 1930 the average was $81.60 for men and $76.71 for women. By 1956 the state department of education had set up a system whereby a teacher is paid according to the amount of education and training he has received. The ease with which a master of arts degree now can be procured at some of the colleges of the state has inspired many teachers to secure that degree. For a beginning teacher with the master's degree the salary is $2,520 for a ten months' year, while a teacher with that degree and fifteen years of experience can earn a maximum of $3,360. Principals receive an additional $4.50 per month for each full-time teacher up to and including fifteen teachers. The salary for county superintendents also has increased considerably. In 1915 this official was paid $2,250, in 1930 he received $2,200, and in 1956 a superintendent with a master of arts degree in school administration and sixteen years of experience is eligible for a salary of $5,403. County and state supplements make it possible for a person with these qualifications to receive over $6,000 per annum. Statistics for these years also show the disappearance of the log schoolhouse, and the consolidation of many of the smaller schools where several were in the immediate proximity of one another. While in 1896 fifty-two of the buildings were of log, in 1915 more than half of these had disappeared, and by 1930 not a log building remained in the county. In the latter year 75 of the buildings were frame, three were of brick, and one was of stone.

Of the many other things which a comparison of statistics will indicate, one other should be noted. That is the rapid entrance of women into the teaching profession and the disappearance of men. It has been observed that in the years before 1900 men predominated in the profession. In 1915, however, there were only 27 white and two colored men, and 65 white and five colored women. By 1930 the number of white men had dwindled to 17 and the number of colored men to one. On the other hand there were 100 white women and 12 colored women in the same year. In recent years the introduction of vocational agriculture courses and competition in athletics among the schools has increased the number of men in the profession. In the 1955-1956 term there were 28 men and 115 women teaching in the schools of Dickson County, and the number of students exceeded four thousand, nearly 400 of which were Negroes.

During Dickson County's 150 years its people have never slighted the subject of education. J. Alton Barksdale, former commissioner of education of Tennessee, former principal of Charlotte High School, and now Dean of Instruction of Tennessee Polytechnic Institute, recently observed that many of the people of Dickson County are far ahead culturally and intellectually of many of the people in surrounding counties. This he attributed to the ever present interest in education and especially to the many private schools which once exsited, such as Glenwylde, Cloverdale, Edgewood, Dickson Normal College, and others, at which the parents and grandparents of the present generation were educated. Many of those educated in the schools of the county have gone on to succeed in instiutions of higher learning throughout the country. Many have distinguished themselves and rendered great public service at the bar, in the hospital, in the pulpit, in the classroom, and in places of business.

Honorable Frank Goad Clement, Governor of the State of Tennessee. Mr. Clement is the only governor Dickson County has ever produced

Hon. James A. Weems,
County Judge

Hon. Wilson Blake Leech (1868-1945) prominent lawyer, attorney general, financier.

Hon. Henry Collier Leech (1881—)

Honorable Henry Collier Leech and Honorable Joseph B. Weems were two pioneers in the writing of a Dickson County history. Mr. Leech was born in Charlotte, studied law at Cumberland University, and practiced law and edited a newspaper in Charlotte. He practiced law in Nashville, and attained considerable success in a variety of business operations there. His great, great grandfather, Edward Leech, was one of Dickson County's first settlers. He now resides in Chattanooga, and is a member of the Dickson County Historical Society.

Some prominent citizens of White Bluff

One of the most progressive towns of the county is White Bluff. Pictured are some of the prominent citizens of the town. They are, seated, left to right: R. B. Hunter, J. W. Delonas, R. B. Thompson, Earley Harris, Newell Jackson. Standing, left to right: A. W. (Pidge) Wiley, J. K. St. Clair, Walter Jones, L. M. Deal, Clarence Larkins, Roy Sullivan, Calvin Larkins, J. H. Beck, Frank Howell, and Carner Brown.

Directors of Bank of Dickson

The Bank of Dickson is the newest of the Dickson County banks. It is ably managed and beautifully furnished. Directors and officers appearing above are, left to right: Dr. Walter Bell, Mark Wade, Carney Nicks, Ferrell Dennison, Wayne Sensing, R. P. Beasley, Glen Hamilton, and Harry Wynns.

Most of the members of the Dickson County Court and some of the county officials.

Pictured are most of the members of the county court and some of the other county officials. Seated, left to right: A. H. Bibb, H. W. Corlew, Rufus Tidwell, Horace Pickering, C. W. Harris, D. D. Robertson, William Matlock, B. F. Nesbitt, W. R. Berry, Billy Matthews, J. J. Finch, R. A. Wright, Melvin Harris. Second row: Max Davenport, R. B. Hunter, Robert Stone, Joe A. McMillan, J. W. DeJonas, D. B. Greer, James A. Cooksey, E. H. Meek, L. L. Brown, Ray Pack, Earley Harris, D. K. Walker, Robert Daniel, Claude Dickson. Third row: Claude Powers, Ray Stuart, W. B. Work, Earl Hall, V. N. Loggins, Pruett Kelly, Warren Hill, James A. Weems, J. W. Galloway, Horace Swift, Clarence Baker, Hubert Redden, J. C. Erranton, Malcolm Frazier, T. T. Sugg, Melvin Powell, and J. B. White. Magistrates not present when the photograph was made are: Corbie Adcock, Charles E. Bruce, Mark Wade, Nathan Miller, and Edd Brown.

CHAPTER XII

Growth of Urban Areas and the Struggle for Political Supremacy

THE BUREAU of the Census classifies all urban areas with population of 2,500 or more as cities. There is no accepted way of classifying towns, villages, and communities. Through general understanding, however, a "town" has been accepted as an urban area somewhat smaller in population than a "city," but somewhat larger than a "village." The terms "town" and "village" both imply a relatively compact community having a dozen or more homes and such necessary institutions as churches, schools, and places of business, all of course in limited numbers. The term "community" implies a much larger geographical area, probably having a radius of several miles, but tending to cluster about a small central group of homes, or a school, or a church, or some other primary bond. If these general definitions be accepted and applied to Dickson County, only Dickson properly can be termed a city. Urban areas such as Charlotte, White Bluff, Burns, Vanleer, and Slayden are all incorporated with charters from the state of Tennessee, and could be classified as towns. Areas such as Bellsburg, Cumberland Furnace, Pond, Tennessee City, Sylvia, and others might be termed towns, villages, or communities according to an individual's preference. White Oak Flatt, Jackson's Chapel, Colesburg, Sycamore, Eastside, Mt. Lebanon, Mt. Sinai, Liberty, and probably a dozen others might best be termed communities. The usual pattern of settlement in Dickson County has been for a particular area to become inhabited because of some economic pursuit, timber in particular, after which churches and schools would be established. After that, although the original economic pursuit might vanish or become secondary and no longer serve as a primary bond, new economic pursuits, a church, school, or perhaps merely sentiment might serve to hold the community together. According to one source, the timber industry was the primary reason for the formation of many of the Dickson County communities.[1] Although timber is no longer a primary economic factor, other pursuits have succeeded sufficiently to hold the communities together and in many instances to cause growth.

Much has been said of Charlotte in the earlier chapters. The town had been established in 1804 as a county seat. Seeking a central location, the commissioners empowered to select a proper place for the location of a courthouse and jail chose the valley in which the town now stands, and in 1804 selected a man named Ash to survey the area and to draw the plat. The construction of a courthouse and other public buildings was paralleled by the establishment of many places of business, and during the first few decades of the nineteenth century many people belived that the town would grow to city proportions. It was not incorporated until over three decades after its founding, but as early as 1817 "An act for the Regulation of the Town of Charlotte," was passed by the state legislature. The measure provided for the election of seven commissioners of the town, all of whom were required to be owners of lots and residents of the town for at least six months. The commissioners, once elected, were empowered to call on the inhabitants to work the roads and to collect fines from all who refused to work, to "prevent encroachments in the streets or public square," to abate nuisances, to tax property 25 cents on the hundred dollars of valuation, to tax billiard tables five dollars each, and to tax "each white poll 25 cents and each black poll . . . 50 cents." The commissioners were to receive no compensation for their services.[2]

The town grew considerably in the 1830's. During that decade it was considered as a possible site for the permanent location of the state capitol, and when the matter was brought before the state legislature the town received a sizable number of votes, though not the necessary majority. A glimpse of Charlotte in the 1830's has been left by Jesse Daniel, a prominent citizen of the post Civil War days. Daniel, writing in the *Dickson County Press* in 1886, told of visiting Charlotte twice weekly as a youth in order to deliver meal and flour from his father's mill on Cedar Creek. He had seen in the Charlotte of the 1830's a flourishing "metropolis" wherein the prominent citizens of the county congregated. He remembered that

Greenbery Adamson was a blacksmith, Esquire [John] Eubank and Thomas Epps were tailors and their shop was on the north side of the public square. Count Adamson, a brother of Greenbery, was also a tailor, musician, and the politest man in town. The merchants in Charlotte at that time were B. A. and T. L. Collier, and Hicks and Mitchell on the north side of the square; Gould, Voorhies and Kelly, on the west, and club-footed Robert Steele on the South side. Thomas Massey and Stephen Smith, grocers, the former on the east, and the latter in a little red house between the Steele's and the jail, on the South. Field Farrow, a large fat man, was County Court Clerk, and Richard Waugh, Register. Field Farrow was succeeded by William Hightower as Clerk, and he by Thomas J. Kelly.... The first Chancery Court Clerk whom I remember was the venerable John C. Collier. The Circuit Court was held by Judge Humphreys, in the old Tracy Academy building [for a while following the destruction of the courthouse in the tornado of 1830].... The old hotel standing... on the southside of the square... was run by Maj. J. P. Hardwicke....[3]

Considerable growth continued to the time of the Civil War. The entire South received a setback during the war and the reconstruction period, however, and in the years which followed Charlotte was never able to revive ante-bellum growth qualities. For several decades following the war citizens of foresight ardently tried to secure a railroad for the town, but to no avail. The conservative nature of many of the people, a spirit of depression and defeat caused by the war, and economic depression experienced by Charlotte as well as the whole South, were sufficient to defeat all railroad proposals. Perhaps the nearest the town came to getting a railroad was in the early 1890's when the Louisville and Nashville considered an extension of their line at Clarksville to connect with the Nashville, Chattanooga, and St. Louis road in the vicinity of Dickson. A subscription of $10,000 probably would have been sufficient to insure the railroad, according to a Charlotte newspaper, but was never raised. The editor of the paper pleaded with the citizenry, insisting that the town never would grow and develop without adequate transportation facilities, but his voice was that of one crying in the wilderness.[4] The people of the late nineteenth century watched with apparent helplessness as adjoining towns took business, industry, railroads, and finally part of the court sessions. Apparently not a great deal of interest was aroused by the efforts of Dickson, White Bluff, Burns, and Sylvia to take the county seat until 1927, when Dickson and Charlotte locked horns in a bitter man-to-man duel.

During the twentieth century small growth has been evidenced. In recent years, under the direction of Asa Hickerson, L. J. Browning, Wayne Sensing, Graham Hicks, Ray Stuart, Ray Dillingham, and many others, improvements have been made. Because of the recent incorporation of surburban areas, the population today is about 600. A clinic has been erected, streets have been paved, and town officials have considered a program of expansion to include waterworks. Charlotte no doubt will always remain a picturesque town, in some ways reminiscent of ante-bellum days. Mildred Luton, "poet laureate" of Dickson County, has captured this thought in her poem, "Charlotte Town," which is as follows:

> Green hills encircle Charlotte Town.
> From shaded heights one sees
> Far, far below the cobbled streets,
> The domes among the trees;
>
> And driving down from Dicksonville,
> A dozen miles away,
> The trees and spires of Charlotte Town
> Are like a mixed bouquet.
>
> Along the streets of Charlotte Town
> Quaint shops proclaim their wares:
> Pentecost and Dillingham
> Fresh Cantaloupes and Pears!
>
> Oh, would that I were there today,
> I'd buy myself a pear
> And eat it 'neath a sugar tree
> Upon the cobbled square.
>
> The village folk would stop to chat
> For no one ever hurries,
> And visions of old friends would pass
> And wave to me from surreys.

Dickson has shown the most phenomenal growth of all urban areas.

As mentioned, during the Civil War a railroad track was laid through the county, bisecting the present area of Dickson. The town was established because of the need for a railroad stop. With only a few crude buildings in 1865, Dickson was given the name of Sneedsville, for an engineer on the Northwestern Railroad. The devastated conditions of the South following the Civil War brought thousands of Northern people into the Southern states to take advantage of the cheap land which the natives were forced to sell in order to eke out a bare livelihood. Hundreds came into Sneedsville from Pennsylvania and Ohio, chiefly, and by 1868 had constituted a good-sized settlement. In that year C. Berringer, of Allegheny, Pennsylvania, who had already bought much of the land in the present fifth civil district, platted some lots and placed them upon the real estate market. Shortly thereafter it was discovered that a town in Hancock County also bore the name Sneedsville, and during the early 1870's the name was changed to "Dickson."[5]

The town owed its early rapid growth mainly to two factors, good transportation facilities, and an aggressive citizenry having a moderate amount of capital. Although Dickson was connected with Nashville to the east and with several points to the west by the Nashville and Northwestern Railroad, the people during the 1870's under the direction of a Major Falconett raised a subscription of $10,000 and secured Dickson as the northern terminus of the Nashville and Tuscaloosa Railroad. This line served the southern part of the county, and connected the town with Centerville.[6] Thus with transportation connections to the east, west, and south (the northern connection was not to come until the 1890's), Dickson began a period of growth for the next few decades excelled by few other towns in Middle Tennessee. Six years after Berringer platted the first lots, the Nashville *Union and American* published a special article in which tribute was paid to the growing town of Dickson. "Dickson has a population of 150," the editor wrote, and had even established a hotel kept by a Mr. McCutcheon. Especial tribute was paid to the Pennsylvanians who had settled in and around the little town. "They have made a great many changes for the better," he wrote. Their farms are in a good state of improvement . . . their fences are neat and free from briars, . . . and their stables are put up after the fashion of the Old Pennsylvania Dutch barn." The many improvements these people made, coupled with the fact that the Nashville and Northwestern Railroad ran through the town, caused the price of land in the vicinity to rise phenomenally. "Very little land can be had on the railroad for less than $15 per acre," the editor wrote, while "west of Charlotte it sells for 2 or 3 dollars per acre." In the immediate vicinity of Dickson 15 acres had been sold for $850.[7] Four years later many places of business were in operation. W. H. Crutcher, McFarland & McCreary, J. C. Donnegan and Moore, Joseph McWilliams, A. Myatt, William Pickett, John Alexander, Miles H. Mayes, J. R. Spicer, W. H. Mathis, J. A. Thomas, and John Rickert, all, had general merchandise stores where a customer could buy almost anything to suit his fancy from pills and petticoats to plows. J. T. Henslee specialized in drugs, but also handled a general stock. N. George sold hardware. Nopp and Loafbourn had established a flour and corn mill, and Levi Sylvis had opened a shoe repair shop. Many others had established, or were making plans to establish, business, and to participate in the growth and development of the town.[8]

Dickson was incorporated in 1873, and a man named Petty is said to have become the first mayor. For the greater part of the first decade there is no evidence to indicate anything but harmony between the city fathers and their constituents. In 1882, however, two factions developed and were known as the "Corporationists" and the "Anti-Corporationists." The former was led by Mayor J. W. Clark, a local liquor dealer, and sought to preserve the corporate government for the town. The Anti-Corporationists asserted that the tax money was spent improperly, that the town was operated in the interest of the liquor traffic, that no general good came from incorporation, and that the city's charter, therefore, should be revoked. The city was in debt and needed badly certain tax money which was past due, but those who opposed the corporation sought to cripple the government by refusing to pay taxes. The difference broke into the open in April, 1882, when the mayor and alderman served writs of attachment upon the property of those who were delinquent. The Anti-Corporationists then filed suit charging that the mayor and aldermen had not been elected legally, and were not the proper persons to collect taxes. The case was heard before Squires Baker, Smith, and Adcock, with Charlotte attorneys W. L. Grigsby and Jacob Leech for the Corporationists, and Hardin Leech for the opposing group. After several hours of argument a decision was given in favor of the Anti-Corporationists. The editor of the *Dickson County Press* sought to pour oil on troubled waters, advising that "some of our best citizens are engaged on each side" and that they should be able to settle the matter without further litigation.[9]

The controversy subsided for several months, and in October of the same year the mayor and aldermen determined to pursue different tactics. They decided to appeal to the patriotism and civic pride of the citizens rather than to seek to force them to pay taxes. "If we continue to pull back and try to destroy our corporation," the Mayor said, "we will soon have no town." He insisted that everyone should come forward and pay his taxes without further bickering.[10] The Anti-Corporationists in the meantime had drawn up a petition in which the sheriff was requested to hold an election to determine whether the citizens wanted to surrender the charter. Many advantages of an unincorporated town were cited in the petition. The mayor and board of aldermen (consisting of Clark, J. A. Thomas, J. R. Bryan, W. M. Legg, James Maley, J. M. Myatt, and E. Y. Andrews), then filed a bill in chancery in which they sought to enjoin the sheriff from holding an election. They stated that they had been legally elected, that they had proceeded in good faith to repair the sidewalks, work the streets, set out shade trees, and preserve the order of the town. They further cited the fact that under their administration the town had grown considerably and that the population had increased to nearly 800. They alleged that "certain parties who were candidates for alderman and were defeated" had "banded themselves together with a few others," and were intent upon breaking down and destroying "the municipality of said town of Dickson . . . by refusing to pay their taxes, and now by petitioning the Sheriff to hold said election. . . ."[11] The injunction, if granted at all, was a temporary one, however, for the people decided against the corporation.[12] In November an injunction was served prohibiting further proceedings of the mayor and board of aldermen.[13]

For the next two decades Dickson continued as an unincorporated town, but Clark's prediction that the town would be destroyed did not come true. Rather, it grew considerably, as new places of business were established. But the sidewalks and streets deteriorated, and several years later again there developed an active movement to incorporate the town. County Superintendent B. F. Harris wrote to the *Press* to express his favor of incorporation, for he believed it would discourage prohibition. Harris' letter was answered by "Demos" who called the superintendent a "whiskey head," and took him to task for wanting to discourage prohibition. Harris replied in the next issue, challenging "Demos" to reveal his identity, and denying that he was a "whiskey head."[14] In 1892 and 1893 mass meetings were called to discuss incorporation, and were supported vigorously by *The Critic*, a newspaper edited by T. B. Loggins and others. "There are scarcely no sidewalks in town—we need streets, sidewalks, and fire protection," the editor wrote.[15] It was in 1899, however, before incorporation came, and Dr. C. M. Lovell, physician and bank official, served as the first mayor under the new charter.

A careful sifting of the available evidence fails to reveal an isolated cause for the fifteen years of bickering; perhaps there were several reasons for it. Certainly the able educator, T. B. Loggins, believed that incorporation would bring many advantages to the town. However, it is quite probable that the liquor issue was a vital one, if not the main one. This is borne out in the Harris-"Demos" correspondence, and the fact that Mayor Clark, who so ardently supported incorporation, was a local liquor dealer. A state law then on the statute books prohibited the sale of intoxicating liquors in unincorporated towns, and many small towns of the state were able to close their saloons simply by abolishing their charters. It is interesting to note that Charlotte had a controversy of a similar nature but of much smaller proportions during the early nineties, in which the liquor question was the sole issue. A picture of the town in the early nineties is given by Henry C. Leech, then a young man:

> For a long time we had a filthy little town. Public drunkenness, profanity, fights among horse traders on the public square, and all such conduct when sessions of the courts or other events brought to town enough of the rabble to spend their hard-earned dimes at our three open saloons . . . seemed to be the order of the day.

The Charlotte saloons, operated by Oscar R. Leech, William H. Butler, and William R. Hudson, must have been elaborate, as evidenced by contemporary descriptions. These saloon operators, together with Attorneys Jacob Leech, T. H. Grigsby, and W. L. Cook; and H. A. Bibb, Thomas H. W. James, C. V. Austin, John Collier, and others, petitioned the Forty-eighth general assembly of the state not to abolish the town charter. W. Blake Leech was then the county representative and, supported by Thomas C. Morris, Major I. M. Bowers, L. L. Leech, William C. Collier, Dr. A. G. Castleman, and others, he sponsored legislation to abolish the town's charter and thus rid the place of its saloons. The petition of the liquor advocates was not accepted by the legislature, for Leech's measure was local legislation which passed with little difficulty.[16]

While the city fathers of both Dickson and Charlotte bickered with those who would destroy them, others seemed to go about their businesses in a normal way. Dickson was growing, and every year it brought forth new evidence of expansion. In June, 1882, while the corporation argument was brewing, the editor of the *Press* paid tribute to the people of Dickson whom he described as "peaceable, industrious, law abiding, enterprising, and hospitable." They always strove

to help . . . any enterprise which will be beneficial to their town and community. From a business point of view they are not behind the age and generation, and have gained an enviable reputation for their willingness to "tote fair," and do business in a business-like manner every time. They are also a moral people as well as a social and business people.

By the time that article was written (June, 1882), there were at least the following merchants in business: Henslee & Coleman, "druggists and dealers in paints, oils, glass, varnishes, groceries, etc., etc."; J. R. Spicer, general merchandise and groceries; W. M. Hooper, "the old reliable merchant," general merchandise; J. L. Ankeny, general merchandise and groceries; Edwin George, hardware; Steinau & Alexander, "enterprising produce merchants . . . who pay cash for all kinds of country produce"; J. A. Thomas, general merchandise; M. F. Womack, groceries; A. Myatt, "the old pioneer merchant"; W. M. Askins, "handler of a very fine line of wines, brandies and liquors of all kinds, and tobaccoes"; J. W. Clark, whiskies, tobacco, and groceries; Maley & Donelson, butchers; Lee Shawl, "the genial blacksmith"; A. F. Scott, manufacturer of wagons and carriages; Joseph Davis, manufacturer of wagons and grain cradles; Levi Sylvis, boot and shoe maker; and T. F. McCreary, operator of Dickson Star Mills, in which "every Dicksonite takes a commendable pride and interest." L. D. Wright and John W. Griner were dentists, Drs. Cullum and Derryberry maintained medical offices together, and E. Y. Andrews sold insurance. Most of the merchants advertised regularly in the press. In 1882 Henslee and Coleman, in addition to offering bargains in drugs and paints, offered eight pounds of coffee for one dollar. J. W. Clark handled "all grades" of whiskies and brandies, all of which he guaranteed to be "from one to seven years old." Christopher Naegle, the town barber, advertised shaving, hair cutting, and shampooing, all of which he pledged to do "in an artistic and workmanlike manner."

There were four white and two Negro churches in Dickson in 1882. Z. W. Moore was pastor of the Methodist Episcopal Church (South), G. Parks of the Methodist Episcopal Church (North), S. F. Thomas of the United Presbyterian, and W. C. Barnett of the Lutheran Church. All churches were of frame construction except the Lutheran, which was brick.

Will J. Conant was editor and publisher of Dickson's only paper, the *Dickson County Press*. That paper was a seven column, four page, news sheet, selling at $1.50 per year, and described as being "independent in politics." Mails were received from and carried in all directions. The following schedule was announced in 1882: Westward bound arrives and departs at 9:50 A. M.; Eastward bound arrives and departs at 5:20 A. M.; North for Charlotte, Cumberland Furnace and other parts, leaves at 6:00 A. M. and arrives at 6:00 P. M.; Southward bound leaves at 8:00 A. M. and arrives at 4:00 P. M.[17]

Ten years later the population had nearly doubled. The editor of *The Critic* estimated it at 1,200 to 1,500 in the first issue of his paper, published February 2, 1893. By that time a stave factory employing over a dozen men and turning out up to 20,000 staves per day, and a planing mill valued at $10,000 and employing a dozen men, had been established. The Dickson Bank and Trust Company (later known as the Citizens' Bank) had been founded in 1890 with a capital stock of $25,000 and with stock selling at fifty cents per share. Its officers and board of directors in 1893 included J. R. Bryan, P. O. Wilkie, Edwin George, W. A. Hopkins, J. S. Murrell, J. A. Myatt, William Davis, C. M. Lovell, J. L. Ankeny, E. E. Miller, B. Z. Henslee, and W. H. McMurry. The bankers advertised that they would accept deposits as low as 25 cents, and that in addition to banking, would act "as guardian and administrator of estates, and do all kinds of business conducive to a sound banking business."[18] The need for capital and credit in an expanding economy meant growth for the bank. By 1907, at which time its officers were W. B. Leech, president, C. M. Lovell, vice-president, and W. H. McMurry, cashier, the total resources were listed at nearly $160,000. In the meantime, in 1903, the First National Bank was established and capitalized at $25,000. Organized by Pitt Henslee and J. A. Myatt, the bank's first directors chosen from stockholders who held $1,000 or more in stock, were, in addition to Henslee and Myatt: C. M. Turner, J. G. Henslee, J. C. Foster, L. M. Sensing, J. R. McClelland, J. A. Turner, John T. Overby, F. O. Watts, E. H. Stone, H. B. Horner, S. E. Hunt, W. H. Greer, and S. G. Holland. An establishment known as the Dickson National Bank, founded around 1912 with Tom Halbrook as president and Oury Harris as cashier, merged with the First National in 1914.[19]

The expanding need for credit over the county resulted in the founding of other banks. The Bank of Charlotte was established in 1905 and within a few years enjoyed remarkable growth. A little over a year after it began operation its deposits increased from $11,000 to $37,000, which reflected the confidence of the people in the institution. Its president in 1905 was W. L. Cook, with O. R. Leech as vice-president, and Oury Harris and F. H. Hickerson as cashiers.[20] Other banks in more recent years have been established at Vanleer, Slayden, White Bluff, Charlotte, and Dickson.

During the first half of the twentieth century Dickson has continued to grow and expand, although growth of the last fifty years has not been as rapid as that of the first forty. By the end of the first quarter of the twentieth century the town could boast of a population of nearly 3,000. Its industrial growth had continued at a steady pace, and it could claim a dozen or more manufacturing establishments. The A. H. Leathers Handle Factory, which shipped handles of all kinds over the United States and to Europe, was the oldest. A raincoat factory, producing a thousand coats daily and having an annual payroll of $50,000 for one hundred people, had been established. Also, over 250 women worked at the Dickson branch of the American Cigar Company and carried home an average weekly payroll of $3,000. The manner in which the cigar factory was acquired for the town is indicative of the spirit of the people of Dickson. Realizing that before industry would come material concessions would have to be made, the people raised a public subscription of $4,000 and erected a building which was leased to the factory for ten years. Lights, water, and heat were to be furnished by the city.[21] The Coca-Cola Bottling Works and the NuGrape Bottling Works had been established, and the Dickson Wholesale Grocery had been founded. Numerous grocery stores, of which H. G. Tomlinson's and J. E. Tidwell's were the oldest, and general merchandise stores, clothing stores, hardware stores, drug stores, restaurants, and other places of business had been established. By the end of the first quarter of the century all of the important streets had been paved with a heavy coating of asphalt, and the power plant, which cost $250,000, had been expanded greatly. The plant had been established at the conclusion of the World War, but had proved inadequate by the early twenties. In 1923 it was expanded to include three units, whose combined horsepower was 650. Business houses and homes were supplied current at eleven cents per kilowatt-hour, and they paid to the city sufficient amounts to net an annual profit of $12,000.[22]

Perhaps the depression of the early thirties struck Dickson as hard as any other city of its size in the country. The Citizens' Bank, the raincoat factory, the cigar factory, and other places of business fell completely under the financial catastrophe, and many other businesses suffered considerably. Nevertheless, by 1940 the population was still increasing, the census taker having enumerated 3,504 persons in that year. At present (1956) the population is estimated at 4,000 or more. Today it has more places of business than ever before in its ninety years of existence.

As has been mentioned, White Bluff was established during the Civil War by Federal soldiers. It is located about eleven miles southeast of Charlotte, and was on the Nashville and Northwestern railroad. There was a good wagon road from Charlotte to White Bluff, extending on to Nashville, which afforded adequate transportation facilities. The town, which took its name from the White Bluff Iron Forge which at one time operated near the present location of the town, did not grow as rapidly as Dickson, but sufficiently rapid for it to be incorporated under the laws of the state in 1870.[23] Among the first business houses were those operated by Morton and Wright, Charlton and Hicks, Jackson and Harris, George W. Collier, F. E. Willey, and others. A hotel, established and operated by Mrs. Thomas Overton, was in use during the 1880's and after. A town correspondent writing in one of the Nashville papers in 1873 stated:

Our little town is steadily improving. Several buildings are going up and others in contemplation; amongst the latter are a church, a schoolhouse, and an Odd Fellows' Hall.[24]

Churches were established at White Bluff rather early. The Methodist Episcopal (South), the Cumberland Presbyterians, the Christians, and the Baptists were among the early groups to found churches at, or in the immediate proximity of, the town. Much difficulty in establishing schools was experienced during the early period. Several years after a school building finally was erected, it was destroyed by fire. This was in 1879, and for nearly a decade thereafter little effort was made to reestablish an institution of learning.

Little interest was shown in a corporate form of government, and for several decades thereafter it would be permitted to die, then to be renewed, and then to expire again. In recent years much civic pride has been shown in White Bluff, and the people have exhibited a progressive spirit equivalent to that shown by any community in Dickson County. A recent disastrous fire has awakened the people to the needs of a water system and a good fire prevention system. In recent years water works have been supplied the town, and fire engines purchased. The present mayor is C. B. Thompson, who takes much pride in the town of 506 population. He is ably supported by the entire community.

Two other towns having their origin during the Civil War are Burns and Tennessee City, the latter of which was first called Gillam. Burns lies about five miles east of Dickson, and has evidenced some growth in recent years. Moses Tidwell, who owned much of the land where the town now stands, began to erect houses in the vicinity shortly after the establishment of the railroad. In 1868 William Wadkins opened a general store, and soon J. C. Donegan, Neilly & Stephens, Larkins & Son, J. C. Alspaugh, F. F. Tidwell, and various others also established stores. A Primitive Baptist Church was the first to be established in the town, but soon a Methodist, Church of Christ, and others were built. Perhaps the largest single business operation in Burns has been the Allen Lime Company. In May, 1883, the *Dickson County Press* announced that "The Dickson Lime Company has purchased a very fine stone quarry near Burns' Station, and are now making active preparations for the erection of kilns."[25] This group operated the kilns for awhile, and then sold out to the Allen Lime works. The kilns were in operation until comparatively recent times. In 1952 the people of Burns became interested in incorporation, and secured a charter from the state. The present mayor of Burns is A. E. Lampley, under whom the people have manifested much civic pride and spirit. The population in 1950 was 421.

Tennessee City is located on the Memphis-to-Bristol highway, about ten miles west of Dickson. It became a stopping place for locomotives after the building of the railroad, and shortly after the close of the war it had a population of about fifty people. Early places of business were operated by Pickett & Moody, Jesse Haywood, Daniel Rice, and William Moody. The first physician to practice at Tennessee City was W. A. Moody, who had been prominent in the Democratic Party in the county before the war. In 1886, one of the many Northern capitalists interested in Southern lands purchased several thousand acres in the vicinity of the village. His name was W. A. Schoenfeld, and he had visions of making of Gillam a great Southern metropolis. He platted a town consisting of over 20,000 lots, and petitioned the postmaster-General to change the name from Gillam to Tennessee City. His wishes were complied with in April, 1866,[26] and the town has been known by that designation ever since. Schoenfeld apparently believed that the new name would act as a magnet in drawing Northern settlers, but he was to be disappointed. Tennessee City even to this day remains a small village with little over one hundred people.

Two towns to become quite progressive in recent years are Vanleer and Slayden. Vanleer received its name from Anthony Wayne Vanleer, iron master who purchased Cumberland furnace from Montgomery Bell. The town is located on property which was owned by Vanleer. Both Vanleer and Slayden are post-Civil War towns, and both are now incorporated. The mayor of Vanleer is V. G. Seals, while Ace Potts heads the town of Slayden. In 1950 Vanleer had a population of 243, and Slayden had a population of 90. An outstanding citizen of Vanleer until his death several years ago was Norman Eubank. He was cashier and a director of the Peoples' Bank, and was an enterprising civic leader. For many years he was a member of the county court, in which proceedings he took an active part. He was also a representative to the state legislature for several terms, and represented the twenty-third senatorial district for one term.

Much has been said about Cumberland Furnace in connection with the iron works there. The depression brought to a conclusion further operation of the iron works, and during the Second World War the historic old monument to pioneer ingenuity was dismantled and the scrap contributed to the war effort. The community has continued to remain intact, however, and has grown. Many of the people are farmers, while others commute daily to work in Dickson, Clarksville, or Nashville.[27]

Amid the expansion and development of the urban areas of the county there existed gaity and sorrow. Lack of fast automobiles and drive-in movies did not hinder the younger generation from having a "good time." For example, around Christmas, 1882, the young ladies of Dickson gave the young men a "necktie party." The men, not to be outdone, a few weeks later reciprocated with a "handkerchief party" for the girls, which took the form of a masquerade ball. The local press gave the affair ample publicity:

> The gentlemen and a portion of the ladies were dressed in fancy costumes representing different characters, and as the gay colors of their costumes mingled together it formed a delightful scene, and it was not an unusual sight to see a fierce (?) cowboy with gun strapped across his shoulders, promenading with a Gypsy queen.[28]

A week later a party was given at the home of James Maley and was reported to have continued until the "wee, small hours."[29] The home of R. B. Stone in Cumberland Furnace was a scene of much gaity in that area. Youth from over the county sometimes would congregate at the Stone mansion, and often would be entertained by strains from the fiddle of Poe Caldwell, one of the leading musicians of the Barton's Creek neighborhood.[30]

Activities around churches also occupied a large part of the social life of the people. Childrens' Day exercises, dinners on the ground, preaching services, and other functions often drew both the pious and the impious. Activities at the Charlotte Methodist church at one time became so appealing that one scribe felt called upon to share with the public his joy in attending the services. He wrote to the editor of the *Press*:[31]

> Seldom if ever has it been my pleasure to attend a more enjoyable occasion than the entertainment given at the Charlotte Methodist Episcopal Church last Tuesday evening. The supper was excellent, the music superb, and Brother Comer's speech rivaled the best. The young ladies were so attractive that I was constrained to exclaim:
> My willing heart would gladly stay
> In such a place forever.

Athletic events of a modern flavor began to interest the people of the county more and more after the Civil War. On September 7, 1882, a Dickson newspaper reported that "the first match game of baseball ever played in Dickson" had just taken place between the Nails' Creek Nine and the Dickson "Seed Ticks." Each player seemed "to exert himself to the utmost." The first two innings of play were calm enough, and at the conclusion of the second inning the score was tied. During the third inning, however, the Ticks opened up both barrels and scored 15 runs, and in the fourth inning they scored 33 times. As the score now stood 50 to 2 in favor of the Dickson team, the Nails' Creek boys, led by Morgan Brown, W. D. Galloway, J. B. Tidwell, F. P. Tidwell, and others, decided that they had had enough for the day and refused to continue the humiliating affray. Will J. Conant, Will Murrell, W. S. Swift, and W. F. Davis, had been the heroes of the massacre and were to lead the Ticks to many victories in the seasons to come.[32]

Crime and disaster appeared not infrequently in the towns of Dickson County. In 1881 the murder of a recluse named James P. Cloudy occurred near Burns, and the crime wreaked fear in the hearts of the people of the neighborhood. Cloudy, a bachelor, had been found dead on the morning of January 25, and had been struck on the head a number of times with a dogwood stick which lay nearby and which was described by attending officers as "about four feet long and one and one-half inches thick." Esquire John M. Stuart, W. H. Meek, Dillard Brown, Ben Oliphant, Moses Garton, Daniel Harris, and Samuel C. Brown, were among those who constituted a jury of inquest which pronounced the crime murder. Several weeks later a nineteen-year-old youth named Andrew Jackson White was arrested in Nashville, was given a preliminary hearing at which Meek testified, and was committed to jail. On March 21 the grand jury, of which D. E. Balthrop was foreman, met and found a true bill. Sheriff W. M. Kirk was ordered to proceed at once to Nashville to convey the accused to the Charlotte jail. Hearings on the case began July 21, and must have attracted a wide audience. On July 23 the jury found the defendant "guilty of murder in the first degree as charged in the indictment." He then was sentenced to be hanged. The Sheriff was commanded

to take the defendant to the county jail and him safely keep until the 26th day of August next when he shall take him the said defendant from thence and within one mile of the courthouse of Charlotte between the hours of one and three o'clock and there hang him by the neck until he is dead, and that he pay the costs of this prosecution.

On July 18 White was tried for larceny and sentenced to eight years in the penitentiary. Court costs in the larceny and murder trials exceeded $500 which White was ordered to pay. An appeal to the supreme court failed to gain for White a stay of execution, but shortly before the day set for the hanging the governor commuted the sentence to life imprisonment because of White's youthfulness. White then served 30 or 40 years of his sentence, which was shortened on account of good behaviour. Once out of prison he lived his remaining days in Nashville a model citizen.[33]

In the year following White's crime Andrew Crockett, a Negro, was shot and killed at the Dickson depot by an unknown assailant. Governor Alvin Hawkins offered a reward of $100, and several men were arrested and questioned, but there was no immediate solution to the crime. The editor of the *Press* wrote that the wrath of the people had become aroused, and promised that they would "leave no stone unturned to ferret out the guilty party."[34] Later in the same year Hardin Leech, young Charlotte lawyer, inflicted a near-fatal wound upon a Negro named Gil Clemens in Clark and Beasley's Saloon in Dickson. The editor of the *Press* gave the following account of the affray:

Leech, who had been drinking quite freely, went into the saloon with a party of friends, when he met Clemens, who was leaning up against the bar. Leech told him to move along and give his party room. This he would not do, and after some words, Leech left the saloon, telling Clemens that he would see him again. In about ten or fifteen minutes he returned, and ordered Clemens out. After more talk Leech took hold of Clemens and pushed him to the side door, drew his revolver and fired at him twice. Clemens then turned around and grasped the pistol and they struggled into the saloon again, when the pistol was taken away from them. Leech then gave himself up to the officers and procured bail....[35]

During the 1890's there were two crimes which surpassed all others, and which provoked mob action. In 1892 James Thompson of Vanleer was murdered by a telegraph operator named Daniel. Daniel allegedly had emptied an automatic pistol into Thompson's body, which killed him instantly. The felon escaped arrest temporarily, and passed through Charlotte and thence to Burns where he boarded an eastbound train, but he was taken off the train and arrested in White Bluff. From there he was transported to Charlotte and jailed. According to one newspaper, "the killing caused considerable excitement among the citizens ... and talk of lynching was freely indulged." Thirty men guarded the jail to prevent mob violence.[36] In the same year James Wynn of Burns murdered his wife with a double-bit ax while she lay sleeping, and seriously wounded her 12-year-daughter with the same instrument. After committing the atrocious crime he went into a wooded area nearby and attempted to commit suicide by the use of both a dirk and a pistol, but he was not successful. Several days later he was found hiding near Burns and was taken into custody. A mob quickly formed and made plans to lynch the culprit. The sheriff, however, with his prisoner secretly departed Burns and headed for the Charlotte jail, but was overtaken by the mob at Colesburg and forced to release Wynn. The murderer then was hanged from a nearby tree. "It was quick work to fling a rope around his neck and stretch him up to an elm which stood nearby," the editor of a Dickson paper wrote. "While the people ... sympathize with the mob in the course which was taken, the prevailing sentiment over the county seems to be a condemnation of the manner in which justice was meted out," the editor concluded.[37]

Fire has proven a destructive force to the towns of the county, and has occurred more frequently than crime. Mention has been made of the fire in White Bluff during the early 1870's when the school was burned, and of the catastrophe of the 1940's which devoured much of the town. The city of Dickson, however, has experienced more fires than any of the other urban areas. Perhaps the most disastrous fires came during the ten-year period of 1895-1905. In January, 1895, a "small fire" consumed the residence and photo gallery of John T. Moore and resulted in a loss of about $2,500. Spread of this fire was prevented by hasty action of neighborhood "volunteer firemen." Several months later a larger fire occurred, spread rapidly, and resulted in a loss of property valued at over $50,000. Holland Brothers' grocery store, the office of the Dickson Planing Mill, T. A. Wyatt's produce store, Dr. McCreary's drug store, and a livery stable were destroyed by this fire of an unknown origin.[38] Two years later the Dickson Foundry and Machine Shop was entirely destroyed by fire—an industry described by a newspaper editor as "the most important enterprise in town." Several homes also were destroyed. The origin of the fire was not determined, but some people believed that tramps had built a fire near the machine shop and that it had spread over the entire establishment.[39] Perhaps the most disastrous fire of all occurred in 1905 when much of the business area was burned. This catastrophe is still discussed on the streets of Dickson by elderly citizens. Ralph Freeman and others believe it began in a candy kitchen situated in the present location of the Bank of Dickson. Many places of business were destroyed, including the Dickson *Verdict*, a newspaper which was published by Charles and Harry Bevan, who formerly were associated with the Ruskin settlement. Some time was required for the rebuilding of the town. In 1907 when the general assembly of the Cumberland Presbyterian Church convened in Dickson, the mayor and aldermen addressed a message to the body welcoming it to the city but apologizing for the poor condition of town facilities which they said was the result of recent fires.[40] Other fires of a less disastrous nature have occurred since that time, and modern fire prevention methods have been the main reason why they have not been more damaging.

Fire mercilessly brought death to a thirteen-year-old Burns girl in 1886. The child, a daughter of J. W. Watson, had her dress ignited from an open fireplace in her own home. She dashed out of the house and ran aimlessly until a neighbor overtook her and beat out the blaze. The child, badly burned, lingered for about twelve hours before death came.[41]

A most interesting chapter in the history of the towns of Dickson County has been the struggle among the urban areas, principally Charlotte and Dickson, for the location of the county seat. For the first half century of the county's existence Charlotte was the undisputed location of the seat of justice, inasmuch as there were no other towns in the county to rival it. Because of its being the county seat, Charlotte was a flourishing rural town in the ante-bellum days and was a favorite spot for state political leaders to meet voters of Dickson and surrounding counties. The Civil War and its aftermath brought railroads and new settlers from the North, however, and by the turn of the century at least Burns, White Bluff, Sylvia, and Dickson had sought to wrest from Charlotte the apple of her eye, and Dickson had partially succeeded. As early as 1870 Representative A. D. Nicks had secured the passage of a bill which authorized the people to vote on a change of county seat from Charlotte, to Burns, Sneedsville, or White Bluff.[42] All three were located on the Nashville and Northwestern Railroad, and many people contended that this made them more accessible and more desirable as a county seat than was Charlotte. Three years later Jacob Leech introduced a bill in the house authorizing the citizens of Dickson County to vote for or against a change in the county seat.[43] Neither attempt resulted in a removal.

The question erupted again in the 1890's. Dickson by this time was a growing young metropolis and readily accessible by railroads, while Charlotte allegedly had only tradition behind it. At that time a settlement known as Sylvia was being built, five miles east of Charlotte.

Sylvia was located on the Mineral Branch Railroad, (the line which connected the Nashville, Chattanooga, and St. Louis Road at Pond with the Louisville & Nashville at Clarksville), and showed promise of growth. The Sylvia citizens claimed (inaccurately) that their town was located in the exact center of the county, and that this fact, coupled with its accessibility by rail, made it the ideal location for the county's capitol. By 1894 the controversy had become quite heated, and had aroused the attention of people in the neighboring counties. The editor of a Clarksville paper well described the situation:[44]

... There are two candidates for the place provided it is moved from Charlotte. They are Dickson and Sylvia. The latter is a new town on the line of the Clarksville Mineral road, and it is said to be exactly in the center of the county. Sylvia is not known to fame, and its population is something less than Brooklyn. It sprang into existence when the road was built, and it has not yet elected a board of Mayor and Aldermen. Nevertheless, it is in the race and Dickson and Charlotte will find in it a strong competitor. The reason that the sentiment is against Charlotte is the fact that the town is so difficult of approach. A man to attend court in that town from a distance is compelled to go overland and the roads are very rough.... Dickson is on the Northwestern road, and is on the edge of the county. Sylvia, as stated above, is on the Mineral, and is in the center of the county. It would cost no more to build a courthouse and jail there than it would at Dickson and the town of course would build up, should it be selected by the voters as the county site. The property owners of Dickson will make a hot fight to carry the election in their favor, and those of Charlotte will not be idle either. With Sylvia occupying the central ground, there are some who predict that she will walk off a winner.

While Sylvia, Burns, and White Bluff were never entirely successful, Dickson did achieve a victory in 1899. In that year an act was passed whereby a courthouse was erected in that town and the county's business was divided between Charlotte and Dickson. Under this act the circuit and chancery courts would be held in Dickson and the county court in Charlotte. The arrangement was never satisfactory, however, and rivalry between the two towns continued. In 1902 the editor of a Charlotte paper called for a return to the days when the county was blest with unity. Citing the old adage "united we stand, divided we fall," the editor claimed that the division was stifling enterprise, industry, politics, and religion.

Let us lay down our prejudices [he wrote]; let us come together as a unit, and let us work for each other's benefit, and instead of trying to tear down, let us strive to build up. Let the so-called North be a mutual benefit and help to the so-called South, and vice versa. If we will do this, you have no idea how much more pleasant it will be, and how much more influence Dickson County will wield abroad. Let us work together in harmony and we can accomplish much good.[45]

For the next quarter of a century war and recurring depression and prosperity kept the issue smoldering in the background. In 1926 and 1927, however, it erupted in great fury. By this time it had become apparent that several thousands of dollars would have to be spent for maintenance and repair of both courthouses in Charlotte and in Dickson. At the October, 1926, session of the county court a resolution was presented calling for an appropriation of $32,000 for the erection of a new courthouse at Dickson and for the repair of the one at Charlotte. After considerable debate it was defeated by a vote of 18 to 13.[46] Three monts later, in January, 1927, the same resolution was introduced, but was tabled without debate. The faction desiring a new courthouse at Dickson was not to be underestimated, however, for it then presented a motion by which J. T. Halbrook, J. R. Baker, Dan Beasley, and Graham Robertson, with a fifth man to be selected by them, would constitute a committee for the purpose of selecting a site for a new courthouse in Dickson. The motion, which carried no provision for an expenditure of money and which did not call for a direct committal of the court members either way, was passed by a comfortable majority. The committee reported as directed at the next term of court, and its decision was that "the original lot that the old courthouse is situated on" was the best location. The committee members stated that a clear and undisputed title to the property, signed by the wife and each heir of C. Berringer, was held.[47]

Much "politicing" had transpired in the county during the interim between the January and April sessions of the court, and many people became convinced that the taxpayers, already groaning under the burden of having to maintain two separate seats of justice, would not support the sale of bonds in an amount sufficient to erect a new courthouse at Dickson and also repair the one at Charlotte. Therefore, the magistrates passed a resolution calling for a referendum on August 4, 1927, at which the people would decide between Dickson and Charlotte for the location of the county seat. Should the proposed move from Charlotte to Dickson fail to carry, the special court at Dickson would be abolished and all the courts would revert to Charlotte. The resolution was as follows:[48]

Whereas, in order to settle, once for all, the County Seat question, in order that we may have one County Seat and one County Town, either at Dickson or Charlotte, and to do away with the extra trouble, expense and worry because of the two Court systems, which has been the bone of contention in our County for the past 25 years;

Therefore, be it resolved by the Quarterly Court assembled on this, the 4th day of April, 1927, that an election be and is hereby called, to be held at every voting precinct in Dickson County on a day to be fixed by this Court, or the election commissioners, said day to be the 4th day of August, 1927, for the purpose of voting on the removal of the County Seat from Charlotte to Dickson, Tennessee, said election to be held and supervised by the election commissioners of Dickson County, Tennessee, and according to the laws of such cases.

Be it further resolved by this Court, that in case the removal of the said County Seat from Charlotte to Dickson does not receive the ... necessary majority to remove said County Seat, then and in that event the Special Court at Dickson is to be abolished, and all the Court is to revert back to Charlotte, as before the Special Court at Dickson was created.

Thursday, April 4.

The passage of this resolution was a signal for the beginning of a cold war of huge proportions, as the "Southside" of the county arrayed its forces in an effort to pluck the prize from the "Northside." Much unnecessary bitterness, detrimental to every section of the county, resulted, as fact and exaggerated rumor vied with one another in the minds of the voting public. Those desiring Dickson as the permanent location sought to impress upon the people that the town of Dickson had become the market center of the county, that the center of population was in Dickson or in the immediate vicinity of Dickson, that Dickson was more readily accessible to the people than was Charlotte, that the courthouse at Charlotte had been condemned and that a new courthouse would have to be built somewhere anyway, and that Dickson in many others ways was by far the more desirable location. Their story was told by personal contact, through the press, and by tracts and leaflets, large quantities of the latter on several occasions having been dropped from an airplane—then a novelty indeed.

The Charlotte propagandists were not idle. They sought to show that if Dickson was the market center of the county it was a poor one indeed, since most of the farmers took their produce to Nashville markets. They also showed, through leaflets widely distributed, that a county court committee composed of Joe Crosby, Joe Halbrook, N. H. Eubank, and others had examined the courthouse structure at Charlotte and had pronounced it to be in perfect condition. Their examination had taken place in 1925. In order to convince the taxpayers that they did not intend to appropriate money for a new courthouse at Charlotte in case the county seat removal failed, twenty-four magistrates signed a statement pledging their vote against any increase in taxes for the purpose of building a new courthouse at Charlotte.[49]

One prominent citizen, now living in Dickson but then living in Charlotte, assumed leadership in the campaign for Charlotte, and claimed that he mailed out thousands of leaflets over the county in an effort to convert voters. Shortly before the election he hastily penned a letter to W. Blake Leech to inform Leech that some "inside information" on the aims of the Dickson faction had been discovered. "We are inside on their dearest secret," he wrote. The secret was "their hope to get a city hall in the new courthouse in exchange for the perfectly worthless jail they have over there." He asked for a contribution from Leech, who probably had already spent several hundreds of dollars on the campaign, in order that pro-Charlotte information might be disseminated widely by tract and leaflet.[50]

To the great majority of people living in and around Charlotte the courthouse was the lifeblood of the town, and many were convinced that to remove it would leave the historic old county seat little more than a ghost town. Perhaps the strongest and most convincing argument the Charlotte faction had was that there would be no increase in taxes if the county seat were retained at Charlotte, while a removal to Dickson would necessitate the floating of bonds approaching $50,000 in amount for the erection of a courthouse at Dickson. In one leaflet, disseminated widely a few days before the election, the Charlotte forces stated:[51]

Why will you vote more debts and taxes on yourself and on your children, when there is absolutely no need of it? What has Dickson to offer you? Increased debts and more taxes. What does the town of Charlotte offer? A courthouse and jail without increase in debts or taxes.

Attention, Tax-Payers!

The Historical Court House at Charlotte is the Object of Attack by a Ring of County and City Politicians at Dickson.

This court house, founded in 1804 by Montgomery Bell, Robert Dunning, Sterling Brewer and John Davidson, is falsely reported condemned. Mr. Taxpayer, a majority of the magistrates are pledged not to vote any more taxes or increase the county debts to build a new court house at Charlotte if the Dickson politicians fail to remove the county seat. This historical court house is solid, substantial and will serve the county for years to come without cost to taxpayers. It is adequate for the county business, but it is true there is no leather-cushioned, steam-heated loafing place for the politicians.

Why Will You Vote More Debts and Taxes on Yourself and on Your Children, When There is Absolutely No Need of It?

The County Has an Outstanding Debt of Half a Million Dollars

on which we are paying $30,000.00 interest annually. This is $2,500.00 monthly and $85.00 each day, and you still owe the debt for your children to pay. Will you vote to increase this debt and interest charge? You do not have to---the county is well provided with a court house and a new jail.

What Has Dickson to Offer YOU?
INCREASED DEBTS AND MORE TAXES.

What Does the Town of Charlotte Offer?
A Court House and Jail Without Increase in Debts or Taxes

Think, Count the Cost, and Vote Against Removal of the County Seat!

PUBLICITY COMMITTEE

July 25, 1927.

Propaganda leaflet used by Charlotte faction in county seat strife.

Also, sentiment no doubt swayed some in favor of Charlotte. Much was said of the town's early history and, particularly, of the fact that Andrew Jackson once had held court in Charlotte. The Dickson faction on the other hand contended that the vast majority of the citizens would be better and more conveniently served if the seat of justice were at Dickson rather than at Charlotte. They saw in Dickson a rapidly growing metropolis whose growth would be aided vastly by the location of the county courthouse.

On voting day many citizens who had not voted for years rallied to the polls to express their preference for the location of the prize plum of the county. People throughout Middle Tennessee awaited the outcome with anxiety, for some saw within this contest a modified revival of the old Jefferson-Hamilton struggle of agrarianism versus industrialization and rural life versus urban life. The news of the approaching referendum had been publicized in both Nashville papers, and two days before it was held the Nashville *Tennessean* used its choicest editorial spot for a lengthy comment on the implications of the election.[52]

Finally, when all the votes had been tallied, it was found that a majority had voted for removal, but not the necessary two-thirds which was required by law. Nearly 5,000 people cast a record vote, with 2,734 indicating a preference for Dickson and 1,983 voting for Charlotte. A vote of 3,145 would have been necessary for removal, and thus the attempt was lost by a count of 411. As many people suspected, Districts 1, 2, 3, 4, 5, and 13 voted overwhelmingly for Dickson, while the "northside" districts voted for Charlotte. District by district the vote was as follows:[53]

District Number	For Dickson	For Charlotte	District Number	For Dickson	For Charlotte
1	155	0	8 (Cum. Fce.)	4	254
2	102	1	8 (Hamble)	3	79
3	114	2	9 (Slayden)	6	156
4 (Burns)	238	3	9 (Vanleer)	12	179
4 (Brown's)	67	0	10	0	98
5	1,683	46	11	66	72
6 (Charlotte)	4	552	12	82	90
6 (Sylvia)	32	48	13	163	3
7	1	205	14	0	35
			15	2	160

Although statements had been made during the campaign to the contrary, none truthfully could deny that the courthouse at Charlotte, while not in a dangerous condition, was showing considerable wear after one hundred years of use. Also, many people argued that it was too small and inadequate a building in which to conduct all of the county affairs. Consequently, in the early 1930's the present modern and expansive structure was erected. In 1955, when it began to show signs of wear, the county court appropriated several thousand dollars for repair and beautification of the building and grounds, and today the courthouse is one of the best among rural counties in the entire state.

CHAPTER XIII

Dickson Countians in Two World Wars

IN ALL WARS in which the United States has engaged, a call to the colors brought a large contingent of Dickson County men to the defense of their country's honor. This especially was true in both World Wars when the Allied powers became involved in struggles with powers whose designs were to conquer the free world and subject it to their fiat. The seeds from which the first World War germinated had been sown decades before the actual firing commenced in 1914. The major powers of Europe for years had depended upon a "balance of power" to keep the peace. On one side were Germany, Italy, and Austria-Hungary, whose agreements as to military cooperation dated back to the time of our Civil War; on the other were Great Britain, France, and Russia—ancient enemies driven together by the rise of Bismarck and Germany. By 1914 these nations, the former three known as the Triple Alliance and the latter three as the Triple Entente, stood like two pugilists in the ring awaiting the sound of the gong to begin the fight. Imperial rivalry also had pushed the groups apart. England, France, and Russia had old established empires to which they had added liberally during the last decades of the nineteenth century. Germany, only recently unified under Bismarck, also desired a "place in the sun" and under the aggressive Kaiser Wilhem II was willing to risk all in an effort to obtain it. Shortly after 1900, the major European powers began an extensive expansion program, and Germans freely talked of *"der tag,"* which generally was interpreted to mean the day when they would attain what they believed to be their rightful place among nations of the world. The Balkans, ever a powderkeg in European diplomacy, proved to be the spot where the catastrophe actually began, when on June 28, 1914, the heir to the Austrian throne was assassinated in Bosnia. Within the next few weeks events hastily transpired, and by early August, Germany moved troops to the Belgian frontier for an invasion of France. The breath-taking speed with which Europeans had plunged into war left the American people aghast. While government officials began to prepare for American defense, many of the American people talked of "leaving Europe to her quarrels," while others began mentally to take sides one way or another.

A cursory survey of the Dickson County *Herald* for the period indicates no great amount of interest in the European happenings in the early stages of the war.[1] Buying and selling continued as usual, and social affairs apparently continued without interruption. The same was true for the years of 1915 and 1916. By early 1917, however, more interest was manifested. The entrance of the United States into the struggle caused excitement. On April 4, the Senate declared war by a vote of 82 to six, and two days later the House concurred by a vote of 373 to 50. The editor of the *Herald*, in the issues of April 6 and April 13, gave front page publicity to the declaration, and called upon loyal Americans everywhere to rally to the aid of their country. The full implication of the war became more and more apparent as the people became aware that their country was now involved in its first major war since 1865. Within a few weeks they began to mobilize for Red Cross contributions, food conservation, and other ways in which they could help their country at war. By mid-May an organization of which Pitt Henslee and R. E. Corlew were chairman and secretary, respectively, was under way with the assigned task of "selling" the war to the people of Dickson County. They promptly announced extensive speaking engagements for themselves and others to take place in every civil district of the county. The speakers stressed the need for raising larger crops and vegetable gardens, for conserving fuel and food, and for giving liberally to the Red Cross. By the following month the Red Cross campaign was in full swing, and in the issue of June 29, the *Herald* released the names of those who had given generously to the drive. H. T. Cowan and Pitt Henslee headed the list with $100 each, and scores of others followed with gifts ranging from fifty cents to one hundred dollars.

The war was brought even closer to home when on May 18 the Congress passed a Selective Service Act by which men between the ages of 21 and 30 were compelled to register for possible call to service. (The law later was amended to include men between the ages of 18 and 45.) Many Americans had predicted that some of their fellow citizens would not obey the draft laws but that riots comparable to those occurring in the North during the Civil War would ensue. Even Speaker of the House Champ Clark on one occasion exclaimed that there was "precious little" difference between a conscript and a convict. Two weeks after the passage of the law Dickson County Sheriff T. J. Coleman announced the date and places of registration and the officials to be in charge. Adequate precautions would be taken to keep peace, he said, and called upon all the people to cooperate. "Slackers" were warned that they would be under surveillance. "The police of the city, and the county officers are all commanded to see to it that every man is registered if between the specific ages," he advised. Coleman further ordered the officers to "force any man who looks between the ages to show his registration card" if he was suspected of avoiding the draft. By August the first draft numbers had been drawn in Washington, and the names of 302 Dickson County men with numbers corresponding to those drawn in the nation's capital were published in the *Herald*. Earl Choate headed the list. By the first of the following month it was announced that 85 per cent of the County's quota of men, 151, would leave September 19 and October 3, and that the rest would depart shortly thereafter.

The 62 men who left for Camp Gordon, Georgia, on September 19 were given a send-off which probably few had experienced before. Automobiles were scarce in Dickson County at the time, but the local citizenry insisted that each of the 62 men be given a "joyride out Yellow Creek Pike" before being taken to the Dickson courthouse to hear speeches by Colonel R. J. Kelley and R. E. Smith of Ruskin-Cave College, S. E. Hunt, Pitt Henslee, and others. Shortly before they departed the men were served food by the United Daughters of the Confederacy and the Parent-Teacher Association. As Conscripts Joe Ferguson, S. A. Freeman, and Ellis Schmittou made certain that each of their buddies was safely on the train, 1,500 parents and friends wept and shouted words of encouragement to the Dickson County boys who embarked upon an unknown course to defend their country's honor. "The boys were sent away with a smile," a *Herald* reporter wrote.

On October 3, sixty more men departed, and joyrides and "a feed at the Halbrook" Hotel were extended Harry Leathers, Verlie Deason, Norman Nicks, and the other 57 men who left for Camp Gordon.

The editor of the *Herald* announced that he would publish communications from the boys from time to time, and the first of the articles addressed to the folks back home was written by Joe Ferguson of Slayden and S. A. Freeman of Dickson, and published October 12. They wrote that camp life was not as bad as some had reported. "We fear our people are worrying too much about us. They seem to think we are having all work and no rest and no fun. This is a mistaken idea, and we are enjoying ourselves," they cautioned the homefolk. A sizeable contingent of Dickson County men, Freeman wrote on October 19, was to be transferred soon to Camp Sevier near Greeneville, South Carolina. Shortly thereafter he wrote from Camp Sevier, where he was a member of the 105th Trench Mortar Battery.

Another group was transferred to Camp Jackson near Columbia, South Carolina, at about the same time. On December 21 Benjamin C. Greer and Gilbert D. Freeman wrote that they had just arrived at Camp Jackson and that the arrangements were most satisfactory. They had been assigned to the 324th Infantry, and were getting a steady diet of "beans and bacon." Like the men at Camp Gordon, they advised friends not to worry about them for they intended doing their duty. "It's you we are fighting for, mothers, sweethearts, and friends," they advised, ". . . and we won't be back until it's over 'over there.'"

In the meantime the people back home settled down to peacetime mobilization. Pitt Henslee, chairman of the war bond drive, announced a program for the sale of bonds in which every person would be expected to participate. R. E. Corlew, chairman of the food pledge-card campaign, announced sixteen meetings with at least one in every civil district in the interest of food conservation. Joe B. Weems, Mrs. Dockie Shipp Weems, S. E. Hunt, Frank Frazier, Mrs. Pitt Henslee and many others were scheduled to appear at one or more of the meetings for brief addresses. "This nation is not only expected to feed its soldiers, but to feed the Allies also," the chairman advised. Several weeks later County Fuel Administrator J. S. Johnson announced that Dickson County faced a fuel famine. "The winter has just begun," he wrote, "yet there is very little coal on hand." The Dickson power plant had only a two-days supply on hand, and the *Herald* editor prophesied that "there will be women and children found frozen in their fireless homes" unless something was done. People were advised to conserve fuel in every way possible, to close off parts of their homes not in actual use, and to lend efforts toward the procurement of more wood and coal.

While Henslee, Corlew, Johnson, and many others worked on peacetime mobilization, H. H. Self of the First National Bank was instrumental in organizing a National Guard for Dickson County. Much publicity was given to the raising of the Guard, and draft board officials J. M. Larkins and C. M. Lovell stated that those joining the Guard would not be drafted. On December 21, Self announced that 104 men had placed their names upon the National Guard roster and that a unit had been formed. Colonel R. J. Kelley, vice-president of the Ruskin-Cave College, stated that while the same broad curriculum would be offered at his college, emphasis would be placed upon military science.

The columns of the *Herald*, then being edited ably by Ralph A. Freeman, were devoted freely to the war effort. Editorials appeared intermittently. One appearing in the issue of January 4, criticized those who were taking much time in trying to state and define the war aims, and insinuated that they should spend more time in trying to bring the hostilities to a successful conclusion. "An accurate statement of this country's war aims is not of nearly so much importance as the accuracy of the aims of the boys in the trenches," the editor wrote. In the same month he encouraged people to raise more hogs. "Pork production may be the turning point of the war for victory," he wrote, and announced the promotion of "Hog Sales Day" at Dickson and Charlotte for the purpose of promoting the raising of more swine. A "Hog Edition" was soon to be published, and hog advertisements would appear in the *Herald* free for all who got their announcements in by a specified date. In nearly every issue of the paper readers were urged to buy war bonds and stamps and to aid the Red Cross by giving liberally. The occasional reports of the Red Cross making huge profits, which tend to crop up in every war, were stoutly refuted by the *Herald* editor and Pitt Henslee. Henslee issued a statement in which he termed the reports "propaganda." The April 26, issue proclaimed "Corn and Egg Day" on which all who could not contribute money to the Red Cross were urged to bring corn and eggs that would be sold and the proceeds given to the Red Cross. In June the editor placed in the middle of the front page a huge streamer proclaiming the largest War Bond drive yet launched. Dickson County's quota was $418,380, and the combined efforts of all would be necessary to raise this amount, he emphasized. The *Herald* announced the receipt of "slacker blanks" to be furnished those in charge of the war savings drive, which were to be used "to take down the names of all persons not attending the meetings, or who do not pledge themselves to buy War Savings stamps, or who pledge too small amounts." Joe B. Weems, Pitt Henslee, R. E. Corlew, J. A. Clement, Frank S. Hall, and others appeared at places throughout the county in the interest of the campaign. For awhile the campaign seemed to move rather slowly and "slackers" were given the blame. On October 18, the Executive Committee of the Fourth Liberty Loan of which Pitt Henslee was chairman published a special notice to slackers. It read:

SLACKERS TAKE NOTICE

It has been agreed by the Executive Committee ... that all who are able to take bonds, and do not, their names will be published next week, and a copy of the paper mailed to the Government.

Apparently such was sufficient to drive the slackers to action, for shortly thereafter Henslee announced that Dickson County had "gone over the top" and had subscribed more than its allotment.

The columns of the Dickson County *Herald* were open to any and all who might desire to contribute comments and opinions on the war. Of the many schemes for winning the war, one of the most unique was contained in a letter signed by "Clod Hopper" of Charlotte, and published April 26. The writer believed that a hasty cessation of hostilities might be attained by capturing all women associated with the German Kaiser and preventing them from advising or influencing the Kaiser in any way. "The power that brought on this war is woman," he wrote. "Capture the Kaiserine and this war will end as suddenly as it began." Women had driven Kaiser Wilhelm to commit "every heinous crime his murderous mind could conceive. He has courtmartialed and shot women, burned Belgian girls at the stake, bayoneted children, and ... seems to glory in his inhuman deeds ... ," it was alleged.

While the war was on the minds of all, the people "back home" tried as best they could to "carry on" in a reasonably normal manner. The Twentieth Century Mothers Club of Dickson still held its regular meetings, and pie suppers, barbecues, and dinners on the ground continued to be held throughout the county. The silent movies drew crowds in Dickson, as the antics of Fatty Arbuckle and the dramatic performances of Mary Pickford thrilled Dickson County movie goers. A local political campaign with almost as many fireworks as then were being displayed on the Marne took place in 1918, with Frank Frazier and Joe B. Weems as candidates for county judge, and Frank S. Hall and Henry T. V. Miller for state representative. Frazier accused Weems of being a tool of the W. R. Hudson machine, which Weems denied. Hudson, as colorful and powerful a political figure as the county ever had, had held various offices, including that of county judge for sixteen years, sheriff, circuit court clerk, and magistrate. He was still a potent force in 1918, and his support, coupled with Weems' general popularity, won the election for Weems. In the Miller-Hall race, Miller, having defeated R. L. Leech in the general election of 1916, was the incumbent; Hall, a young lawyer who had recently moved to Dickson from Hickman County, was the challenger. Miller's father was a native German, and rumors were spread that the candidate was not a loyal American citizen. This Miller hotly denied in a full column statement published in the *Herald* on July 18, and countered with the claim that Hall was a "draft dodger." He described Hall as a "lawyer who has done nothing . . . in behalf of the war effort," but who, having become eligible for the draft in Hickman County, had come to Dickson County in order to avoid the draft in Hickman. Miller published:

> Mr. Hall is not justly a citizen of Dickson County. He has never voted in any election in Dickson County, has never paid taxes in Dickson County, and owns no property in Dickson County. But being an artful dodger he comes here from Hickman County hoping to be elected to the Legislature when it is doubtful if he could be elected to any office in Hickman County, where he is best known.

Hall was described as the son of a wealthy planter who would put thousands of dollars into his son's campaign for representative, and who might even stoop to an attempt to buy his son out of military service.

In the following issue of the *Herald* Hall answered the attack by describing it "libelous" and by presenting several signed affidavits. One such affidavit was signed by the chairman of the draft board of Hickman County, who stated that Hall had been deferred because he had a wife and child. The chairman further decried the insinuation that the elder Hall's money could exclude any man from the draft and declared Miller's allegations an insult not only to the Hickman County draft board but to the government of the United States also. Another statement presented by Hall was signed by J. A. Larkins, chairman of the Dickson County draft board, who agreed with the Hickman ruling, and condemned Miller for his remarks insulting to both the draft board of Hickman County and to the government of the United States. Hall stated that he had no other intention but to go when called into military service, that he had two brothers already in the service, that he was a taxpayer of Dickson County, and that he was in the process of building a home in the first civil district of the county. O. N. Moody earlier had announced his intention of entering the race for representative, but withdrew in June, and pledged himself to give to the Red Cross an amount equal to that which he would have spent on the campaign. Ignoring the Miller-Hall feud, he wrote of his withdrawal and concluded:

> Every fiber of my being is dedicated to winning this war. Why? Because everything we hold near and dear to us is at stake—our homes and firesides, and the safety of our women and children. God bless our women.

Hall went on to win the election overwhelmingly and to become one of the most powerful political leaders in the state. He has held several important political positions including that of speaker of the house of representatives. Miller likewise later achieved considerable prominence.

While people at home tried as best they could to live a normal life, men continued to answer the draft calls and to entrain for service.

Eighteen white and 16 colored men departed May 3, and on July 26 twenty-five men left for Camp Gordon. On May 10 Private S. A. Freeman advised the *Herald* readers that he and his buddies soon would sail for Europe where they promised to make short work of the Kaiser. "We are preparing to cross the pond and lick the Kaiser," he advised the Dickson County friends. "It is our determination when we do get to Germany to drive those Huns back to Berlin, and then clear off the face of the earth," he wrote.

As the men were sent to Europe in increasingly large numbers the ravages of war were felt in Dickson County as never before. The "Spanish Influenza" which struck in the fall of 1918 accounted for more deaths than did the bullets and bayonets of the Germans. Lucian Thomas Berry, for whom the American Legion Post in Dickson later was named, died of pneumonia on September 30, 1918 at the age of 23, and a few weeks later William Luther Browning, only son of Mr. and Mrs. L. J. Browning, died "somewhere in France" of measles and bronchial pneumonia. One of the saddest cases of all was that of Esquire and Mrs. J. N. Peeler, of the second civil district, who in a period of three months lost three sons. The people back home were stricken with influenza, also. Dr. Ewing Larkins of Charlotte, his wife, and infant son died in a period of a few weeks from the dreaded disease. Many articles appeared in the *Herald* on how to treat influenza and pneumonia. The patient usually was advised to go to bed, remain quiet, call the doctor, and use of plenty of Vaporub and Calatabs.

The war came to end on November 11, 1918, and the next issue of the *Herald* carried headlines announcing "Germany Accepts Allies Terms; World War Ends." The editor advised that although the war in Europe was over, there should be no relaxation of the war effort on the home front. Wynns Brothers and others published advertisements in which they urged the people not to relax until every boy "is safe back at home." Two weeks later the county paper was published on Thanksgiving Day. The editor wrote in that issue:

Many of us began to be thankful about a month before Thanksgiving Day. The weight of a great anxiety has been lifted from those whose relatives have been in war service in the field.... Amid our rejoicings there should sound a note of deep sympathy for those who have been maimed on the battlefield and for the families of the killed.

The transition "back to normalcy" for the people of Dickson County was rapid. Less than a month after the war was over Pitt Henslee announced an increase in the sugar allotment from three pounds to four pounds per month, per person. Controls would be dropped entirely soon, he said. By January and February of the following year business was booming and real estate in the vicinity of Dickson brought high prices. The county court considered the construction of a new and more elaborate jail at Charlotte, G. W. Dodson purchased the T. B. Loggins property on which the Dickson Normal College had been operated, and some farm land in the vicinity of Dickson was selling for $120 per acre. By 1919 a highway, which would span the state from

Memphis to Bristol, was planned. Some people in Dickson County favored it and some opposed it, but the County, like the entire nation, was on the precipice of a huge highway construction program which was to dominate the interests of the American people for years to come.

During the two decades between the two world wars the people experienced the ten fat years and the ten lean years in much the same manner as did the people of the entire nation. Economic expansion is discussed in another chapter. Politically, several Dickson Countians rose to prominence during the period. Frank S. Hall, in 1923 at the age of 32 became speaker of the house of representatives of Tennessee, and was the first and only person from Dickson County ever to receive that honor. The legislature of 1923 had among it many young Tennesseans who later rose to prominence, over whom Hall presided ably. Among them were Prentice Cooper, of Shelbyville, who later became governor; I. D. Beasley, of Carthage, who until his recent death was one of Tennessee's most prominent and colorful political figures; Walter M. Haynes, of Winchester, later to become lieutenant governor of the state; and Lois Bejach, of Memphis, whose distinguished career of public service has led him to his present position of member of the court of appeals. All were under 30 except Bejach, who was 36. In the following year Hall, now a well known political personality, entered the race for congressman from the seventh congressional district. The county court endorsed him as a man in whom the people of the district might safely repose the "utmost confidence in his honesty, ability, and integrity."[2] Hall, together with Edward E. Eslick and C. W. Turner, opposed the incumbent, W. C. Salmon. The fact that Hall, Turner, and Salmon were from the northern part of the district and only Eslick, of Giles County, was from the southern part, insured victory for Eslick, who campaigned hard and impressed many with his oratorical abilities. In the district as a whole, Hall finished fourth, but in the county he ran nearly 600 votes ahead of his nearest opponent. The victorious Eslick ran a poor fourth in Dickson County.[3]

William Loch Cook was another Dickson Countian who rose to prominence during the period between the wars. He was appointed a justice of the supreme court in 1923. Cook had practiced law in Charlotte, had served in the house of representatives, and had been elected circuit judge in 1908.

W. M. Leech and W. C. Cook were two other Dickson Countians who were candidates for positions in political subdivisions larger than the county level. Both ran for positions on the State Democratic Executive Committee from the seventh congressional district, Leech being a candidate in 1942 and Cook in 1944. Both lost, Leech being defeated by a tremendous majority. He polled only 4,890 votes, while two opponents, A. B. Bryant and C. D. Walton, polled 9,289 and 10,312 respectively. Cook fared better than Leech two years later but also was unsuccessful. He polled 4,319 votes, to 5,098 for Bryant and 5,589 for Walton.

Of the county races during the interim between the wars perhaps that for county judge in 1934 was the most interesting. In that year Clark Leech, a member of the county court and a practicing attorney of Dickson, and W. M. Leech, Charlotte attorney, became engaged in what the editor of the *Herald* called the "show of the marathon." Both were young and desirous of victory and launched vigorous campaigns. Over four thousand votes were cast in the election, which was far more than had been cast in any previous contest for the post. W. M. Leech was victorious, but only by a slim margin of about 200 votes. Both men ran strong on their respective sides of the county, and Clark Leech polled over one thousand votes in the city of Dickson alone. W. M. Leech ran stronger in the rural areas, however, and this proved to be his margin of victory.[4]

The Second World War and the part played in it by the people of Dickson County still are too well in the minds of the people to need much recapitulation. It will be remembered that the phenomenal rise and agggressive policies of Adolf Hitler by 1938 had placed him in full and complete control of Germany and the Sudetenland, and on the precipice of what he hoped would be world conquest. By September of the following year his Nazi troops had goose-stepped into Poland almost unhindered, and several months later crushed the massive Maginot line between France and Germany as though it had been made of cardboard. While Charles A. Lindbergh and others of pacifist temperament believed the Allied cause to be hopeless and openly sought to keep the American people from expressing anti-German sentiments for fear that Hitler might be offended, the prevailing sentiment of the vast majority of the American people was pro-Ally from the beginning. The United States began immediately to prepare for war. On September 16, 1940, President Roosevelt signed the Selective Service Act, and the draft which had been used so effectively in the First World War was resurrected. Before the first contingent of Dickson County men could be called to the defense of the colors under this act, however, the National Guard was inducted into federal service. The Dickson County unit, known as Company E of the 117th Infantry of the Thirtieth Division, departed for Fort Jackson, South Carolina, to begin a period of service which for many was not to end until cessation of hostilities five years later. Many of the men transferred into other units in the months and years after induction, but all served with distinction. Many were wounded on the field of battle, and some gave their lives.

The official American entrance into the war came on December 8, 1941, on the day following the surprise attack by the Japanese on Pearl Harbor. Germany and Italy declared war on the United States on December 11, and on the same day Congress responded with separate declarations against those countries. By 1942 the people of Dickson County were witnessing the departure of more and more of their sons for military service. This war, of course, was felt considerably more than was the First World War. There was scarcely a home in Dickson County which did not have a son, husband, or other loved one in the war. Many families had as many as three sons in the service, and a few had even more. Mrs. William W. White of Burns had six sons in the service—Marshall D., Wesley W., Robert T., and Walter B., who were in the Navy; Olin K., with the Coast Guard; and Marcus L., in the Army.

While the men marched off to war, the home front appeared very much like it had been in the First World War. There were the same appeals for the purchase of war bonds, for gifts to the Red Cross, and for the conservation of food, fuel, and electricity. Gus Lanier, Negro writer for the *Herald*, expressed the general sentiment found in many of the issues of the *Herald* when he advised the people on March 10, 1944, "If you are interested in the soldiers and want to help shorten the time when they will come home, ... give all you can to the War Fund Drive." Sugar, gas, shoes, and other commodities were rationed to a much greater extent than had been the case 25 years before, and the people felt the pinch of war far more. Industry experienced a great dearth of manpower, and those who for various reasons were not called into military service could find jobs readily at good wages. The Nashville, Chattanooga, and St. Louis Railroad and the DuPont Company at Old Hicksory, not infrequently published advertisements in the *Herald* for workers. The N. C. and St. L. would not only pay well but would give time and one-half for overtime, and free passes on trains. The DuPont Company advertised for "male or female" laborers.

By 1944 scarcely an issue of the county paper appeared without including an account of the death or the wounding of a Dickson County soldier. The issue for August 18, 1944, announced that "Casualties among local youth continue to mount as Armies blast Nazis on French fronts." The writer told of the recent wounding of T/Sgt. Louis Story (who later was killed), S/Sgt. Wayman McClurkan, and S/Sgt. Claude Creighton, all of whom had left Dickson with the National Guard in 1940; and of Lynn Cochran for the second time, Earl C. Mackey, and others. Many men were decorated on the field of battle. Billy Speight was awarded a battle field commission. Naval Lieutenant James A. Weems, present county judge (1956), was cited for gallantry at Tarawa and earlier had been awarded the Silver Star. T/Sgt. Paul M. Corlew was awarded the Distinguished Flying Cross and the Air Medal with three oak leaf clusters, and Carney Nicks received the Bronze Star medal and the Silver Star. Many received the Purple Heart for wounds received in action, and many, in addition to those mentioned above, received awards and were cited for gallantry and intrepidity in duty.

The people back home felt the war with increasing intensity throughout 1944 and early 1945. Herbert Tallent wrote a regular weekly column entitled "With the Armed Forces" in which he told of the happenings to Dickson County men in service. Annie Lee Williams, a member of the faculty of Dickson High School and a regular columnist for the *Herald* expressed the sentiments of many early in 1945 when she wrote, "War is a fantastic, unreal thing to those of us who stay at home. ..." Betty Adcock, a senior at Dickson High School in 1945 published an essay in the *Herald* in which she sought to capture the spirit of those who had made the supreme sacrifice. She wrote:

We are the War Dead. We are many in number. Our purposes were and are great. We did not want to die. Our petty lives went unnoticed among the masses, but to us our future stretched before us like a broad and beautiful highway. Gradually the picture began to change and almost imperceptibly fade. Then with the suddenness of lightning our future was completely gone.

We went in many ways. The Dieppe raid claimed many of us. Pearl Harbor was only the beginning of the long "missing in action" list.... Wherever we may be, the spirit with which we fought and the ideals for which we died shall not perish from the earth!

The *Herald* issue of February 23, 1945, paid special tribute to 43 Dickson County men who had made the supreme sacrifice. Less than two months later the paper devoted much of its front page to a tribute to the Commander-in-Chief whose untimely death had shocked the world. The editor saw in Franklin D. Roosevelt a "great American" who would be recorded in the pages of history as "one of the greatest statesmen of the ages," and whose greatness rested primarily in his fight for the common man.

Less than a month later the *Herald* proclaimed the defeat of the Axis in Europe. On May 11, the unconditional surrender of the enemy was announced in the columns of the county paper as having occurred four days earlier. The people were urged to remain diligent, for the Japanese remained an enemy "even more ruthless than the one just defeated...." Within three months, on August 6, about one-half of Hiroshima was destroyed by an atomic bomb, and three days later Nagasaki met with even greater destruction at the hands of the American Air Force. Russia, then an American ally, declared war on Japan by the time of the dropping of the second bomb, and proceeded to drive quickly into Manchuria. Japan surrendered on August 14, although the surrender documents were not signed until September 2, which date President Truman officially designated as V-J Day. The main problem now became that of getting the men home, and the *Herald* each week told of the arrival of Dickson County men on "stateside" and of the many celebrated homecomings.

Military hostilities now yielded to domestic and foreign problems of broad and serious scope. The menace of fascism was now replaced by what many considered to be an even greater menace—communism. Korea was divided for occupational purposes between Russia and the United States, but within five years after the close of World War II a struggle began between the North Koreans (pro-Communist), and the South Koreans (anti-Communist). While the Korean War was not of the scope of either World War I or World War II, it was of sufficient size to take a large number of Dickson County men to the battlefield for the third time in a little over a quarter of a century.

A discussion of military activities would be incomplete without brief reference to the veterans organizations of the county, particularly the Lucian Berry Post Number 115 of the American Legion. This chapter was formed April 16, 1921, with Joe F. Crosby as commander and

Herbert S. Tallent as adjutant, and became the first veterans' organization in the county. Twenty-seven veterans were charter members, and they launched the organization upon a successful venture. By 1952, when Warren G. Medley was commander, membership reached 660. The charter members are as follows:

Lee R. Baker	Alfred L. White
Mack Dudley	J. G. Barber
S. V. Garton	Sam A. Freeman
Claude L. McCorpin	W. J. Martin
Lloys S. Robinson	Cullom Redden
Dr. H. P. Spencer	William B. Saeger
D. Talmage Taylor	Herbert S. Tallent
J. A. Brake	Hugh T. Wynns
Thomas D. Devine	J. F. Crosby
H. Rye Leech	W. R. Foster
Thomas A. Pack	Carney Murrell
Lester Rogers	William R. Robinson
Arthur Speight	Curtis F. Sheley
	C. A. Tutor

The Post is ably supported by the unit of American Legion Auxiliary, which was organized in 1926. Mrs. W. O. Hake was its first president. The two organizations sponsor many worthy projects over the county annually.

In addition to the Lucian Berry Post Number 115, there is the White Bluff American Legion Post Number 140, which was organized at the close of World War II. It reached a peak membership of 104 in 1946, at which time Warren Hill was commander. Shortly after World War II ended the Harry Murrell Chapter of Disabled American Veterans was organized, and in 1945 the Sensing Brothers Post of Veterans of Foreign Wars was established. Wilbur F. Marsh, who had been among the first to cross the English Channel on D-Day as he led a company of infantry, and who was wounded in action and decorated on several occasions, became temporary commander and assumed much of the responsibility for the chapter's organization. It is the only post in the county named for two men—Benjamin C. Sensing and Arnold Sensing, sons of Mr. and Mrs. Drury Sensing of the Greenwood Community.

Forty-two men in the First World War and 62 men in the Second World War gave their lives in order that the American way of life might not perish. Their names were cast in a bronze memorial plaque and placed on the east side of the War Memorial Building in Dickson, as a most fitting memorial to the honored sacrifice they made. Their names also appear in Appendix E of this volume.

The War Memorial Building itself is a tribute to all Dickson County men who gave their lives in the service of their country. It was made possible by an appropriation of $15,000 from the State of Tennessee and a like sum by the county. Because of the untiring efforts of Joe F. Crosby, Dickson County representative, and others, the state appropriated its part in 1929. It was 1933, however, before the building was completed and officially dedicated. The building today houses the Dickson County Library, in charge of Mrs. A. N. Hines.

CHAPTER XIV

Recent Developments

PERHAPS the most important political development in recent years was the election of a native son, Frank Goad Clement, as governor of the State of Tennessee. Clement was born and reared in Dickson, and also lived for brief periods in Scottsville, and Kyrock, Kentucky, and Lebanon, Tennessee, during his early years. He was graduated from Dickson High School in 1937, where he attained an enviable record as a public speaker. After studying for two years at Cumberland University, Clement entered the Vanderbilt University Law School, where he was graduated in 1942 with an LL. B. degree. He then served with the Federal Bureau of Investigation for one year before entering military service. After his discharge from the army he established law offices in Dickson and Nashville and quickly came to the attention of state administration leaders who saw in him one whose oratorical abilities could render him a strong asset to any political cause. He was appointed as general counsel for the railroad and public utilities commission and served for four years before resigning to enter private law practice. In 1949 he was elected State Commander of the American Legion, and in the same year was named "young man of the year" by the State Junior Chamber of Commerce. He announced his candidacy for governor nearly two years before the election of 1952 and opened his campaign in Gallatin in May, 1952.

In his opening address at Gallatin Clement severely indicted the Browning administration in a lengthy bill of particulars which he filed with the people of Tennessee. This address and others that followed drew large audiences, and the young lawyer held them entranced with his spellbinding oratory. The Nashville *Banner*, which had backed Senator Clifford Allen in 1950, hastily left the Allen camps desolate in order to give the full impact of its influence to the Clement candidacy.

Incumbent Gordon Browning, a political warhorse of many seasons, sought in 1952 a fourth term as governor—a thing others had sought but which only two, John Sevier and William Carroll, had attained a century and a quarter ago. Browning had made at least two serious political blunders during his stormy political career, and added a third of equal proportions during the campaign. These made him a ready target for the oratorical artillery of Clement. During his first term as governor (1937-1939), he had sought the enactment of a unit bill which, although popular among some in the rural counties, was clearly out of step with the times. His action was lambasted by the urban press, which played an important role in his failure to achieve re-election in 1938. His second serious political error came early in 1952 when he lease-purchased the Memorial Hotel from men close to his administration. The building was to be used for much needed office space, but it was purchased at a price allegedly far higher than that for which buildings of similar size and construction could be bought. His third serious political blunder came (through no fault of his own) at the Democratic convention in Chicago, in 1952, when he and the Tennessee delegation supported the "loyalty oath" in their effort to secure the nomination of Estes Kefauver for President, to which oath some of the Southern delegates vigorously objected. Browning was said to have "sold out the South" in this, the alleged "Chicago betrayal," and thus alienated the support of the strong Dixiecrat element of West Tennessee. These political mistakes, especially the Memorial Hotel deal, became grist for the Clement mill. The young Dickson Countian's superb radio and television personality, coupled with his skillful platform performances, drew large audiences from the time of his opening address at Gallatin to the close of his campaign via radio on the morning of the election.

The incumbent was opposed not only by Clement, but by two other prominent Tennesseans, Senator Clifford Allen of Nashville, and Clifford Pierce of Memphis. Allen had made a surprisingly good race in 1950, and many believed that he had a chance for election in 1952. As the summer progressed, however, the contest became a bitter man-to-man duel. On election day, August 7, 1952, Clement polled over 300,000 votes, and won the election by over 55,000 votes.

Once inaugurated, the governor launched a program too well known to recapitulate here. Several Dickson Countians received appointments to high posts in state government. W. M. Leech was named to the important cabinet position of commissioner of highways. Leech, a Charlotte native, had practiced law in Charlotte, and had served two terms as county judge. Shortly before his appointment to the governor's cabinet he had been elected by a substantial majority to the Limited Constitutional Convention, which convened in Nashville in April, 1953. James Edwards was named warden of the penitentiary, but later resigned.

Various others received responsible posts, among whom are E. W. Adcock, Dowl Miller, Maurice Harris, and others. During the second Clement administration, to be discussed presently, Robert Clement, father of the governor, became the second Dickson Countian in history to serve on the supreme court of the state when he received a temporary appointment. Miss Anna Belle Clement, the governor's sister, who had been active in her brother's initial campaign for governor, became prominent in Democratic circles of the state.

In 1954 Governor Clement was re-elected by an overwhelming majority. His opponent again was Gordon Browning. The former governor waged a vigorous campaign, but his tactics were outmoded and overshadowed by those of the youthful Dickson Countian. To his skillful platform appearances the governor added his record in office and a promise of no increase in taxes, all of which brought to him the largest number of votes ever received by a gubernatorial candidate in a Democratic primary.

In 1956 Governor Clement was selected by the Democratic National Committee to deliver the keynote address to the Convention members, on August 13, 1956. In the address he severely indicted the Republican Administration. It was the first keynote address ever delivered by a Tennessean. Although it did not achieve for him the Vice-Presidential nomination as many had hoped, it did help him to acquire national recognition.

From a business and industrial point of view, the recent additions of the K. F. Kline Company, Incorporated, and the Diebold Company, Incorporated, stand foremost. The Kline Company manufactures a variety of warehouse equipment, including lockers for schools, offices, and industrial use; steel shelving for use in stock rooms, storage rooms and warehouses; and parts for storage bins and storage cabinets. It began operation in Dickson in January, 1953, and today employs about 60 persons. The Diebold concern acquired the interests of the Kline Company in October, 1955, and will manufacture microfilm equipment, bank vaults, and safes, in addition to continuing the manufacture of the Kline products. Fred Bean, who has been the general superintendent of the Kline concern, will continue in that capacity with the Diebold Company, according to an announcement from Diebold's Canton, Ohio, headquarters.

Another enterprise recently added is Dickson's first and only radio station, WDKN which is operated by Billy Potts. It operates on a frequency of 1260 kilocycles, and is on the air seven days each week during the daylight hours.

Two large factories of Dickson, established during the 1930's, today are operating at full capacity. The Henry I. Siegel Company, Incorporated, began operation in 1933, and today manufactures trousers and shirts. The plant employs nearly 600 persons, of whom 505 are women, and had a payroll during the year of 1955 of over one and one-quarter million dollars. Ernest Siegel is manager of the plant. The other "old timer" in Dickson is the Dickson Manufacturing Company, which began operation in 1930. In that year it began with only 20 employees in a building which had housed the Cigar Company. In 1956 it employed 300 persons, mostly women, and has an annual payroll of over a half million dollars. J. Mitchell Hayes is in charge of the plant and is a part owner.

The oldest enterprise in Dickson is the Leathers Handle Factory, which was established by A. H. Leathers when he and his wife came to Dickson from Pennsylvania in 1897. Leathers operated the business until his death in 1933, when members of his family took charge. For some years they manufactured baseball bats, in addition to handles of all types and flooring, and the "Dixie Swatter" came to be used by baseball teams over the country. Today the concern employs 65 people and has an annual payroll of over one hundred thousand dollars.

There are a number of smaller industries in Dickson that employ from a half dozen to 25 persons, including the Tennessee Valley Furniture Industry, Stewart Lumber Company, Central Lumber Company, Dickson Laundry, Myatt's Laundry, Coca Cola Bottling Company, Taylor Machine Works, and the John B. Leathers Lumber Company.

Industries in Dickson County employ over one thousand people and have a payroll of over two million dollars. The County's location and ample labor supply make it an excellent location for the addition of more industrial establishments.

The Montgomery Bell Park, located on Highway No. 70 between Dickson and White Bluff, brings thousands to its recreational facilities annually. The park was begun in 1934 when the Federal government, undertook to create a park in each of the three grand divisions of Tennessee. Thanks to the efforts of Joe B. Weems, E. S. Payne, and many other prominent Dickson County citizens, the park was located in Dickson County and was named for the iron master whose energetic spirit still haunts the hills of Middle Tennessee. Approximately 3,892 acres were acquired from the estate of Epps Jackson and others, and was developed into a rustic park by men working under the various New Deal agencies, chiefly the Civilian Conservation Corps. Two large lakes, one 54 acres in size and the other 28 acres, have been developed. In 1951 a hotel large enough to offer overnight accomodations for fifty persons was opened, and its dining facilities have become very popular. Summer camps are maintained for both boys and girls, and boating and fishing have interested many people, both old and young.

Educationally, much progress has been made in recent years, as the people have become more conscious of the educational needs of their children and of the crowded conditions and inadequacies of the existing school plants. At the April, 1956, meeting of the county court legislation was enacted which will provide important changes in the educational facilities of the County. The legislation was based upon a study and recommendation of a committee composed of the county judge and representatives from the board of education and the county court. The committee found the Sylvia school to be in a "deplorable condition" and the Colesburg building to be "old, in poor condition, and not large enough." The Charlotte, Burns, and White Bluff buildings were found to be overcrowded and inadequate. The erection of another elementary school at Dickson was strongly advised. The report of the committee, which was adopted with small modifications, called for expenditures of three quarter million dollars.

Doctors Lawrence Jackson, J. T. Jackson, and William Jackson operate the largest medical clinic in the county.

Dickson County has been fortunate in having able public officials from the earliest days to the present. The names of most of them appear in the Appendix of this volume. Brief biographical sketches of some of the present officials follow:

James A. Weems is the present county judge. He is a graduate of Vanderbilt University and of the law school of the University of Virginia; he is a combat veteran, having served with the United States Navy. Judge Weems is the son of the late Joe B. Weems, beloved county judge who served from 1918 to 1934, and Dockie Shipp Weems, well known civic leader and teacher who once was voted the outstanding high school speech teacher in the United States. Mr. Weems is a lawyer. The judge is the chief magistrate of the county, judge of the juvenile court, and presides over meetings of the county court.

V. N. Loggins is clerk of the county court. Born in 1908, Mr. Loggins was elected to his position in 1954 by a large majority. His official duties are to keep the minutes of the county court, issue all licenses, issue letters of administration, and keep probate records, wills, and so forth.

Pruett Kelly is the trustee. He was born in 1910 in Humphreys County, but moved at an early age to Dickson County. He was elected in 1952 by a substantial majority, and again in 1954. His duties are to collect all property and utility taxes.

Claude Powers holds the office of circuit court clerk. Mr. Powers, a native Dickson Countian, is one of the oldest officials in point of service, having held his present office continuously since 1934. He keeps the records of the circuit court, including both criminal and civil jurisdiction.

Warren Hill was elected sheriff in 1950, and has ably served in this capacity since that date. He was born in Dickson County in 1900, and lives at Dickson today. He is the chief law enforcement officer of the county. He was succeeded in 1956 by James (Bud) Weems.

Charles Marsh, Jr. became county register in 1950, and is now serving his second term. He was born in 1923 in Vanleer, but moved to Charlotte at an early age. He is a graduate of Austin Peay State College, and a veteran, having served in the European theatre of operations during the Second World War. His duties are to record deeds, mortgages, and other instruments which are required by law to be registered or that one might desire to have registered.

Tom T. Sugg is the present superintendent of public schools. Born in 1904, Mr. Sugg was elected to his present position fifty years later. He is responsible for the successful operation of the public schools of the county, and also is secretary of the board of education. Serving with him are Mrs. Mary Eubank Sensing, supervising teacher; J. C. Erranton, attendance teacher; Mrs. Carlene Brown, materials and textbook clerk; and A. C. Spicer, maintenance and transportation supervisor.

J. B. White is the present clerk and master. He was appointed to the position by Chancellor Sam Marable in 1941, upon the death of the incumbent, J. J. Taylor. He is a lawyer, and is a director of the First National Bank of Dickson. He keeps the records of the chancery court, and performs other judicial functions.

A. Dalton Brown is the present tax assessor. He was born in 1888 in the third district, and took office in 1950, and was re-elected in 1956. He had served as a member of the county court from 1936 to 1948. He assesses values on all real property in the county.

Earl Hall is the county road supervisor. Born in 1906, Mr. Hall is a native of the White Bluff area. He first took office in 1948. His duties include the building and supervising of repair of the roads of the county.

Dr. Mary Baxter Cook is head of the county health department. She is a graduate of the Vanderbilt Medical School. Her duties are to supervise the health and welfare of the people of the county.

Mrs. Albert Hines is the county librarian. She maintains the library at the War Memorial Building, which includes thousands of volumes.

The members of the county board of education are: M. F. Powell, chairman, Cumberland Furnace; John D. Sensing, Cumberland Furnace; M. G. Frazier, Dickson; E. D. Buttrey, White Bluff; J. E. Horton, Charlotte; Graham Hicks, Charlotte; and James H. Nicks, Dickson.

The magistrates of the county play a very important role in county affairs and county government, as they compose the legislative body of the county when in session, and are judicial officers for their respective districts. They convene quarterly, and also may be called into extra sessions from time to time when conditions warrant. Brief biographical sketches of the present (1956) magistrates follow.

D. K. Walker and Corbie Adcock serve the first civil district. Both are farmers. Squire Adcock is relatively a newcomer to the court compared with Mr. Walker, who has served for nearly 20 years as a magistrate from the first district. Both live on RFD No. 1, Dickson.

Hubert Redden and Charles E. Bruce are representatives from the second civil district. Both are farmers, and both were elected in 1954. Both live on RFD No. 2, Dickson, and both are well respected in their communities.

A. H. Bibb and Rufus Tidwell represent the third district. Mr. Bibb was born in 1886, and was first elected in 1954. He lists his address as RFD No. 1, Burns. Mr. Tidwell was born in 1903, is a farmer, and was elected in 1954. He and Squire Bibb ably represent their district.

E. H. Meek, Sr., and Lynn Brown are magistrates from the fourth district. Mr. Meek was born in 1881, and is a retired Railroad Agent of the Nashville, Chattanooga, and St. Louis Railroad. He was elected in 1953 shortly after Burns was incorporated, and is Burns' first magistrate. Mr. Brown also lives at Burns, is a farmer by occupation, and has served eight years as magistrate.

Melvin Harris, John W. Galloway, and Dr. B. F. Nesbitt serve the fifth district. Mr. Harris was born in 1879, and he and Squire Galloway are the oldest men on the court. Most of his life has been devoted to public service. He has served the county in the capacity of both trustee and county court clerk. He is the father of Dorris, Garner, Maurice, and Brooks—all prominent Dickson County citizens. Mr. Galloway is the corporation magistrate for the City of Dickson. He was born in 1879, and has served as magistrate for six years, having been elected in 1951. Dr. B. F. Nesbitt is the only physician on the court, being an optometrist by profession. He is a director of the First National Bank, chairman of the board of public utilities of Dickson, a past president of the Tennessee Optometrist Association, and has held other positions of public trust.

Hubert W. Corlew, Joe McMillan, D. B. Greer, and D. D. Robertson represent the sixth district. Mr. Corlew is the oldest, both in years and in point of service. Always a very popular magistrate, he led the ticket in votes both in 1948 and again in 1954. He is a retired farmer. Mr. Robertson is next in point of service. He was elected first in 1948 by a large vote, and was re-elected in 1954. D. B. Greer is the other magistrate from the district-at-large. Born in 1903, Squire Greer for many years has taken an active part in civic and church affairs. A man of unimpeachable integrity, he was elected in 1954 by a large vote. Mr. McMillan is the magistrate for the town of Charlotte, which is in the sixth district. Squire McMillan is the youngest magistrate in the district, and with one exception is the youngest on the entire court, having been born in 1918. He is the son of Hon. J. A. McMillan, who was the Charlotte magistrate for some years prior to his death in 1936, and Eva Leech McMillan; thus he comes from two of the county's oldest and best respected families. He was elected in 1954, and from the beginning he has exerted an important influence upon good county government.

Charlie Warner Harris and Horace Pickering are the seventh district magistrates. Both are farmers, and both live on RFD No. 1, Charlotte. Mr. Harris long has been prominent in civic and church affairs, and at one time served as deputy sheriff. He has served for eight years, and Mr. Pickering for four years.

Horace Swift and Nathan Miller are the able magistrates from the eighth district. Both are serving their second terms. Both live at Cumberland Furnace, are highly respected citizens, and take an active part in the affairs of their county and community.

James A. Cooksey, Max Davenport, W. R. Berry, and R. F. Stone are magistrates from the ninth district. Mr. Cooksey has served as magistrate for a total of 13 years, and first became a member of the court in 1931. Between that date and the present he has been a member of the board of education, and has held other important posts. He lives at Vanleer. Mr. Davenport lives at Slayden, and is a merchant there. He is also recorder for the town of Slayden, and has been a member of the county court since 1952. Squire Stone is a farmer, and lives on RFD No. 2, Cumberland Furnace. He has been a member of the court for nearly six years, and is considered one of the court's ablest members. Squire Berry was elected to his first term in 1954. He lives in Vanleer, and once served as deputy sheriff and jailer.

Claude Dickson and J. J. Finch are the tenth district magistrates. Mr. Dickson is the older in point of years and service, being 75 years of age and having served on the court for 13 years. Mr. Finch, who lives on RFD No. 1, Vanleer, began his second term in 1954.

Billie Matthews and William Matlock represent the eleventh civil district. Mr. Matthews is an active farmer and manufacturer of lumber and crossties, and lives near Vanleer. He is serving his second term. Mr. Matlock is a farmer of the Edgewood Community, and was elected to his present office in 1954.

The twelfth district, which includes White Bluff, has three magistrates. They are J. W. Delonas, E. N. Harris, and R. B. Hunter. All live in White Bluff. Squire Delonas has served on the court for 20 years, and recently began his fourth term. Squire Harris has been in public life for many years. He is a retired mail carrier, a former member of the county board of education, and a magistrate during the administration of W. R. Hudson. He began his present term in 1954. Squire Hunter is the youngest of the three. He is an aircraft metal worker for a Nashville concern, and also is assistant city recorder of White Bluff. He was elected to the court in 1954.

R. A. Wright and Clarence Baker represent the thirteenth district. Squire Wright is the dean of the county court, having been a member for 35 years. He was born in 1882, was elected a magistrate when 38 years of age, and has served continuously since. He is a retired farmer. Mr. Baker is a blacksmith, and has served on the court since 1954. Both men are residents of Tennessee City.

Ray D. Pack and Edd Brown are from the fourteenth district. Mr. Pack is the youngest man on the court and takes an active part in its proceedings. Both he and Squire Brown list their address as RFD No. 1, White Bluff. Both are highly respected citizens in their community.

The fifteenth district is served by W. B. Work and W. R. Daniel. Both are farmers, and both are experienced men on the court. Mr. Work was elected a magistrate first in 1940, but resigned shortly thereafter to become tax assessor for Dickson County. He became a member again in 1954, and has been a magistrate for over a decade. Squire Daniel first was elected in 1940, and has served since then. He takes an active part in court affairs. Both men are farmers, and both are well respected citizens of their community.

Many people born and reared in Dickson County have not confined their activities to local affairs, but have made their mark in the world outside the county. To enumerate all of them would prove an insurmountable task. A few, however, compiled with the help of members of the Dickson County Historical Association, and others, are enumerated below.

A score or more have attained high places in the Christian ministry. W. B. Taylor, now deceased, for many years pastored the McKendree Methodist Church in Nashville. Dr. H. Thornton Fowler, a graduate of Charlotte High School, is the present pastor of the church. His brother, Fort, is also an outstanding Methodist minister, and at present is president of Martin College. Lexie Freeman is another who has held important posts in the Methodist Church. Robert Jackson, Charlotte native, is the present pastor of the Riverside Church of Christ, Nashville, and is a popular evangelist. Jewell R. Smith is treasurer of the Methodist Publishing House.

Several hundred Dickson County natives have filled important educational posts outside of Dickson County. Dr. C. N. Stark, who holds a Ph.D. degree in agriculture from Cornell University, where he taught for many years, is the present head of the department of agriculture of Middle Tennessee State College, Murfreesboro. Dr. Fort Fowler is president of Martin College. Dr. H. N. Williams, who has earned a half dozen degrees from various educational institutions, is a professor of law at Mercer University, Georgia. R. B. Stone, now a teacher at Martin College, was for many years superintendent of schools of Giles County. Curtis Sheley is a teacher at State Teachers' College, Conway, Arkansas; Paul Moody teaches biology in Wesley College, Mitchell, South Dakota; Marion Edney heads the biology department of the University of Kentucky; Barron Stuart teaches at a college in New Mexico; John Breeden teaches at David Lipscomb College, Nashville; Leon Bibb is professor of industrial arts of Austin Peay State College; Walter E. Erranton is principal of a high school in Lemon Springs, North Carolina. One of the most successful educational careers has been that of Dr. Mildred English, who attended public schools in Dickson and graduated from the Dickson Normal School. She has held many important positions, among which was educational advisor to the German people after World War II. She is now a professor of elementary education at George Peabody College, Nashville.

Hundreds of Dickson Countians also have excelled in the field of business. Wilbur Sensing is a steel company executive in Nashville, and his brother, Thurman, is executive secretary of the Southern Manufacturing Association. Harding E. Williams is president of a Bank in Morristown, Tennessee. A. W. (Pidge) Willey, brother-in-law to Williams, for many years has been prominently connected with the First American National Bank, Nashville. Daniel Webster Johnston, of White Bluff, is a vice-president of the Third National Bank of Nashville. Richard Hawkins is president of the Northern Bank, Clarksville. Miss Beulah Elliott several years ago became the first woman ever to become an officer of the First American National Bank, Nashville. Buford Wall has made an outstanding record with the First National Bank of Clarksville. Roscoe Buttrey is president of a bank in Jacksonville, Florida. J. E. Crain is an outstanding Nashville contractor. Hundreds of others have carved out successful business careers throughout the United States.

Dr. Leslie G. Myatt is among those prominent in the medical profession. He is head of the staff at City Hospital, Bridgeton, New Jersey. Dr. Noel Hunt is a dentist in Chattanooga. Dr. Robert Thompson is a dentist in Lewisburg, Dr. Robert Gilliam practices dentistry in Oak Ridge, and Harry Bryan is a dentist in Memphis. Dr. W. J. Sugg is a Nashville dentist. Dr. Horace Gray is a Memphis physician. Dr. Podge Beasley is a Franklin dentist. Approximately two score others have made a name for themselves in medicine. Joe Lee Parrish is probably the most outstanding cartoonist. He began his career with the Nashville *Tennessean*, and is now with the Chicago *Tribune*. Ed Sugg, a member of the Dickson County Historical Society, has been outstanding in the field of law and government service, and is now in Washington.

Two top men in the military profession are General George H. Weems of the United States Army, and Captain P. V. H. Weems of the Navy. Both were born in the northern part of the county at the Dickson-Montgomery county lines. General Weems, recently retired, is a graduate of West Point and saw considerable action in the First World War. Later he became a professor of military science at Davidson University, and at West Point. During the Second World War he was in command at Fort Benning, and at the time of his retirement was chief of the Georgia Military District. Captain P. V. H. Weems, also retired, served in both World War I and World War II and was decorated for his service in both. He has been outstanding in the field of navigation, and founded the Weems system of navigation, which is used extensively in the Navy. He has also written several books on navigation, some of which are widely used. The men are brothers of the late Judge Joe B. Weems, and are uncles of the present county judge, James B. Weems.

While many other Dickson Countians in a variety of fields could be named and their accomplishments listed, this seems sufficient to give persons not familiar with the county and the people an adequate impression of the accomplishments of the Dickson County people in areas outside the county.

Footnotes

CHAPTER I

[1] John Haywood, *The Civil and Political History of the State of Tennessee* (Nashville, 1891), 88, 90.
[2] Philip M. Hamer, *Tennessee, A History* (Washington, 1933), I, 11.
[3] Joseph H. Parks, *The Story of Tennessee* (Oklahoma City, 1952), 2.
[4] William E. Myers, "Indian Trails of the Southeast," in *Forty-Second Annual Report of the Bureau of American Ethnology to the Secretary of the Smithsonian Institution* (Washington, 1924–1925), 852–53.
[5] *Ibid.*, 852.
[6] The original journal kept by Donelson may be seen in the Department of Archives, State Library, Nashville.
[7] Deeds of Dickson County, Book D, 398; Nashville *Clarion and Tennessee State Gazette,* September 1, 1814.
[8] Thomas P. Abernathy, *From Frontier to Plantation in Tennessee* (Chapel Hill, 1932), 197.
[9] James Phelan, *History of Tennessee* (Boston, 1889), 179.
[10] The date 1793 has been accepted generally for the establishment of this furnace, although some, notably James B. Killebrew and Samuel Cole Williams, have claimed that the date is too early. See Killebrew, *Introduction to the Resources of Tennessee* (Nashville, 1874), 705; and Williams, "Early Iron Works in the Tennessee Country," *Tennessee Historical Quarterly* (Nashville), VI (1947), 44.
[11] This name was applied later to iron works in Stewart County, held principally by John Bell and others.
[12] Phelan, *History of Tennessee,* 168; Abernathy, *From Frontier to Plantation,* 132.
[13] Abernathy, *Frontier to Plantation,* 138.
[14] John Allison, "The Mero District," *American Historical Magazine* (Nashville), I (1896), 116.
[15] Cartter Patten, *A Tennessee Chronicle* (Chattanooga, 1953), 93.
[16] Goodspeed Publishing Company, *History of Tennessee ... wtih an Historical Sketch of Dickson ... [and other] counties* (Nashville, 1886), 211. Hereinafter cited merely as "Goodspeed."
[17] Patten, *Tennessee Chronicle,* 124.

CHAPTER II

[1] House *Journal,* 1803, p. 37.
[2] *Public Acts,* 1803, Chap. LVI, 112–115.
[3] *Biographical Directory of the American Congress, 1774–1949,* (Washington, 1950), 1085.
[4] See Samuel C. Williams, "Tennessee's First Military Expedition, 1803," *Tennessee Historical Magazine,* VII First series (1922), 179–80; also John Spencer Bassett (ed.), *Correspondence of Andrew Jackson* (Washington, 1926), 48, 64, 81, 89, 169.
[5] Stanley J. Folmsbee, *Sectionalism and Internal Improvements in Tennessee, 1796–1845* (Knoxville, 1939), 34.
[6] *Ibid.*, 34 ff.
[7] Senate *Journal,* 1803, p. 154; House *Journal,* 1803, p. 143; Minutes of County Court, 1803–1807, pp. 1–2.
[8] *Ibid.*, 5 ff.
[9] *Public Acts,* 1804, Chap. XXXIX, 50–2.

[10] Elizabeth F. Ellet, *Pioneer Women of the West* (Philadelphia, 1852), 63-4.
[11] Thomas F. Mathews, *General James Robertson, Father of Tennessee* (Nashville, 1934), 213.
[12] Ellet, *Pioneer Women of the West*, 78.
[13] *Ibid.*, 78.
[14] Minutes of the County Court, 1803-1807, p. 17. The story of Montgomery Bell is developed largely from the following sources: Montgomery Bell Papers, collected by Mrs. Isaac Boyd of New York, deposited in the State Library; Thomas C. Morris' article in the *Dickson County Press*, August 12, 1886; typewritten statements taken from various publications on Bell in Henry C. Leech collection; and Robert E. Corlew, "Some Aspects of Slavery in Dickson County," *Tennessee Historical Quarterly*, X (1951), 224-48.
[15] Nashville *Impartial Review and Cumberland Repository*, April 7, 1808.
[16] *Ibid.*
[17] William L. Cook, "Furnaces and Forges," *Tennessee Historical Magazine* (Nashville), IX (1925), 192.
[18] *Ibid.*, 192 ff; Goodspeed, 921; papers in Henry C. Leech collection.
[19] The correct spelling of the name was Pattison. It frequently appeared as "Patterson," however.
[20] Nashville *Whig*, July 3, 1824.
[21] J. B. Killebrew and J. M. Safford, *Elementary Geology of Tennessee* (Nashville, 1876), 178-79; also *Introduction to the Resources of Tennessee* (Nashville, 1874), 242, 788-89, 796-98; also Dawson A. Phelps and John T. Willett, "Iron Works on the Natchez Trace," *Tennessee Historical Quarterly*, X (1953), 309-22.
[22] Blake Leech to Mrs. Isaac S. Boyd, August 2, 1928 and Nov. 20, 1928. Montgomery Bell Papers.
[23] Minutes of Circuit Court (1839-1845), 175. (WPA Copy).
[24] Nashville *Impartial Review and Cumberland Repository*, May 16, 1807.
[25] *Ibid.*, August 27, 1807.
[26] Nashville *Politician*, August 8, 1845.
[27] Blake Leech to Mrs. Isaac S. Boyd, November 20, 1928, Montgomery Bell Papers.
[28] *Id.* to *Id.*, May 28, 1931. Montgomery Bell Papers.
[29] Nashville *Banner*, May 11, 1955.
[30] Mrs. Isaac M. Boyd.
[31] House *Journal*, 1822, 2d Session, 99, 147.
[32] Nashville *Whig*, July 3, 1824.
[33] Montgomery Bell's Will written in July, 1852; copy in Montgomery Bell Papers.
[34] Compiled statement and inventory, in *ibid*.
[35] Leech to Mrs. Boyd, August 2, 1928, in *ibid*.
[36] Parks Marshall to Mrs. Boyd, March 19, 1926, in *ibid*.
[37] Judge Robert Ewing to Dr. James Vance, October 28, 1926, in *ibid*.

CHAPTER III

[1] John Alexander Kerr, W. J. Latimer, H. G. Lewis, and E. H. Bailey, *Soil Survey of Dickson County, Tennessee* (Washington, 1928), 321. Pamphlet published as an extract of *Soil Survey Report*, Ser. 1923, No. 11, United States Department of Agriculture, Bureau of Chemistry and Soil.
[2] *Ibid.*, 309.
[3] Abernathy, *Frontier to Plantation*, 200-01.
[4] *Ibid.*, 201.
[5] *Public Acts*, 1806, Chap. XV, 46-9.
[6] Albert C. Holt, "The Economic and Social Beginnings of Tennessee," *Tennessee Historical Magazine*, VII (1922), first series, 278.
[7] *Impartial Review and Cumberland Repository*, June 27, 1807.
[8] *Ibid.*, August 23, 1806.
[9] John Wooldridge (ed.), *History of Nashville, Tennessee* (Nashville, 1890), 243.
[10] *Ibid.*, 243-44.
[11] *Seventh Census, Population*, 1850, p. 587.
[12] William H. McRaven, *Life and Times of Edward Swanson* (Nashville, 1937), 91.

FOOTNOTES   215

[13] Goodspeed, 924.
[14] *Impartial Review and Cumberland Repository*, March 1, 1805.
[15] *Ibid.*, December 13, 1805.
[16] Nashville *Clarion and Tennessee State Gazette*, September 1, 1814; J. B. White, article in *Dickson County Herald*, May 31, 1956.
[17] *Impartial Review and Cumberland Repository*, May 24, 1806.
[18] *Public Acts*, 1807, Chap. XLVI, 81–2.
[19] *Ibid.*, Chap. XLIV, 79–80.
[20] *Impartial Review and Cumberland Repository*, April 24, 1807.
[21] William N. Chambers, "Thomas Hart Benton," *Tennessee Historical Quarterly*, VIII (1949), 328.
[22] *Ibid.*, 329.
[23] C. L. Grant, "The Public Career of Cave Johnson," *ibid.*, X (1951), 197.
[24] Minutes of County Court, 1803–1807, pp. 45, 130.
[25] Goodspeed, 924.
[26] Clarksville *Gazette*, March 18, 1820.
[27] *Ibid.*, February 2, 1820.
[28] Holt, "Economic and Social Beginnings of Tennessee," 37.
[29] Minutes of County Court, 1803–1807, p. 39.
[30] *Ibid.*, 68.
[31] *Impartial Review and Cumberland Repository*, July 12, 1806.
[32] Folmsbee, *Internal Improvements in Tennessee*, 16. For a contemporary description of road conditions in 1834, see Nashville *Republican and State Gazette*, November 27, 1834.
[33] Folmsbee, *Internal Improvements in Tennessee*, 8; Holt, "Economic and Social Beginnings of Tennessee," 85.
[34] Census, Schedule I, Population (unpublished).
[35] Records of Turnbull Primitive Baptist Church in Burns, Tennessee, *passim*.
[36] *Ibid.*
[37] Thaddeus C. Blake, *The Old Log House* (Nashville, 1878), 10.
[38] Minutes of County Court, 1803–1807, p. 102.
[39] Edward Scott (ed.), *Laws of the State of Tennessee including those of North Carolina now in force in this state from the year 1715 to the year 1820, inclusive*, 2 vols (Knoxville, 1821), 1, 592; Minutes, Circuit Court, 1842–1852, April Session, 1846.
[40] *Public Acts*, 1817, Chap. CXI, 124.
[41] George Roulstone (ed.), *Laws of the State of Tennessee, 1792–1801* (Knoxville, 1803), 155.
[42] *Public Acts*, 1803, Chap. LXVI, 112–14.
[43] Will Book of Dickson County, Book A, 1–2.
[44] *Ibid.*, 12.
[45] *Ibid.*, 46.
[46] *Ibid.*, 55.
[47] *Ibid.*, 1–2.
[48] *Ibid.*, 12, 68, 293.
[49] *Public Acts*, 1803, Chap. LXVI, 112–115.
[50] *Ibid.*
[51] Nashville *Clarion and Tennessee State Gazette*, August 19, 1817; Patten, *A Tennessee Chronicle*, 114.

CHAPTER IV

[1] For further discussion of the cultural influence of church groups in Middle Tennessee, see F. Garvin Davenport, "Culture vs. Frontier in Tennessee, 1825–1850," *Journal of Southern History*, V (1939), 18–33.
[2] Patten, *A Tennessee Chronicle*, 163; H. N. McTyeire, *A History of Methodism* (Nashville, 1884), 439, 444.
[3] Francis Asbury, *Journal* (New York, 1852), Vol. III, 278.
[4] Davidson County Tennessee Wills and Inventories I, 162; Davidson County Court Minutes, Book A, 152–53 (WPA copies in State Library).
[5] Abernathy, *Frontier to Plantation*, 210.
[6] Details of the Great Revival may be found in many good religious histories. Perhaps the best account is to be found in Catharine C. Cleveland, *The Great Revival in the West* (Chicago, 1903).

7 B. W. McDonnold, *History of the Cumberland Presbyterian Church* (Nashville, 1899), 84.
8 Abernathy, *Frontier to Plantation*, 217.
9 Goodspeed, 937.
10 Sarah Bell to Anne Jane Bell, December 1, 1837. Bell Papers, in custody of Mrs. Walter Bell, Sr., Vanleer, Tennessee.
11 Sarah Bell to Anne Jane Bell, November 17, 1838. Bell Papers.
12 Goodspeed, 937.
13 Walter Brownlow Posey, *Presbyterianism in the Old Southwest* (Richmond, 1952), 8.
14 W. Woodford Clayton, *History of Davidson County, Tennessee* ... (Philadelphia, 1880), 201.
15 Goodspeed, 938.
16 When the writer examined these records in 1948 they were in the custody of Henry J. Deal who lives near Burns, and who graciously permitted the author to examine them at his leisure.
17 F. Garvin Davenport, "Culture Versus Frontier in Tennessee, 1825-1850," *Journal of Southern History*, V (1939), 31; J. H. Spencer, *A History of Kentucky Baptists from 1769 to 1885*, 2 Vols., (Cincinnati, 1885), I, 575.
18 Henry J. Deal, lifelong member, stated recently to the author that his mother witnessed the "accident" which caused the friction.
19 C. D. Bell to Anne Jane Bell, August 1, 1838. Bell Papers.
20 Sarah B. Bell to Anne Jane Bell, December 1, 1837. Bell Papers.
21 Id. to Id., November 17, 1838. Bell Papers.
22 Census, 1860 (Unpublished), Schedule VI (Social Statistics).

CHAPTER V

1 Census, 1820 (Unpublished), Schedule I.
2 *Public Acts*, Chap. CXI, 124.
3 *Ibid.*, Chap. CLXIII, 159.
4 This story about Brewer is taken largely from the writer's article in the Dickson County *Herald*, April 5, 1956.
5 General Index to Deeds, Davidson County, 1784-1871, p. 78 of WPA copy in State Library. The Deed was filed November 3, 1796.
6 R. H. Rovers, *The Life of Robert Paine, D.D., Bishop of the Methodist Episcopal Church, South* (Nashville, 1884), 173.
7 Nashville *Clarion and Tennessee Gazette*, July 25, 1820 ff.
8 Rovers, *Life of Robert Paine*, 174.
9 *Ibid.*
10 Census, 1820 (Unpublished), Schedule I.
11 Nashville *Whig*, October 24, 1820; William L. Cook, "Forges and Furnaces," *Tennessee Historical Magazine*, IX, First Series, (1925-26), 190.
12 Cook, "Forges and Furnaces," 190.
13 Nashville *Whig*, October 24, 1820, *passim*.
14 Census, 1850 and 1860 (Unpublished), Schedule I.
15 James Killebrew, *Introduction to the Resources of Tennessee* (Nashville, 1874), 238, 303.
16 Census, 1820 and 1840 (Unpublished), Schedule I.
17 Killebrew, *Introduction to Resources*, 235.
18 *Ibid.*, 236-37.
19 Census, 1820 (Unpublished), Schedule I.
20 Nashville *Republican and State Gazette*, June 2, 1830.
21 Phelps and Willett, "Iron Works on the Natchez Trace," 313 ff.
22 *Ibid.*, 315 ff; Dickson County Will Book A, 183-95.
23 Nashville *Republican and State Gazette*, June 2, 1830.
24 Census, 1830 (Unpublished), Schedule I.
25 Nashville *Republican and State Gazette*, June 9, 1830.
26 *Ibid.*, June 2, 1830.
27 Census, 1850 (Unpublished), Schedule I.
28 Nashville *Republican and State Gazette*, August 15, 1828.
29 Census, 1830 (Unpublished), Schedule I.
30 *Ibid.*

³¹ Eastin Morris, *The Tennessee Gazetteer or Topographical Dictionary* (Nashville, 1834), appendix XV.
³² *Public Acts*, Chap. CCXLI, 358–62.
³³ *Ibid.*, Chap. CCXC, 423–27.
³⁴ Hamer, *Tennessee, A History*, II, 447. For report and extensive debate on the question, see House *Journal*, 1837–38, p. 705 ff.
³⁵ *Public Acts*, 1833, Chap. XXXIV, 30–32.
³⁶ Material for this discussion on the tornado comes from the following sources: Nashville *Republican and Gazette*, June 2, 9, 1830; Goodspeed, 925; and Dorsey L. Castleman, "History of the Charlotte Tornado A Century Ago is Reproduced," Dickson County *Herald*, May 30, 1930.
³⁷ Chase C. Mooney, "Some Letters from Dover, Tennessee, 1814 to 1855," *Tennessee Historical Quarterly*, VIII (1949), 182.
³⁸ *Public Acts*, 1837–38, Chap. XXI, 50–51.
³⁹ Material on the slave Wiley comes from Goodspeed, 929–30, and from common legend often repeated in the county. County records for these dates are nonexistent.
⁴⁰ Nashville *Banner and Daily Advertiser*, December 26, 1833.
⁴¹ *Public Acts*, 1833, Chap. XCVII, 52.
⁴² *Ibid.*, Chap. LXXXVIII, 99–100.
⁴³ *Ibid.*, Chap. I, 19–23; Resolution No. 3, p. 196; Resolution No. 21, p. 210.
⁴⁴ *Ibid.*, Chap. IV, 34.
⁴⁵ *Ibid.*, 1837–38, Chap. LIX, 85.
⁴⁶ Will Book A, 45–49; 55; 69–70.
⁴⁷ Census, 1840 (Unpublished), Schedule I. Of the number given, 371 paid all or part of their tuition, while 73 depended upon the state or the county to pay all expenses.
⁴⁸ *Ibid.*

CHAPTER VI

¹ Will T. Hale and Dixon L. Merritt, *A History of Tennessee and Tennesseans*, 8 vols. (Chicago, 1913), I, 292.
² Nashville *Impartial Review and Cumberland Repository*, March 10, 1808.
³ Census, 1820, 1830, 1840, 1850, 1860, Dickson County (Unpublished), Schedule I.
⁴ *Ibid.*
⁵ Corlew Family Bible, in possession of Hubert Corlew, Charlotte, Tennessee. Avery Craven in his *The Repressible Conflict* (University, Louisiana, 1939), writes of Virginia, Massachusetts, and Vermont families which exceeded the dozen mark. Of an Iowa family which had 23 children Craven states that this was "probably exceptional but not unique." p. 44 ff.
⁶ Newspaper clipping in Henry C. Leech collection. No date.
⁷ Census, 1820 and 1830, Dickson County; Census, 1850, Davidson County (Unpublished), Schedule I.
⁸ Will Book A, 183–97.
⁹ *Ibid.*
¹⁰ *Ibid.*, 2.
¹¹ *Ibid.*, 55–60.
¹² *Ibid.*, 93.
¹³ *Ibid.*, 129–30; Book B, 25.
¹⁴ Will Book A, 258–59.
¹⁵ Minutes of County Court, 1803–1807, p. 39.
¹⁶ *Ibid.*, 68, 147.
¹⁷ Bill of sale, Taylor to Hardin, in possession of writer.
¹⁸ Minutes of Circuit Court, 1837, pp. 21–2.
¹⁹ Administrators Report, copy among papers of Henry C. Leech collection. The "Boy Sam" lived to a ripe old age and is remembered today by some of the older citizens of the County. "Uncle Sam," as he came affectionately to be known to many whites in the post Civil War days, married Mary, daughter of Dinah, who had belonged to the Dillahunty family. To this union was born Cora who, during the Reconstruction period, married a Negro from the North named Lanier. Their children, McPherson, Gus, Emmett, and Charlie, are remembered especially for their humble conduct in the presence of white people. Gus, who began a business career in Charlotte as a barber, died in Dickson in 1947, at which time he was a well

respected businessman and correspondent among the Negroes for the Dickson County *Herald*.

[20] Deed Book H, 23.

[21] Administrator's Book in Records of County Court, 1846, p. 2.

[22] *Report of the Comptroller of the Treasurer of the State of Tennessee to the House of Representatives*, 1838, 1841, 1843, 1845, 1847, 1849, 1851, 1853, 1855, 1857, 1859.

[23] Nashville *Whig*, September 27, 1814.

[24] Nashville *Clarion and Tennessee State Gazette*, September 2, 1817.

[25] Minutes of Circuit Court (1839–1845), 197-8.

[26] William L. Cook, "Furnaces and Forges," 190-92.

[27] Eubank to Hardin, dated January 8, 1846, in Henry C. Leech papers.

[28] Abernathy, *Frontier to Plantation*, 286.

[29] Cook, "Furnaces and Forges," 191.

[30] Minutes of Circuit Court (1839–1845), 197-98.

[31] *Ibid.*, 201.

[32] Minutes, County Court of Williamson County, 1800–1812, Vol. I, Part I, 191, 235 (WPA copy).

[33] Goodspeed, 929-30.

[34] Ulrich B. Phillips, *American Negro Slavery* (New York, 1918), 485-86.

[35] *Public Acts*, 1836, Ch. XLIV, 145-46.

[36] Harvey Wish, "The Slave Insurrection Panic of 1856," *Journal of Southern History*, V (1939), 206 ff.

[37] *Ibid.*, 210.

[38] *Ibid.*

[39] Nashville *Banner*, November 27, 1856.

[40] Wish, "The Slave Insurrection Panic of 1856," p. 211.

[41] *Ibid.*, 213.

[42] *Ibid.*, 212.

[43] *Ibid.*

[44] Caleb P. Patterson, *The Negro in Tennessee, 1790–1865* (Austin, Texas, 1922), 50.

[45] Wish, "The Slave Insurrection Panic of 1856," 212.

[46] Will Book A, 121.

[47] *Ibid.*, 178 (July 10, 1846).

[48] Will Book B, 113.

[49] Will Book A, 133-34.

[50] *Ibid.*, 220-21.

[51] James H. McNeilly, *Religion and Slavery* (Nashville, 1911), 19.

[52] *Ibid.*

[53] Old newspaper clipping among papers of Henry C. Leech collection, said to have been written by a reporter who watched the Negroes assemble in front of the First Presbyterian Church in Nashville.

[54] Typewritten copy of a statement by W. McLain, in Journal of the Executive Committee of the American Colonization Society, in Montgomery Bell Papers, State Library.

[55] *Ibid.*

[56] Perhaps the best treatment of this may be found in Frank L. Owsley, *Plain Folk of the Old South* (University, Louisiana, 1949).

CHAPTER VII

[1] *Public Acts*, 1842, Second Session, 9.

[2] Census, 1840, Schedule I (Unpublished). References to population in this chapter come from this source unless otherwise designated.

[3] Blanche Henry Clark, *The Tennessee Yeoman, 1840–1860* (Nashville, 1942), 108–140, gives a full account of the agricultural awakening in the state.

[4] *Ibid.*, 117.

[5] Census, 1850 (Unpublished), Schedule IV (Agriculture).

[6] *Ibid.*

[7] Clark, *Tennessee Yeoman*, 120.

[8] Census, 1850 (Unpublished), Schedule IV.

[9] *Census*, 1850, p. 587; *Census*, 1860, p. 133. Census cited in this manner, of course, refers to the published census reports.

[10] Census, 1850 (Unpublished), Schedule IV.
[11] *Census*, 1850, p. 585; 1860, p. 132.
[12] Census, 1850 and 1860 (Unpublished), Schedule IV.
[13] *Census*, 1850, p. 586; 1860, p. 133.
[14] *Ibid.*, 1860, p. 133.
[15] Clark, *The Tennessee Yeoman*, 130.
[16] *Ibid.*, 132.
[17] *Census*, 1850, p. 585; 1860, p. 132.
[18] Census, 1850 (Unpublished), Schedule I.
[19] Nashville *Banner*, November 21, 1837.
[20] William L. Cook, "Forges and Furnaces," 191. A much more elaborate statement made by Mockbee to Cook appears here. Mockbee settled in North Carolina after the Civil War, but later moved to Memphis. He was an occasional visitor in the home of a Mrs. Watkins at Cumberland Furnace where Cook met him and had him write the statement appearing here.
[21] Phelan, *History of Tennessee*, 357.
[22] Nashville *Republican*, November 24, 1836.
[23] Sarah Bell to Anne Jane Bell, August 7, 1839. Bell Papers.
[24] *Ibid.*
[25] Thomas B. Alexander, "The Presidential Campaign of 1840 in Tennessee," *Tennessee Historical Quarterly*, I (1943), 36-7.
[26] *Whig Almanac and Politician's Register* (New York, 1845), 70.
[27] *Ibid.*, 69-70. Johnson became Postmaster General under Polk in 1845.
[28] Statement by Leonard Lane Leech, Dickson County lawyer and farmer, to Anne Somers Gilchrist, in "Charlotte News" by Dorsey L. Castleman, Dickson County *Herald*, July 29, 1954. Leech made this statement in 1898 when 83 years of age.
[29] *Ibid.*
[30] *Ibid.*
[31] *Whig Almanac*, 1853 (New York, 1855), 58.
[32] Nashville *Union*, May 15, 1845.
[33] J. G. Harris, Esquire, "Eulogy Delivered at Charlotte, Tennessee, July 17, 1845 on the Life of Jackson," in B. N. Dusenbery, *Monument to the Memory of General Andrew Jackson* (Philadelphia, 1846), 316-32. This work contains a dozen or more addresses given over the country in honor of Jackson. Other speeches included herein were delivered in Washington, Philadelphia, New York, Baltimore, Richmond, and Pittsburgh. Charlotte was the smallest town in which a major eulogy was delivered.
[34] Nashville *National Union*, November 20, 1848.
[35] *Ibid.*, September 25, 1848.
[36] *Ibid.*
[37] *Ibid.*
[38] *Ibid.*, November 20, 1848.
[39] Nashville *Daily Union and American*, November 11, 1856.
[40] House *Journal*, 1843-44, p. 46.
[41] Census, 1860 (Unpublished), Schedule I.
[42] *Ibid.*
[43] *Census*, 1850, p. 579.
[44] Census, 1840 (Unpublished), Schedule I.

CHAPTER VIII

[1] The name later was changed to Dickson. The spelling of the name varies. At least the following spellings have been observed: Sneedville, Sneedsville, Sneadville, Sneadsville, Smeedville, and Smeedsville.
[2] The name later was changed to Tennessee City.
[3] Census, 1860 (Unpublished), Schedule VI (Social Statistics).
[4] *Ibid.*
[5] *Ibid.*
[6] Census, 1860 (Unpublished), Schedule I.
[7] *Ibid.*
[8] *Ibid.*
[9] *Ibid.*

[10] Patten, *A Tennessee Chronicle*, 154.
[11] Goodspeed, *Humphreys County*, 882–83; *Dickson County*, 447–48.
[12] Census, 1860 (Unpublished), Schedule I.
[13] January 20, 1860.
[14] *Ibid.*, January 31, 1860.
[15] February 10, 1861.
[16] *Ibid.*, February 22, 1861.
[17] James Welch Patton, *Unionism and Reconstruction in Tennessee, 1860–1869*, (Chapel Hill, 1934), 17.
[18] *Ibid.*, 21; Nashville *Republican Banner*, June 16, 1861.
[19] May 11, 1861.
[20] May 17, 1861.
[21] June 8, 1861.
[22] Goodspeed, 935–36.
[23] *Ibid.*, 936.
[24] Newspaper Clipping in Dickson County Scrapbook, in State Library, Nashville, Tennessee; Robert Selph Henry, *"First with the Most" Forrest* (New York, 1944), 63; General Thomas Jordan and J. P. Pryor, *The Campaigns of Lieut.-Gen. N. B. Forrest* (New Orleans, Memphis, and New York, 1868), 99–101.
[25] Henry, *Forrest*, 63; Diary of John H. Wharton, Civil War Soldier, in "Civil War Correspondence" in State Library, Nashville, 11. Compiled and copied by WPA, 1938.
[26] Wentworth Morris, "The Davie Home and the Register of the Federal Military Prison at Clarksville," *Tennessee Historical Quarterly*, VIII (1949), 248–251; Goodspeed, *Humphreys County*, 883.
[27] ORA, *Official Records of the Union and Confederate Armies in the War of the Rebellion*, Series I, XXIII, part I, 146.
[28] Goodspeed, 936.
[29] *Ibid.*
[30] "Civil War Correspondence, Middle Tennessee." WPA Copy, (copied by Roy Gentry) pp. 47–8.
[31] See letters in Bell collection, particularly letter to his wife, dated September 27, 1864. He was held at Camp Morton, Indiana, near Indianapolis.
[32] Goodspeed, 1337–53.
[33] *Ibid.*, 943.
[34] Thomas B. Alexander, *Political Reconstruction in Tennessee* (Nashville, 1950), 249.
[35] *Ibid.*
[36] Newspaper clipping in Dickson County Scrapbook, in State Library, Nashville.
[37] For one of the most complete accounts, see *Testimony Taken by the Joint Select Committee to Inquire into the Condition of Affairs in the Late Insurrectionary States*, 13 vols. (Washington, 1872). Volume XIII includes testimony taken in Tennessee. This report is commonly known as *Ku Klux Conspiracy*.
[38] Nashville *Daily Press and Times*, March 3, 16, 25, 26, 31, 1868.
[39] *Ibid.*, March 31, 1868.
[40] For a detailed discussion of the work of Northern teachers in the entire South, see Henry Lee Swint, *The Northern Teacher in the South, 1862–1870* (Nashville, 1941).
[41] Barnum to Brvt. Lt. Col. James Thompson, Asst. Commissioner of Bureau of Refugees, Freedmen, and Abandoned Lands, in Henry Lee Swint (ed.), "Reports from Educational Agents of the Freedmen's Bureau in Tennessee, 1865–1870," *Tennessee Historical Quarterly*, I (1942), 63.
[42] *Ibid.*
[43] Nashville *Daily Press and Times*, March 26, 1868.
[44] *First Report of the Superintendent of Public Instruction of the State of Tennessee* (Nashville, 1869), pp. xli, cxxxvii, clxxxxv; *Appendix to Senate Journal*, 1868, p. 306.
[45] *Ibid.*, Appendix, p. cxii ff.
[46] *Census, 1870*, Vol. I, 61, 371.
[47] Two historians have written at some length on this problem. They are: C. G. Belissary, "Tennessee and Immigration, 1865–1880," *Tennessee Historical Quarterly*, VII (1948), 229–248; and W. B. Hesseltine, "Tennessee's Invitation to Carpetbaggers," East Tennessee Historical Society's *Publications*, No. 4 (1932), 102–114.
[48] *Senate Journal*, 1868, *Appendix*, 85.

FOOTNOTES

⁴⁹ *Ibid.*, 93.
⁵⁰ *Ibid.*, 94–5.
⁵¹ (New York, 1868), 66–7.
⁵² April 22, and September 11, 1867; February 14, 1868; Hesseltine, "Tennessee's Invitation to Carpetbaggers," 107.
⁵³ Material for the remainder of this chapter comes from Schedule I (Population), of the unpublished census records for 1870.
⁵⁴ Information supplied by Miss Eleanora Miller, Charlotte, Tennessee.

CHAPTER IX

¹ *Census*, 1870, *Population*, part I, 61, 371; *ibid.*, 1900, part II, 520; *Bulletin 8* (Negro Population), 220–21.
² *Census*, 1900, part II, 520.
³ May 8, 1885.
⁴ Nashville *Banner*, May 1, 1885.
⁵ T. C. Morris in *Dickson County Press*, August 12, 1886.
⁶ Clarksville *Semi-Weekly Tobacco Leaf-Chronicle*, April 22, 1890.
⁷ Nashville *Banner*, March 14, 1898; Clarksville *Daily Leaf Chronicle*, March 15, 1898.
⁸ *Census*, 1880, *Statistics of Agriculture*, 86, 87, 132, 169, 204, 241, 308, 309, 310, 311.
⁹ August 12, 1886.
¹⁰ The unpublished records for 1890 and thereafter have not yet been released by the Federal government, and thus this information for the succeeding years is not immediately obtainable.
¹¹ Census, 1870 and 1880 (Unpublished), Schedule I.
¹² W. L. Cook, "Furnaces and Forges," 191.
¹³ Clarksville *Semi-Weekly Tobacco Leaf*, May 25, 1886.
¹⁴ Quoted in *Ibid*.
¹⁵ Dickson *Home Enterprise*, February 17, 1899.
¹⁶ Nashville *Daily American*, April 23, 1880.
¹⁷ *Ibid.*, February 17, 1899.
¹⁸ *Ibid*.
¹⁹ *Ibid.*; *Dickson County Press*, August 27, 1897.
²⁰ Dickson *Democrat*, May 20, 1886.
²¹ *Dickson County Press*, August 12, August 27, September 17, 1891.
²² Grace Leab, "Tennessee Temperance Activities, 1870–1899," East Tennessee Historical Society's *Publications*, No. 21 (1949), 67–8. Also see J. Eugene Lewis, "The Tennessee Gubernatorial Campaign and Election of 1894," *Tennessee Historical Quarterly*, XIII (1954), 110 ff.
²³ R. R. Hancock, *Hancock's Diary: or, A History of the Second Tennessee Confederate Cavalry, with Sketches of First and Seventh Battalions; also, Portraits and Biographical Sketches* (Nashville, 1887), 583.
²⁴ Goodspeed, 944–45.
²⁵ April 6, 1886.
²⁶ Clarksville *Semi-Weekly Tobacco Leaf-Chronicle*, August 26, 1890.
²⁷ *Dickson County Press*, August 27, 1891.
²⁸ February 17, 1899.
²⁹ The Dickson *Critic*, February 2, 1893.
³⁰ Clarksville *Semi-Weekly Tobacco Leaf*, August 26, 1884.
³¹ Clarksville *Semi-Weekly Tobacco Leaf-Chronicle*, March 24, April 3, 1891.
³² *Ibid.*, March 25, 1890.
³³ *Ibid.*, July 31, 1894.
³⁴ Clipping from an unidentified newspaper in Dickson County Scrapbook, State Library, Nashville.
³⁵ *Dickson County Press*, March 23, 1882.
³⁶ Clarksville *Semi-Weekly Tobacco Leaf*, December 4, 1888, citing the *Press*.
³⁷ Cited in *Ibid.*, August 26, 1884.
³⁸ *Ibid.*, January 13, 1888.
³⁹ Cited in *Ibid.*, January 24, 1888.
⁴⁰ Cited in *Ibid.*, February 21, 1888.
⁴¹ *Ibid.*, April 2, 1889.
⁴² Quoted in *Ibid.*, November 19, 1889.
⁴³ *Ibid.*, May 30, June 6, 1890.

44 *Ibid.*, November 4, 1890.
45 *Ibid.*, May 12, November 24, 1891.
46 Nashville *Union and American*, October 29, 1870.
47 *Ibid.*, April 5, 1872.
48 *Ibid.*, November 5, 1874.
49 Goodspeed, 947, 1345.
50 *Tennessee Law Review*, XVI (1941), 853–55.
51 Newspaper clipping dated September 6, 1929, in Henry C. Leech collection.
52 House *Journal*, 1873, pp. 359, 266.
53 Nashville *Daily American*, December 18, 1877.
54 *Ibid.*, November 4, 1880.
55 *Ibid.*, June 5, July 9, 1880.
56 *Ibid.*, October 11, 1882.
57 Clarksville *Semi-Weekly Leaf-Chronicle*, April 4, April 18, 1890; Columbia *Herald, passim.*
58 *Dickson County Press*, September 17, 1891.
59 Charles A. Miller, *The Official and Political Manual* (Nashville, 1890), 279.
60 *Ibid.*, 282, 287, 293.
61 Nashville *Banner*, August 7, 1894.
62 Nashville *Daily American*, July 9, 1880.
63 *Ibid.*, July 10, 28, 1880.
64 Miller, *Official and Political Manual*, 258.
65 *Journal of Tennessee Constitutional Convention* (Nashville, 1871), 397–98.
66 Goodspeed, 1346; George W. Stanbery, II, "The Tennessee Constitutional Convention of 1870," 1940, Master's Thesis at University of Tennessee, Knoxville, 47.
67 Dickson *Home Enterprise*, February 17, 1899.
68 Goodspeed, 1337–38.
69 Dickson *Home Enterprise*, February 17, 1899.
70 *Ibid.*

CHAPTER X

1 Howard H. Quint, *The Forging of American Socialism* (Columbia, South Carolina, 1953), 175.
2 A. M. Simons, "J. A. Wayland, Propagandist," *Metropolitan Magazine*, XXXII (1913), 25.
3 *The Coming Nation*, No. 204, April 17, 1897.
4 Quint, *American Socialism*, 177.
5 *Ibid.*, 179; *The Coming Nation*, No. 101, April 27, 1895.
6 *The Coming Nation*, No. 35, December 30, 1893.
7 Quint, *American Socialism*, 189.
8 *The Coming Nation*, No. 64, July 21, 1894.
9 *Ibid.*, No. 28, November 11, 1893.
10 Grace Sloan, "Tennessee: Social and Economic Laboratory," *Sewanee Review*, XLVI (1938), 313–14.
11 *The Coming Nation*, No. 58, June 9, 1894.
12 Records of Register, Dickson County, Deed Book Y, 339.
13 Sloan, "Tennessee: Social and Economic Laboratory," 315.
14 *The Coming Nation*, No. 218, July 27, 1897.
15 *Ibid.*, No. 204, April 17, 1897.
16 Records of the Clerk and Master, Book 6, pp. 536–39; Book 7, p. 84; Nashville *American*, July 27, 1899.
17 *The Coming Nation*, No. 204, April 17, 1897.
18 *Ibid.*, No. 289, December 3, 1898.
19 "The Ruskin Cooperative Colony," *The Independent*, LI (1899), 193.
20 *The Coming Nation*, No. 115, August 3, 1895.
21 *Ibid.*, No. 180, October 31, 1896.
22 *Ibid.*, No. 181, November 7, 1896.
23 Helen Dahnke, "Ruskin—A Brief Utopia in Rural Tennessee," *The Nashville Tennessean Magazine*, March 20, 1932, p. 1.
24 Editorial comment in *American Monthly Review of Reviews*, XVI (1892), 606, commenting on John Southworth, "The Ruskin Settlement" in *Home Magazine*, October, 1897; Sloan, "Tennessee: A Social and Economic Laboratory," 319–20.

25 Dahnke, "Ruskin—A Brief Utopia," p. 1.
26 *The Coming Nation*, No. 238, December 11, 1897.
27 Editorial Comment in *American Monthly Review of Reviews*, XVI (1892), 606.
28 *The Coming Nation*, No. 101, April 27, 1895.
29 *Ibid.*
30 Isaac Broome, *The Last Days of the Ruskin Cooperative Association* (Chicago, 1902), 37.
31 *The Coming Nation*, No. 89, February 2, 1895; No. 90, February 9, 1895; No. 100, April 20, 1895.
32 *Ibid.*, No. 89, February 2, 1895.
33 Dahnke, "Ruskin—A Brief Utopia," 16.
34 *Ibid.*, 16; *The Coming Nation*, No. 208, May 15, 1897.
35 *The Coming Nation*, No. 204, April 17, 1897.
36 Casson, "The Ruskin Cooperative Association," 194–95.
37 *Ibid.*
38 *The Coming Nation*, No. 93, March 2, 1895.
39 *Ibid.*, No. 85, January 5, 1895.
40 *Ibid.*, No. 99, April 13, 1895.
41 *Ibid.*, No. 73, October 13, 1894.
42 *Ibid.*, No. 211, June 5, 1897.
43 Casson, "The Ruskin Cooperative Association," 194.
44 Dahnke, "Ruskin—A Brief Utopia," 1; Casson, "The Ruskin Cooperative Colony," 192.
45 Letter from Mrs. Irene Charlesworth Johnson to the writer, September 9, 1955.
46 *The Coming Nation*, No. 73, October 13, 1894.
47 *Ibid.*, No. 114, August 3, 1895.
48 *Ibid.*, No. 204, April 17, 1897; Quint, *American Socialism*, 193; Sloan, "Tennessee: Social and Economic Laboratory," 325. The original thousand-acre tract had been purchased in the name of J. A. Wayland, Trustee, and when Wayland departed he transferred full and complete title to the Ruskin Cooperative Association. As a matter of fact, he had made a conditional transfer soon after the purchase of the land and the chartering of the Association. The condition was that the Association would agree to have by December 15, 1894 (six months after purchase) "no less than 20 persons permanently employed" and to have made "valuable improvements." Before he left in July, 1895, however, he made a complete transfer of the thousand acre tract "for consideration of the sum of one ($1.00) dollar." Records of the County Register, Deed Book X, 602–03; Book Y, 401.
49 Quint, *American Socialism*, 209.
50 *Ibid.*, 192–93; *The Coming Nation*, No. 114, August 3, 1895.
51 *The Coming Nation*, No. 231, October 23, 1897.
52 Broome, *The Last Days of the Ruskin Cooperative Colony*, 107.
53 Letter from Mrs. Irene Charlesworth Johnson to writer, September 9, 1955.
54 Broome, *The Last Days of the Ruskin Cooperative Colony*, 27.
55 Casson, "The Ruskin Cooperative Colony," 193.
56 Nashville *American*, July 27, 1899.
57 Records of the Clerk and Master, Books 6 and 7, *passim*.
58 Nashville *American*, July 27, 1899.
59 *The Coming Nation*, No. 355, March 24, 1900, quoted in Sloan, "Tennessee: A Social and Economic Laboratory," 326.
60 *Ibid.*, No. 330, September 16, 1899, quoted in *ibid*.
61 Dahnke, "Ruskin—A Brief Utopia," 1.
62 Broome, *The Last Days of the Ruskin Cooperative Association*, 168; Nashville *American*, July 27, 1899.
63 *Ibid.*, 22.
64 *Ibid.*, 21.
65 Braam, "The Ruskin Cooperative Colony," *American Journal of Sociology*, VIII (1903), 667–80.
66 *Ibid.*
67 Nashville *American*, July 27, 1899.
68 Nashville *Banner*, July 27, 1899.
69 Letter from Mrs. Irene Charlesworth Johnson to writer, September 9, 1955.
70 *The Coming Nation*, No. 472, March 21, 1903; No. 512, January 1, 1904.

CHAPTER XI

[1] Goodspeed, 939.
[2] Mrs. John Trotwood Moore, "The First Century of Library History in Tennessee, 1813-1913," *East Tennessee Historical Society's Publications*, No. 16 (1944), 5-6; *Public Acts*, 1815, pp. 29-30; *Public Acts*, 1817, p. 84.
[3] *Public Acts*, 1807, Chap. LVI, 93.
[4] Nashville *Whig*, July 7, 1823.
[5] Register's Records, Deed Book H, 22.
[6] *Ibid.*, Book 38, p. 121.
[7] Nashville *Union and American*, June 25, 1872.
[8] Announcement among Bell papers.
[9] *Report of Public Schools of Tennessee* (Nashville, 1876), 45; Notice of opening of 82nd Session of Cloverdale, 1897, among Bell papers.
[10] Census, 1840 (Unpublished), Schedule I.
[11] Will Book B, 214-23.
[12] *Ibid.*, 275, 293-94.
[13] Wills and Inventories of Humphreys County, 1838-1844, part 2, p. 630. WPA Copy in State Library. The will was written December, 1843 and probated March, 1844.
[14] *Public Acts*, 1847-48, Resolution 27, pp. 439-40. Resolution was passed January 31, 1848.
[15] *First Report of the Superintendent of Public Instruction of the State of Tennessee* (Nashville, 1869), Appendix clxxxxv, cxxxvii.
[16] *Report of the Public Schools of Tennessee*, 1876 (Nashville, 1876), 31, 40, 43, 57, 58, 59, 60.
[17] *Ibid.*, 1886, pp. 26, 38, 42, 44, 46, 131.
[18] *Ibid.*, 1882, p. 56; 1887, p. 193.
[19] *Ibid.*, 1895, p. 145.
[20] *Ibid.*, 1896, pp. 114, 115, 122, 126, 133, 136, 148.
[21] Cited in Clarksville *Semi-Weekly Tobacco Leaf-Chronicle*, April 28, 1891.
[22] *Dickson County Press*, September 17, 1891.
[23] *Semi-Weekly Tobacco Leaf-Chronicle*, December 8, 1891.
[24] Dickson *Home Enterprise*, February 17, 1899.
[25] *Announcement of the Dickson Normal College and Commercial Institute* (Dickson, 1904), 3, 4, 5.
[26] *Ibid.*, 1906, p. 4.
[27] *Ibid.*, 5.
[28] *Ibid.*, 1909, *passim*.
[29] *Ibid.*, 1911, p. 6.
[30] *Ibid.* For source material on Dickson Normal College the writer is indebted greatly to Mrs. Alice Hickman Davies, Martin, Tennessee, who provided him with much data and helpful comments and suggestions. Mrs. Davies was a former instructor at the school.
[31] *The Bugler* (Dickson, December, 1919) published by students of Dickson Central High School, 5, 6, 10.
[32] See advertisements appearing in *Dickson County Press* in August and September, 1891.
[33] Deed Book 29, pp. 348-49; 573-76. The author is indebted to Mr. Edgar Nesbitt for much information on the College. Mr. Nesbitt's ancestors were some of the first to come into the county, emigrating from Scotland. His father and uncle were on the first board of trustees of Ruskin-Cave College.
[34] *Bulletin of Ruskin-Cave College*, n/d. The writer is indebted to Mrs. Blake Loggins, now deceased, for much source material on the college, and for the use of the Bulletin herein cited.
[35] Statistics for the dates cited are taken from the reports of the State Superintendent (Commissioner of Education), and from information supplied from the office of the present county superintendent of Dickson County.

CHAPTER XII

[1] "A History of Dickson County," mss., compiled in 1945 by teachers of Dickson County.
[2] *Public Acts*, 1817, Chap. XIV, 24-6.
[3] *Dickson County Press*, August 12, 1886.
[4] *Ibid.*, October and November, 1889, *passim*.
[5] In the House *Journal* for 1870-1871 the town was still referred to as Sneedsville. See pp. 13-14.

[6] "Dickson, Tennessee—On the Broadway of America," *The N.C. & St. L. Railway News Item,* January 15, 1930.
[7] June 11, 1872.
[8] Goodspeed, 944.
[9] *Dickson County Press,* April 6, 1882.
[10] *Ibid.,* October 19, 1882.
[11] *Ibid.,* October 26, 1882.
[12] Town records for this period have been destroyed.
[13] *Ibid.,* November 23, 1882.
[14] *Ibid.,* June 30, July 7, and July 14, 1882.
[15] *The Critic,* February 9, 1893.
[16] Statement and petition among Henry C. Leech Papers.
[17] *Dickson County Press,* February 16, June 15, 1882.
[18] *The Critic,* February 2, 1893; *Dickson County Press,* May 29, 1890.
[19] Dickson County *Herald,* August 27, 1953.
[20] Statement of condition of Dickson Bank and Trust Company, June 29, 1907; Statement of condition of the Bank of Charlotte, December 31, 1906. Both statements appear on printed cards.
[21] Nashville *Tennessean,* April 5, 1925.
[22] *Ibid.,* Clipping in Henry C. Leech papers.
[23] *Public Acts,* 1869–70, Chap. XXIV, 252.
[24] Nashville *Union and American,* April 29, 1873.
[25] May 31, 1883.
[26] Clarksville *Semi-Weekly Tobacco Leaf,* May 4, 1886.
[27] Much of the material on the early history of the towns, other than that cited in footnotes, comes from Goodspeed, 943–47.
[28] *Dickson County Press,* January 18, 1883.
[29] *Ibid.,* January 24, 1883.
[30] Clarksville *Semi-Weekly Tobacco Leaf,* August 7, 1888; Clarksville *Semi-Weekly Tobacco Leaf-Chronicle,* July 18, 1890, July 23, 1891.
[31] *Dickson County Press,* March 23, 1882.
[32] *Ibid.,* September 7, 1882.
[33] Nashville *Daily American,* February 2, 1881; Minutes of Circuit Court, 1881, pp. 276, 279, 290, 310, 323–26; Execution Docket, 1881, pp. 13–14, 20–22.
[34] *Dickson County Press,* February 16, 1882.
[35] *Ibid.,* June 15, 1882.
[36] *Ibid.,* June 9, 1892.
[37] *Ibid.,* July 28, 1892. Ralph A. Freeman believes that the *Press* was guilty of inaccurate reporting, and that the lynching took place on the White Bluff hill a short distance from Charlotte.
[38] Nashville *Daily American,* January 2, 1895; October 6, 1895.
[39] Clarksville *Semi-Weekly Tobacco Leaf-Chronicle,* April 22, 1897.
[40] *Minutes of the General Assembly of the Cumberland Presbyterian Church,* 1907, p. 35.
[41] Clarksville *Semi-Weekly Tobacco Leaf,* April 16, 1886.
[42] *House Journal,* 1870–71, pp. 33–34, 344, 398; *Public Acts,* 1870, p. 119.
[43] *House Journal,* 1873, p. 244.
[44] Clarksville *Semi-Weekly Tobacco Leaf-Chronicle,* May 25, 1894.
[45] *Dickson County Press,* October 9, 1902.
[46] Minutes of the County Court, 1926, p. 163.
[47] *Ibid.,* 1927, pp. 175, 188.
[48] *Ibid.*
[49] Leaflet in Henry C. Leech Papers.
[50] Letter to W. Blake Leech, July 13, 1927, in Henry C. Leech Papers.
[51] Leaflet in Henry C. Leech Papers.
[52] Nashville *Tennessean,* August 2, 1927.
[53] Paper in Henry C. Leech Papers.

CHAPTER XIII

[1] Most of the information for this chapter is taken from the files of the Dickson County *Herald,* for the dates indicated. Election figures and results, except as otherwise noted, are taken from the Tennessee *Bluebook.*
[2] Minutes of County Court, 1919–1924, p. 503.
[3] *Herald,* August 8, 1924.
[4] *Ibid.,* July 13, August 10, 1934.

APPENDIX A

POPULATION AND AREA
DICKSON COUNTY

Year	Whites	DICKSON COUNTY County Slaves	Total Population	TENNESSEE Total Population
1810	—	—	4,516	261,727
1820	3,885	1,305	5,190	422,823
1830	5,596	1,669	7,265	681,904
1840	5,387	1,687	7,074	829,210
1850	6,286	2,118	8,404	1,002,717
1860	7,781	2,201	9,982	1,109,741
1870	—	—	9,340	1,258,520
1880	—	—	12,460	1,542,359
1890	—	—	13,632	1,767,518
1900	—	—	18,635	2,020,616
1910	—	—	19,955	2,184,789
1920	—	—	19,342	2,337,885
1930	—	—	18,491	2,616,556
1940	—	—	19,718	2,915,841
1950	—	—	18,805	3,291,718

POPULATION OF DICKSON COUNTY MUNICIPALITIES 1910–1950

Municipality	1910	1930	1940	1950
Burns	—	—	—	421
Charlotte	236	291	470	478
Dickson	1,850	2,902	3,504	3,348
Slayden	—	162	164	90
Vanleer	—	243	206	243
White Bluff	419	464	522	506

POPULATION OF INCORPORATED DICKSON COUNTY MUNICIPALITIES COMPARED WITH CERTAIN OTHER MUNICIPALITIES WITHIN THE IMMEDIATE VICINITY

City or Town	Population (1950)	City or Town	Population (1950)
BURNS	421	Franklin	5,475
Centerville	1,136	Hohenwald	1,703
CHARLOTTE	478	McEwen	710
Clarksville	17,695	SLAYDEN	90
DICKSON	3,348	VANLEER	243
Dover	547	Waverly	2,102
Erin	290	WHITE BLUFF	506

LAND AREA AND POPULATION OF DICKSON COUNTY COMPARED WITH THAT OF OTHER NEARBY COUNTIES

County	Area (in Square Miles)	Population (1950)
Hickman	613	13,353
Houston	207	5,318
Humphreys	555	11,030
DICKSON	486	18,805
Stewart	484	9,175
Montgomery	543	44,186
Williamson	593	24,307

APPENDIX B

SLAVEHOLDINGS FOR SELECTED YEARS

RESIDENTS OF DICKSON COUNTY HAVING FIFTEEN OR MORE SLAVES IN 1820

Name	Number Slaves	Name	Number Slaves
R. C. Napier	37	Nehemiah Scott	20
Montgomery Bell	83	Daniel Williams	21
A. W. Vanleer	43	James Goodrich	34
Thomas Collier	23	Benjamin Sturdivant	16
Christopher Strong	15	Robert West	27
George F. Napier	15	Christopher Robertson	22
Elizabeth West	25	Sterling Brewer	17
Shadrach Bell	29	Thomas Whitmill	44
George Ross	54	I. Henry	17

RESIDENTS OF DICKSON COUNTY HAVING FIFTEEN OR MORE SLAVES IN 1840

Name	Number Slaves	Name	Number Slaves
William Hogans	21	John R. Hudson	28
Minor Bibb	17	Spencer T. Hunt	19
Christopher Strong	19	William S. Fentress	50
Russ Bowen	18	Nancy W. Ellis	18
Daniel Leech	23	Henry A. C. Napier	32
William Ward	26	Epps Jackson	16
James W. Christian	30	John J. Bell	17
Shadrach Bell	25	Benjamin C. Robertson	50
George Cooksey	15	John L. Patterson	17
Sarah Eleazer	22	Anthony Vanleer	114
Belfield N. Carter	21	Elias W. Napier	70

APPENDIX C

PUBLIC OFFICIALS OF DICKSON COUNTY [1]

COUNTY JUDGES

Name	Date Served	Name	Date Served
W. R. Hudson	1902–1918	W. M. Leech	1934–1950
Joe B. Weems	1918–1934	James A. Weems	1950–

(The office of County Judge was created in 1902. Before that time a county chairman was elected on an annual basis from among the members of the county court. Among those serving as County Chairman during the quarter century prior to 1902 were: E. T. Hicks, John T. Baker, H. J. Larkins, M. V. Smith, B. J. McCaslin, W. B. Williams, J. T. Hudson, and others.)

COUNTY COURT CLERKS

Name	Date Served	Name	Date Served
David Dickson	1803–1812	H. J. Larkins	1894–1906
Field Farrar	1812–1836	T. R. Dickson	1906–1918
William Hightower	1836–1842	Melvin Harris	1918–1930
Thomas J. Kelly	1842–1843	Lee Mathis, Jr.	1930–1938
Thomas McNeilly	1843–1859	Lee Peeler	1938–1946
T. C. Morris	1859–1865	Carney Nicks	1946–1954
F. M. Binkley	1865–1870	V. N. Loggins	1954–
T. K. Grigsby	1870–1894		

PUBLIC OFFICIALS OF DICKSON COUNTY [1]

SHERIFFS

Name	Date Served	Name	Date Served
Robert Weakley	1804–1806	D. L. Matlock	1866–1872
David Hogan	1806–1808	J. W. Hutton	1872–1877
Michael Molton	1808–1810	W. M. Kirk	1877–1882
Edward Pearsall	1810–1811	Rufus Ferebee	1882–1884
James Read	1811–1813	S. M. Grigsby	1884–1888
Joseph Wingate	1813–1815	W. H. Matlock	1888–1890
Clark Spencer	1815–1817	H. J. Larkins	1890–1896
Drury Christian	1817–1819	W. R. Hudson	1896–1900
Richard Batson	1819–1825	M. D. Corlew	1900–1906
David McAdoo	1825–1826	S. A. Tidwell	1906–1908
William Hightower	1826–1828	R. D. Eubank, Jr.	1908–1912
George Smith	1828–1835	T. J. Coleman	1912–1918
Robert Livingston	1835–1838	J. T. Petty	1918–1921
George W. Tatum	1838–1840	(Resigned January 3, 1921)	
Thomas McMurry	1840–1846	M. O. Stuart	1921–1922
W. J. Mathis	1846–1852	W. H. Hickerson	1922–1928
W. L. White	1852–1853	Will Ellis	1928–1934
G. W. Clarke	1853–1854	W. E. Hutton	1934–1940
J. W. Hutton	1854–1860	H. L. Hammon	1940–1946
John V. Walker	1860–1861	Claude Creighton	1946–1948
Eli Wylie	1861–1865	Percy Corlew	1948–1950
M. G. Harris	1865	Warren Hill	1950–1956
(served two weeks)		James (Bud) Weems	1956–
W. G. McMahan	1865–1866		

COUNTY REGISTERS

Name	Date Served	Name	Date Served
James Walker	1804–1816	T. R. Dickson	1918–1927
Molton Dickson	1816–1823	(Died in office)	
Richard Waugh	1823–1842	Mrs. T. R. Dickson	1927–1928
Henry A. Bibb	1842–1848	(Elected by County Court to fill out	
L. L. Leech	1848–	unexpired term of husband, but	
(Served one month)		resigned shortly after election.)	
E. E. Larkins	1848–1856	L. J. Browning	1928–1930
J. P. Priestly	1856–1860	(Elected by County Court to fill out	
E. E. Larkins	1860–1874	unexpired term.)	
Henry A. Bibb	1874–1894	W. H. Jordan	1930–1942
J. W. Fielder	1894–1918	Burley B. Underhill	1942–1950
		Charles Marsh, Jr.	1950–

TRUSTEES FROM 1886 TO PRESENT

Name	Name
R. D. Eubank	B. C. Nicks
T. R. Dickson	R. M. Holland
Melvin Harris	Henry Sensing
J. M. Thompson	Mrs. Lucy Heard Wright
W. C. Doty	Mrs. Henry Sensing
H. Slayden Hunt	Pruett Kelly

SUPERINTENDENTS OF PUBLIC SCHOOLS

Name	Date Served	Name	Date Served
T. F. McCreary	1869–1874	S. E. Hunt	1897–1901
L. L. Leech	1874–1878	H. G. Gilbert	1901–1903
T. F. McCreary	1878–1882	R. E. Corlew	1903–1905
W. G. McMillan	1882–1885	W. A. White	1905–1907
B. F. Harris	1885–1888	R. E. Corlew	1907–1930
Robert (Bob) C. Jackson	1888–1891	W. E. Luther	1930–1936
W. G. McMillan	1891–1893	Minor Stuart	1936–1945
H. C. Richardson	1893–1895	W. H. Garrett	1945–1954
Agnes Shipp	1895–1897	Tom T. Sugg	1954–

PUBLIC OFFICIALS OF DICKSON COUNTY [1]

REPRESENTATIVES

Name	Date Served	Name	Date Served
John Coleman	1809–1811	W. B. Leech	1893–1895
Sterling Brewer	1811–1813	H. C. Richardson	1895–1897
William Easley	1813–1817	W. L. Cook	1897–1899
Robert C. Daugherty	1817–1819	Pitt Henslee	1899–1901
Abraham Caldwell	1819–1821	S. E. Hunt	1901–1905
Molton Dickson	1821–1823	W. T. Crotzer	1905–1907
Richard Batson	1823–1827	J. T. Hudson	1907–1909
John Reed	1827–1831	F. F. Tidwell	1909–1911
Bowling Gordon	1831–1833	J. T. Hudson	1911–1913
George Smith	1833–1835	T. R. V. Schmittou	1913–1915
Robert McNeilly	1835–1837	J. E. Mathis	1915–1917
John Eubank	1837–1847	H. T. V. Miller	1917–1919
William A. Moody	1847–1855	Frank S. Hall	1919–1921
W. J. Mathis	1855–1857	J. A. Larkins	1921–1923
F. T. V. Schmittou	1857–1859	Frank S. Hall	1923–1925
William L. White	1859–1865	N. H. Eubank	1925–1929
A. D. Nicks	1865–1867	Joe Crosby	1929–1931
M. J. J. Cagle	1867–1869	N. H. Eubank	1931–1935
A. D. Nicks	1869–1873	D. Ray Stuart	1935–1937
Jacob Leech	1873–1875	Hale Crow	1937–1939
J. J. Pollard	1875–1877	Earl Brown	1939–1941
Jacob Leech	1877–1879	Frank S. Hall	1941–1945
G. W. McQuary	1879–1881	Roy Donegan	1945–1947
H. H. Buquo	1881–1883	H. N. Williams	1947–1949
W. J. Mallory	1883–1885	J. Minor Stuart	1949–1951
N. B. Sugg	1885–1887	Robert Littleton	**1951–1957**
Hardin Leech	1887–1891	Lee Mathis	1957–
R. J. Work	1891–1893		

SENATORS

Name	Date Served	Name	Date Served
Duncan Stewart	1805–1807	R. E. Thomas	1897–1899
Parry W. Humphreys	1807–1809	J. C. Hobbs	1899–1901
John Shelby	1809–1811	R. L. Leech	1901–1903
James B. Reynolds	1811–1815	W. A. Bell	1903–1907
Robert West	1815–1817	W. T. Thomas	1907–1909
Sterling Brewer	1817–1819	G. W. Turner	1909–1911
James R. McMeans	1819–1821	W. W. Patterson	1913–1915
Sterling Brewer	1821–1823	J. A. Clement	1915–1917
Robert Weakley	1823–1829	N. M. Nichols	1917–1919
Henry Frey	1829–1831	J. W. Rice	1919–1921
Bowling Gordon	1831–1833	E. G. Collier	1921–1923
Thomas Shaw	1833–1839	W. O. Hake	1923–1925
Stephen C. Pavatt	1847–1851	Jim Spencer	1925–1927
Samuel B. Moore	1851–1853	S. C. Lewis	1927–1929
W. C. Whitthorne	1853–1857	F. S. Hall	1929–1931
Thomas McNeilly	1857–1863	J. M. Spencer	1931–1933
Joshua Frierson	1865–1867	N. A. Link	1933–1935
Jesse E. Eason	1867–1869	Clint B. Jones	1935–1937
W. A. Moody	1869–1873	N. H. Eubank	1937–1939
Mitchell Trotter	1873–1875	L. F. Stone	1939–1941
H. M. McAdoo	1875–1879	Frazier Riggins	1941–1943
Vernon F. Bibb	1879–1885	John W. Anderson	1943–1945
D. B. Thomas	1885–1887	S. E. Hunt	1945–1947
Jacob Leech	1887–1889	W. H. Wiseman	1947–1949
J. D. Sensing	1889–1891	Frazier Riggins	1949–1951
George Tubbs	1891–1893	Jack Saunders	1951–1953
Hardin Leech	1893–1895	Wayne Sensing	1953–1955
J. R. Winbourn	1895–1897	Joe H. Spencer	1955–1957
		William D. Howell	1957–

PUBLIC OFFICIALS OF DICKSON COUNTY [1]

TAX ASSESSORS (since 1908)

Marvin Taylor	1908–1912
R. D. Eubank, Sr.	1912–1916
G. L. Tatum	1916–1920
J. M. Scott	1920–1928
R. D. Loggins	1928–1932
Guy Oakley	1932–1936
J. R. Harris	1936–1944

(Harris resigned near the beginning of his second term, and R. B. Work was elected by the county court to fill out the unexpired term.)

R. D. Loggins	1944–1948
Frank Jackson	1948–1950
Dalton Brown	1950–

CIRCUIT JUDGES

Name	Date Served
Mortimer A. Martin	1836–1852
W. W. Pepper	1852–1861
Thomas W. Wisdom	1861–1865
John A. Campbell	1865–1869
James E. Rice	1869–1878
Joseph C. Stark	1878–1886
A. H. Munford	1886–1892

Name	Date Served
W. L. Grigsby	1892–1900
D. B. Bell	1900–1908
W. L. Cook	1908–1923
J. D. G. Morton	1924–1936
Dancey Fort	1936–1952
W. P. Puryear, Jr.	1952–

ATTORNEYS GENERAL

William K. Turner	1836–1842
W. B. Johnson	1842–1848
V. S. Allen	1848–1850
J. M. Quarles	1850–1858
W. E. Lowe	1858–1862
James E. Rice	1865–1869
W. J. Broaddus	1869–1870
T. C. Mulligan	1870–1878

B. D. Bell	1878–1886
W. R. Elliott	1886–1889
H. C. Carter	1889–1894
W. Blake Leech	1894–1902
R. L. Peck	1902–1910
Edd Bowman	1910–1934
W. C. Howell	1934–1950
Reeder Parker	1950–

CLERKS OF CIRCUIT COURT

John C. Collier	1836–1842
Robert McNeilly	1842–1862
James E. Justice	1862–1866
Henry C. Collier	1866–1870
J. A. Dodson	1870–1886

R. A. Sugg, W. R. Hudson, J. A. Dodson, and R. L. Leech served during the period 1886 and 1902. Hudson did not serve a complete term, and Leech served for about a term and one-half. The exact dates are indeterminate.

J. J. Taylor	1902–1910
T. E. Gray	1910–1918
L. J. Browning	1918–1926
D. Ray Stuart	1926–1934
Claude Powers	1934–

CHANCELLORS

Name	Date Served
Milton Brown	1834–1842
Andrew McCampbell	1842–1846
Terry H. Cahal	1846–1850
A. O. P. Nicholson	1850–
(Presided over two sessions)	
John S. Brien	1851–1854
Samuel D. Frierson	1854–1855
Stephen C. Pavatt	1855–1861

(From 1861 to September, 1865 records show "as no Chancellor appeared, the Clerk and Master, Henry C. Collier, adjourned the Court until Court in course.")

Name	Date Served
Robert H. Rose	1866–1868
J. W. Doherty	1868–1871
G. H. Nixon	1871–1886
Andrew J. Abernathy	1886–1903
J. W. Stout	1903–1936
S. A. Marable	1936–

This court was created in 1834.

CLERKS AND MASTERS

Valentine S. Allen	1834–1842
John C. Collier	1842–1853
Henry C. Collier	1853–1865
Richard M. Baldwin	1865–1871
Henry C. Collier	1871–1880
W. W. Collier	1880–
(served four months)	

W. L. Grigsby	1880–1892
I. M. Bowers	1892–1899
Horace J. Bowers	1899–
(Served two months)	
W. G. McMillan	1899–1911
J. J. Taylor	1911–1940
J. B. White	1941–

[1] Names and dates of service of sheriffs, registers, senators, representatives, circuit judges, attorneys general, and circuit court clerks, to 1886, are taken from Goodspeed's *History of Tennessee*.... Names and dates of service of senators and representatives since that date are taken from the Senate and House *Journals*. Names and dates of service of county superintendents come from the state superintendent's *Reports*. All other names and dates are taken from the county records found in the courthouse at Charlotte. Several people have aided in the collection of these data. Some of the old records proved hard to read. Two or more sources in a few cases are in disagreement as to names and dates of service of officials. For these reasons the author makes no pledge of complete accuracy, but he believes the great majority of names and dates are correct.

APPENDIX D

OFFICIAL VOTE IN DICKSON COUNTY FOR PRESIDENT FROM 1836 TO PRESENT

Year	DEMOCRATIC PARTY Candidate	Votes Received	WHIG OR REPUBLICAN PARTY Candidate	Votes Received
1836	Van Buren	426	Harrison, Webster, White, and Mangum, all ran on the Whig ticket	203
1840	Van Buren	653	Harrison (Whig)	396
1844	Polk	706	Clay (Whig)	339
1848	Cass	674	Taylor (Whig)	386
1852	Pierce	607	Scott (Whig)	323
1856	Buchanan	816	Fremont (Repub.)	382
1860	Douglas (Northern Democrat)	86	Bell (Constitutional Union)	135
	Breckinridge (Southern Democrat)	465	Lincoln (Repub.)	0
1864				
1868	Seymour	144	Grant	292
1872	Greeley	917	Grant	394
1876	Tilden	1,341	Hayes	446
1880	Hancock	1,169	Garfield	497
	Weaver (Greenback-Labor)	202		
1884	Cleveland	1,339	Blaine	561
1888	Cleveland	1,511	Harrison	765
1892	Cleveland	1,385	Harrison	494
	Weaver (People's)	312		
1896	Bryan	1,938	McKinley	841
1900	Bryan	1,691	McKinley	728
1904	Parker	1,490	Roosevelt	828
1908	Bryan	1,499	Taft	899
1912	Wilson	1,698	Taft	445

(Roosevelt ran on Progressive ticket, and polled 293 votes)

Year	Candidate	Votes	Candidate	Votes
1916	Wilson	2,105	Hughes	1,008
1920	Cox	2,145	Harding	1,472
1924	Davis	1,648	Coolidge	516
1928	Smith	1,428	Hoover	891
1932	Roosevelt	2,007	Hoover	369
1936	Roosevelt	2,022	Landon	402
1940	Roosevelt	2,784	Willkie	527
1944	Roosevelt	2,379	Dewey	600
1948	Truman	2,337	Dewey	485
1952	Stevenson	4,196	Eisenhower	1,415

SOURCES: W. Dean Burnham, *Presidential Ballots, 1836–1892*. Johns Hopkins Press, 1955. Also, Edgar Eugene Robinson, *The Presidential Vote, 1896–1932*. Leland Stanford University Press, 1934. Also, *Tennessee Blue Book*, 1932 to 1952.

OFFICIAL VOTE FOR GOVERNORS IN THE DEMOCRATIC PRIMARIES

(For years where records are readily accessible)

Year	Major Candidates and Votes Received By Each		
1928	Horton 1,038	McAlister 591	Pope 763
1930	Horton 1,373	Gwinn 1,272	
1932	McAlister 874	Patterson 591	Pope 1,391
1936	Browning 1,658	Dossett 1,000	
1938	Browning 1,197	Cooper 1,613	
1940	Cooper 1,869	Dempster 385	
1942	Cooper 530	J. Ridley Mitchell 1,465	
1944	McCord 937	Neal 142	
1946	Browning 1,560	McCord 968	
1948	Browning 2,437	McCord 754	
1950	Browning 2,506	Allen 2,451	
1952	Clement 4,875	Browning 954	Allen 578
1954	Clement 5,067	Browning 1,069	

APPENDIX E

DICKSON COUNTY MEN WHO MADE THE SUPREME SACRIFICE
WORLD WAR I

Ashworth, Richard
Berry, Lucian
Breeden, Lawrence
Browning, Wm. Luther
Buckner, Clyde I.
Buttrey, Dorsey
Carter, James L.
Carter, William C.
Carter, Jeff T.
Clifton, Samuel J.
Dunnagan, Sam R.
Donaldson, Rawleigh
England, Zuma
Field, Thomas C.
Goodwin, Sam Virgil
Herbison, Ellie T.
Hooper, Pearlis
Hudgins, Walter T.
James, Hugh S.
Knott, Charles I.
Lyle, Justin
McCollum, George K.
Manley, Walter C.
Martin, Roy
Martin, William E.
Moore, Elijah
Nesbitt, Athie
Oakley, Frank
Oakley, James
Outlaw, Grover
Pack, Phillip
Peeler, William E.
Shawl, Dudley
Sheley, James C.
Stuart, Olin D.
Taylor, Aretus
Tidwell, George L.
Welch, Mark
Woodard, Selkirk
Adams, McKinley, Col.
Hutton, John Brady, Col.
Spicer, Ulysses, Col.

APPENDIX F

DICKSON COUNTY MEN WHO MADE THE SUPREME SACRIFICE
WORLD WAR II

Adams, Carl
Adcock, Curtis
Ashworth, Fred W.
Baker, William N.
Bellar, Robert
Black, James L.
Bone, Thomas
Bradford, Elmer
Brown, Joe H.
Boaz, Robert E.
Browning, Archie
Brunet, Frank
Buchanan, Allen
Burgess, Larry L.
Cannon, Newton
Capps, Charles T.
Daniel, Robert E.
Dickson, Nolie
Edgin, James W.
Edwards, Phillip M.
Field, Minor
Foster, Wesley B.
Franklin, Howard
Finch, Austin
Gentry, Allie G.
Gray, John L.
Hood, William R.
Hood, John F.
Hudson, E. W.
Kelley, Woodrow W.
Lamastus, **Dudley B.**

Lamb, Mike
Lankford, James D.
Larkins, John M.
Lowe, James Y.
Luther, Delbert G.
Luther, John W.
McElhiney, Cecil R.
Martin, Oscar L.
Miller, William T.
Mitchell, Van J.
Murrell, Harry
Osborne, James
Ostrander, Andy L.
Patey, Randall
Sensing, Arnold
Sensing, Benjamin C.
Sizemore, William E.
Skeggs, George
Spahr, Raymond
Stinson, Roy L.
Stokes, Granville
Stokes, John Hugh
Story, Louis E.
Taylor, Clyde M.
Tidwell, Lamdon C.
Tuggle, Joe W.
Underwood, Leamond
Vetter, Adrian F.
Walton, Mack
Hall, James E. (Col.)
Hopson, Nelson (Col.)

STATEMENT ON BIBLIOGRAPHY

A detailed bibliographical essay consisting of five pages has been omitted for the sake of economy. Scholars interested in a bibliography are referred to the detailed footnotes, pages 213 to 225.

INDEX

Academy, provided for in 1806, 154
Adcock, Betty, 202–203
Adcock, Corbie, 210
Adcock, D. W., 83
Adcock, E. W., 206
Adcock, M. V., Confederate soldier, 106
Agricultural pursuits, 1870–1900, 116
Allen, Clifford, candidate for governor, 206
Allen, Gabriel, member of County court, 20
Allen, Valentine S., 155
American Legion, charter members of, 204
Amusements, 39
Anderson, William, 84
Armstrong, J. C., 156
Austin, Calvin F., Confederate soldier, 106
Austrians, settled, 1870–1900, 115

Banks, Dickson Bank and Trust Co., 180; First National, 180; pictures of directors and officials of First National, 136; pictures of directors and officials of Bank of Dickson, 171; of Vanleer, Slayden, White Bluff, Charlotte, and Dickson, 180–181.
Barksdale, J. Alton, 168
Barton's Creek, early settlers on, 17; furnaces on, 23; Bell's grist mill on, 23; mentioned, 29.
Bate, William B., governor, speaks in Charlotte, 129
Batson, Rich, sheriff, 36
Baxter, Jere, supported for governor, 129
Baxter, Robert, 60
Baxter and Hicks, operated iron works, 62
Bean, Fred, 207
Beasley, D. E., picture of, 136
Beasley, R. P., picture of, 171
Beck, J. H., picture of, 171
Baker, Clarence, 211
Bell, Montgomery, early settler, 17; member of county court, 20; develops iron works, 23 ff; offers rewards for runaway slaves, 26–27; seeks to sell property, 27; sends

Bell, Montgomery *(Continued)*
    slaves to Liberia, 28; dies a recluse, 28; picture of, 33; ruthless slave-driver, 45; slaveholder, 71; mentioned, 116
Bellsburg, 12, 173; Mount Liberty Church at, 47
Bell, William B., Confederate soldier, 107; 155
Benton County, 91
Benton, Thomas Hart, practices law in Charlotte, 35
Berringer, C., 176
Berry, Michael, preacher, 48
Berry, W. R., 210; picture of, 172
Bevan, Charles and Harry, 122
Bibb, A. H., 210; picture of, 172
Bibb, Leon, 211
Bibb, Minor, early settler, 17, 36, 53, 70
Bibb, Major V. F., 90
Bibb, Vernon F., 129
Bird, William C., 67
Blount, Governor William, 15
Boone, Daniel, 13
Bowers, H. J., 148
Bowers, Isaac M., settles after Civil War, 107; 122
Braam, J. W., appraises Ruskin settlement, 151
Bragg, General Braxton, troops under, 104
Bratton, W. M., 165
Breeden, John, 211
Brewer, Sterling, member of county court, 20; buys slave, 37; prominent in politics, 58–59; seeks saline streams, 59; discouraged and disillusioned, 60; dies in poverty, 60.
Bright, Frank, picture of, 136
Bruce, Charles E., 210
Bryan, James, 165
Bryan, Coleman, and Company, 120
Broome, Isaac, at Ruskin, 148
Brown, A. Dalton, biographical statement, 209; picture of, 172
Brown, Governor Aaron V., speaks in Charlotte, 93–94
Brown, Carner, picture of, 171
Brown, Edd, 211

Brown, George W., 118
Brown, John, early settler, 17
Brown, Lynn, 210
Browning, Gordon, governor, 205
Browning, L. J., 175, 228, 230, picture of, 135
Browning, William L., killed in World War I, 199
Brownlow, William G., 109
Burns, 182
Bushwhackers, killed, 110
Buttrey, E. D., 209
Buttrey, L. E., picture of, 136
Butler, James L., 83
Butler, W. H., operates saloon, 120

Cagle, M. J. J., 113
Caldwell, Abraham, early settler, 17
Caldwell, Poe, 184
Carroll Furnace, 23
Casson, Herbert N., 140, 145
Castleman, A. G., 155
Castleman, Dorsey L., 66; picture of, 134
Cathey, Elias N., 81
Cedar Creek, 173
Central Lumber Co., 208
Charlesworth, W. H., 140, 143
Charleville, Jean de, 11
Charlotte, 12; named for Charlotte Reeves Robertson, 14; committee appointed to lay out and establish, 21; in 1810, 31; courts in, 41; partly destroyed in 1830, 65; memorial services for Andrew Jackson, held at, 92; proposed as capital of state, 95; General Nathan Bedford Forrest in, 105; guerrilla warfare in, 105; in state of alarm in Civil War, 105; mentioned, 109; newspapers in, 121–122; seeks railroads, 125 ff.; early history of, 173 ff.; vote for courthouse location, 192
Charlotte Female Academy, 69
Charlotte Hotel, 40
Cheatham County, 24
Cherokees and Chickasaws, 12
"Chickasaw Trace," 12
Churches, 48; (also, see name of church desired)
Civil War, 100, 157
Claiborne, Thomas, Jr., practices law, 35
Clark and Erskine College, 156
Clark, J. W., Dickson mayor, 176 ff.
Clarksville, 16; road to from Charlotte, 38; 43, 63; Negro-white fracas in, 110
Clement, Anna Belle, 206

Clement, Frank Goad, candidate for governor, 205; elected governor, (in 1952) 206, and (in 1954) 207; delivered Democratic keynote address in 1956, 207; picture of, 169
Clement, J. A., 197
Clement, Robert, 206
Clifton, James K., 81
Climax Sample Rooms, saloon, 120
Cline, G. H., 81
Cloudy, James P., murdered, 185
Cloverdale, established, 155; closing of, 160
Coca-Cola Bottling Company, 208
Cochran, Lynn, 202
Coffee County, 112
Coleman, W. S., 118
Colesburg, 173
Collier, Benjamin A., 63
Collier, Christopher, returns after war, 107
Collier, Henry, 97
Collier, John C., Whig, 90
Collier, T. L., 99
Collier, Theodore M., 63
Collier, W. C., 98
Collier, William, 35
Columbia, road to, from Charlotte, 38
Coming Nation, The, editorial policy of, 142
Conant, Will J., 180
Connecticut, 113
Cook, Mary Baxter, 209
Cook, Richard C., peddler, 68
Cook, W. L., locates trace, 12; describes Cumberland Furnace, 117, mentioned, 149; favors saloons, 179; member Supreme Court, 135; picture of, 135
Cook, W. C., candidate for State Democratic Executive Committee, 200
Cook, Reverend Valentine, 58
Cooksey, George, 85
Cooksey, James A., 210; picture of, 172
Cooper, Prentice, 200
Cording, Captain J. B., Confederate leader, 103
Corlew, Benjamin, 47, 71
Corlew, Hubert W., 210; picture of, 172
Corlew, John, farmer, 86
Corlew, M. D., 71, 228
Corlew, Paul Maynard, decorated for gallantry, 202
Corlew, Percy, 228
Corlew, R. E. (Bob), elected school superintendent, 160; on Dickson Normal faculty, 163; mentioned, 165, 194, 195, 228; picture of, 135

Corlew, Robert E., picture of, 134
Corlew, William, 75; files suit for slaves, 76
Cotton, grown, 30; not successful in Dickson County, 31
Counties, Davidson, Sumner, Montgomery, Robertson, Houston, Hickman, Humphreys, Stewart, 16
County court, first meeting, 20; organization of, 40
County seat, struggle for, 187 ff.; vote on removal of, 192
Courfman, Felix, 83
Courthouse, planned in 1806, 32
Courts, in Charlotte, 41
Cowan, H. T., 194
Craft, Jesse, member, county court, 20
Craighead, Thomas B., 15
Crain, J. E., 212
Creighton, Claude L., 202, 228
Crockett, Andrew, murdered, 185
Crotzer, W. T., 121
Crow, Hale, 229
Cullum, W. E., 131
Cumberland Furnace, Negro-white fracas at, 110; after Civil War, 117; seeks railroad, 125; mentioned, 183
Cumberland Iron Works, 15
Cumberland Presbyterian Church, organized, 46; sanctuary erected in Charlotte, 56
Cumberland Valley Land and Improvement Company, 166

Daniel, Jesse, 173
Daniel, Robert, picture of, 172
Daniel, W. H., 97
Daniel, W. R., 211
Davenport, Max, 210
Davidson County, Dickson County carved from, 11
Davies, W. J., 162
Davis, J. L., 97
Davis, William B., robbed in Charlotte, 67
Deal, L. M., picture of, 171
Deason, Verlie, 195
Delaware, 113
Delonas, J. W., 211; picture of, 171 and 172
Democratic Party in Dickson County, 89, 92; loyal to Jackson, 90-91
Democratic-Whig rivalry, 91-92
Democrats, successful, 1870-1900, 127
Dickson, city of, established, 176; early history of, 176-177; struggle over incorporation, 177 ff.; newspapers in 121 ff.; vote for courthouse, 192

Dickson Academy, 161
Dickson Brick Company, 119
Dickson, Claude, 210; picture of, 172
Dickson County, in Highland Rim, 11; iron furnaces established in, in 1793, 14-15; after 1783 a part of Davidson County, 16; carved from Montgomery and Robertson, 16; legally established, 19; Indian raid in, 31; population, in 1810, 31; Scotch Covenanters in, 47; Churches in, 55; total population, in 1820, 57; population origin, in 1850, 82; occupations of people in 1850, 83; agricultural products, 1850, 84; population origins from 1870 to 1900, 115
Dickson, David, first county court clerk, 21
Dickson Laundry, 208
Dickson Library Company, 154
Dickson Normal, established, 161; decline of, 165
Dickson, Joseph, first will recorded, 41-42
Dickson, Martha, sues Montgomery Bell, 26
Dickson, Molton, early settler, 17; establishes store in Charlotte, 35
Dickson Oil Company, formed, 118
Dickson Roller Mills, 119
Dickson, William, Dickson County named for, 19
Dickson, Colonel William, Sr., 19
Diebold Company, 207
Dillingham, Ray, 175
Dismukes, G. C., 122
Doak, William, member of county court, 20
Dodson, Demps, shot by Federals, near Charlotte, 106
Donelson, John, 14
Dotson, George C., school teacher, 69
Doughty, Victor A., 122
Dover, road to, from Charlotte, 38; mentioned, 63; slaves hanged at, 78; slave insurrection at, 78
Drouillard, J. P., 60, 117
Dull, 12
Dull, Will, 119
Duplin County, North Carolina, William Dickson born in, 19

Eastside, 173
Edgerton, Graham, 121
Edgewood Normal, founding of, 160
Education, in Ruskin Cooperative Association, 143; early development of,

Education, in Ruskin *(Continued)* 153 ff.; recent progress, 208; Negro, after Civil War, 111; (see Chapter on Education)
Edwards, James, penitentiary warden, 206
Elliott, Beulah M., bank official, 212
Ellis, E. W., 97
English, Dr. Mildred, educator, 211
Erranton, J. C., picture of, 172
Erranton, Walter, 165
Erranton, Walter E., 211
Eubank, John, 64, 83, 229
Eubank, R. D., returns after Civil War, 107
Ewing, Finis, 46
Ewing, Judge Robert, 28

Farming, 1870–1900, 116
Ferguson, Joe, 195
Finch, J. J., 211
Forrest, General Nathan Bedford, moves troops through Cumberland Furnace and Charlotte, 104
Fowler, Fort, 211
Fowler, H. Thornton, 211
Franklin, road to, from Charlotte, 38; mentioned, 63
Frazier, Frank, viii, 195; candidate for county judge, 197
Frazier, Malcolm, picture of, 172
Freedman's Bureau, 110
Freeman, Lexie, 211
Freeman, Ralph A., 121; publishes *Herald*, 122; picture of, 136
Freeman, Samuel, newspaper publisher, 121; dies, 121
Freeman, S. A., 195
"French Lick," 11
Fuqua, J. Benjamin, locates trace, 12
Furnaces, iron, manner of operation, 25

Galloway, John W., 210
Garner, Colonel William, slain by Indians, 31
Garner's Creek, 31
Garrett, W. H., 228
Garrett, William, 85
Garton, Mark, 114
Garton, Moses, 81
Gentry, Brother, on Turnbull Creek, 53
Gentry, Hon. Hartwell, viii; picture of, 134; Mrs. Hartwell Gentry, picture of, 134
Gentry, Thomas, early settler, 17
Gentry, William, early settler, 17
Georgia, 113
Germans, in Dickson County after Civil War, 112–115

Gilbert, B. C., school official, 160
Gillam, 96, 115
Glenwylde High School, 165
Goodlett, Clifton, picture of, 134
Goodrich, James, 42; writes will, 69
Gray, David, 97
Gray, John, Turnbull settler, 39
Gray, Thomas, 53
Great Revival of 1800, 45
Greer, Ben, 195
Greer, Miss Bessie, picture of, and member Dickson County Historical Society, 134
Greer, D. B., 210; picture of, 172
Grigsby, T. K., 84, 97; Confederate leader, 103; returns after war, 107
Guerin, Dr. Claud, 160
Guerin, Walter, 160
Guerrillas, in Charlotte, 105

Hake, Mrs. W. O., 204
Hall, Earl, biographical statement, 209; picture of, 172
Hall, Frank S., 197; candidate for legislature, 197–198; speaker of house of representatives, 200
Hamilton, Glen, picture of, 171
Hammon, John, 50
Hampton High School, 166
Hardin, Joab, 63; writes will, 72; mentioned, 84
Hardin, Sarah Ann, 73
Hardwicke, John James, 63
Harper, T. M., 155
Harpeth River, Moundbuilders on, 12
Harpeth River, 24
Harris, B. F., school official, 158
Harris, Charlie Warner, 210; picture of, 172
Harris, E. N., 211; picture of, 172
Harris, J. R., 230
Harris, Jeremiah, speaks in Charlotte, 92–93
Harris, Mark, 40
Harris, Maurice, 206
Harris, Melvin, 210; picture of, 172
Harvey, Lemuel, member of early county court, 20
Hayes, J. Mitchell, 207
Henry County, 91
Henslee, Dr. J. T., 118
Henslee, Pitt, 194
Hickerson, Asa, 155, 175
Hickerson, Bob, edits *Herald*, 123
Hickman, Alice Evans, on Dickson Normal faculty, 163
Hickman County, carved from Dickson County, 35; population, 38

INDEX

Hicks, Graham, 175, 209
Hicks, R. H., 121
Hicks, S. C., 121
Hicks, W. E., 98
Hicks, W. R., 62
Hiland, M. M., threatened by Ku Klux Klan, 112
Hill, Warren, biographical statement, 209, 228
Hines, Mrs. A. N., 204, 209
Historical Society, picture of, 134
Hogan, John C., 118
Hogg, John, receives first grant of land, 15
Holland Brothers, 119
Holland John, in Charlotte, 36
Horton, J. E., 209
Houston County, 16
Howell, Frank, picture of, 171
Howell, W. C., 230
Howell, William D., 229
Hudson, George H., 118
Hudson, W. R., operates saloon, 210; sheriff, 149; mentioned, 197
Humphreys County, 16; population in 1810, 38
Humphreys, Parry W., 35
Humphries, John, 42
Hunt, Spencer T., slaveholder, 70; 157
Hunt, S. E., 155, 195
Hunter, R. B., 211; picture of, 171 and 172
Hurt, R. N. P., 98
Hutton, Henry, preacher, 48
Hutton, W. E., sheriff, 228

Institutes, teachers, 159
Irish immigration, 83, 115
Ishmael, Leland, viii, 123

Jackson, Andrew, friend of William Dickson, 20; used Bell's cannon balls at New Orleans, 24; memory of honored, 92
Jackson, Epps, 208
Jackson, Dr. J. T., 208
Jackson, Dr. Lawrence, 208
Jackson, Newell, picture of, 171
Jackson, Peter, 69
Jackson, Robert, 211
Jackson, Dr. William, 208
Jackson's Chapel, 173
James, Colonel William, 165
Jones, Walter, picture of, 171
Jarman, Robert, manufactures cotton gins, 30
Jewell Cave, discovered, 123
Johnson Cave, 35, 91

Johnson, J. S., 196
Johnson, Mrs. Irene Charlesworth, appraises Ruskin, 145, 146, 152
Johnson's Creek, early settlers on, 17, 29; distilleries on, 36
Johnston, D. W., 212
Jones' Creek, early settlers on, 17; furnaces on, 23; mentioned, 23, 29
Joslin, Benjamin, 30

Kelley, William, 98
Kelly, Pruett, biographical statement, 208; 228; picture of, 172
Kelly, R. J., 166
Kentucky, 113
Killebrew, James B., 115
King, Samuel, 46
Kirfman, J. N. H., 98
Kirkman, Florence, 60
Kirkman, General Hugh, visited by bushwhackers, 109–110
Kirwine, Major, Federal officer in Charlotte, 106
Ku Klux Klan, 109

Lampley, Jacob, 42, 157
Lanier, Isaac H., iron master, 63
Larkins, A. N., 97
Larkins, Calvin, picture of, 171
Larkins, Clarence, picture of, 171
Larkins, Clark, 47
Larkins, Ebenezer E., schoolmaster, 73, 83, 155
Larkins, Dr. Ewing, 199
Larkins, J. M., 97, 196
Larkins, James, Jr., 63
Lawson, W. H., at Ruskin, 143, 150
Leathers, A. H., 207
Leathers, Harry, 195
Leech, Beulah McLean, viii
Leech, Clark, viii; candidate for county judge, 201
Leech, D. R., 156
Leech, Daniel, maintains distillery, 36; slaveholder, 70
Leech, Edward, early settler, 20; dealings with Montgomery Bell, 27
Leech, Hardin, 149
Leech, Henry Collier, viii, 122; describes Charlotte, 178; picture of, 170
Leech, Herbert, 127
Leech, Jacob, 86, 97, 127; career, 127–129; favors saloons, 179
Leech, Leonard Lane, describes Montgomery Bell, 25; mentioned, 28, 47, 97–98; school official, 158
Leech, Oscar R., operates saloon, 120
Leech, R. L., 122, 149, 197

Leech, W. Blake, viii; describes Montgomery Bell, 27; mentioned, 122, 130; biography, 131, 148; bank president, 180; mentioned, 190; opposes saloons while in state legislature, 199; picture of, 170
Leech, W. M., candidate for State Democratic Executive Committee, and also for county judge, 200; appointed commissioner of highways, 206; mentioned, 227
Leech, William W., dies, 124
Liberty Community, 173
Littleton, Robert, 229
Lloyd, Henry Demarest, speaks at Ruskin, 144
Loggins, R. D., 230
Loggins, T. B., 159; leaves Dickson Normal, 165
Loggins, V. N., biographical statement, 209; 227; picture of, 172
Louisiana, 113
Lovell, Dr. C. M., 118, 119, 196
Luther, George, 86
Luther, W. E., 228
Lutheran Church, 56
Luton, Mildred, 175

McAdow, Samuel, 39
McCaslin, Mrs. Lester, picture of, 134
McClelland, W. J., 97
McClurkan, Wayman, 202
McCreary, L. T., physician, 114
McCreary, T. F., school official, 111, 157, 163
McLean, Ephraim, 46
McMillan, Joe A., Sr., 210
McMillan, Joe A., viii, 210, picture of, 172
McMillan, Eva Leech, 210
McMillan, W. G., school official, 159
McMillan, Miss Willie G., picture of, 134
McMurry, W. H., 163, 180
McNeilly, Robert, 79, 97
McNeilly, Thomas, 83, 95, 97
Mallory, Captain W. J., Confederate leader, 103; 131
Marable, S. A., 230
Marsh, Charles, Jr., biographical statement, 209; 228
Marsh, Wilbur, wounded and decorated in World War II, 204; picture of, 134
Marshall County, Negro-white fracas in, 110
Marshall, Park, 28
Martin, James, early settler, 17
Mathis, Lee, Jr., 227
Mathis, W. J., 83

Matlock, William, 211; picture of, 172
Matthews, Billie, 211; picture of, 172
Maury County, Negro-white fracas in, 110
Mayhew, Mrs. George, viii
Meek, Christopher, school teacher, 69, 85
Meek, E. H., Sr., 210; picture of, 172
Medley, Warren G., 204
Miller, A. E. C., 114
Miller, Arthur, 164
Miller, Augustus, 114
Miller, Dowl, 206
Miller, Miss Eleanora, picture of, 134
Miller, Elmer E., 114
Miller, Henry T. V., 197-98; picture of, 133
Miller, Idilla, 114
Miller, Lawrence Edgar, 114
Miller, Lincoln, 114
Miller, Miss Lola, picture of, 134
Miller, Nathan, 210
Miller, P. A., 98
Miller, Virgil, 114
Missouri, 113
Mitchell, Gordon, picture of, 136
Mitchell, Kenneth, picture of, 134
Mitchell, Mrs. Vina, picture of, 134
Mockbee, Howard, 87
Mockbee, John H. B., describes iron works, 88
Montgomery Bell Park, 208
Montgomery County, 16; population in 1810, 38
Moody, Paul, 211
Moody, O. N., 198
Moody, W. A., 83
Moore, John Trotwood, questionnaires, 80-81
Morris, Thomas C., lawyer, 97, 127, 131, 149
Morton, Colonel George H., settles in White Bluff, 107
Moundbuilders, in county, 12
Mt. Lebanon, 173
Mt. Sinai, 173
Municipalities, population of, 226
Myatt, Alston, 88
Myatt's Laundry, in Dickson, 208
Myatt, Dr. Leslie G., 212
Myatt, Miss Mayme, viii

Napier, Elias, 63
Napier family, settled, 61
Napiers, owned many slaves, 61
Napier, George F., 61
Napier, Henry A. C., 61
Napier, John R., early settler, 17

INDEX 241

Napier, John W., 61
Napier, Richard C., member of early county court, 20
Napier, Richard, sues George F. Napier, 76
Napier, William C., 88
Nashville *Banner*, appraises Ruskin, 151
Nashville *Tennessean*, appraises Ruskin, 151
Negroes, church membership, 54
Negro-white fracases, 110
Negro education, after Civil War, 111
Nesbitt family, early settlers, 17
Nesbitt, Dr. B. F., 210; pictures of, 136, and 172
Nesbitt, Nathan, buys slaves, 37
New York, 113
Newspapers, after Civil War, 121; at Burns, 123; seek industry, 125
Nicks, A. D., Conservative Unionist, 109; representative, 187
Nicks, B. C., 228
Nicks, Carney B., decorated for gallantry in action in First World War, 202; mentioned, 227; picture of, 171
Nicks, James, 209
Nicks, Norman, 195
Norris, William, 42

Oil, in County, 118; on farm of George W. Brown, 118
Overton, Thomas W., 63

Pack, Ray D., 211; picture of, 172
Paine, Reverend Robert, 58
Palace of Happiness, saloon, 120
Parker, Anne, granddaughter of John, captured and sold into Indian slavery, 49
Parker, Daniel, 48
Parker, John, organizes Turnbull Baptist Church, 48
Parker, Reeder, 230
Parker, W. A., bank director and oil distributor, picture of, 136
Parish, A. G., 83
Parrish, Joe Lee, cartoonist, 212
Payne, E. S., 208
Peeler, Lee L., 227
Peeler, J. N., 199
Petty, Thomas, early settler, 17
Pierce, Clifford, candidate for governor, 206
Pickering, Horace, 210; picture of, 172
Piney River, early settlers on, 17; 23
Pitts, Judge John A., 128, 149
Pollard, R. V., 162
Pond, 173

Population movements, after Civil War, 112
Potts, Billy, 207
Powell, M. F., 209
Powell, Melvin, picture of, 172
Powers, Claude, biographical statement, 209; 230; picture of, 172
Primm, Uncle Harry, picture of, 34
Promised Land, 12
Pulaski, Negro-white fracas in, 110
Puryear, W. P., Jr., 230

Railroad construction, Irish employed, 98 ff.; 1870-1900, 125 ff.
Rape, Gustavus, 84
Ray, D. E., 167
"Rebels," captured in Charlotte, 106
Redden, Hubert, 210
Red Rover, saloon, 120
Reeder, R. E., edits Burns paper, 123
Representatives, in legislature, 1870-1900, 131
Richardson, T. H., picture of, 134
Roads, established in 1806, 37
Roberts, Augustin, 64
Robertson, Charlotte Reeves, town of Charlotte named for, 14; character described, 22
Robertson County, 16
Robertson, D. D., 210; picture of, 172
Robertson, James, comes to Middle Tennessee, 13; establishes furnace in Dickson County, 14; endorses Dickson County gin manufactures, 30
Robertson, Samuel Graham, bank president, picture of, 136
Rogers, Gertrude, 163
Rogers, Lida, 164
Rogers, Thomas, discovers Jewell Cave, 123; 149
Ruskin Colony, 12; script used for money, 141, seeds of dissent, 147; suit for dissolution, 148; dissolved and moves to Georgia, 149; appraisals of, 150 ff.; final move, 152; (See Chapter, "A Socialist Colony Comes and Goes")
Ruskin-Cave College, established, 166; illustration, p. 52
Russell, Edmund, 50
Russell, Wiley, member Historical Society, picture of, 134
Russell, William, member of early county court, 20
Rutledge, W. M., bank official and automobile dealer, picture of, 136
Rye, Governor Tom C., in Charlotte, 131

Saloons, 120
Schmittou, Ellis, 195
Schmittou, F. T. von, 95
Schools, early, 42
Secession sentiment in Dickson County, 101 ff.
Self, H. H., 196
Sensing, Arnold, 204
Sensing, Benjamin, 204
Sensing, Donald, 164
Sensing, John D., supports Buchanan for governor, 130
Sensing, Thurman, 212
Sensing, Wayne, 175; picture of, 171
Sensing, Wilbur, 212
Shelbyville, 65
Sheley, Curtis, 211
Shipp, Agnes, school official, 159, 228
Shipp, Dockie (Mrs. Joe B. Weems), 164
Siegel, Ernest, 207
Silver, discovered near White Bluff, 118
Slackers, in World War I, 197
Slayden, early History of town, 173; 183
Slayden, C., 97
Slayden, Dr. W. W., 160
Slaveholdings, in County, 70–71
Slavery, important in iron furnaces, 70; established in Middle Tennessee, 70
Slaves, hired, 75; insurrections of, 1836 and 1856, 76 ff.; Minor Bibb's, 54; Moses Parker's, 54; prices in County, 72–73; runaways, 75; sent to Liberia, 28, 79; total number, 226
Smith, Mrs. Ann, picture of, 134
Smith, Bessie, 164
Smith, Jewell R., 211
Smith, R. E., 166; strict disciplinarian at Ruskin-Cave College, 166
Smith, Q. M., 167
Smith, R. E., 195
Sneedsville, established and named, 107
Soule's Chapel, 48
Speight, Billy, 202
Stark, Dr. C. N., 211
St. Clair, J. K., picture of, 171
Steam Forge 23
Stephenson, Guy, 167
Stewart, Charles, gives land for county seat, 21
Stewart County, 16; population in 1810, 38
Still, Mrs. Grace H., picture of, 134
Stone, E. H., 155
Stone, Ida, 162
Stone, Colonel Robert B., manages Cumberland Furnace, 117
Stone, R. B., 122, 167, 211; picture of, 172
Stone, R. F., 210
Strong, Christopher, maintains distillery, 36; slaveholder, 70; 156
Strong's Branch, 84
Strong's Hill, 84
Stuart, Barron, 211
Stuart, Henry, 98
Stuart, J. Minor, viii; 228–229; picture of, 134
Stuart, John M., 185
Stuart, M. O., 228
Stuart, Madge Roberts, picture of, 134
Stuart, Mrs. D. Ray, picture of, 134
Stuart, D. Ray, viii, 175, 229, 230; picture of, 134 and 172
Sugg, Ed, 212
Sugg, N. B., 131
Sugg, Tom T., biographical statement, 209, 228; picture of, 172
Sugg, William, member Dickson County Historical Society, picture of, 134
Sugg, Dr. W. J., physician, picture of, 133
Sugg, Dr. W. J., Jr., 212
Sullivan, Roy, picture of, 171
Sulphur Fork Creek, 48
Sumner County, 16, 37
Swift, George, 83
Swift, Horace, 210; picture of, 172
Sycamore, 173
Sylvia, 12, 173, 187–188

Tallent, Herbert, viii, 202, 204
Tax rate, early, 32
Taylor Machine Works, 208
Teachers, salaries, 167
Teas, William, member of first county court, 20
Tennessee City, 173, 182
Tennessee County, Dickson County at first a part of, 15
Tennessee Iron Works, 62
Thedford, Captain William, Confederate leader, 103
Thompson, C. B., 182; picture of, 171
Thompson, James, murdered, 186
Thompson, T. T., 19
Tidwell, E. H., 155
Tidwell, Edward, early settler, 17
Tidwell, J. E., 181
Tidwell, Rufus, 210
Tomlinson, H. G., 181
Topp, Robertson, Memphis Whig speaks in Charlotte, 94
Tornado of 1830, 64; described, 65–67
Tracy Academy, 69, 89; established, 155
Troops, Dickson County, at Stone's River, 103; at Fort Donelson, 103; Federal, take Charlotte, 106

Tubbs, George, early settler, 17, 73
Turnbull Baptist Church, organized, 48; rules of decorum, 49–50; Negroes admitted, 54
Turnbull Creek, early settlers on, 17; furnaces on, 23
Turner, Howard W., school teacher, 69
Tuthill and Pattison, 119

Underhill, C. H., 155

Van Fleet, Dr. Walter, at Ruskin Colony, 143
Vanleer, 173; early history of town, 183
Vanleer, Anthony, iron master, 37, 60, 85
Vanleer, Bernard, 60
Voorhies, 95; establishes school, 154

Wade, W. T., 159
Wade and Loggins, at Edgewood, 160; at Dickson Normal, 161
Wages, in 1860, 98
Walker, B. F., 162
Walker, D. K., 210; picture of, 172
Ward, William, early settler, 17
Waugh, Richard, first Postmaster of Charlotte, 37
Waverly, 64
Wayland, Julius Augustus, biography, 137–139; purchases land in Dickson County, 139; forms corporation called Ruskin Cooperative Association, 140; critical of ministry, 144; suicide, 146
Weakley, Sheriff Robert, 31
Weems, General George H., 212
Weems, Judge James A., viii, biographical statement, 209; decorated for gallantry in World War II, 202, 227; picture of, 134, 169, and 172
Weems, Miss Jamey, youngest member of Dickson County Historical Society, picture of, 134
Weems, James (Bud), 228
Weems, Joe B., viii, 195, 208, 277; picture of, 134

Weems, Mrs. Dockie Shipp, viii, 195; picture of, 134; (see also Shipp, Dockie)
Weems, Captain P. V. H., naval officer, 212
Wharton, John H., of Cannon County, describes Charlotte, 105
Whig-Democratic rivalry, 91–92
Whig Party, in County, 89
White Bluff, 109; silver ore discovered near, 118; early history of, 181–182
White Bluff, picture of prominent citizens, 171
White Elephant, saloon, 120
White Oak Flatt, 173
White, Beedy, Turnbull settler, 39, 50
White, J. B., biographical statement, 209; writes Introduction; 230; pictures of, 134, 136, and 172
White, Mrs. William W., sons in service, 202
Wiley, Negro slave executed for murdering master, 67
Willey, William D., shot by Federals during Civil War near Charlotte, 106
Willey, A. W. (Pidge), 212; picture of, 171
Williams, Annie Lee (Mrs. Floyd B.), viii, 202; picture of, 134
Williams, Dr. H. N., 211
Wilson County, 107
Wilson, Albert, 165
Wilson, E. B., on Dickson Normal faculty, 163; operates Dickson Normal after Loggin's departure, 165
Wingate, Joseph, establishes hat shop in Charlotte in 1808, 36
Wisconsin, 113
Woodward, James and Elizabeth, 83
Woods Valley, 165
Work, R. J., 130
Work, W. B., 211; picture of, 172
World War I, Dickson County men in, 194–195
Worley Furnace, 23; named for slave, 72
Wright, Dr. L. D., 123
Wright, Mrs. Lucy Heard, 228
Wright, R. A., 211; picture of, 172
Wynn, James, lynched, 186

www.ingramcontent.com/pod-product-compliance
Lightning Source LLC
LaVergne TN
LVHW091537060526
838200LV00036B/642